Japanese and American Agriculture

Japanese and American Agriculture

Tradition and Progress in Conflict

EDITED BY

Luther Tweeten, Cynthia L. Dishon,
Wen S. Chern, Naraomi Imamura,
and Masaru Morishima

Westview Press

BOULDER · SAN FRANCISCO · OXFORD

This Westview softcover edition is printed on acid-free paper and bound in library-quality, coated covers that carry the highest rating of the National Association of State Textbook Administrators, in consultation with the Association of American Publishers and the Book Manufacturers' Institute.

Copyright © 1993 by Westview Press, Inc.

Published in 1993 in the United States of America by Westview Press, Inc., 5500 Central Avenue, Boulder, Colorado 80301-2877, and in the United Kingdom by Westview Press, 36 Lonsdale Road, Summertown, Oxford OX2 7EW

A CIP catalog record for this book is available from the Library of Congress.
ISBN 0-8133-8700-0

Printed and bound in the United States of America

∞ The paper used in this publication meets the requirements
of the American National Standard for Permanence of Paper
for Printed Library Materials Z39.48-1984.

10   9   8   7   6   5   4   3   2   1

Contents

Preface

This project had origins in 1987 in communication between Yutaka Yoshioka, Chairman, Japan International Agricultural Council, and Kenneth Farrell, Vice President for Agriculture and Natural Resources, the University of California-Berkeley. Projects were proposed in "long-term food and consumption trends" and "a comparative analysis of farm structure in the United States and Japan" (letter from Farrell to Yoshioka, April 20, 1987).

Proposals and counterproposals were sent back and forth but the project accelerated after Professor Wen Chern of The Ohio State University learned of the project from Professor Naraomi Imamura of the University of Tokyo on a visit to Tokyo in September 1989. Because of pressing administrative responsibilities precluding an active role in the project, Kenneth Farrell recommended to Professor Imamura that the project be carried out with Professor Chern and associates.

To provide a match between U.S. and Japanese interests in the project, Professor Chern (whose interest was primarily in consumption/demand) enlisted the involvement of Professor Luther Tweeten of The Ohio State University, whose interest was in farm structure and output supply response. Professor Imamura (whose interest was in structure/supply) worked closely with Professor Masaru Morishima of the University of Tokyo, whose interest was food consumption/demand. Thus the team leadership was complete.

On the American side, considerable professional input on food demand and consumption came from the S-216 regional committee. Professional input also came from the NC-181 regional committee studying determinants of size and structure in American agriculture.

Several members of the team met in a pre-conference meeting on "Comparative Analysis of Food Demand/Consumption and Agricultural Structure/Supply in the United States and Japan" in March 1990 in Columbus, Ohio, to outline a research proposal and course of future action.

Members of the team also met in August 1990 at the American Agricultural Economics Association (AAEA) meeting in Vancouver, B.C., to finalize plans for the Discussion Group and Symposium in Tokyo. The team members sponsored a symposium at that AAEA annual meeting.

The collaborative arrangement culminated in a one-day symposium and four discussion-group sessions during the International Association of Agricultural Economists Conference in Tokyo in August 1991. Approximately 50 people attended each session. In total, 21 papers were presented. These papers plus the introduction and summary constitute the contents of this monograph. In addition to formally presenting these papers, participants from both sides engaged in useful exchanges and interactions.

Grants from the Cooperative State Research Service and the Farm Foundation were very helpful in facilitating the project. We are deeply grateful for their assistance.

The interaction provided by the project on consumption/demand and farm structure/supply has stimulated efforts to improve data, analytical tools, and the way issues are defined and researched. While much has been accomplished, much remains to be done as analysts of the two leading world economies collaborate to improve knowledge and decisions regarding food and agriculture.

Luther Tweeten and Wen S. Chern

1

Overview
Luther Tweeten

The United States and Japan are the world's largest economies. They enjoy the highest per capita income among major economies. Food and agriculture is the largest industry in each country.

That industry in each country is beset by problems. Japan's high-cost farming industry supplies less than half the country's food supply and is heavily protected from foreign competition. Japan is concerned about dependence on foreigners for food and about retaliation by other countries against Japanese food import barriers. American agriculture is highly efficient, and is competitive in world markets, but Americans feel that family farms are in jeopardy and that foreign trade barriers deny them rightful benefits of their comparative advantage in agriculture.

This brief introduction has emphasized differences in perceived problems between countries. The two countries also share many similarities. Differences and similarities are examined in the following pages. This overview has two main sections: one on agricultural structure/supply and the other on food consumption/demand. The special case of rice in Japan also is discussed.

But first I digress to reach the heart of much of the American-Japanese *angst* over food and agriculture. There is a clash of values, not so much *between* the two countries as *within* each of the two countries. The conflict is over tradition versus progress.

Tradition Versus Progress

The U.S.-Japan agricultural story documents the epic conflict between progress, technology, and markets on the one hand and culture, heritage, and tradition on the other. Economic development depends on three elements -- attitudes/culture, institutions, and natural resources (Tweeten and Brinkman, p. 60). Of these, attitudes are especially important. America and Japan are richly endowed with the work/savings ethic and entrepreneurial zeal, making economic progress inevitable. The two countries have experienced spectacular economic success and are the envy of the world. Who could find fault with such success? The answer is "a great many people."

The very essence of economic progress is *change*. Technology and markets are highly impersonal -- that is their strength and their weakness. The strength is that markets do their job without respect to ancestry, titles, and connections. Markets cause Schumpeterian *creative destruction* central to continuing renewal essential for growth. As a consequence, economic progress has sharply diminished the ravages of hunger, disease, drudgery, cold in winter, and heat in summer. It has created middle- and upper-class societies that have moved beyond merely satisfying physical needs to search for self-realization, self-fulfillment, enlightenment, and happiness.

The problem with the change brought by technology and markets is that it erodes treasured values and traditions. The loss is rarely more apparent than in food and agriculture. Economic progress in Japan is endangering a rural culture based on irrigated rice. That culture tamed but respected nature and its rhythms of seedtime and harvest. To survive, that culture valued competition within groups but valued a common front to threatening outsiders. That culture taught the importance of conservation and wise use of natural resources. It taught the importance of the family and community for survival. Rice mimicked human existence itself, teaching respect for planting (human reproduction), care of younger rice plants (nurturing and teaching children), and the bounty of the harvest (appreciation of the benefits of honest toil and wisdom of elders). Rice culture emphasized sharing the safety net with those less fortunate. The family and the village community were ideally suited to make decisions of when to share and when to withhold.

The family and village could understand supply, demand, and marketing when rice was produced and consumed locally. Later, when inputs needed to be purchased from outsiders and rice needed to be sold to outsiders to pay for inputs, markets became inscrutable, even sinister, and seemingly beyond the control of rice farmers and villagers. For rural people, it was easy to feel exploited by outsiders when prices were low due to an unfavorable supply-demand balance. For urban people, it was easy to feel insecure when rice supplies depended on people they didn't know. And the greatest insecurity seemed to be to depend on foreigners for staples.

American society also is taken with its agrarian heritage. It too celebrates the rhythms of nature, marking critical times with Easter (the promise of rebirth and growth in the Spring) and Thanksgiving Day (the realization of harvest in the Fall). Winter symbolizes death, but the human spirit seeks at least temporary relief and a glimpse of hope for renewed life celebrated at Christmas. American society, like Japanese society, prizes the family farm as a symbol of an earlier, simpler time when people were close to nature, revered Mother Earth, and when the closeknit, intact family above all else valued honesty, hard work, and respect for neighbor and God. But in contrast to the collectivistic society fostered by the irrigated rice culture of Japan, the independent family farm of America fostered an individualistic culture.

The Hegelian dialectic in economic development is apparent. Thesis and antithesis constantly are in opposition. It is not that the thesis (technological and inputs needed to be purchased economic progress) is bad and the antithesis (culture, tradition, heritage) is good. Both are good and both are bad.

Social scientists are frustrated when confronting values in conflict. The usual approach is to inform regarding advantages and disadvantages of economic progress versus tradition and of the individual versus the collective, then let an informed society, through dialogue and the political process, make decisions.

That political decision process can be distorted even under the heroic assumption that social scientists have provided all worthwhile objective information to make decisions. One problem is that special interest groups with money and power use propaganda, campaign contributions, and other means to bias the political process to serve their ends. A second problem is that a correct political decision for Japan alone or for the United States alone may not be correct for the two countries viewed jointly or for the world. For example, in our interdependent global economy the world community is poorly served by the European Community's decision to export its instability by dumping internal agricultural shocks on world markets. Worldwide, there may be too little empathy with Japanese consumers' concerns about food security in a nation depending on foreigners for most of its food -- and with its biggest suppliers 6,000 miles away. Markets don't adequately respond to such concerns.

The conflict between economic progress and tradition, and the market interventions pursued to preserve tradition permeated the discussions and symposium in which the papers contained in this monograph were presented. Japan has benefitted perhaps more than any other from open world trade. The visceral response of foreigners to Japan's trade barriers is to retaliate with barriers to imports from Japan. That is an inappropriate response because the big cost of trade distortions are paid by the nations which perpetrate them. Perhaps a compromise can be reached so that Japan can feel food secure while foreign countries can have access to markets. Later, I propose a compromise.

Structure/Supply

The most notable conclusion from Chapters 2 through 8 is the striking similarity in structural changes in American and Japanese agriculture despite very different agricultural support policies in the two countries. The same forces of technology and markets have brought substitution of capital for labor in both countries. Both countries have adjusted to the forces of technology and markets by migration from farms and by part-time farming. America especially emphasized outmigration and farm enlargement whereas Japan especially emphasized part-time farming.

Both countries tried very hard to slow change through public policies to help preserve small family farms and rural towns. The pressures for change, some originating from the governments' own policies of science and technology, proved frustratingly difficult to circumvent, however. Japan conducted a thorough land reform after World War II and created a situation where the land rental and sales markets do not function well. Farms remain small, averaging about one hectare per family. Such small farms cannot compete globally without transfers from consumers and taxpayers. These transfers totalled 5.3 billion yen ($36.7 billion) in 1987, or 79 percent of farm receipts (Webb *et al.*, p. 161). That compares with transfers to U.S. farmers of $36.0 billion in the same year, or 33 percent of their farm receipts. A paradox is that Japan is at once the largest food importer and the most protected food importer in the world.

According to Tsuboi (Chapter 4 Appendix), traditional small farms are consistent with environmental stewardship in Japan: "Human activities which do not depend on high technology and large organizations are generally compatible with preservation of the natural environment." In seeming contrast, Tweeten (Chapter 5) found that mid-size or larger family farms are more consistent than are small farms (under $100,000 sales per year) with soil conservation, economic efficiency, low poverty rates, and community vitality in the United States.

Despite government interventions, Japanese farmers have made adjustment responses predicted by neoclassical economic theory. Imamura *et al.* show that output value share of rice has fallen while the shares of livestock, vegetables, and fruits have increased sharply since 1955. Those adjustments seem consistent with market efficiency. Given the shortage of affordable housing and the very high value of land for urban real estate, the shift of farmland to urban development also is consistent with efficient markets.

In summary, although rates of change differ between the U.S. and Japan, agriculture in both countries is characterized by

- Fewer and larger farms.
- Fewer full-time commercial farms.
- More capital intensity, more technological sophistication, more dependence on nonfarm inputs, and more productivity per unit of land and labor.
- More dependence on off-farm jobs, income, and part-time farming.
- A declining share of the national economy and population.
- More scrutiny of agriculture for environmental soundness.
- Increasing average age of operators.
- Declining numbers of mid-sized, full-time farms compared to large farms and part-time small farms.

A variant of *Dutch Disease* operates in Japan. Nonfarm industry product-ivity growth supplies massive foreign exchange earnings, raising the value of the yen. As a consequence, agricultural imports become cheaper in Japan. Japan's agriculture has not been able to increase productivity to remain competitive. Opportunities for adjustment to larger farms could help, but at a social cost to displaced farmers. Studies of supply response to incentives (see Chapters 15 and 16) have been fewer in Japan than in the United States, but leave no doubt that farmers in both countries respond to economic incentives.

The process of growth through industrialization reduced farm numbers in Japan and the United States by approximately 0.1 percent per year from 1910 to 1940. American agriculture then made major adjustment in the 1950s and 1960s. Japanese agriculture delayed its adjustment but farm numbers declined 1.9 percent annually in the 1980s -- double the American rate! B.F. Stanton (Chapter 7) projects that American farm numbers will decline slowly between 1987 and 2000 -- about 0.6 percent annually. Based on past trends shown by Kada and Goto (Chapter 3), the rate of decline for Japanese farms may be somewhat greater.

Issues of sustainability of farms and rural communities are discussed for Japan by Kada and Goto and for the U.S. by Hallam and Dibooglu. Sustain-ability has social, economic, and environmental dimensions. Their chapters inform the debate; conflicts in values over tradition versus progress will have to be settled by markets and the political process.

Food Consumption/Demand

Food consumption/demand addressed in Chapters 9 to 14 confronts issues of the tangible and intangible as in the case of farm structure/supply.

Intangibles are of interest because, as in farm structure, markets and tradition are in conflict. The traditional Japanese diet is almost ideal, being high in complex carbohydrates and fiber from rice and in high grade protein from fish. The diet is low in fat. The longevity of the Japanese testifies to their superior diet. At issue is whether, with affluence and open trade, the Japanese will shift to a "modern" diet that is relatively high in sugar and fat, and lower in fiber.

Food consumption is mature and saturated in terms of total calories in both the U.S. and Japan. The composition of diets is of special interest. Morishima *et al.* (Chapter 8) note that the major changes in Japanese food consumption have been "a decrease in starchy food and increases in major livestock products, oils and fats, processed foods, and food away from home." Fujita (Chapter 9) cites restaurants, non-grain crops, livestock, meat and dairy products, processed fish, and beverages as growing sectors in Japan.

Senauer *et al.* (Chapter 10) observe that "Eating patterns around the world seem to be moving in directions that will make them increasingly similar across countries in the future." Tendencies toward global homogenization of food consumption are brought about by international communication, transportation, advertizing, entertainment, and by the rising cost of time and the falling cost of travel. Aging population, affluence, smaller families, women in the labor force, and greater nutritional awareness also are homogenizing food consumption patterns. Japan is moving toward an American diet and Americans are moving more to a Japanese diet of more fish and complex carbohydrates.

Critical issues for the future are the extent to which genetic engineering can create leaner hogs and beef, and lower cholesterol eggs. Can food technology develop flavor enhancers that will substitute for fats and salt (Price *et al*., Chapter 11)? It is likely that many of the world's advances in food production and processing technology will be made in Japan and the United States.

The theory and practice of demand estimation (Chapters 12 and 13) are more advanced than that of supply estimation (Chapters 15 and 16). Supply parameter estimates are crude, partial, and differ widely even under similar conditions for the same crop. The parameters of domestic demand for food have been estimated with greater elegance, precision, and comprehensiveness.

Japan and the United States have substantial data and rapidly improving analytical capabilities and techniques to study food demand (Chapters 12 and 13). Problems are apparent, however. Analysts have emphasized estimating demand models more than making accurate forecasts. They have not reconciled demand and supply models -- demand has been estimated at retail and supply at the farm level. Forecasting models in which supply and demand interact must have consistent parameters at the same market level.

Other problems remain in demand estimation. Changes in tastes, preferences, and food industry structure that shift demand curves are difficult to sort out from movement along demand curves. The appropriate choice of functional form of demand system is not always clear. Export demand elasticities are estimated with even less precision than farm output supply elasticities. The influence of exchange rates, border measures (tariffs, etc.), and economic growth on export demand is elusive indeed.

In Chapter 17, Yamaji and Ito express doubts whether freer markets in Japan could move the country in needed directions: to commodities more favored by consumers, to enlarged farms realizing economies of size, and to land and other resources in uses most favored by society. They seem sympathetic to views that every country has a right to self-sufficiency. Ozawa (Chapter 18) lists many of the reasons why rice is so important to Japan. His list extends beyond food security and culture. He notes that paddy fields hold reserve water, prevent floods, and reduce soil erosion. The rice policy restrains movement of people to cities. Oga in Chapter 20 emphasizes that Japan has opened its market more than any other country in recent decades. From an American perspective, Wailes *et al*. reply to many of the concerns and assertions raised about rice in Japan in earlier chapters.

At issue is whether to pursue self-sufficiency or food security -- an issue addressed by Wailes *et al.* in Chapter 19. A case can be made that a country has greater food security from self-reliance (ability to buy food abroad *or* produce it at home) than from self-sufficiency. Self-reliance means buying power to go into world markets where there has been plenty of food every year for many decades rather than rely on local production which frequently falls short of needs.

In Chapter 21, Hayes details how technology has changed for chilled beef exports. Now it is technically and economically feasible to ship meat over long distances and still preserve its quality. He concludes that U.S. meat exports will replace feedgrain exports and raise the value-added component of exports.

Conclusions and Proposals for Policy Compromise

In summary, markets in Japan and the United States have worked pretty much as predicted by economic theory. Markets have moved in the direction of economic efficiency and consumers' preferences. But markets do not reflect intangibles. Concern was particularly evident among Japanese social scientists that their country was losing a prized heritage of rice culture, family farms, and self-sufficiency in food. American social scientists also recognize the importance of family farms and rural communities to the American heritage. An impressive 82 percent of all Americans including three-fourths of those in large cities agree that "The family farm must be preserved because it is a vital part of our heritage" (Tweeten, pp. 77-79).

Most American farms today are either commercial operations that are a business rather than a way of life or small part-time farms operated by persons who make their living in nonfarm occupations. The American farmer today finds it ever more difficult to fulfill the image of the archetypical rugged, independent individual who represents the qualities of self-reliance, commitment to democracy, social cohesion, and the backbone of social and economic vitality for rural communities. He must share his decision making with banks, government, and others.

Preservation of symbols of rice culture and some degree of food self-sufficiency is an intangible but entirely appropriate concern to the Japanese. It is true that farm policies become an international concern when actions of one country, be it the U.S. or Japan, arbitrarily affect the other as in the case of agricultural policy. I suspect Americans would show a concern for self-sufficiency if they depended on foreigners for over half of their calories as the Japanese do.

Striving for self-sufficiency by high prices creates a dilemma for Japan: High rice prices designed to stimulate supply restrict consumption. Other imported grains substitute for rice, reducing overall self-sufficiency.

Changes in public policy can diminish problems of rice self-sufficiency and family farm loss.

In the following proposal, I look for a compromise at once respecting Japan's concern for food (rice) security and America's concern for access to markets abroad. The proposal is an attempt to break a trade impasse that has been expensive to Japan and the U.S.

I offer three suggestions.

1. To resolve the rice food security problem but promote more open markets elsewhere, I propose that every nation be allowed to be self-sufficient in *one* main staple crop. In Japan, that would be rice. In return for that concession, the country would be bound by certain restrictions:

   • Only direct payments from the Treasury tied to output could be used to induce producers to supply national self-sufficiency needs. Consumers would buy the main staple and indeed all other food, goods, and services at world prices -- no distortions except for health and safety would be allowed in consumer markets. On the supported staple, the government would need to pay a cash supplement from the Treasury to producers equal to the difference between the world price and the self-sufficiency price.

     Payments would have limits (1) for individual farmers to encourage diversification and targeting of small farmers and (2) in aggregate to avoid excess production.
   • The country could only achieve self-sufficiency in the commodity up to the per capita amount prevailing before the change in policy. Imports would fill the gap between the additional consumer demand generated by lowering price from the initial level to the world level. If a country chose to export, it could not subsidize any production. Hence the U.S. could not subsidize wheat if it chose to continue to be an exporter of that commodity.

   The requirement that direct payments for self-sufficiency must come from taxpayers rather than consumers would be a severe political constraint, avoiding excesses and abuses of the program. The political system might have difficulty sustaining payments when national budget pressures are severe. Restriction of the program to one staple commodity not exported especially suits the program to East Asia. With free trade in all other commodities, social (deadweight) cost of the program is small and much overshadowed by gains from overall freer world trade while honoring legitimate concerns regarding food dependency.

At issue is whether world rice supplies would be adequate to supply Japan's needs under open world markets. Oga (Chapter 20) notes that the Japanese consumers favor japonica rice which has a rather thin world market. Questions were raised about the ability of the world to meet Japan's rice needs with an open market.

Wailes *et al.* appear to be confident. Japonica and indica rices are substitutes in production in some world regions. An open world market would generate a frenzy of research to adapt japonica varieties to areas previously producing indica rice or other crops. The issue of whether japonica rice can be supplied by imports need not be decided by government officials. For example, the Mississippi Delta, the major indica rice growing area of the United States, once produced substantial japonica rice and could again if markets provide incentives to do so. The argument that restrictions are needed because foreigners cannot supply desired rice varieties is best resolved by markets.

2. My second proposal addresses the need to preserve the traditional family farm and the skills that attend it. Given the demise of family farms as we have known them, an appropriate response in Japan and the United States is to establish *living history* farms. Examples already exist in Iowa. The concept is to as faithfully as possible reproduce typical farms as they existed in the 1800s, 1920s, 1930s, or other periods. These would be established across each country as necessary and affordable to give people an opportunity to observe traditional family farms of earlier epochs. The cost to operate such farms would be paid partly by fees on visitors. Other costs would be paid by taxpayers and by market receipts. The Treasury cost of such farms would be high enough to constrain their numbers and share of production to a level that would not distort trade or drive out modern farms. I doubt that either Japan or the U.S. would support more than a few dozen living history farms.

3. The final suggestion is for an open-ended U.S.-Japan free trade agreement (see Gleckler and Tweeten). Other countries would be allowed to join if they too agreed to remove trade barriers. The two major world economies would set an example to the rest of the world of cooperation and close economic relations. Such agreement might give assurances of dependable supplies of food for Japan (proposal 1 also would help) and dependable supplies of (say) microprocessors for the United States. Together, the two countries could make major leadership in science and technology to improve worldwide living standards and food security. If enough countries joined, the result could be widespread free trade despite the disappointing outcome of the Uruguay Round.

The book leaves many issues unresolved regarding food and agriculture in Japan and the United States. The issues raised in this book and many additional issues need analysis, dialogue, and resolution. Regional research in food and agriculture has an impressive record of success in the United States as explained by Robinson *et al*. They go on to explain in Chapter 22 how procedures that have worked for regional and interregional agricultural research in the United States could be extended to international research cooperation. American and Japanese analysts interacting to prepare this book gained great respect for each others data, analytical capabilities, problems, and dilemmas. Improved research arrangements between countries could help find solutions to the latter.

References

Gleckler, James and Luther Tweeten. 1990. The economic impact of a U.S.-Japan free trade agreement. Pp. 87-104 in Luther Tweeten, ed., proceedings of *Realizing Opportunities for Farm and Food Product Exports to the Pacific Rim*. Columbus: Department of Agricultural Economics and Rural Sociology, The Ohio State University.

Tweeten, Luther. 1989. *Farm Policy Analysis*. Boulder, CO: Westview Press.

Tweeten, Luther and George Brinkman. 1976. *Micropolitan Development*. Ames: Iowa State University Press.

Webb, Alan, Michael Lopez, and Renata Penn. 1990. Estimates of producer and consumer subsidy equivalents. Statistical Bulletin No. 803. Washington, DC: ERS, U.S. Department of Agriculture.

2

Japanese Agriculture:
Characteristics, Institutions, and Policies
Junko Goto and Naraomi Imamura

Why is rice such an important crop in Japan? Why can't the Japanese accept a more open-door policy in agricultural trade? Why do many urban consumers support the status quo in agriculture, despite their awareness that food prices in Japan are some of the highest in the world? Why is the Ministry of Agriculture so concerned about the majority of part-time farmers whose income is more dependent on nonfarm activities than on farming?

The many myths and facts about Japanese agriculture require careful examination and explanation. In this chapter, we focus on the description and analysis of recent changes in Japanese agricultural structure and the relationships between agricultural structure and policies in Japan. To facilitate the understanding of these issues, some background of Japanese agriculture and farm structure will be presented.

History and Characteristics

The following historical points highlight the importance of rice. *Rice* has been the dominant and most important crop in Japan for centuries. Peasants, the majority of the population until the end of the 19th Century, paid their taxes mainly in harvested rice. The power of local lords before the Meiji regime (1868-1912) was measured by the amount of rice produced on their land. Rice was equivalent to money in the Edo period (1600-1868). The authorities, both national and local, had a keen interest in increasing rice production. Peasants themselves strove for increased yields and improved techniques. Therefore, since this early modern period, Japanese agricultural development has been characterized by "overdevelopment" of rice production.

Another historical characteristic of Japanese farms is that they are very *small* in size. An average size of about one hectare per farm has been constant for more than a hundred years. Japan is a land-scarce country. Two-thirds of the total land area of 370,000 square kilometers is mountainous and covered by forests. The rest of the country (alluvial lowlands, coastal plains, valley bottoms, and plateaus) has been devoted intensively to agricultural, residential, industrial, and transportation uses. Hillsides and narrow valleys were also converted to paddy terraces and dry fields. By the end of the Edo period, frontiers for agriculture were nearly exhausted except in Hokkaido. Due to such topographical limitations, one farm usually consists of several plots of paddies and dry fields which are scattered in the vicinity. The physical characteristics of Japanese farms are often referred to as the "small, fragmented, and scattered" field pattern.

Irrigation is another key characteristic of Japanese agriculture. Rice is grown in wet paddies which must be inundated for the growing period from May to September (the growing season varies from south to north and by altitude). Located in the monsoon area of East Asia, Japan receives about 1,800 millimeters of rainfall per year. Preventing floods and controlling and managing water resources has been a matter of life and death for both farmers and the state. In an effort to achieve these goals, an elaborate network of irrigation systems has been constructed throughout the country. The distribution of water and the maintenance and operation of local irrigation facilities has been the responsibility of the villages. The village community, the basic unit of rural settlement, functions both as a body of local autonomy and as an administrative subordinate. It protects and dictates the livelihood of member families. Irrigation farming with the small and dispersed field pattern requires village-level cooperation and coordination, indispensable in carrying out farm operations, although competition among villagers has been persistent at the same time.

Part-time farming has changed the internal structure of the farm economy. Part-time farming or by-employment is not new among Japanese farm families. But the nature of part-time farming changed during the high growth period of 1955-1970. During this period, off-farm jobs became the primary source of income for the majority of farm households. Common forms of off-farm work changed from casual to more regular, long-term, and full-time employment. Economically speaking, agriculture became a supplementary activity for the family and was principally under the care of married women and older men. Younger people resist making farming their major occupation. They become part-time family farmers, unwilling to give up farming because it is valuable as a way of life and because farmland is an important family asset. Rice is the most widely grown crop among part-time farmers.

The *family farm* obsession in Japan has ties with the history of agricultural development. From the early modern period onward, the family farm, no matter how small or who owned it, was the operating unit. Tenancy but not a landless laborer class existed in prewar Japan. Although the nonfarm commitment drastically changed the income structure and made the contribution of many farm families to agricultural output quite small (except for rice), part-time farm families are not excluded from the family farm category which continues to receive special political support. At the village level, farming remains a way of life among part-time farmers. They usually participate in the maintenance of irrigation canals and village roads and cooperate with other farmers. While part-time farmers are often viewed as an obstacle to farm adjustment and rationalization, their role in maintaining village solidarity and practicing resource stewardship is appreciated by the increasingly urbanized society.

In the Edo period, the national government (shogunate) and the provincial governments (han) made special efforts to raise rice production. Several means were used to achieve this goal. First, new land was devoted to cultivation. Because Japan is such a mountainous country, most of the flatland, on which it is easy to control water with existing technology, was already developed. What was left included plateaus which were not accessible by river water, steep hillsides which required costly terracing, and floodplains and adjacent lowlands of rivers which people thought uncontrollable at that time. Technical advances, government investment, and a large amount of labor input converted this unutilized land to paddies. Construction and maintenance of canals, ditches, weirs, headworks, and other irrigation facilities became one of the most important tasks for the governments and for the farmers themselves, as their livelihood depended on how much they could raise and how much they had after paying their taxes.

Until the end of the 19th Century, agriculture was the leading sector in the national economy. In 1873, agriculture accounted for 77 percent of the total labor force and produced enough food for the entire population. When Japan had nothing else to export, agriculture earned foreign exchange from such exports as raw silk, tea, and rice. Following the Land Tax Reform enacted in 1873, the land tax collected from rural areas supported the new state. Surplus agricultural production financed industrialization.

Several agricultural statistics remained stable from the early Meiji period for about the next century. Total farmland comprised about 15 percent of the total land area of Japan, or six million hectares, which meant that the expansion of agricultural land had almost reached its physical limit by the early Meiji period. The size of the farm population remained fairly stable up to 1955. Total farm households remained unchanged at around 5.5 million, total farm population was around 30 million, and the population employed in agriculture was about 14 million. Finally, as a result of these conditions, the average size of land-holding by farm households remained about one hectare.

Why didn't industrial development affect the farm sector more drastically? The majority of rural-to-urban migration before 1955 consisted of the excess labor (younger sons and daughters) of the farm family. Seldom did a whole family leave the village for the city. The low level of labor absorption capacity and of wages in cities offered few incentives for many rural families to migrate. So, the number of farm households remained virtually unchanged and only the excess labor moved to the cities (Namiki).

The 1910s marked an end to a period when agriculture was the leading sector of the national economy. The outbreak of World War I stimulated Japanese industry. With the small and fragmented land-holding system intact and the labor-intensive and land-saving technology nearly exhausted, Japanese agriculture could not keep up with the rest of the economy. Landlords, who were agents of agricultural modernization in the earlier period, shifted their interest from agricultural to non-agricultural activities. The number of absentee landlords increased gradually. In order to improve irrigation facilities and overcome the inefficiency of the small and fragmented field pattern, the government and leaders in agriculture sought to solicit ideas from farmers for land improvement and consolidation. Although tenant-cultivators as well as owner-cultivators favored innovations to increase yields and labor productivity, landlords often acted as a stumbling block by opposing such schemes.

The livelihood of villagers became more connected with the macro economy. Imported rice from the colonies (Taiwan and Korea) kept the domestic price low. When recession hit, fewer jobs were available in cities and more people had to be fed in the already depressed rural economy. As a result, stratification (internal mobility) among farmers virtually ceased and tenant disputes emerged and spread throughout the country. Some poverty-stricken families had to "sell" their daughters to cities or to move altogether from the home village to new places such as cities in Japan and cities and villages in Korea and Manchuria.

During this period following the end of World War I the foundation of state agricultural policy was laid. The objective of supplying enough food for the growing population was met by squeezing peasants in the new colonies. The focus of agricultural policy in Japan changed from a "food" problem to a "poverty" problem (Hayami). Policymakers tried to relieve the depressed rural economy and alleviate possible rural unrest. Many legislative and administrative measures were set forth to ameliorate farmers' difficulties and distress. Major acts and regulations included the Reclamation Assistance Act (1919), the Rice Act (1921), the New Agricultural Association Act (1922), the Rules for Subsidization of Irrigation and Drainage Improvement Projects (1923), and the Tenant Conciliation Act (1924). The Ministry of Agriculture was established (the Ministry of Agriculture and Commerce was divided) and in 1926 regulations for establishing small owner-operated farms were issued.

If we compare the formation of state policies for agriculture between Japan and the United States, we notice that the Japanese state acted and intervened in agricultural production more than ten years earlier than the United States which began major intervention with the New Deal in 1933. The reason for this difference in state commitment can be found in the rate of industrial growth and the need for state measures to adjust the imbalance between the farm sector and the nonfarm sector. Many of the current agricultural acts and regulations have forerunners in this period. The modern history of Japanese agriculture can be seen as a history of rigorous public intervention and guidance to every aspect of farm life. We will discuss changing focuses and problems of modern farm policy later. The remainder of this section briefly narrates what happened to Japanese agriculture and the farm sector after World War II.

The Depression and World War II brought a serious food shortage crisis to Japan. Total agricultural production dropped sharply beginning in the late 1930s. Imports of rice and sugar from Taiwan and Korea were cut as the war became intense. When the nation surrendered in August 1945, the nonfarm population was barely subsisting under a strict food rationing system. One of the most urgent tasks of the Occupation period (1945-52), therefore, was to get everyone enough to eat.

The agricultural land reform, rigorously implemented throughout the country, abolished absentee ownership by 1950 and transferred two million hectares of farmland (one-third of the total farmland) into the hands of cultivators, mostly former tenants (Dore). Ceiling provisions for cultivating landlords set the limit for individual holdings at 12 hectares in Hokkaido and 3 hectares in the rest of the country. As a result, Japan became a model country of small farm development ("unimodal strategy" by Johnston and Kilby). But this reform did not change the average size of individual farms. The continuity of family management systems and the small fragmented field pattern were simply reinforced by this new egalitarian tenure structure.

Agriculture took leadership in reconstructing the national economy. The immediate goal -- self sufficiency in rice -- was achieved by 1955 and production continued to increase until the mid-1960s. For nearly two decades, Japanese agriculture apparently met both the efficiency and equity objectives. Japanese villages experienced a new period of hope, improvement, cooperation, democracy, and prosperity. As soon as the nation entered the period of high growth, however, the villagers' livelihood experienced a dramatic change. The change involved simultaneous development of two kinds of population movement: one was the typical rural-to-urban migration and the other was a mobilization of the farm population for nonfarm activities without geographical relocation other than daily commuting. Part-time farming began to prevail as the major farming system among farm families. In contrast to the "weak push and weak pull" situation of the pre-war period, a "strong pull and fair push" (for the younger generation) situation dominated the rural out-migration (Namiki). By the early 1960s, Japan became a labor-scarce economy and the dominant sector "did not remove only *excess* farm population," but increasingly took "*needed* labor from the farms" (Bernier, p. 78). The development of labor-saving technologies helped this transition. Small power cultivators and planters permitted so-called weekend farming for rice farmers. Mechanization also created over-investment and debt burden for many families, accelerating the trend away from farming.

Agricultural policymakers began to realize that the relative "success" of the small farm strategy would not last long. They now faced the dilemma of achieving greater economic efficiency in agriculture while also satisfying the equity criteria. No one in agricultural administration and planning welcomed part-time farming which was eventually chosen by the majority of farm families as a strategy of adaptation and survival (and also resistance) to industrialization and urbanization (Jussaume). Most farmers had to engage in part-time farming because the returns from agriculture alone hardly covered the expenses for modern farming, while regular household expenses kept growing. Also, they did not want to withdraw from farming; giving up the land was the last thing they wanted to do. Land is not only a family asset and the most important source of economic security, it also is a symbol of ancestry and tieship to the village. The increase of part-time farming meant that the chances for expansion and consolidation for ambitious full-time farmers were small. They had to resort to more labor-intensive and capital-intensive forms of agriculture.

This is a simplified contextualization of the "structural problem" of Japanese agriculture. You may hear cliches about farming in Japan such as: "farm families prosper, but agriculture fails" and "agricultural cooperatives prosper, but..." Before we proceed to describe major components of the postwar agricultural policy, i.e., the efforts to readjust agriculture to changing social and economic circumstances, let us insert one small section -- a statistical summary of the present structure of agriculture.

Agricultural Structure: An Overview

Economic Position

The total number of farm households has been decreasing steadily since their historical peak in 1950. In 1950, there were 6,170,000 farm households, defined as "agricultural establishments that are identical with households with cultivated land of 10 acres or more in Eastern Japan and of 5 ares (Note: 100 ares = 1 hectare) (approximately 0.12 acres) or more in Western Japan, or households with cultivated land less than the minimum size mentioned above but with farm sales of 10,000 Yen or more during a year prior to the survey data." The minimum sales component of this definition changed almost every five years, i.e., every census year. The size component, however, was raised to 10 ares (0.25 acres) for the entire country in the 1990 census (the minimum sales was raised to 150,000 Yen). By 1975, the total number of farm households had dropped below five million and by 1990 had fallen to below four million. In 1990 there were 3,835,000 farm households, among which 2,971,000 were "marketing farm households" which were defined as farm households with 30 ares (0.74 acres) or more of cultivated land or with farm sales of 500,000 Yen or more. The remaining farm households (864,000) were called "self-sufficient" or non-marketing farm households. The rate of decrease in the number of farms was greater among marketing farms (-10.4 percent during 1985-90) than non-marketing farms (-5.4 percent).

Looking at the farm size distribution and the change in size distribution over the past 20 years, the polarization or stratification tendency is clear. We call this tendency the "squeezed middle." That is, small-scale farms stay relatively stable though they decline slightly in numbers, and large-scale farms increase in absolute number and share. The dividing line increased from 1.5 hectares between 1960 and 1965, to 2.5 hectares between 1970 and 1975, and to 3.0 hectares between 1985 and 1990.

This polarization tendency does not mean that Japanese farms are growing larger at a steady pace. A new class of ex-farm families still own farmland in sizes of 5 ares or more. They no longer farm their land but continue to reside in the same house and own the paddies and other agricultural land. The number of these ex-farm households grew from 443,000 in 1985 to 775,000 in 1990. The farmland under their ownership is more likely to lay idle rather than to be rented to other active farmers. When we limit our discussion to currently active farm households, most farms are still smaller than 1.0 hectare (the average was 0.9 hectare per farm in 1990 in prefectures excluding Hokkaido). In Hokkaido, the average farm size is 10.8 hectares.

Part-time farms continue to dominate farm numbers. In the 1990 census, the definition of full-time and part-time farms changed. Full-time farm households now include farm households of which all members are exclusively engaged in their own farming *including* farming on rented or entrusted land owned by other farmers. Previously, such contract farming was regarded as "other jobs" and, therefore, those farmers who enlarged their operations by lease, rental, and contract agreement were counted as part-time farmers. This change in definition reflects the fact and perception that this kind of farming is increasing in numbers and should be regarded as full-time farming.

In 1990, the share of full-time farms was 15.9 percent of all 2,971,000 marketing farms and 12.3 percent of all 3,835,000 farms including self-sufficient farms. One out of three full-time farms, however, did not have any male family members between the ages of 16 and 64. Full-time farms are divided into (1) single- or two-person households of retired farmers and (2) households which are headed by "professional" farmers with no off-farm jobs. The latter category comprises about one-tenth of all marketing farms.

The share of agriculture in GDP dropped from 7.2 percent in 1965 to 2.0 percent in 1988. In spite of efforts to improve the infrastructure and adopt labor-saving technologies, the labor productivity of agriculture compared to non-agricultural sectors continued to decline and was approximately 25 percent in 1988. When the cost for agricultural inputs such as machinery, feed, fertilizers, chemicals, and fuel rose steadily, the income ratio of agriculture (the ratio of agricultural income to gross agricultural output in percentage) deteriorated. It was 57.2 in 1965 and 35.6 in 1988. How did ordinary farm households survive? During the high growth period, the majority of Japanese farm households became dependent on off-farm jobs. The share of agricultural income in the total farm household income declined steadily from 48.0 percent in 1965 to 16.5 percent in 1988. So-called multiple job holdings are established among farm households.

Part-time farm households are divided into two groups. Class I part-time households earn income mainly from farming and Class II mainly from nonfarm jobs. It should be noted that the definition of part-time farming (and full-time farming) in Japan uses the household as the basic unit and not the individual. The number of Class II part-time families did not decline as fast as that of Class I part-time families. The reason for this is similar to the "disappearing middle" phenomena described in the size distribution above. Most Class II family heads are engaged in long-term and full-time off-farm work, while Class I family heads are faced with the dilemma of either remaining in agriculture at perhaps lower income or devoting more time and energy to off-farm jobs.

When we compare the average household income of farm families to that of urban wage-earners' families, farm families fare better than urban families because multiple job holdings are more widespread among farm family members. Another reason is that more people are working per household in farm families than in urban families because the average size of the household is bigger. Per capita family expenditures of farm households were lower than those of urban wage earners in 1970 but have exceeded urban households by more than 10 percent since 1975. However, per capita family expenditures of full-time farm households with core male farmers were lower than those of urban wage earners by 14 percent in 1988. So per capita income is highest in Class II part-time farm families and lowest in full-time farm families.

Farmland Ownership and Management

Statistics on farmland (cultivated and planted area) are available from the Crop Survey series of the Census of Agriculture. Total acreage of cultivated area declined from 6.12 million hectares in 1960 to 5.24 million hectares in 1990. In 1988 54 percent of total farmland area (5.32 million hectares) is paddies. Upland field crops, permanent crops (orchards, tea, etc.), and pastures comprised 24, 10, and 12 percent, respectively.

More than 90 percent of the total farmland is cultivated by owner-farmers. The ratio of rented land to total farmland increased slightly from 6.4 percent in 1970 to 7.8 percent in 1990. But this level is significantly lower than in other OECD countries such as West Germany and France which had 30.2 percent and 47.6 percent, respectively, in 1982 (Saeki, p. 24). One reason for this low figure is that Japanese farmers do not want to report that land is rented. Although the total area of rented land appears low, the number of farms which rent farmland has increased significantly in the past decade. This is especially true among larger farms (those with 5.0 hectares or more and those with 3.0 to 5.0 hectares). The number of farms that rent farmland outnumbered those that do not in those large farm categories in 1990. Renting land is definitely recognized as a means of enlarging the operation.

At the same time, the ratio of idle farmland to cultivated farmland is increasing at a phenomenal rate. The total area of idle farmland increased between 1985 and 1990 by about 60 percent. Reasons for this growth include the rice diversion program, the drop in the government purchase price for rice, the aging of farm operators, and the shortage of farm operators who want to rent more land. In some regions, the ratio of idle land to total farmland reached as high as one-tenth.

Vertical Coordination

Agricultural cooperatives hold the number one position in providing input and output linkages to farm families in Japan. The history of Japanese agricultural cooperatives dates from the period of the agricultural depression before World War II. The present system developed after the 1947 Agricultural Cooperatives Act. Agricultural cooperatives are divided into two types: general-purpose cooperatives and special-purpose cooperatives. Let us limit out discussion to general-purpose cooperatives.

The characteristics of these farm organizations in Japan can be summarized as follows (Saeki; Imamura) First, they are territorial organizations. The network of cooperatives covers all of the inhabited area in rural Japan. Thus, virtually all farm households belong to the agricultural cooperative in their locality. Agricultural cooperatives are consolidated into larger basic units which are coordinated with units at the prefectural and national levels. Secondly, they cover a wide range of activities such as marketing, purchasing, repairing, storing, processing, contract farming, credit, mutual insurance, housing, and land development. These activities reflect the needs of part-time farm families, which are in many ways identical with those of urban consumers. Thirdly, they act as strong political pressure groups -- the strongest among farmer organizations in Japan. The top-level unit, *Zennokyo*, located in Tokyo, is as influential in lobbying as the *zaibatsu* corporations. Finally, they act as though they are government agencies or extension agencies in disseminating innovations and information to improve farm operations and rural life in general.

Although the position of the agricultural cooperatives has never been seriously challenged by others, several structural changes call for redirection of their activities. First, the number of "associate" members has increased. This is because the number of nonfarm households increased in many farm communities and "associate" newcomers joined the agricultural cooperatives because of the convenience and benefits (especially insurance, credit, and purchasing). Agricultural cooperatives assume the role of general-purpose area cooperatives. Even in communities with little in-migration, farming no longer serves as an integrating theme to coordinate the activities of the cooperative members as more farm families become Class II part-time farmers. The minority, full-time farmers, in turn started to rely on special-purpose cooperatives rather than general-purpose cooperatives.

Japanese agricultural cooperatives today need to clarify the organization's objectives and streamline their operations. Many small cooperatives at the municipality level are planning to consolidate. Success of Japanese agricultural cooperatives in readjusting themselves in this ongoing restructuring processes is difficult to predict. We should note, however, that these farmer organizations have potential for resilience and flexibility.

Corporation farming accounts for only a small share of the domestic food production system. Agricultural operations (enterprises) other than family farms are few in numbers (0.3 percent of all farm enterprises in 1990) and do not account for significant agricultural output except for a few commodities. Those operations include partnerships of family farms, corporations, agricultural cooperatives, local governments, schools, and other public bodies. There were about 11,620 of these units in 1990, of which 7,473 were commercial (for marketing purposes) units. The contribution of these non-family operations were greatest in livestock farming: 30.2 percent in fattening hogs, 47.0 percent in broilers, and 50.1 percent in layers (share of non-family operations in numbers of animals produced).

On the other hand, the role of corporations in distribution and processing is increasing dramatically. This development of the food industry lies outside of the traditional food producer-distributor line. The diversification of consumer needs, i.e., preference for variety, high-quality, and processed food; the growing interest in "healthy" and "safe" food; the popularity of fast food and food-away-from-home; and other factors support the growth of the food industry which increasingly relies on imported food. The share of sales of raw food produced in Japan is currently about one-quarter of the total output value of the food supply system.

Human Resources

Statistics on farm operators are complicated and confusing. The Census of Agriculture has three definitions of farm operators. The broadest category is "persons engaged in own-farming." This refers to farm household members 16 years of age and over who are engaged in their own household's farming, no matter how little the engagement is. In addition, this definition includes those who are engaged mainly in other jobs. "Population engaged in farming" refers to those who either exclusively work on farms or who have other jobs but spend more days on their farm. We will call these persons the agricultural working population. "Principal persons engaged in farming" refers to persons who mainly do work and are engaged mainly in farming. The last groups is closest to "farm operators" in the word's usual sense, but include those who have auxiliary jobs other than farming.

Previously, we stated that the population employed in agriculture stayed relatively stable at 14 million persons for a century. This number is the agricultural working population, the "population engaged in farming" described above. In 1960, 17.7 million farm household members were "engaged in own-farming," 14.5 million constituted the agricultural working population including farm wives and the elderly, and 11.8 million were farm operators. These numbers declined drastically during the next 30 years. In 1990, 10.4 million people were engaged in farming, 5.7 million were in the agricultural working population, and only 3.1 million were farm operators.

If we describe the "average" farm family situation in 1990, there were 0.8 farm operators, 1.5 agricultural working population persons, and 2.7 persons engaged in farming per household. This transition from earlier statistics can be explained by the spread of "multiple job holding" among farm families and by the aging of the farm population. Average household size declined from 5.3 persons per farm in 1965 to 4.5 persons per farm in 1990. Farm families have been bigger than the national average which was 4.1 in 1965 and 3.0 in 1989. Among the 4.5 persons per farm in 1990, 3.1 were working population, of which 1.5 were engaged in agriculture and 1.6 in nonfarm jobs. If a farm family is a three-generation family, the grandfather may be retired from non-farm work but work on that farm with the grandmother. The younger couple is likely to hold off-farm jobs, but help the farming operation occasionally (especially for rice planting and harvesting).

The average age of the farm population is advancing faster than that of the nation's total population. The aging index (share of persons of 65 years old and over to total population) of the farm population reached 20.0 percent in 1990 compared to 11.6 for the nation in 1989. The aging of persons engaged in farming is even more advanced. Elderly people on farms are more likely to spend more days on farms. More than half of persons engaged in farming are over 50 years of age.

Numbers of farm households without successors have been increasing. The farm household succession and inheritance problem is perceived to be one of the most serious farm problems in Japan. Of the farms responding to the 1990 census, 2.03 million indicated that they have successors (16 years old and over) at home and 1.80 million indicated that they have no successors at home. Some 372,000 households out of the 1.80 million had successors away from home. So, about 1.40 million farm households were without successors.

The meaning of "successors" is very ambiguous. It refers to those who take responsibility as the next family head of the particular household (which happens to be a farm household) and does not necessarily mean that they commit themselves to farming. Thus, the real successors of farming are few in number.

Natural and Environmental Resources

The concerns over the relationship between the food problem (surpluses and shortages) and the environment are growing among Japanese citizens and corporations. With regard to Japanese rice farming, such arguments as below are popular among agricultural interest groups and are supported by a fair number of consumers.

The highly productive Japanese paddy field also serves to preserve the national land and the environment through fostering water resources and preventing flood...there is a need to deepen our awareness of the function that Japanese agriculture has in conserving our national land and the environment. There is also a need to examine the forms of agriculture that come into harmony with the environment and humankind, keeping in mind the necessity to improve productivity [MAFF, 1990b, p. 10].

The history of traditional agriculture in Japan may be proof of its sustainability. The maintenance of paddies in plains and valleys might be as effective as forests in mountains in preventing floods and saving soil and water resources. We should be critical, however, when listening to such claims. The modernization of agriculture in Japan, in the era of technological innovations (mechanization, chemical input, field consolidation, irrigation and drainage improvement, etc.), was no exception to modernization elsewhere in changing and destroying nature. If caring about the *environment* is going to be one of the major rationales for the survival of *agriculture*, then the relationship between these two must be studied carefully.

Postwar Agricultural Policy: An Overview

The overall structure of Japanese agricultural policies and programs can be classified into four areas: policies for (1) ownership, use, and transfer of agricultural land; (2) supply-demand adjustment and price control of agricultural commodities (mainly rice); (3) agricultural subsidies to promote land improvement projects and to encourage structural adjustment; and (4) agricultural cooperatives and other organizations. Another classification is found in the state agricultural budget: (1) production measures; (2) structural measures; (3) price control and farm income measures; and (4) others, including measures for farmers' welfare, agricultural organizations, and farm surveys. What follows is not a category-by-category explanation but an overview of the major concepts and policy measures implemented during the postwar period.

Following the agricultural land reform, the 1952 Agricultural Land Act firmly established the principle of postwar agricultural policy. Three components of farming -- land ownership, farm management, and farm labor -- are all under the control of a family farm. Other types of farm management were discouraged. This principle, often referred to as the triplicity principle of postwar agricultural policy, worked well in the earlier period.

Land reform not only gave former tenants new incentives to invest in their individual operations, but it also brought an ideal social environment to the village level to materialize land improvement and other development projects. The government encouraged and supported grassroots initiatives for production expansion and modernization. The concept of river basin resource management and development was applied in many regions. The construction of multipurpose dams contributed to reducing flood damage, improving irrigation systems (and thus increasing rice production), supplying water for municipal and industrial uses, and generating electricity.

Equity considerations plus political pressure pushed the government to raise the price support level for rice. Price control of rice was institutionalized with the 1921 Rice Act following the Rice Riots in 1918. During the war and recovery period, the government controlled and supported the price of rice under the Food Control Act of 1942. The policy objective was to ensure that farm household incomes would not fall behind urban household incomes ("parity price"). Agricultural cooperatives and other farm organizations formed a strong interest group for raising producer prices annually. Because postwar conservative governments (LDPs) relied heavily on rural votes, the protection of rice and other agricultural subsidies had political importance. Japanese farmers used to grow crops such as wheat, barley, buckwheat, and soybeans as a second crop after the rice harvest. But this practice had almost died out by 1970 because the domestic production of those crops received almost no protection, and, therefore, could not compete with imports. Between 1960 and 1975, Japanese self-sufficiency rates for wheat declined from 39 to 4 percent and for coarse grains from 66 to 2 percent. While the per capita consumption of rice decreased steadily due to the westernization of eating habits, self-sufficiency rates over 100 percent have been measured only for rice since 1960.

In short, the 1960s and 1970s were characterized by a skewed development of rice production supported by mechanization and other technological progress under an increasing amount of government protection. However, agricultural protection was not as high as that in other advanced economies in 1955. But by 1965, after a series of annual increases in producer prices for rice during the high growth period, Japan became the leading industrialized country in level of support for agriculture.

Given the reluctance of the majority of farm families to give up their land, the efficiency goal of reducing production cost per unit by rationalization was pursued in various ways but without much success. For example, the Ministry of Agriculture launched an ambitious plan with the passage of the Basic Agricultural Act of 1961. The act stated that the objective of agricultural policy was to create, through specialization and diversification, independent farms, called "viable farms," large enough to survive without off-farm wage employment and without government subsidies. The initial target was to create one million "viable farms" by 1970. But this policy never worked. The majority of households chose to work off the farm and to keep a small piece of land on which to grow rice.

Farming was not an economically attractive option for young people. Shortly after the Basic Agricultural Act was passed, the urban-rural income disparity started to shrink and, in fact, reversed. Comparing per capita household income, for example, farm households have fared better than nonfarm worker households since 1975. This was not because of improvements in agricultural productivity, however, but mostly because of the increased job opportunities within commuting distance and the hefty price support for rice. The ratio of agricultural income to the total household income of farm families declined as we saw in the previous section. Of course, some farmers intensified production of non-rice products such as vegetables, fruits, livestock, poultry, and flowers in order to survive without nonfarm jobs. This diversification and intensification caused the value share of rice in total agricultural production to fall from 47.4 percent in 1960 to 37.9 percent in 1970 and then to 28.8 percent in 1988.

In summary, the economic reality of Japanese agriculture was the emergence of small landholders whose income came more and more from non-agricultural sources. By preserving the family farm tradition, the equity goal was maintained at the expense of the efficiency goal. Most farm families were, as far as the household economy was concerned, not very different from working class families in the nonfarm sector.

During the late 1960s, excess capacity of rice production became a financial problem for the government. The strict administrative control over production and marketing since the Food Control Act of 1942 made the concept of demand and supply adjustment alien to Japanese rice producers. The government not only had to support the difference between the producer price and consumer price each year, but had to deal with the left-over rice from the previous years' production as well. In 1969, the Ministry of Agriculture developed two policy innovations: (1) the introduction of a category of rice (usually high quality rice) to be distributed and marketed without government intervention (called *jishu-ryutsu-mai*, meaning voluntarily distributed rice), and (2) a voluntary acreage reduction program under which farmers received 20,000 Yen per 0.1 hectare taken out of production. This voluntary program was not popular and the Ministry had to introduce a mandatory program for the curtailment of rice production in 1971. This time, all of the farmers had to fallow approximately 10 percent of their rice acreage, irrespective of their size, specialization, location, and status (full-time or part-time).

To find a niche in industrial society, agricultural policymakers had to redefine policy objectives for themselves. In 1970, the Ministry of Agriculture announced a new policy direction under the title of promoting *sogo-nosei* (comprehensive agricultural policy). The new goals were to (1) encourage individual viable farmers, (2) encourage group farming, including part-time farmers, (3) encourage the smooth retirement of non-viable farmers, (4) streamline the processing and marketing mechanism, (5) ensure parity for farm households, (6) stabilize agricultural commodity prices, (7) help creation of nonfarm income sources, and (8) provide physical improvement of rural areas including non-agricultural infrastructure and community development.

The emphasis shifted from agriculture per se to rural affairs in general. Policies within the Ministry of Agriculture itself were not well coordinated. The Agricultural Promotion Areas Act of 1969 was to protect agricultural land as much as possible from urban and industrial expansion. The Act for Promotion of Industry in Farm Areas of 1971, on the other hand, encouraged industrial decentralization to the countryside which caused a large-scale conversion of farmland to industrial uses. In the absence of other agencies with implementation powers and money, the Ministry of Agriculture assumed the leading role in upgrading standards of living in rural areas. Through various subsidy schemes for structural improvement of agricultural, forestry, and fisheries communities, a significant sum of taxpayers' money (classified as the agricultural budget) was directed to non-agricultural aspects of rural infrastructure such as roads, sewage, drinking water, community halls, children's parks, and sports grounds. In this regard, Ministry of Rural Affairs would be a better title than Ministry of Agriculture, Forestry, and Fisheries.

This qualitative shift in agricultural policy reflects the changing environment of public policies in the 1970s when the emphasis of public guidance for regional development shifted to more balanced and environmentally sound growth and to the enrichment of social and cultural life in both urban and rural areas. Regionalization and regionalism were advocated by leading intellectuals and practitioners in planning.

During this overall restructuring period following the oil crisis of 1973, the Ministry of Agriculture faced the difficult task of readjustment. Rice producers still received an increase in price supports. For example, the producer price of rice rose 30 percent in 1974. Calder (p. 270) contrasted the case of Japan with other advanced nations: "In Western Europe sharp cutbacks in support for agriculture followed the oil shock in 1973, but Japanese conservatives did not follow. ...Japan did not cut support prices for food gains, such as rice, until the late 1980s."

Government expenditures to support domestic rice production (and non-production) were acknowledged to be one of the three big sources of the national deficit, called the "Three K's": *Kome* (rice), *Kokutetsu* (Japan National Rail), and *Kenpo* (National Health Insurance). The Council of Administrative Reform under Doko Mitsuo's powerful chairmanship advocated a retrenchment of public spending. Agricultural spending became an easy target in the campaign for a reduced role for government. In 1982 and for the first time in its postwar history, the total budget of the Ministry of Agriculture did not exceed in nominal terms that of the previous year. Foreign pressure to open up agricultural markets was another factor urging policy innovations in agriculture.

Regionalization (*chiiki-nosei*) became a leading concept in agriculture as well. Regional variations in crop production, farm structure, infrastructure, and land improvement were taken into consideration in formulating agricultural policies. In 1978, the former rice control measure was replaced by a diversion policy called *tensaku* which gave subsidies for growing specified non-rice crops on paddies. Simple fallowing was discouraged. While the former policy had been applied unilaterally throughout the country, prefectures were now assigned different quotas for diversion acreage. This regionalized acreage control system continues today. In 1987, those prefectures where rice was important in supporting viable farm units were assigned lower diversion quotas (16-20 percent), while others received high quotas (21-30 percent). In the field of promoting the structural improvement of rural communities, the Ministry of Agriculture respects local needs, encourages local initiatives, and welcomes policy and planning innovations from below.

The shift away from agriculture, however, did not cease in spite of the overall recession and slower growth after the oil shock in 1973. The Japanese economy went through a period of tough restructuring, changing from a dependence on heavy industry to a diversified combination of high-tech and light industries plus the traditional leading sectors of automobile, machinery, and steel. But the trend toward a more decentralized industrial structure only contributed to the stability of part-time farming. Part-time farming and urbanization (rising price of farmland) continued to obstruct the consolidation and improvement of agricultural operations. The government advocated the use of lease agreements for enlarging farm size. But the majority of part-time farm families were reluctant to lease out their land because they feared a possible loss of their family asset. Even such ideas as group farming and the machine bank, which did not interfere with the tenure structure, were not very well received by ordinary farm families.

Conclusion: Efficiency Versus Equity in Japanese Agriculture

Japan was a late developer among capitalist economies. The drive for efficiency has been strong in all sectors. At the same time, distributive policies in the form of agricultural policy, small business policy, and regional development policy (for special regions such as mountain villages, depopulated areas, and outer island areas) have been given rather consistent political attention, especially in the postwar period.

Compared to commonplace agricultural policies adopted in other advanced economies, Japanese agricultural policy has had an orientation toward equalizing productive capacity between advanced regions and backward regions, and between progressive farmers and mediocre farmers. In order to upgrade the production capacity of irrigation agriculture with its small-scale and fragmented tenure structure, the Ministry of Agriculture adopted the land consolidation method initiated in Germany before 1900 and devised subsidy programs for which any territorial group of farmers could voluntarily apply. Even in the prewar period, the Ministry of Agriculture was characterized as a "subsidy distribution" ministry. This system of volunteerism and formation of groups as the beneficiaries of agricultural subsidies has been consistent throughout the 20th century. Another characteristic of agricultural policy in Japan is that subsidization is mainly for fixed capital formation on a collective basis. That is, many subsidy programs promote field consolidation, land improvement, drainage improvement, and construction of access roads and other production facilities. Subsidies seldom provide direct income transfers. During the postwar shift to a highly industrialized society, the notion of parity and price support of rice was introduced to maintain farm family income.

One may argue that the reason for this equity focus stems not so much from humanitarian concern but from elite concern for the survival and maintenance of the overall efficiency of the national economy. Japanese capitalists, politicians, and bureaucrats realize that it would be more costly in the long run to pursue a radical form of economic restructuring that would put the vulnerable and weak sectors and factions of its economy in jeopardy and despair.

In reviewing the postwar agricultural policy, we have observed the tensions between the efficiency goal and equity goal. It is extremely difficult to clearly identify where the swing is between these two goals. One reason is that these two are not mutually exclusive. The other is that a given policy at any one time usually has elements which contradict each other. And policymakers are never articulate -- they say at best that they want to meet both the efficiency goal and equity goal. Since the late 1980s, the swing has been towards greater efficiency, and the waning of equity concerns is harshly affecting rural Japan. At the same time, the support for agriculture from the social, environmental, and cultural concerns has been strong. A careful and critical examination is needed on many fronts.

References

Australian Bureau of Agricultural and Resource Economics. 1988. *Japanese Agricultural Policies: A Time of Change*. Canberra: Australian Government Printing Service.

Bernier, B. 1988. The Japanese peasantry and economic growth since the land reform of 1946-47. Pp. 78-90 in E.P. Tsurumi, ed., *The Other Japan: Postwar Realities*. Armonk, NY: M.E. Sharpe.

Bray, F. 1986. *The Rice Economies: Technology and Development in Asian Societies*. New York: Basil Blackwell.

Calder, K.E. 1988. *Crisis and Compensation: Public Policy and Political Stability in Japan, 1949-1986*. Princeton, NJ: Princeton University Press.

Dore, R.P. 1959. *Land Reform in Japan*. London: Oxford University Press. (Reprinted in 1985.)

Fukutake, T. 1980. *Rural Society in Japan*. Tokyo: University of Tokyo Press.

Hayami, Y. 1988. *Japanese Agriculture Under Siege: The Political Economy of Agricultural Policies*. New York: St. Martin's Press.

Hayami, Y. and Vernon W. Ruttan. 1985. *Agricultural Development: An International Perspective*. Revised and expanded edition. Baltimore: The Johns Hopkins University Press.

Imamura, Naraomi. 1991. Kyo-kyo-kyo: Nippon Nogyo no Tenkai Ronri o motomete (Community, competition, and cooperation: In search for the way out for Japanese agriculture). Pp. 1-98 in Naraomi Imamura, Shoji Inuzuka, and Kazushige Kawai, eds., *Nogyo no Katsuro o Sekai ni miru (Redirecting Japanese Agriculture with a Global Perspective)*. Tokyo: Nosangyoson Bunka Kyokai.

Imamura, Naraomi and Kazuo Morozumi. 1989. *Nogyo Hogo no Rinen to Genjitsu (Agricultural Protection in Theory and Reality)*. Tokyo: Nosangyoson Bunka Kyokai.

Johnston, B.F. and P. Kilby. 1975. *Agriculture and Structural Transformation: Economic Strategies in Late-Developing Countries*. London: Oxford University Press.

Jussaume, R.A., Jr. 1991. *Japanese Part-Time Farming: Evolution and Impacts*. Ames: Iowa State University Press.

Kada, R. 1980. *Part-Time Family Farming*. Tokyo: Center for Academic Publications.

Kelly, W. 1982. *Irrigation Management in Japan: A Critical Review of Japanese Social Science Research*. Cornell East Asia Papers No. 30. Ithaca, NY: China-Japan Program and Rural Development Committee, Cornell University.

Kuroda, T. 1990. Urbanization and population distribution policies in Japan. *Regional Development Dialogue* 11(1):112-129.

Latz, G. 1989. *Agricultural Development in Japan: The Land Improvement District in Concept and Practice*. Geography Research Paper No. 225. Chicago, IL: Committee on Geographical Studies, University of Chicago.

Ministry of Agriculture, Forestry, and Fisheries (MAFF). 1990a. *The State of Japan's Agriculture 1989: A Summary Report*. Tokyo: MAFF.

Ministry of Agriculture, Forestry, and Fisheries (MAFF). 1990b. *Annual Report on Agriculture, FY 1990 (excerpts)*. Tokyo: MAFF.

Ministry of Agriculture, Forestry, and Fisheries (MAFF). 1990c. *Structural Changes in Japan's Agriculture*. (Japan's Agricultural Review, Vol. 18.) Tokyo: Japan International Agricultural Council for the MAFF.

Ministry of Agriculture, Forestry, and Fisheries (MAFF). 1990d. *Nogyo Hakusho Fuzoku Tokeihyo for FY 1990 (Annual Report on Agriculture, Statistical Appendix)*. Tokyo: Norin Tokei Kyokai.

Ministry of Agriculture, Forestry, and Fisheries (MAFF). 1990e. *The 65th Statistical Yearbook of Ministry of Agriculture, Forestry, and Fisheries, 1988-89*. Tokyo: MAFF.

Ministry of Agriculture, Forestry, and Fisheries (MAFF). 1990f. *Pocket Norinsuisan Tokei 1990 (Statistical Handbook for Agriculture, Forestry, and Fisheries 1990)*. Tokyo: Norin Tokei Kyokai.

Ministry of Agriculture, Forestry, and Fisheries (MAFF). 1990g. *1990 Census of Agriculture, Preliminary Results*. Tokyo: MAFF.

Miyamoto, Kenichi, ed. 1990. *Hojokin no Seijikeizaigaku (The Political Economy of Subsidy)*. Tokyo: Asahi Shinbunsha.

Moore, R.H. 1990. *Japanese Agriculture: Patterns of Rural Development*. Boulder, CO: Westview Press.

Nakane, C. 1967. *Kinship and Economic Organization in Rural Japan*. London: Athlone Press.

Namiki, M. 1960. The farm population in the national economy before and after World War II. *Economic Development and Cultural Change* 9(1) (Part 2):29-42.

National Land Agency (Kokudo-cho). 1989. *Kokudo Riyo Hakusho (Annual Report on National Land Use)*. Tokyo: Government Printing Office.

Ogura, T. 1980. *Can Japanese Agriculture Survive?* Tokyo: Agricultural Policy Research Center.

Ohkawa, K. and H. Rosovsky. 1960. The role of agriculture in modern Japanese economic development. *Economic Development and Cultural Change* 9(2):43-68.

Rural Development Planning Commission. 1981. *Rural Planning and Development in Japan*. Tokyo: Rural Development Planning Commission.

Saeki, Naomi. 1989. *Nogyo-Keizaigaku Kogi (Agricultural Economics Lecture Notes)*. Tokyo: Tokyo University Press.

Smith, T. 1959. *The Agrarian Origins of Modern Japan*. Stanford, CA: Stanford University Press.

Statistics Bureau, Management and Coordination Agency. 1990. *Japan Statistical Yearbook 1990*. Tokyo: Government Printing Office.

Takahashi, Akiyoshi. 1987. Noson seisaku to noson mondai (Rural policy and rural problems). Pp. 83-118 in Otohiko Hasumi, Eiji Yamamoto, and Akiyoshi Takasashi, eds., *Nihon no Shakai (Japanese Society)*. Volume 2. Tokyo: Tokyo University Press.

Tamamki, Akira, Isao Hatate, and Naraomi Imamura. 1984. *Suiri no Shakai-kozo (Social Structure of Irrigation Development)*. Tokyo: United Nations University (Tokyo University Press).

Wailes, Eric J., S. Ito, and Gail L. Cramer. 1991. *Japan's Rice Market: Policies and Prospects for Liberalization*. Fayetteville: University of Arkansas and Arkansas Agricultural Experiment Station.

Waswo, A. 1977. *Japanese Landlords: The Decline of a Rural Elite*. Berkeley: University of California Press.

3

Present Issues of Sustainable Land Use Systems and Rural Communities in Japan

Ryohei Kada and Junko Goto

Introduction

This chapter discusses the history and future directions of land use systems and rural communities in Japan. The first section addresses land use systems with an emphasis on agricultural uses. It discusses the changes which have occurred in Japanese agriculture over the last several years, mainly since the country entered into its period of high economic growth and industrial development. Some of these changes have been welcomed but some have not. For example, increased yields and quality have been welcomed but problems of over-production and soil fertility deterioration have not. The second section provides an overview of Japanese rural communities. After a brief history, the section addresses current problems of the rural communities. The section concludes by addressing the sustainability of the communities, and policies under consideration for maintenance of the communities.

Japanese Agriculture

The term "sustainability" is quite new to Japanese agriculture. Sustainable development lacked urgency because Japan's rice-based agriculture has been a nearly sustainable system enabling farmers to produce rice in the same paddy fields year after year. However, this sustainable system has been gradually changing since the early 1960s when Japan entered a highly industrial economic development stage. The rice production system has also changed from one of relatively low input and output to one of high input and output. As Japanese agriculture has rapidly increased its intensity of use per unit of land area, problems have emerged such as soil fertility deterioration and soil and groundwater pollution. Recently, the Japanese people have become more concerned about these issues because global environmental problems such as global warming and desertification have become serious issues.

Locational and Climatic Conditions of Japanese Agriculture

Japan consists of four major islands surrounded by several smaller ones stretching from north to south over a distance of 3,000 kilometers. Japan can be divided into two climates: the north which experiences a cold season with sub-frigid conditions and the south which experiences hot, humid summers and cold, dry winters. It also includes a temperate monsoon area. Major differences in climate, however, provide Japan with a great variety and abundance of vegetation. Heavy rainfall is an important factor governing Japanese agriculture. Annual rainfall in Japan averages about 1,800 millimeters and ranges from 1,500 to 2,500 millimeters.

The Economic Situation of Japanese Agriculture

Limited land resources for agricultural purposes restricts the development of Japanese agriculture (Table 3.1). About 66 percent of the total land area in Japan is mountainous. Of the remaining 34 percent, 20 percent is used for urban purposes, which leaves only about 14 percent for agricultural use.

Among major agricultural producing countries, Japan has one of the lowest percentages of arable land. Meadows and pasture account for only a tiny percentage of total land area and restrict dairy and livestock production in Japan. The land use figures for Japan basically explain the nature of Japanese agriculture -- the large percentage of forested area and limited arable and pasture land make for a highly intensive farming structure.

Agriculture's share of population in Japan fell from 16 percent in 1970 to about 7.3 percent in 1987. However, it is important to point out that the agricultural labor force is governed by the seasonal nature of agriculture in Japan. Those who find it profitable to work in agriculture over the summer

Table 3.1. Land Utilization, 1986.

	Hectares	
	(1,000)	(Percent)
Arable land	5,358	14.2
Forest and woodland	25,198	66.9
Residential, roads, etc.	7,087	18.8
Total land	37,643	100.0

Source: Adapted by the authors from Ministry of Agriculture, Forestry, and Fisheries (MAFF) data.

months may find it equally profitable to work in industry or other occupations during the winter.

Farm household population fell from 26.6 million in 1970 to 19.2 million in 1988. While the number of persons engaged in farming decreased sharply over this period, the number of persons engaged only in other jobs and those mainly engaged in housekeeping have increased. Persons over 60 years of age make up 39 percent of the agricultural workforce. Farming is becoming increasingly popular among people retired from nonfarm jobs.

Agricultural Production

We now turn to the changing nature of Japanese agricultural production. Rice demand has been declining sharply since the mid-1960s, and the production trend of rice reflects the growing diversification of the nation's dietary habits.

Oversupply problems characterize several major farm products including rice and mandarin oranges. The undersupply of low self-sufficiency commodities such as wheat, soybeans, and feedgrains emphasizes the need for diversification. The decline in the growth of products such as rice is countered by the growth of livestock products, whose share of total agricultural output went from 15 percent in 1960 to 27 percent in 1987. Japan's area for cultivation is small in comparison with its competitors, thus the increase in livestock in an already highly intensive farming system increases the need for feed imports. Commercial production of livestock in Japan started expanding in the mid-1960s, is still in the development stage, and more expansion can be expected in the future.

Agricultural Land Use

The pattern of land use in Japan is changing constantly (Table 3.2). The most noticeable change is the overall reduction in Japan's agricultural land area. Total agricultural land use has been reduced by 8 percent, or from 5,796,000 hectares in 1970 to 5,317,000 hectares in 1988. This reduction is basically a result of the difference between agricultural land expanded and land converted to non-agricultural use ("ruined"). The total area of cultivated land expanded was 23,700 hectares in 1988 and the total area of cultivated

Table 3.2. Japanese Agricultural Land (1,000 Hectares).

	1970	1988
Expanded	63.0	23.7
Converted or idled	116.1	46.6
Artificially transformed	(100.9)	(25.2)
Total	5,796.0	5,317.0

Source: Adapted by the authors from MAFF data.

land converted in the same year was 46,600 hectares, which includes 40,400 hectares of artificially transformed land. In Japan, the strong external demand for agricultural land has more than offset the Japanese government's endeavor to retain the superior land in farms. It is remarkable that upland field area increased by 2 percent while paddy field area decreased by 15 percent during the same period. The increase of upland field area is basically due to the expansion of meadows developed in the mountainous areas (Table 3.3). Meadow land area increased by 122 percent since 1970. The total meadow land area in 1988 was about 636,000 hectares.

In 1988, paddy field area constituted 54 percent of total agricultural land area, hence continued to dominate total agricultural land. Of the 46 percent of upland field area, 24 percent was normal upland field, 12 percent meadows, and 10 percent under permanent field. Although the importance of meadow land to the Japanese economy is growing, in 1988 it still constituted only 12 percent of Japan's total agricultural land area (Table 3.4).

A few words should be mentioned about the Rice Crop Diversion Policy which was initiated in 1971 and the Paddy Field Reorganization Policy which was introduced in 1978. In recent years, the Japanese Government has endeavored to combat the surplus of rice production through diversification (Table 3.5). Total diversified area in 1988 was 817,000 hectares which was 15.4 percent of the total cultivated area.

Table 3.3. Expansion of Meadows (1,000 Hectares).

Year	Acreage
1970	285.7
1975	485.2
1980	580.3
1985	620.8
1988	636.2

Source: Adapted by the authors from MAFF data.

Table 3.4. Composition of Agricultural Land (Percent).

	1970	1988
Paddy field	58.9	54.3
Upland field	41.1	45.7
Normal upland field	25.8	24.1
Permanent field	10.4	9.6
Meadows	4.9	12.0
Total	100.0	100.0

Source: Adapted by the authors from MAFF data.

Table 3.5. Diversification Area of Paddy Field (1,000 Hectares).

	1982	1988
Paddy Field	-672	-817
Diversified Field	+595	+619
Forage crops	+173	+135
Wheat & barley	+113	+134
Vegetables	+110	+120
Soybeans	+96	+96

Source: Adapted by the authors from MAFF data.

Paddy field area diverted from rice production is concentrated in vegetables, soybeans, forage crops, wheat, and barley. For example, in 1988, 817,000 hectares were diverted from rice production and used as follows: 135,000 hectares for forage crops, 134,000 hectares for wheat and barley, and 96,000 hectares for soybeans. The fact that forage crops constitute the largest area of diversification from rice helps the shift towards livestock production. Diversification is also being promoted through the increase of multipurpose paddy fields which can produce a variety of crops as well as rice.

It is not surprising to note that actual planted area fell by 12 percent from 1970 to 1987 (Table 3.6). The major crop reduced was rice, with area decreasing from 2,923,000 hectares in 1970 to 2,146,000 hectares in 1987, or 26.6 percent. Wheat and barley area also fell on a large scale, around 20 percent.

The main increase in aggregate planted area has occurred in forage and manure crops. This area increased from 736,000 hectares in 1970 to 1,089,000 hectares in 1987, a 48 percent increase. The increase is basically from land formerly in rice. It is important to note that Japan has limited options for diversion to other crops from rice basically because of the high cost of production compared to imported product prices. This situation is similar to that faced by the EC. Consequently, the Japanese are particularly interested in recent changes in the Common Agricultural Policy.

Table 3.6. Actual Planted Area (1,000 Hectares).

	1970	1987
Rice	2,923	2,146
Wheat & barley	483	386
Forage crops	736	1,089
Total	6,311	5,533

Source: Adapted by the authors from MAFF data.

An international comparison of farmland acreage relative to population reveals that Japan's greatest disadvantage is land area. The U.S. with just over double the population has 77 times the farmland acreage of Japan. The U.K. with just under half the population of Japan has three times as much farmland. Farming is intensive in Japan to compete with these countries. Farmland acreage per farm household provides evidence: The U.S. has 175.2 hectares per farm household or 146 times that in Japan. The U.K. has 77.1 hectares per farm household in comparison with Japan's 1.2 hectares. The U.K. has 64 times more and France has 25 times more area per farm household than Japan. The intensity is apparent in farmland prices. At 1,372,000 Yen per 10 acres, Japan's farmland is 33 times more expensive than U.S. prices, 16 times French prices, 9 times U.K. prices, and 3 times German prices. High land values offset less area per farm so that Japanese farmers on average have about the same *total value* of property as most European farmers. Very high land prices provide Japanese farmers with a greater problem. Difficulties in expansion mean that production must constantly become more intensive if Japanese agriculture is to compete with imports. Government policies contribute to high land values which in turn make farm area expansion expensive.

Farm Size and Productivity

The issue of farm size and productivity is dictated by this intensive agricultural system. Paddy field area reached its peak in 1965 at 0.7 hectares per farm household before falling to 0.6 hectares in 1988 (Table 3.7). Dairy cattle per household increased 8.4 times -- from 3.4 head per farm household in 1965 to 28.6 head in 1988. Beef cattle increased 7.8 times from 1.3 head in 1965 to 10.2 head in 1988, and hogs increased 35.8 times from 5.7 head in 1965 to 203.9 head in 1988. Layers increased from 27 head in 1965 to 1,356 head in 1988, or 50.2 times. The number of chickens increased 28.6 times, from 892 in 1965 to 25,500 per household in 1988. The number of greenhouses per farm household has also undergone a tremendous increase.

Table 3.7. Change in Farm Size (Per Farm Household).

	1965	1988
Paddy field area (Hectares)	0.7	0.6
Dairy cattle (Head)	3.4	28.6
Beef cattle (Head)	1.3	10.2
Hogs (Head)	5.7	203.9
Layers (Head)	27.0	1,356.0
Chickens (Head)	892.0	25,500.0

Source: Adapted by the authors from MAFF data.

The change in paddy field size can be explained by the Rice Crop Diversion Policy which reduced the total cultivated area of rice. Livestock production will continue to grow.

The long-term change in Japanese farmland acreage can be explained by several factors (Figure 3.1). From the year 700 to the late 16th century, rice yields remained nearly constant at about 1.6 tons per hectare. From that period up until the mid-1870s, rice yields increased gradually. However, the most dramatic increase occurred during the 110 years after the Meiji Restoration in 1868. This was due to strenuous efforts by both the government and the people of Japan. Before World War II, higher productivity was achieved through a number of methods. These included improved rice varieties, use of animal power, and improved fertilization. The small farm management system was also improved through increased use of both fertilizer and labor. Following the war, however, increased production was brought about by labor saving techniques, mainly mechanized farming.

The difference in productivity by cultivation size basically shows that the smaller the area of agricultural production, the longer the hours worked per hectare and the higher the secondary production costs per unit of output. For example, farmers with agricultural areas of less than 0.3 hectare worked 82 hours per 0.1 hectare in 1982. Farmers with more than 5 hectares worked only 32 hours per 0.1 hectare.

Other interesting facts are revealed about present agricultural production and productivity trends. First, agricultural productivity in Japan has improved at a rate similar to other countries under the high-level economic growth of the country during the 1960s. However, the sharp increase in wages and the slow increase in agricultural product prices during the period of stabilized economic growth from 1976-83 created economic incentives for adjustments noted earlier. It is important to note, however, that with the decline in farm population and slowing growth of agricultural production, the circumstances surrounding the improvement of productivity have changed. The annual rate of increase in agricultural production between 1960 and 1970 was 2.3 percent, whereas from 1976 to 1983 it was only 0.9 percent. On the other hand, the annual rate of decline in farm population was 3.7 percent from 1960 to 1970 but only 3.0 percent from 1976 to 1983.

A number of ideas have been put forward for improving agricultural productivity in the future. Expanding farm size would help. This scale expansion could come through an increase in farmland liquidity and a systemization of agricultural production. It is important to devise more efficient means of utilizing agricultural machines and facilities. Second, Japanese agriculture would benefit from the increased use of improved farming technology as a means of increasing efficiency and production. Third, the maintenance of agricultural production and the increased promotion of higher value-added cash crops are considered essential to improve productivity. To achieve this, it is important that Japanese agricultural producers strive for the

38

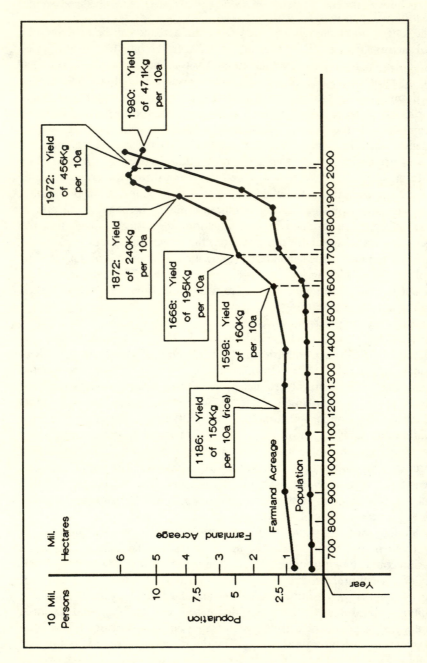

Figure 3.1. Change in Farmland Acreage (10a or 10 ares = .1 hectare).
Source: Adapted by the authors from MAFF data.

following: to undertake domestic production of crops best suited to Japan, to promote development of new demand within the country, to expand agricultural-product exports, and to add more value to cash crops.

Changing Cropping Patterns

Under the monsoon climate conditions of high summer temperatures and high humidity, Japan has high vegetative productivity. The average production of organic matter in Japanese forests, for example, is 13 to 23 tons (on dry matter basis) per hectare, which is as much as tropical forests which produce 10 to 35 tons. These numbers contrast with Mediterranean Europe where average forest production is only between 2.5 and 15 tons per hectare. The high production capacity of nature has enabled Japan to produce rice as the most productive, population-supportive crop for nearly 2,000 years.

In the paddy fields, soil tends to possess several characteristics because rice has been continuously planted for a long time. First, the decomposition of organic matter is slowed in the paddy fields. Paddy fields are covered by water during the summer time, hence decomposition of organic matter in the soil is minimal even under the high temperatures. During the winter time, the soil becomes dryer but organic decomposition is minimal due to the cold temperatures. In addition, rice straws and roots remain, which maintains soil fertility to a certain degree. As a result, rice production tends to be relatively easily stabilized over a long period of time.

Second, ferrous ions are susceptible to deoxidization to ferric ions in a watered paddy field. Then, the acid condition of the soil becomes neutral which makes the rice plants grow well.

Third, phosphorus ions, separated from ferrous compounds, become available for the rice plants under those conditions. Furthermore, many minerals dissolved in the water are supplied to the paddy fields during the irrigation period. These minerals can be conserved and used as nutrients for the growing plants because water does not leak through the base soil of the field. Finally, soil erosion caused by heavy rainfall is minimized when terraced paddy fields are located in a stepwise pattern on the mountain slopes.

For these reasons, Japanese farmers have endeavored to create as many paddy fields as possible out of the total agricultural land. In areas where the winter is not very cold, paddy fields had been utilized to produce barley and other upland crops in winter. This system of crop rotation has been established in parts of Japan for a long time.

Generally speaking, because average farm size in Japan is very small, farmers have tried to produce as much as possible per unit of land and adopted such a crop rotation system. In this system, livestock and human manure as well as decomposed leaves are widely used to supplement soil fertility. This has established a self-contained, recycling system of paddy land use.

However, when Japan entered into the high economic growth period, Japanese agriculture started to change very dramatically. More and more farm household members sought nonfarm employment and the agricultural population started to decline very rapidly. As a result, many rice farmers became part-time farmers, where rice was only produced as a monoculture system.   The remaining farmers tended to be specialized in vegetable production, livestock production, and the like. Among rice farmers, rice was produced only with heavy use of machinery, chemicals, and chemical fertilizers. The intensity of land use declined. In livestock farming, feeds were mostly purchased to increase the number of livestock.

These changes not only have broken down the crop rotation system but also created agricultural pollution problems such as a point-source accumulation of livestock manure from intensive livestock systems. On the other hand, soil fertility on crop farms has gradually deteriorated due to the heavy dependence upon chemical fertilizers.

Demand and policy factors have also influenced the nature of agricultural land use systems in Japan. The most important factor may be the reduction of rice consumption in Japan (Table 3.8). Although rice is still a staple food in the Japanese diet, per capita consumption of rice decreased from the peak of 115 kilograms in 1962 to 72 kilograms in 1988. Japanese people are eating more livestock and dairy products. This demand side change has necessarily reduced rice production acreage.   The Japanese government has used government subsidies to encourage rice farmers to divert rice production to other crops in the paddy fields. However, these crops are not as profitable as rice. Some paddy fields have been idled. As a result, the self-sufficiency rate of food production in Japan has rapidly decreased.

Future Perspectives and Research Needs

To increase the food self-sufficiency rate and to utilize paddy fields more efficiently, one of the most important current agricultural policy goals in Japan is how to reorganize cropping patterns of paddy fields. The Ministry of Agriculture has adopted and implemented a long-term project to remodel the system of land use toward one of a more ecologically adaptive and economically viable system. One of the core plans is to reorganize the use of paddy fields in such a way that combines rice as a main crop with other upland crops such as wheat, barley, soybeans, or forage on a regional basis.

Table 3.8. Japanese Rice Consumption (Kilograms per Year).

Year	Amount Per Capita	Year	Amount Per Capita
1955	110.7	1970	95.1
1960	114.9	1980	78.9
1962 (peak)	118.3	1988	71.9

Source: Adapted by the authors from MAFF data.

To this end, for example, the so-called "manure bank" system is encouraged in each locality to utilize organic manure (substituted for chemical fertilizer) and maintain soil fertility. The basic idea is to create a "regional-basis material cycle" system through cooperation between livestock farmers and cash grain farmers within each region or locality. A number of research projects have also been started by researchers of the government agricultural research institutes and universities to examine the sustainability of alternative land use systems.

Since the high economic growth period, the nature of Japanese agriculture has shifted toward a more energy intensive and resource exploitative system. As a result of the increased use of commercial fertilizers and other agricultural chemicals, yields have increased and stabilized and quality has improved.

At the same time, a number of problems have emerged in this transformation process such as overproduction of rice and other crops, deterioration of soil fertility, and dangers to food safety. These issues are not only raised by the agricultural side but also by consumer groups and the general public of Japan. There is also an increasing concern among Japanese consumers over the safety of agricultural products, both domestic and imported products.

It is a time of change in the system of agricultural production and land use. More and more effort should be devoted toward recreating the viability and sustainability of Japanese agriculture drawing on lessons of the rice-based agriculture which displayed favorable ecological characteristics for centuries.

Introduction to Rural Communities

This section gives a concise introduction to changes in the structure and function of Japanese rural communities. The history and geography of rural settlement in Japan is briefly explained. It is, however, beyond the scope of this chapter to examine in detail the many interpretations of the meaning of the village community which is often debated among Japanese scholars.

In the midst of the protection versus free-trade debate over the future of Japanese agriculture, some protectionists claim that rural communities (or the village community, *sonraku kyodotai*) have been and still are the backbone of Japanese society. During the high growth period, Japan experienced a massive rural-to-urban migration. Currently, urban population, defined as the people residing in the statistical "Densely Inhabited Districts" (DIDs), outnumbers rural population (non-DID) by about 20 percent. But many urbanites maintain a close relationship with their home village. Even for those who have been metropolitanists for generations, the village represents something they value. The survival and preservation of rural communities is deemed to be important not only for the present rural population but also for the entire society. Therefore, there are those who strongly argue that, however marginal the average farming operation is in the macroeconomic sense, it should be protected from foreign pressure and the global restructuring process. The protectionist camp often uses this social and cultural factor -- attachment and adherence to the village -- as one of the several important reasons for supporting Japanese agriculture. Before going on, let us first define rural communities.

Structure of Rural Communities

The term *rural community* in this chapter is a translation of *nogyo shuraku* which is defined as the basic unit of rural settlement discernible by territorial integrity and often characterized by kinship relationships. There are some 140,000 rural communities in Japan today. Many of these communities were established prior to the Meiji Restoration in 1868. The expansion of rural settlement corresponded with agricultural development in early modern Japan, especially the installment of irrigation systems and water control. Therefore, many rural communities carry place names associated with the history of agricultural development. In the Edo period, these rural communities served, at the same time, as a natural village and as an administrative village. The village was a unit of local autonomy, cooperation in irrigation agriculture (i.e. rice farming), and mutual help in the sphere of reproduction. The same village was used as a unit of tax collection (mainly in harvested rice), various forms of coercion and regulation by the authorities, and residence of farmers.

Geographically speaking, there are four types of rural communities as classified by the physical settlement pattern. The *agglomerated settlement* is the most densely populated pattern and is found in an area where human settlement and agricultural development are most advanced, such as in western Japan. The *nucleated community*, the most common pattern throughout the country, is not as dense as the agglomerated community, but is easily identified as a unit with the housing concentration usually surrounded by paddies and other fields. The *dispersed settlement in plains* is a rare pattern of rural settlement in Japan and is found notably in such areas as the Tonami plain and Ooigawa's downstream plain. The reasons for this pattern include fire prevention and military security. In Hokkaido, frontier development necessitated such a settlement pattern in many rural communities. The final pattern is the *dispersed settlement in the hill and mountain areas* -- a common form of human settlement where flatland is only available in small quantities.

Production and Reproduction in Rural Communities

Since the early Meiji period, several reforms and consolidations of local governments have taken place which reduced the number of cities, towns, and villages (municipalities, the lower level of local governments) from more than 70,000 in 1883 to 3,254 in 1985. In spite of these changes in administrative structure, rural communities have persisted as the basic unit of rural settlement. The territoriality did not change much except in urbanized rural communities. The economic foundation of most communities, however, shifted from agriculture to non-agricultural employment in adjacent cities and towns as many farmers became part-time farmers. In many communities, the attention of community life started to shift from cooperation in agriculture to matters of mutual concern to neighbors such as festivals, garbage collection, and road improvement. However, the maintenance of agricultural land and water resources is still an important concern for most rural communities.

It is difficult to generalize the path of transformation for rural communities because of the regional and locational variations.[1] In 1960, the Ministry of Agriculture, Forestry, and Fisheries started to collect various data on all rural communities in the country as a special sub-component of the Census of Agriculture. The total number of rural communities has not changed much in the past 30 years. There were slightly more than 152,000 rural communities in 1960 and about 140,000 in 1990. The rate of decline was faster between 1965 and 1970. Many of the remotest rural communities ceased to exist as a community, while those communities in the metropolitan fringe were absorbed in the urban expansion. Since 1970, the decline has been gradual but found in the same settings as above, i.e., rural-remote and urban-fringe areas.

Japan's high economic growth was characterized by urbanization and industrialization. Industrial development was concentrated along the "Pacific Ocean Belt" megalopolis (from Kita-kyushu to Tokyo); the rest of the country experienced an unprecedented volume of out-migration. Throughout the entire period of high growth, only eight prefectures (Tokyo, Kanagawa, Saitama, Chiba, Aichi, Osaka, Hyogo, and Nara) had population growth rates higher than the national average. The share of population in cities rose from 56.1 percent in 1955 compared to 72.1 percent in 1970 (Table 3.9).

We should be careful in reading such statistics, however. A nationwide amalgamation of lower-level local governments took place around 1955, reducing the total number of cities, towns, and villages from 9,868 in 1953 to 3,975 in 1956. This reorganization increased the tendency of "over-boundedness" of cities. That is, a city often includes rural areas and population and sometimes very sparsely populated mountainous areas as well. In order to statistically differentiate urban and rural population, "Densely

---

[1] If we want to trace the transformation of rural communities from the pre-World War II period to present, a simplified scenario is from an agricultural community with a social hierarchy based on landlordism, owner-tenant stratification, and the household system in the pre-war period, to an egalitarian owner-cultivator community, and finally to an economically differentiated rural community.

Table 3.9. Urban and Rural Population.

Year	Total Population	Share of Population in:		Share of Population in:	
		Cities (% in land)	Towns & Villages	DID (% in land)	Non-DID
	(1,000)	(Percent)		(Percent)	
1950	84,115	37.3 (5.3)	62.7	----	---
1955	90,077	56.1 (18.0)	43.9	----	---
1960	94,302	63.3 (22.0)	36.7	43.7 (1.03)	56.3
1965	99,209	67.9 (23.5)	32.1	48.1 (1.23)	51.9
1970	104,665	72.1 (25.3)	27.9	53.5 (1.71)	46.5
1975	111,940	75.9 (27.1)	24.1	57.0 (2.19)	43.0
1980	117,060	76.2 (27.2)	23.8	59.7 (2.65)	40.3
1985	121,049	76.7 (27.3)	23.3	60.6 (2.80)	39.4
1990	123,612	77.4 (27.8)	22.6	----	---

Source: Census of Population; 1990 from preliminary counts.

Inhabited Districts" have been used since the 1960 Census of Population.[2] The proportion of urban population increased from 43.7 percent in 1960 to 60.6 percent in 1985. Rural population (non-DID population) declined both as a percent of the total population and in the absolute numbers between 1960 and 1980.

---

[2] A "densely inhabited district" is defined as a census enumeration district with a population density of over 4,000 per square kilometer, forming a congregation of more than 5,000 persons together with adjacent districts (DIDs). The population residing in DIDs is considered urban population.

Let us now introduce another measure of urban and rural population. The share of households in rural communities increased gradually from 50 percent in 1960 to 59 percent in 1990. The absolute number of households residing in rural communities increased steadily. These numbers result from two kinds of population movement: one was a loss in remote rural areas and the other was an influx of non-farm households into rural communities in the urban fringe. Because the gain in urbanized (or suburbanized) communities exceeded the loss in remote communities, the total number of households in rural communities grew.

The internal social composition of rural communities changed drastically (Table 3.10). On average, the share of farm households in total households of rural communities decreased from 61.4 percent in 1960, to 23.2 percent in 1980, and to 16.0 percent in 1990.[3] The share of full-time farm households in total farm households decreased from one-third in 1960 to about one-tenth in 1990. Although the average number of farm households per rural community did not decrease rapidly (39 in 1960, 33 in 1980, and 27 in 1990 as shown in Table 3.10), the income structure of these farm households changed

Table 3.10. Number of Rural Communities and Household Composition.

Year	Number of Rural Communities	Average Number of Rural Households per Community		
		Total (*)	Farm Households	Nonfarm Households
1960	152,431	64 (50)	39	25
1965	150,326	86 (54)	38	48
1970	142,699	81 (41)	37	44
1975	142,876	118 (52)	35	83
1980	142,876	141 (56)	33	108
1990	140,144	172 (59)	27	144

Source: Rural Community Surveys, Census of Agriculture.
(*) = Share of the number of households residing in rural communities in nation's total number of households (%).
NOTE: In 1970, groups (concentrations) of non-farm households residing in rural communities but forming separate administrative sub-districts were excluded.

---

[3] The change in the definition of farm households between 1980 and 1990 partially explains the sharp drop in farm numbers in 1990.

sharply. The development of industries in nearby urban centers as well as the improvement of transportation systems helped to smooth this transition so that rural residents did not need to move to cities. The majority of rural communities today are within an hour's commuting distance from the nearest DID. More than 75 percent of rural communities and rural households are less than one hour away from nearby urban centers. The fact that rural residents can commute to cities means that city residents can move to rural areas and commute to cities. As expected, the influx of newcomers to rural communities was adversely related to the distance to the nearest urban center.

Contemporary Rural Problems

According to the Ministry of Agriculture, Forestry, and Fisheries, the present problems of rural Japan can be summarized as follows: (1) insufficient public service provisions, (2) continuing conflicts between agricultural and other uses of land and water resources, (3) difficulty in agricultural restructuring and rationalization, (4) unpromising markets for off-farm jobs, (5) depopulation and aging of the rural population, (6) disintegration of traditional community relationships, and (7) growing demands of urban population for access to and use of rural resources.

Following the announcement of the Fourth National Comprehensive Development Plan, the committee on rural development issues of the National Land Agency reported the planning directions for rural areas: (1) to secure employment and income opportunities for rural residents through promotion of agriculture, forestry, and indigenous industry and through introduction of modern industry; (2) to conserve and promote proper utilization of land and water resources and to improve and modernize the agricultural structure; (3) to enhance the habitability of rural areas as well as improve living conditions and public services; (4) to establish and enhance the networking of human, material, and information capital flows between places, mainly between the city and countryside; (5) to effectively cope with the problems of aging; (6) to foster voluntary citizen organizations to coordinate various initiatives and interests for better rural life; and (7) to maintain the multiple functions of rural areas. In short, the dilemma is how to maintain the social and economic viability of rural communities while encouraging open exchanges and networking with other localities, especially urban areas. Reconciling this dilemma is perceived as the key to a survival strategy for rural communities by both national and local level planners and policymakers.

In the rest of the chapter, we will focus on problems in the urban fringe and remote rural areas. (Problems of communities where the sustain-ability of farming is the main concern were discussed in the preceding section.)

In the metropolitan regions, *konju-ka* ("rurbanization") is underway. Tokyo, Osaka, and Nagoya metropolitan regions absorbed 5.5 million people from other regions during the first half of the 1960s. This rapid pace of urban growth proceeded with almost no public intervention. Land prices rose rapidly in the 1960s and some farmers became instant millionaires. The reduction of total farmland from 6.1 million hectares in 1960 to 5.8 million hectares in 1970 corresponded with the expansion of urban areas. The areas in DIDs grew from 390,000 hectares (1.03 percent of the nation) in 1960 to 640,000 hectares (1.71 percent) in 1970.

To cope with the problems of urban sprawl, the City Planning Act of 1968 and the Agricultural Promotion Areas Act of 1969 introduced new systems of development control. Under the City Planning Act, the Town Planning Area was zoned into the Urbanization Promotion Area and the Urbanization Control Area. Under the Agricultural Act, the piecemeal permission system for farmland conversion was replaced by agricultural zoning which tried to preserve farmland as strictly as possible in the Agricultural Promotion Zone. Drawing these lines became a complex task for local governments with two systems aiming at different goals and administered by separate ministries.

Although located in the urban fringe, many farmers did not want to give up their land and became part-time farmers instead. It became difficult for local groups of farmers to reach a consensus on coordinating individual agricultural operations, including such routine activities as canal and road maintenance, communal forest care-taking, and strategic decisions as applying for land improvement, irrigation improvement, cooperative mechanization, and other subsidized schemes for modernization and adjustment. This individualism among farmers accclerated the tendency for disorderly and fragmented land use patterns. Newcomers in urban fringes were generally families commuting to metropolitan centers who had no understanding of the farmers' problems. Thus, *konju-ka* presented physical, fiscal, and social challenges to the small municipalities in metropolitan fringe areas. Agricultural modernization in such areas became doubly difficult for the minority who remained farmers: internal urbanization converted many family farmers into small-scale landowners who marginally maintain agricultural operations while external urbanization brought conflicts in land use and in social life. It was only recently that the government ministries with overlapping responsibilities began to coordinate their expertise in facilitating rational land use and infrastructure building in urban fringe areas.

What happened in remote rural communities was also problematic, although the nature of the problems differed a great deal from urban fringe problems. Since the 1960s, their problems were of "depopulation" (*kaso mondai*), meaning the social and economic deprivation and environmental degradation of areas which experienced rapid population outflow -- especially of young people. The concerns for economically bypassed or underdeveloped regions led to special area legislation such as the Mountain Village Development Act of 1965 and the Depopulation Areas Special Measures Act of 1970.

During the 1980s, the secondary effect of rapid out-migration from those rural communities became apparent. It is a shift from population decrease because of migration to population decrease because of natural loss (aging and death). Many very remote communities are faced with the threat of extinction. Sometimes, over one-third of the residents in a community are over 65 years of age, often living in single or two-person households. Even for those households where relatively young people remain, part-time farming cannot guarantee a good life because the nature of off-farm work, even if it exists, is very precarious and low-wage in remote rural areas. The local governments (towns and villages) are usually poor and must rely on subsidized programs and projects to survive as a public body and to try to meet the basic needs of residents. At the same time, the recent boom in resort development and "green" tourism has created a new opportunity for remote rural areas. Recognition of the scenic and other amenity and commercial value of country-side resources is becoming a potential solution to *kaso-mondai*.

Conclusions

In early modern Japan, carrying capacity was determined by land area (especially paddy fields), its productivity, and the availability of water. Many farm households supplemented their livelihood by earning cash income from off-farm employment. But that was the supplementary rather than the dominant element managing their lives. Industrialization in the twentieth century brought a kind of "urbanization" to the social and economic life of rural communities. The carrying capacity of a given rural community is determined by the availability and prospect of nonfarm jobs in the vicinity. The future depends not so much on the community's agricultural resource endowment but on macroeconomic and industrialization forces.

We have come a long way from the notion of village-Japan in the free trade versus protectionism debate. Most concerns about the future of agriculture tend to create an ideal image of the village community which is not a fair representation of rural communities today. The village-Japan ideal lives in the heart of many policymakers, bureaucrats, and opinion leaders but some of the national elites want to end the myth.

The income sources of rural community life in Japan have already been transformed in spite of the paternalism and deliberation of the agricultural bureaucracy. But the government has not retired to the background. The development, prosperity, and decline of those rural communities took place in part because of governmental maneuvering to induce non-agricultural development in rural areas, including a part of the agricultural policy called the rural industrialization program. More importantly, living conditions in rural communities have been improved through a myriad of public programs including those under the Ministry of Agriculture. Currently, interests in the development and welfare of rural areas are pursued by at least the following central ministries: Agriculture, Construction, Local Affairs, Education, National Land Agency, Health and Welfare, International Trade and Industry,

Post and Telecommunications, Environmental Protection Agency, and Finance. The lack of a clear sense of direction and leadership has plagued rural planning and policy implementation at the local level. In discussing the "sustainability" of rural communities, there is no single authority which dares to define the term. Many people agree that rural communities must be sustained and that "rural" policy needs to be realigned with agricultural policy. The realignment of such policies should begin with an open-minded and rigorous learning of the diversity and complexity of the problems at the community level. How to weigh and interpret the contribution of agricultural activities to community life in various regional and local circumstances is a difficult task. After that task we can start to talk about who and how to define "sustainability" of rural communities in contemporary Japan.

References

Befu, H. 1965. Village autonomy and articulation with the state: The case of Tokugawa, Japan. *Journal of Asian Studies* 25(1):19-32.

Dore, R.P. 1978. *Shinohata, A Portrait of a Japanese Village*. London: Allen Lane.

Fukutake, T. 1980. *Rural Society in Japan*. Tokyo: University of Tokyo Press.

Hasumi, Otohiko. 1987. Gyosei-son toshiteno shizen-son: Nihon noson-shakai-ron no saikento (National villages as administrative villages: Revisiting theories on Japanese rural society). Pp. 3-32 in Ryukichi Kitagawa, Otohiko Hasumi, and Hiroichi Yamaguchi, eds., *Gendai Sekai no Chiiki-shakai (Communities and Localities in the Modern World)*. Tokyo: Yushindo.

Hebbert, M. 1986. Urban sprawl and urban planning in Japan. *Town Planning Review* 57(2):141-158.

Ishimitsu, K. and J. Goto. 1982. Changing rural areas as the object of rural planning in Japan. *Irrigation Engineering and Rural Planning* 2:28-42.

Jussaume, R.A., Jr. 1991. *Japanese Part-time Farming: Evolution and Impacts*. Ames: Iowa State University Press.

Kornhauser, D. 1982. *Japan: Geographical Background to Urban-Industrial Development*. 2nd edition. London: Longman.

Kuroda, T. 1990. Urbanization and population distribution policies in Japan. *Regional Development Dialogue* 11(1):112-129.

Kusumoto, Yuji. 1989. Shuraku-kukan no seibi-shuho (Land use patterns and planning in rural communities). Pp. 325-342 in Nippon Kenchiku Gakkai, ed., *Zusetsu Shuraku: Sono Kukan to Keikaku (Rural Communities: Their Space and Planning)*. Tokyo: Toshi-bunka-sha.

Latz, G. 1989. Agricultural development in Japan: The land improvement district in concept and practice. Geography Research Paper No. 225. Chicago, IL: Committee on Geographical Studies, University of Chicago.

Ministry of Agriculture, Forestry, and Fisheries. 1987. *Nogyo Hakusho, 1987 (Annual Report on Agriculture, 1987)*. Tokyo: Government Printing Office.

Ministry of Agriculture, Forestry, and Fisheries. 1990. *Annual Report on Agriculture, FY 1990*. (Excerpts: development of market-adaptable agriculture and the revitalization of rural areas (provisional translation).) Tokyo: Government Printing Office.

Ministry of Agriculture, Forestry, and Fisheries. 1990. *Pocket Norinsuisan Tokei 1990 (Statistical Handbook for Agriculture, Forestry, and Fisheries, 1990)*. Tokyo: Norin Tokei Kyokai.

Ministry of Agriculture, Forestry, and Fisheries. 1990. *1990 Census of Agriculture, Preliminary Results*. Tokyo: Ministry of Agriculture, Forestry, and Fisheries.

National Land Agency. 1989. *Kokudo Riyo Hakusho (Annual Report on National Land Use)*. Tokyo: Government Printing Office.

Rural Development Planning Commission. 1981. *Rural Planning and Development in Japan*. Tokyo: Rural Development Planning Commission.

Saito, Hitoshi. 1989. *Nogyo-Mondai no Tenkai to Jichi-Sonraku (The Agrarian Problem and Village Autonomy)*. Tokyo: Nihon Keizai Hyoronsha.

Smith, R.J. 1978. *Kurusu: The Price of Progress in a Japanese Village 1951-1975*. Stanford, CA: Stanford University Press.

Statistics Bureau, Management and Coordination Agency. 1990. *Japan Statistical Yearbook 1990*. Tokyo: Government Printing Office.

Takahashi, Akiyoshi. 1987. Noson seisaku to noson mondai (Rural policy and rural problems). Pp. 83-118 in Otohiko Hasumi, Eiji Yamamoto, and Akiyoshi Takahashi, eds., *Nihon no Shakai (Japanese Society)*. Vol. 2. Tokyo: Tokyo University Press.

Tamaki, Akira, Isao Hatate, and Naraomi Imamura. 1984. *Suiri no Shakai-kozo (Social Structure of Irrigation Development)*. Tokyo: United Nations University (Tokyo University Press).

4

Japanese Farm Structure: Trends and Projections

Naraomi Imamura, Nobuhiro Tsuboi,
and Tokumi Odagiri

Why are the Japanese so sensitive about rice? Why is rice treated as holy in Japan? Why can't the Japanese consider rice simply a market commodity? We can find answers to these questions in the post-16th century social and economic history of Japan. Since 1968, the beginning of rice overproduction, the sense of "free from rice" has been gradually growing among farmers and the nation as a whole. Furthermore, the concept of agriculture in Japan is changing rapidly and as a result the Japanese are for the first time confronting the rice issue.

Historical Perspective

History of Irrigation Agriculture in Japan

Since the 16th century, irrigated rice farming has been a predominant sector of Japanese agriculture. During this period, techniques to control rivers and organizations to manage the techniques and irrigation facilities developed rapidly. Many of the irrigation facilities (except in Hokkaido) were constructed beginning in the 17th century. Uplands, wastelands, and forests were converted to wet paddy fields with irrigation water from rivers and the result was an expansion of paddy field area.

Prior to the 16th century, upland farming was one of the main farming sectors. The vitality of upland farming has decreased gradually since then. Irrigated rice farming has influenced society differently than did upland farming. Farmers cannot develop irrigated farming independently in Japan because they are not allowed to construct and maintain irrigation facilities, other than underground water irrigation systems, themselves. Irrigation farming requires construction of irrigation facilities and these facilities only work well under suitable management and maintenance of the facilities.

Therefore, the success of irrigated farming depends on organizations to manage facility maintenance and irrigation water use. On the other hand, development of upland farming did not require an organization. Therefore, irrigated farming has led to an organization-oriented society.

The nature of an organization-oriented society in an irrigated farming area is characterized by the nature of the irrigation system. We can classify irrigation systems into three categories by the source of the irrigation water. The first type of system is one which uses underground water for irrigation. This system does not require an organization as do the other two systems. Farmers independently can get water to irrigate their fields.

The second type of system requires an organization to control a large river as the source of the irrigation water. These irrigation systems involve large irrigated areas originating from the water source and spreading to the fields through networks of canals. The physical factors associated with this type of system tend to foster large, centralized organizations to control the water source and manage the irrigation system. In these cases, the central government's role is solely investment and organization of the irrigation system.

The third type of system does not require a big, centralized organization but does require a smaller organization. This type of irrigation system is predominant in areas where there are several small rivers such as Japan. In areas where small rivers are predominant, the scale of investment and organization for irrigation facilities is small compared to that in areas of large rivers. A local government or village organization can supervise these smaller irrigation systems without help from the central government. These factors tend to promote the development of self-governing local organizations.

As previously discussed, Japanese society is an organization-oriented society. This means that if a farmer is not a member of an organization, he cannot get irrigation water and cannot survive. Therefore, people are willing to belong to an organization. The nature of Japanese society originates from irrigation systems. This point explains one of the major reasons why the Japanese are so anxious about the downfall of rice farming. This downfall would tend to weaken the irrigation system, its organizational characteristics, and its symbolism so important to Japanese society.

Dual Standard System of Economy — Gold/Silver and Rice Standard

Rice has almost 400 years of history making it similar to the concept of the family farm in the U.S. Rice has had a role in Japanese society since the end of the 16th century. This is an important reason why the Japanese are so concerned about rice. The economy in modern society was based upon the gold standard for decades. Modernization in European countries began under the gold/silver standard system. But when Japan's modernization began in the 18th century, the standard was based on rice and gold/silver. Since the end of the 16th century, rice has played a role in Japanese society. It maintained a real status in social and economic stability longer than that of gold/silver.

During the Edo period, gross production of village communities, local states, and the Tokugawa State was estimated by the amount of rice produced ("Kokudaka System"). The local and central governments collected taxes mainly in rice at a fixed yield. When governments and farmers needed money, they sold some rice. Rice yields directly influenced the economies of farmers, village communities, and local and central governments. Thus rice played a role in the wealth of the nation.

The reason why rice remained the standard for so long is as follows. Since the time rice farming became a predominant sector in Japan's agriculture in the 16th century, rice has been the main food staple. The supply-demand balance for rice was very tight during the Edo period. The Meiji government, which was replaced with the Tokugawa Shogunate in 1868, abolished the rice standard. In spite of the abolishment, rice maintained its former status because it remained the nation's food staple and the main income source for farmers until the 1960s. Furthermore, the supply-demand balance for rice was still very tight.

The overproduction of rice which began in 1968 has continued. This overproduction prompted the government to promote acreage reduction programs. Under these circumstances, the sense of "free from rice" has been gradually growing among farmers and the nation. But the symbolic meaning of rice is still present in the minds of many Japanese. However, we are not insisting that Japan keep its historical notions of rice. The circumstances of rice have been changing rapidly, and we believe that Japan is now in a position to deal with rice as a commodity in the market.

Trends in the Twentieth Century

Changes in Main Agricultural Indices in the Twentieth Century
The area of arable land in Japan increased from 4,470,000 hectares in 1880 to 5,969,000 hectares in 1950 (Table 4.1). Since the peak in 1950, it gradually decreased to 5,516,000 hectares in 1990. Table 4.1 also shows that the number of farm households was 5,417,000 in 1910. (Statistics are not available on the number of farm households before 1907.) The number of farm households peaked at 6,270,000 in 1949 and decreased to 3,835,000 in 1990.

Promotion of the reclamation policy for unemployed people who returned home from overseas possessions by the government directly affected these numbers. Thus, acreage of arable land and the number of farm households peaked in 1950 and 1949, respectively, or 4 to 5 years after the end of World War II. During the 20th century, the average size of a farm household has remained constant at about one hectare. Other data on farm area and numbers were presented in Chapter 3.

Table 4.1. Changes in Japan's Main Agricultural Indices.

Year	Area of Arable Land[a] (1,000 Hectares)	Number of Farm Households[b] (1,000)	Area of Arable Land per Farm Household[c] (Hectares)	Population of Agricultural Workers[d] (1,000)
1880	4,470	---	---	---
1910	5,273	5,417	0.97	---
1920	5,424	5,484	0.99	14,128
1940	5,912	5,390	1.10	14,140
1950	5,969	6,176	0.97	16,132
1960	5,702	6,057	0.94	13,121
1970	5,711	5,342	1.07	9,334
1980	5,611	4,661	1.20	5,484
1990	5,516	3,835	1.44	---

Sources: [a]1880-1970 - Tochi Daichou Menseki; 1980-1990 - Koteisisanzei Daichou.
[b]1880-1940 - Nouji Toukeihyou, MAFF. May be viewed as number of farms assuming one household per farm.
[c]1950-1990 - Nougyou Sensasu (Agricultural Census), MAFF.
[d]Kokusei Chousa (Population Census).

Changes in the Number of Farm Households by Size Class

Most Japanese farms are very small in size (Table 4.2). The share of farms of less than 1.0 hectare was 69 percent and that of farms 5.0 hectares and over was 2 percent in 1990. Prior to World War II, the share of large farms had been increasing. But the trend returned to former levels after World War II because of the land reform. The share of farms 3.0 hectares and over fell from about 4 percent in 1940 to 2 percent in 1950. The government started to promote policies of farm size enlargement under the Basic Agricultural Law in 1961. Since then, farm size has been increasing gradually but it is still small compared to other OECD countries.

Changes in Tenure Patterns

The most serious problem in Japanese agriculture before World War II was tenancy disputes. Landlord-run communities, tenancy, high farm rents, and poverty of tenants prevented development of agriculture and rural communities. The share of tenants in total farm households was more than 25 percent and part-owners accounted for more than 40 percent of total farm households (Table 4.3).

Table 4.2. Number of Farm Households by Size of Cultivated Land (1,000).[a]

Year	Cultivated Land Area per Farm					
	Less than 0.5 Hectares	0.5 - 1.0	1.0 - 2.0	2.0 - 3.0	3.0 - 5.0	5.0 Hectares and Over
1908	2,016	1,764	1,055	348	163	62
1910	2,032	1,789	1,048	322	155	71
1940	1,796	1,768	1,322	309	119	76
1950	2,530	1,973	1,340	208	77	48
1970	2,025	1,614	1,286	255	90	71
1980	1,937	1,311	990	249	102	72
1990	2,627		1,016		112	80

Sources: 1980-1940 - Nouji Toukeihyou, MAFF; 1950-1990 - Nougyou Sensasu (Agricultural Census), MAFF.
[a]See Table 4.1 for total number of farm households.

After World War II, the government carried out land reform under the supervision of the GHQ. As a result, tenants decreased to about 1 percent of total farm households and tenant farmland also decreased to less than 10 percent of total farmland compared to 46 percent before the reform. The problem was solved entirely. Since 1975, farmland rented out has been increasing. But tenants or part-owners have had no large-scale tenancy disputes.

Changes in Production

The main crops in Japan before World War II were rice, wheat, barley, and mulberry for sericulture. Production of vegetables and fruits was minor. Beef and hog production was also small at that time. After World War II, production of vegetables, fruits, beef, dairy, poultry, and hogs increased with growth of the Japanese economy.

Table 4.3. Changes in Tenure Patterns (1,000).

Year	Total	Full Owners	Part Owners	Tenants
1908	5,408	1,799	2,117	1,492
1910	5,417	1,777	2,139	1,501
1940	5,390	1,646	2,286	1,458
1955	6,043	4,211	1,593	239
1975	4,905	4,137	715	53

Sources: 1908-1940 - Nouji Toukeihyou, MAFF; 1955-1975 - Nougyou Sensasu (Agricultural Census), MAFF.

For about 100 years, planted area of paddy fields increased gradually up to 1968 and then peaked at 3,274,000 hectares in 1969, a little less than 56 percent of total farmland (Table 4.4). Rice production in 1968 exceeded demand and the acreage reduction program was started in 1969. The planted area of rice in 1989 was 2,097,000 hectares which was 64 percent of the peak. About 30 percent of the paddy fields was set aside for other crops. The record production of rice in Japan was 14,453,000 metric tons (MT) in 1967. Production then fell to 10,347,000 MT in 1989, 72 percent of the record.

The planted area of wheat reached a record in the first half of the 1940s. Planted area decreased with the growth of imports from the United States after World War II. The least amount of area planted was 75,000 hectares in 1973 but since then area has been gradually increasing with promotion of the acreage reduction program for rice. The main diversion crops for rice are wheat, barley, vegetables, soybeans, and feed crops.

The productivity of crops measured by production per hectare has been gradually increasing for about the last 100 years (Table 4.4). Rice productivity was 2.37 MT in the first half of the 1900s but in the latter half of the 1980s increased to 4.93 MT. In the case of wheat, productivity was 1.07 MT in the first half of the 1900s and 3.52 MT in the latter half of the 1980s.

Table 4.4. Average Annual Planted Area, Production, and Yield of Main Crops, and Number of Livestock.

	1900-1904	1940-1944	1965-1969	1985-1988
Arable Land (1,000 Ha)[a]	5,077	5,880	5,733	5,516
Rice[b]				
Planted area (1,000 Ha)	2,824	3,090	3,265	2,225
Production (1,000 MT)	6,691	9,112	13,612	10,968
Yield per hectare (MT)	2.37	2.95	4.17	4.93
Wheat[b]				
Planted area (1,000 Ha)	469	827	375	258
Production (1,000 MT)	502	1,423	1,016	909
Yield per hectare (MT)	1.07	1.72	2.71	3.52
Meat Production[b]				
Beef cattle (1,000 MT)	31	62	177	560
Hogs (1,000 MT)	5	27	491	1,561

Sources: [a]1900-69 - Tochi Daichou Menseki, Nihon (Teikoku) Toukei Nenkan; 1985-89 - koteisisannzei Daichou Menseki.
[b]Nourinshou Toukeihyou, MAFF.

Table 4.5 shows that production has responded to demand. The share of production accounted for by rice *fell* 23 percent and by livestock and vegetables *rose* 30 percent between 1955 and 1989.

Current Problems

Small Farm Size

Average farm size remained small, 1.2 hectares, in 1990. A farm family can cultivate 15 to 20 hectares of paddy at low cost per unit using highly efficient farm machinery popular in Japan. The mismatch between farm size and productivity is the biggest problem in Japanese agriculture.

The government has promoted the enlargement of farms through various policy measures in the past three decades. One of the main purposes of the Basic Agricultural Law of 1961 was to increase farm size. The size of rice farms has changed little. However, two types of farms, livestock and greenhouses, have increased in size and are now quite large.

Decrease in Newcomers Engaged in Farming

In 1963, an estimated 89,800 farm family entrants chose farming as a career. But in 1990 the number was only 1,800. This low figure shows that Japan needs to be concerned about maintaining the number of active farmers. The government employs various policy measures to promote entry into farming and to maintain and increase the number of active farmers. But these policies are not effective.

Because of government restrictions, in Japan it is very difficult for nonfarm family members and institutions to enter farming. The government protects farm households from competition from corporations. Still, the number of farm households has decreased significantly in the past decade (Table 4.6).

The Aging of Farmers

The rapid decrease of new entrants to farming beginning in the 1960s is consistent with the aging of the current population of farmers. Currently about 3.1 million workers (Kikanteki Nogyo Jujisha) are employed in

Table 4.5. Shares of Gross Agricultural Output Value by Type of Product (Percent).

Year	Total	Rice	Livestock	Vegetables	Fruits	Other
1955	100	52.0	11.2	7.2	4.0	25.6
1970	100	37.9	23.2	15.8	8.5	14.6
1989	100	29.2	27.0	21.0	8.5	14.3

Source: Seisan Nogyo Shotoku Toukei, MAFF.

Table 4.6. Actual Farm Numbers from 1975 to 1990 and Projected Numbers for 2000 and 2010 (1,000).

	1975	1980	1985	1990	2000	2010
Total farm households	4,953	4,661	4,376	3,835	3,120	2,430
Active farm households	1,250	1,033	867	625	500	430

Source: Economic Planning Agency, Sangyo Keizai Shouiinnkai Houkoku.
NOTE: Active farm households are farm households which have one or more
    male workers who are 16 to 60 years old and work 150 days or more
    in farming.

agriculture. About 29 percent of these agricultural workers are 65 years of age and older. In some areas, the aging of farmers and the decrease of new entrants means a decrease in farm households in the near future.

Problems of Family Farms
    The family farm is dominant in Japan. There are only a few corporations in farming. And many of these corporations are groups of family farms and their sizes small.
    Younger generations fail to enter farming not because of low income in farming. Even if they can become high-income earners in farming, or if they are the successors of high-income family farms, many of them still will not enter farming. Many of them prefer to work in corporations which provide satisfying work for them.
    Farming utilizes various kinds of technology from production to marketing. In family-farm dominated agriculture, a family which has only one operator and one or two workers is a farming unit. The operator of the farm has to master the various kinds of technology required. He has no chance to get on-the-job training due to the farm being a family/independent-based activity. Working for a corporation makes getting on-the-job training easier.

Projection into the Twenty-First Century

Difficulty of Projections
    The government liberalized imports of beef and oranges 100 percent in 1991. Now, the government and farmers are confronted by the issue of "liberalization of rice." Liberalization will change Japan's rural areas and agriculture based on rice farming.
    Import liberalization, price support levels, and zoning laws could change the trends which have dominated Japan's agriculture. So it is very difficult to project from past trends into the 21st century. Many changes have occurred

in the last five years. Most results of the agricultural census of 1990 are not yet available. This is another reason for difficulty in projecting from past trends.

Farm Numbers in 2010

The Economic Planning Agency of the government announced the projected number of farm households in 2010 in July 1991 (see Table 4.6). It used the results of the 1990 agricultural census to make these projections. Numbers of total farm households, 3,835,000 in 1990, are projected to decrease to 3,120,000 in 2000 and to 2,430,000 in 2010.

The Ministry of Agriculture, Forestry, and Fisheries classifies total farm households into several categories. The "active farm household" category is a farm household which has one or more male farmers who are 16 to 60 years of age and work 150 days and more in farming. The number of active farm households was 625,000 in 1990. The numbers are projected to decrease to 500,000 in 2000 and to 430,000 in 2010.

Number of Agricultural Workers in 2010

Table 4.7 shows the number of agricultural workers in 2010 as forecasted by the Economic Planning Agency in July 1991. This projection was also based on the results of the census conducted in 1990. Numbers of farm family members, 17,296,000 in 1990, are projected to decrease to 14,400,000 in 2000 and to 11,320,000 in 2010. The ratio of farm family members 65 years and older to all farm family members was 20 percent in 1990. In that same year, that ratio for total households in Japan was 12 percent. The ratio of farm households is projected to increase to 27 percent in 2000 and to 29 percent in 2010. And the ratio of total households is projected to increase to 17 percent in 2000 and to 21 percent in 2010.

The number of active farmers who worked 150 days and more in farming was 3,127,000 in 1990. The number is projected to decrease to 2,300,000 in 2000 and to 1,660,000 in 2010. The ratio of active farmers 65 years and older to all active farmers was 48 percent in 1990. This ratio is projected to increase to 56 percent in 2000 and 2010. These trends show that aging of farm family members is a serious problem in rural areas.

Implications of Past Trends and Projections:
Issues of Common Property, Competition, and Cooperation

Basic Character of Traditional Village Communities

Small-dispersed-fields, plot-to-plot irrigation, long irrigation canals, and traditional village communities are the main factors of irrigated rice farming in Japan. Irrigated rice farming has characterized the Japanese farm and rural structure for centuries. Irrigated farming and its systems were

60

Table 4.7. Number of Agricultural Workers in Selected Years.

	1975	1980	1985	1990	2000	2010
Family farm members	2,319.7	2,136.6	1,983.9	1,729.6	1,440.0	1,132.0
Percent 65 years old and older	13.7	15.6	17.3	20.0	27.4	29.0
Active farmers[a]	488.9	412.8	369.6	312.7	230.0	166.0
Percent 65 years old and older	24.3	27.8	36.4	48.2	56.1	56.0
Male	229.7	203.6	187.0	162.2	130.0	102.0
Percent 65 years old and older	32.3	35.1	43.2	54.4	58.5	56.9
Female	259.1	209.2	182.6	150.5	100.0	64.0
Percent 65 years old and older	17.2	20.6	29.5	41.5	53.00	54.6

Source: Economic Planning Agency, Sangyo Keizai Shouinkai Houkiku.
[a]Active farmers are farmers who work 150 days or more in farming per year.

mentioned earlier. This section explains the nature of traditional village communities called "Mura."

Mura were self-governing communities as well as the basic organizations of the central or local governments that ruled the people in the Edo period (1600-1868). Mura had rights of tax collection, police authority, and jurisdiction. Thus, Mura had all rights except military authority. Each had individual customs or rules to keep the community in order and to maintain the irrigation system.

Tokugawa Shogunate and individual local governments in the Edo period employed minimum rules to maintain the uniformity of Japan or each state. The governments seldom interrupted the self-governing rights of the Mura. Each Mura had an elected village headman to enforce the customs and rules.

Mura displayed their abilities as self-governing organizations for controlling irrigation water and maintaining irrigation facilities. Rice production was a matter of life and death for the Mura. Irrigation was the key factor of rice production. As control of the irrigation system was the most important facility of the Mura, the nature of irrigation systems influenced the character of the communities.

Monoblock Coexistence of Collectiveness and Competitiveness

A farmer could not invest in and maintain irrigation facilities without help from other farmers. However, the farmer could cultivate rice under the collective efforts of many farmers maintaining and managing an irrigation system. The local Mura was the basic organization of farmers which integrated their individual efforts into collective ones. So, the irrigation water was the public property of the Mura. Thus farmers had a need to belong to the Mura in order to secure irrigation water for their paddy fields. If a farmer wanted more water, he could not get it unless it was secured for the Mura first, not for himself. This organization of farmers as a community is called "More Water for the Interest of Mura" (Waga Mura ni Yori Ooku no Mizu wo). This is one of the important origins of Japanese collectiveness.

The interrelationship of farmers through irrigation water was characterized not only by their collectiveness but their competitiveness. The farmers had a need to secure irrigation water for their own paddy fields but only after they got water for the Mura. This interrelationship is called "More Water for the Individual Interest" (Gaden Insui). This is one of origins of Japanese competitiveness.

Collectiveness and competitiveness are disparate concepts and usually do not coexist. But in Japan, the two principles did coexist. The existence is not separate but monoblock. This is a very important principle upon which traditional Japanese rural communities are based.

Rural communities or Mura were not the only organizations for irrigation systems in Japan. Larger organizations consisting of several Mura were called "Mura Federations" (Mura Rengo). Usually a Mura could not control a river and get water by itself. So several Mura would unite in an effort to control the river. The main canal from the river was the common property of several Mura, that is, the federation.

The principle of monoblock coexistence of collectiveness and competitiveness was not confined to Mura communities. The principle also applied to the organization of the federations. Each Mura could not secure irrigation water from the river individually. The Mura had to collectively form a "Mura Federation" to get water from the river. But after they got the water into the main canal which was the common property of the federation, they competed to get more water for each Mura.

The theory of monoblock coexistence of collectiveness and competitiveness is an important characteristic of Japanese society. Japanese unite against existences outside their organization and compete with each other inside their organization. This theory helps to explain why Japan has adapted well to a market economy.

Issues in Transition from the Monoblock to Cooperativeness

The small, dispersed field pattern of farming remains a serious problem in organizing farmland and farm machinery effectively. Enlargement of farm size and economical use of large machinery requires consolidation of fields. But it seems impossible to overcome the problem by the market system or the traditional land reform method. We need the cooperation of farmers.

The oversupply tendency for rice may continue in the future and more area will be diverted from rice to other crops. Under these circumstances, the sense of monoblock coexistence of collectiveness and competitiveness based on irrigated rice farming is losing its influence on farmers. Furthermore, part-time farmers who have no interest in monoblock coexistence are becoming the predominant members of the farming sector.

The sense of monoblock coexistence of collectiveness and competitiveness is not visible to the younger generations of the community who have no interest or experience in irrigated rice farming. If farmers want to effectively manage farmland, they have to cooperate with these part-time farmers. But it is very difficult for them because the part-time farmers have little sense of monoblock coexistence.

It is very important for full-time farmers to create a new sense of cooperation to overcome problems before monoblock cooperation disappears entirely from rural communities. The new principle must be visible to every kind of farmer. It may not be the "monoblock coexistence of collectiveness and competitiveness" which was based on the experiences of history, but it may be a cooperativeness based on mutual understanding and benefit.

References

Imamura, Naraomi, ed. 1991. *Nogyo no Katsuro wo Sekai ni Miru* (*Redirecting Japanese Agriculture with a Global Perspective*). Tokyo: Nosangyoson Bunka Kyokai.

Masamura, Kimihiro, ed. 1988. *Kodo Sangyo Shakai to Kokka* (*Highly Industrialized Society and the Nation*). Tokyo: Chikuma Shobo.

Ministry of Agriculture, Forestry, and Fisheries. 1990. *Structural Changes in Japan's Agriculture*. Tokyo: Japan International Agricultural Council for MAFF.

Sasaki, Takashi. 1985. The role of village collective management traditions in the formation of group farming: Case study in Japan. *Regional Development Dialogue*, Vol. 6, No. 1. Nagoya, Japan: U.N. Center for Regional Study.

Tamaki, Akira. 1977. *The Development Theory of Irrigation Agriculture*. Tokyo: Institute of Developing Economies.

Tamaki, Akira. 1982. *Nihon no Shakai Sisutemu* (*Japanese Social System*). Tokyo: Nosangyoson Bunka Kyoukai.

APPENDIX

Limitations and Potential of Family Farms in Japan: Can Japanese Family Farms Survive?
Nobuhiro Tsuboi

Introduction

Family farms predominate in Japan. The farms have been transferred from generation to generation through inheritance. Today, difficulties in transferring the management of the farm to succeeding generations are increasing. The difficulties are evidenced in the aging of farm operators and in the underutilization of farm resources including the expansion of idle farmland. The difficulties in transferring farm management and resources will become more serious in the future.

In this chapter, I discuss the "limitations of family farms," specifically that full-time family farms with reasonable income are not being transferred to the next generation. Limitations of family farms also include the difficulty of transferring farm resources among farms. For the purpose of this discussion, family farms are defined as farms on which most of the required labor is supplied by family members and which derive a reasonable income from farming.

In Eastern Asia, family farms face problems similar to those in Japan. In the United States and Western Europe, attention is focused on family farms from the viewpoint of environmental problems or revitalization of rural areas. Agricultural reforms in China, Eastern Europe, and the former Soviet Union will be influenced by the development of family farms. I hope that this research on the "limitations and potential of family farms" will contribute to the promotion of structural reforms in agriculture worldwide through international research cooperation and interdisciplinary research among various fields.

Background of the Problem

In Japan, the limitations of family farms are caused mainly by the recent industrialization. These problems include liberation of family members from compulsory succession in farming activities; underdevelopment of farmland markets; and traditional, small-scale, and dispersed field patterns.

Liberalization of family members from compulsory succession in farming activities. Until the end of the 1950s, social and family pressures were so great to transfer farm operation and ownership from generation to generation that the process could be called compulsory. However, since the 1960s, farm families have changed their behavior and the new generation has not accepted compulsory succession. Nowadays, the members of the next generation, even the eldest son, are able to choose jobs according to their own preferences and abilities. As a result, they may abandon farming to take other jobs even if they must commute to the workplace from their homes. This leads to under-utilization of farm resources. In addition, as fewer members of the succeeding generation become engaged in farming, the farm population is gradually becomes older (Appendix Figure 4.1) and producing fewer replacements.

Underdevelopment of farmland markets. The main farm resources in Japan are human capital, farmland, irrigation water, and machinery. Among these resources, farmland and irrigation water have little mobility among owners due to the underdevelopment of the markets. The lack of suitable markets constrains farmers' organization of labor, machinery, other resources, and technology.

If the members of the next generation want to become engaged in farming, they can access farm resources despite lack of markets because they inherit resources. However, if they plan to enlarge their farm after the succession, it is very difficult for them to buy or rent additional land due to the under-development of farmland markets. They may be unable to acquire an economic unit, defined as a farm that utilizes resources efficiently by achieving economies of size, and that earns labor-management-equity returns comparable to returns in the nonfarm economy. As a result, the next generation is likely to abandon farming.

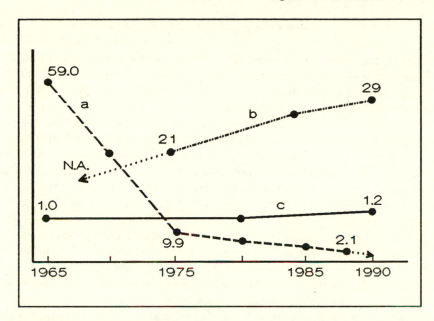

Appendix Figure 4.1. Number of Members of the Next Generation Becoming Engaged in Farming, Ratio of Farmers More Than 65 Years Old, and Average Farm Size in Japan.
Source: Pocketbook of Agricultural Statistics, edit., MAFF.
NOTE: a = Number of members of the next generation becoming engaged in farming (1,000 persons).
        b = Ratio of farmers more than 65 years old only engaged or mainly engaged in farming to all farmers in category (%).
        c = Average farm size (hectares).

Traditional, small-scale, and dispersed field pattern. The average size of a farm, about 1.2 hectares, is divided into 13.4 parcels on the average which are not aggregated but are dispersed among parcels belonging to other farms. This farmland system is well known as the "small dispersed field pattern" in Japan. Although Japan has no suitable farmland markets, occasionally farmers must sell or lease their farmland. However, due to the "small dispersed field pattern", farmers who want to buy or rent land to enlarge their farm cannot obtain additional land in suitable areas for farming.

As members of farm families select jobs other than farming, surplus farmland increases. But active farmers cannot utilize such land efficiently due to the difficulty of enlarging farm size for the reasons previously stated. These factors are disincentives for the successors of farm families to continue the farm operation or for newcomers to become engaged in farming.

New Problems for Family Farms

Since the 1960s, the government through various policies has promoted development of a farmland market and aggregation of small dispersed fields. It is anticipated that in the near future the problems of underdeveloped land markets and farm fragmentation will be solved.

Recently, two new factors have appeared to which the government and researchers have paid little attention. A discussion of these factors follows.

Shift in the sense of commitment to and identification toward organizations and away from families or communities. The farmer's strong sense of commitment to and identification with families and communities has shifted to organizations such as corporations. This trend is most obvious among the younger generation.

In this chapter, I define the sense of commitment to and identification with groups as follows: (a) an identity with the target, norm, and value of the group; (b) a willingness to work for the sake of the group; and (c) a strong desire to remain a member of the group. Corporations are defined as groups which have a specific purpose in common with members.

One of the main causes of the shift in the sense of commitment is the change in the character of society from a "property-dominated society" to a "corporation-dominated society". In highly industrialized societies such as Japan, the main factor which determines the social status, social function, and income of individuals is the corporation to which the younger generation especially wants to belong.

The younger generation feels a lack of status when employed in family-based businesses such as family farms and family retail dealers. This feeling in Japan is fostered by a social insurance system treating family-workers disadvantageously compared with corporation-workers. This is also one of the reasons why the new generation of farm families and other people do not select farming as a main full-time occupation.

Predominance of organizations promoting technical innovation in a highly industrialized society. A modern highly industrialized society is characterized by the rapid development of technological innovations by corporations which can afford the time and capital for the research and development of technology. Technological innovations include the development of management skills and devices, new products, marketing, and organization of resources for operation. Efficiency is realized by internal specialization and integration of work in an organization. In an era of rapid technological innovation, family-based businesses cannot contribute to innovations due to their small capacity for research and development. Until the 1960s, family farms in Japan played an important role in technological innovations in specific fields (i.e., plant breeding). However, they have little opportunity to play that role in a highly industrialized society. That lack of opportunity is another factor discouraging future generations of farm families from continuing to farm and of nonfarm families from entering farming.

Arguments Against the Concept
"Limitations of Family Farms"

There are some arguments against the concept of "limitations of family farms." These include:

1. Collective organization of farming units or group farming may enable operators to overcome the limitations of family farms.
2. Family farms will survive with the support of business activities undertaken by agricultural cooperatives.

Group farming may overcome the inefficiency of farming operations caused by small size farming to some extent. For the promotion of group farming, it is necessary for the farmers to understand accurately the situation and characteristics of family farms in a highly industrialized society. To combine the individual operator or manager of family farms into a group is very difficult due to his independent nature. The formation and survival of farm operator groups needs more skillful incentives and sensitive principles than those for corporation workers.

I believe that the principles can be defined by analyzing carefully the limitations of family farms. However, since many researchers pay little attention to the situation of family farms in highly industrialized societies, they do not understand and cannot solve the problems of the limitations of family farms.

As agricultural cooperatives are organized to supplement the activities of individual farms, business activities of the cooperatives are expected to solve the problems of family farms. Although widely accepted, this concept does not meet the characteristics of farming in Japan: Many members of cooperatives are older, less active farmers.

Structural defects of agricultural cooperatives also inhibit remedial policies. Agri-cooperatives in Japan have many full-time farmer members. But the majority of the members of agri-cooperatives in Japan are smallholders and part-time farmers who derive little income from farming, and have little concern for the development of farming. It is very difficult to implement effective measures to develop and support full-time farmers who are in the minority.

For the successful reorganization of the agri-cooperatives, it is necessary for the cooperative managers and members themselves to understand accurately the problems of family farms and shortcomings of the agri-cooperatives. However, most members and managers have a limited understanding of and little interest in these matters. This makes it very difficult to reorganize agri-cooperatives. Many family farmers may leave farming before reorganization occurs.

The Potential of Family Farms: Hypotheses

Even if family farms are facing difficulties in highly industrialized societies and the number of family farms is decreasing, I believe that family farms may survive because they have important favorable characteristics as follows:

1. The activities of family farms are compatible with the preservation of the natural environment.
2. Family farms provide a relatively large labor absorptive capacity.
3. Highly industrialized societies are aware of the need to recover human values estranged from their organizations and activities.
4. In the future, human activities not restricted to commitment to and identification with groups will become important.
5. The family activities appear to have effects on social stability.

Human activities which do not depend on high technology and large organizations are generally compatible with the preservation of the natural environment. Family-based farming meets such environmental requirements due to the relatively low level of technology applied and small scale organization.

In the 21st century, employment will become a serious problem worldwide due to the increase in population. In the Third World, Eastern Europe, and Russia, this problem is already critical. In these regions the governments are promoting agricultural reform. If agricultural reform leads to an additional flow of unemployed people from rural areas, the social and economic development programs will be further delayed.

In the highly industrialized societies, the sense of commitment to and identification with groups is shifting from families or communities to organizations such as corporations. However these corporations which are characterized by a strong bureaucratic and hierarchical structure may alienate people from human values and may make people reconsider the advantages of family-based groups and activities.

In the beginning of industrialization, it was considered that family-based economic activities would decline. However, even in highly industrialized societies, there is a change of values helping some family-based activities to persist not only in Japan but in the United States and countries such as those of Western Europe in which industrial development started earlier. Philosophers predicted that before the 21st century, many human beings may reject identification with groups such as corporations and return to traditional identification with family (including family farms) and small community. Therefore, family farms may provide a new approach to the post-modern society.

In the 21st century, the *stability* of societies may become an important concept along with liberty and democracy. The family as a fundamental unit may provide social stability. Family-based activities may play similar important roles while their large labor absorptive capacity preserves and promotes the stability of society.

Conclusions

Family farms in Japan face the limitations mentioned above. Although there are fewer family farms, they offer some promise for the future. Therefore, we must carefully follow the trends of family farms in Japan. To achieve this objective, new methods for studying the problems of family farms and other family-based activities need to be developed.

Economic vitality is necessary but not sufficient for survival of family farms. I believe that other factors, such as the social factors mentioned above, are key factors for the survival of family farms. Because the problems of limitations and potentialities of family farms involve various fields of science, interdisciplinary research is essential.

Similar problems to those of family farms appear in other sectors such as retail dealers, fisheries, and forestry in Japan. Similar problems appear in the farming sector of the East Asian countries. Because the problems appear to be worldwide, international research cooperation will contribute to knowledge and solutions.

References

Aoki, Tamotsu. 1988. *Negativeness of Culture* (in Japanese).

Drucker, Adolf. 1969. *The Age of Discontinuity - Guideline to Our Changing Society*.

Mito, Tadashi. 1971. *Drucker: Liberty, Society, and Management* (in Japanese).

Mito, Tadashi. 1972. *The End of Property-Dominated Society* (in Japanese).

Tarrant, John J. 1976. *Drucker: The Man Who Invested in the Corporate Society*.

5

American Agriculture: Organization, Structure, Institutions, and Policy
Luther Tweeten

Introduction

The American public spends billions of dollars each year on commodity programs and trade restrictions to achieve a desired farm structure. Whether that money and effort is well spent depends on answers to basic questions addressed herein. Before listing and addressing these questions, I define the terms "farm structure" and "family farm". Unless otherwise stated, the discussion refers to American agriculture.

Farm Structure

Structure here refers to size, number, type, legal organization, and tenure of farms. Structure includes institutional arrangements: markets in which farmers buy and sell and public policies that regulate, tax, subsidize, or in other ways shape agriculture. Past interventions include land distribution (e.g. Homestead Act of 1862), public research, education, commodity program, and trade policies.

The Family Farm Ideal

The family farm is the focal point of much of the structure debate. The many Americans who prize the family farm do not necessarily agree on its definition, however. To many Americans, the family farm *ideally* is a crop and/or livestock producing unit where the operator and his/her family (see Tweeten (1984) for definition and Sumner for a protest to that definition):

- *control most of the decisions.* (The sole proprietorship legal organization is preferred to a large corporation, coordination by the market is preferred to vertical integration, and ownership by the operator is preferred to tenancy.)

- *supply over half of the labor.*
- *supply over half of the equity capital.*
- *derive over half of their income from farming.*

Society ideally would like to have *as many family farms as possible* subject to the constraint that food be provided efficiently at affordable cost, particularly for the benefit of low-income consumers. The public would like to see family farms *receive comparable economic rewards* to those of nonfarmers. And it wants farmers to *practice sound environmental stewardship.*

An *economic unit* is defined as a farming operation just large enough to provide full-time employment for a farm family (with some seasonal hiring in and out), realize most economies of farm size, and realize a family income comparable to that of nonfarm families.

Key Questions
Key questions addressed in this paper include:

1. If current trends continue, will the family farm survive?
2. What is the impact of public policies and other forces on farm structure?
3. What are the economic, social, and environmental costs to the nation of changes in agricultural structure, including loss of the family farm?

Will the Family Farm Survive?

Family farm survival depends on economic vitality and economies of size as well as other factors. Subsidiary questions include:

- Is survival of the family farm threatened by low income, low prices, low wealth, low rates of return on farming resources, and economies of size?
- Do commodity programs help or hinder survival of family farms? Does the trend toward a more market-oriented agriculture apparent in 1990 farm legislation and ultimately an absence of farm price and income supports, supply controls, and trade interventions threaten family farm survival?
- What public policies would be necessary to maintain or increase the number of family farms? Would economic benefits exceed economic costs of such policies?

Economic Vitality
In measuring economic vitality, it is essential to recognize the diversity of American agriculture. Although annual crop and livestock sales volume is not necessarily the best indicator of farm size, the measure's ready availability

suggests its use in examining farm income, the balance sheet, and rates of return.

Income and Expenses. Several observations are apparent from the 1989 data in Table 5.1:

1. Farm production as measured by receipts is highly concentrated on large farms. Large farms (sales over $250,000 per farm) accounting for 5.2 percent of all farms accounted for 55.4 percent of production as measured by cash receipts from crops, livestock, and other farm-related income. Rural residences (sales under $10,000 per farm) accounting for 47.0 percent of all farms accounted for only 2.8 percent of production.
2. Government payments are greatest *per farm* on large farms but are greatest *per unit of production* on medium and small farms. Payments

Table 5.1. Income and Expenses of Farms by Economic Class, 1989.

Item	Value of Sales ($1,000)				
	Large	**Medium**	**Small**	**Rural Residences**	
	$250 & Over	**$100 to $250**	**$10 to $100**	**Less than $10**	**Total**
	(1,000)				
Number of farms	113	211	828	1,019	2,171
(% of all farms)	(5.2)	(9.7)	(38.1)	(47.0)	(100.0)
	(Dollars per farm)				
Cash receipts	817,372	164,706	42,014	4,599	76,734
(% of all receipts)	(55.4)	(20.9)	(20.9)	(2.8)	(100.0)
Government payments	28,611	16,630	4,640	297	5,015
(% of all payments)	(29.7)	(32.2)	(35.3)	(2.8)	(100.0)
$ payments/$ receipts	[0.03]	[0.10]	[0.11]	[0.06]	[0.07]
Gross cash income	845,983	181,336	46,654	4,896	81,749
Cash expenses	564,805	118,137	33,777	5,982	56,570
(% of all expenses)	(52.0)	(20.3)	(22.8)	(4.9)	(100.0)
Net cash income	281,178	63,199	12,877	-1,086	25,179
Off-farm income	22,920	17,531	23,394	31,246	26,485
Total cash income	304,098	80,730	36,271	30,160	51,664
(% of cash income)	(30.6)	(15.2)	(26.8)	(27.4)	(100.0)

Source: USDA, January 1991.

averaged $28,611 per large farm but only $0.03 per dollar of production in 1989. Payments averaged $16,630 per medium-size farm but $0.10 per dollar of production. Payments to rural residences averaged only $297 per farm but $0.06 per dollar of production.

3. Cash farm expenses were less concentrated on large farms than was output. Large farms accounting for 55.4 percent of production accounted for 52.0 percent of cash expenses in 1989. Rural residences with only 2.8 percent of production accounted for 4.9 percent of cash expenses. Costs for operator and unpaid family labor, management, and equity capital are not included. Such costs are more concentrated on small farms than are cash expenses. It follows as shown later that full economic costs per unit of production (valued at what resources would earn elsewhere -- opportunity cost) are much higher on small farms than on large farms (see Tweeten, 1989a, p. 93).

4. Income per farm compares favorably with income of nonfarmers. In economic equilibrium, a reasonably well-managed, adequate size farm is expected to earn at least as much as similar resources earn elsewhere. In 1989, total cash income of small farms and rural residences averaged near the $34,213 median income of all U.S. families (Council of Economic Advisors, p. 320). The medium-size farm (sales of $100,000 to $250,000), which I call the *quintessential family farm*, represents an economic unit. It is large enough to employ a full-time operator and family supplemented by minimal hired labor in peak periods. That quintessential family farm, with net cash income from all sources averaging $80,730 in 1989, had favorable income -- judging by almost any standard. Large farms did much better but many support more than one operator family, hence sales classes in Table 5.1 exaggerate differences in income *per family*.

5. Off-farm income is critical to the economic livelihood of the majority of farm families. Small farms and rural residences, accounting for 85 percent of all farms, on average received the majority of their income from off-farm sources. Many such families might be properly classified not as farmers but as machinists, mechanics, physicians, teachers, or by whatever other occupation supplies most of their income.

6. Rural residences had negative net farm income in 1989, even before subtracting costs of operator and unpaid family labor, management, and equity capital. I discuss later why that loss, and the fact that total resource costs tend to be about double farming returns, does not necessarily imply economic disequilibrium.

The year 1989 was above average. However, net income from all sources of families on the quintessential family farm consistently exceeded median U.S. income in the late 1980s. Poverty is rare on *commercial* farms (sales over $100,000) because such firms cannot exist for long without considerable net worth and assets.

Balance Sheet. Notable observations from balance sheet data in Table 5.2 are that:

1. Farming is a highly capital intensive industry. Assets per farm averaged $447,827 over all farms and $810,318 on medium size farms in 1989.
2. Debt per farm averages well below assets per farm. The debt-asset ratio for all farms, 15 percent in 1989, was low by nonfarm industry standards and suggests a strong financial position.

   Approximately 5 percent of farms were judged to be financially vulnerable, defined as debt-asset ratios over 40 percent and negative cash flows. However, that percentage is probably *structural*: It is quite normal for some operators to be highly leveraged to get started in farming or be beset by bad luck or poor management even in a generally prosperous farming economy.
3. Large farms operate with higher debt-asset ratios than do small farms. Differences in leverage among farm sizes in 1989 were less than in previous years, however. Debt-asset ratios averaging 15 percent over all farms in 1989 were considerably lower than typical debt-asset ratios of 50 percent or more for nonfarm firms.

   Neither large nor small farms are utilizing their considerable potential borrowing capacity (credit worthiness) to invest in productive assets. Small farms frequently lack profitable investment opportunities.

Table 5.2. Balance Sheet (Including Operator Household) of Farms by Economic Class, December 31, 1989 (Dollars per Farm).

| | Value of Sales ($1,000) | | | | |
| | Large | Medium | Small | Rural Residences | |
Item	$250 & Over	$100 to $250	$10 to $100	Less than $10	Total
Assets	1,598,381	810,318	419,313	268,348	447,827
(% of all assets)	(18.6)	(17.6)	(35.7)	(28.1)	(100.0)
Debt	253,938	130,976	63,560	36,317	67,234
(% of all debt)	(19.7)	(18.9)	(36.0)	(25.4)	(100.0)
Equity	1,344,442	679,341	355,752	232,031	380,592
(% of all equity)	(18.4)	(17.4)	(35.6)	(28.6)	(100.0)
Debt-Asset ratio (%)	15.9	16.2	15.2	13.5	15.0

Source: USDA, January 1991, p. 86.

Caution, apparent in 1989 data in Table 5.2, originated in part from financial stress experienced in the mid-1980s.

4. Wealth as measured by equity is high among farmers. In 1989, net worth averaged $380,592 over all farms. More meaningful for commercial agriculture is wealth of the quintessential medium-size family farm, $679,341. Wealth for types of U.S. households based on 1984 data updated to 1989 using the Consumer Price Index is shown in Table 5.3. The average U.S. farm had a net worth approximately 10 times that of the median net worth of all U.S. households. The quintessential (medium size) family farm had a net worth 10 times that for any category recorded in the Survey of Income and Program Participation, householders age 55-64. Differences might be narrowed but probably not erased if human capital were accounted for. Because medium and large farms receive a substantial portion of government commodity program benefits as noted earlier in Table 5.1, it follows that government programs transfer dollars from taxpayers to farm families of considerably higher income and wealth.

Economies of Farm Size. Figure 5.1, derived from farm income and balance sheet data, shows full economic costs per dollar of production (including annualized costs of operator's management, equity capital, and labor) by economic sales class for all U.S. farms. Economies of size are prominent. It costs $2 to produce $1 of output on small farms and under $1 to produce a dollar of output on large farms. *Most economies of size are realized on a quintessential family size farm* with sales of $100,000 to $250,000 per year. However, on average an additional 10 percent reduction in costs can be obtained on larger farms, in part because of market economies (purchasing inputs at a discount, selling produce at a premium). I have been constructing unit cost curves at approximately 5-year intervals since 1960 and find a remarkable similarity among curves over time. The recurring pattern is that adequate size farms are approximately breaking even (covering all costs) while small farms are losing money.

Table 5.3. U.S. Household Wealth.

U.S. Household Type	1989 Wealth
All	$38,987
Married	59,811
College graduate	72,105
Age 55-64	87,915

Source: Bureau of the Census, 1989, p. 459.

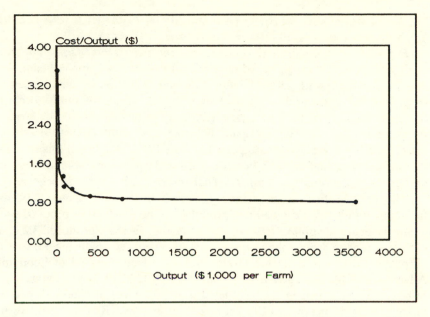

Figure 5.1. Cost per Unit of Farm Output by Economic Size Class of Farms, 1990.
Source: Basic data from USDA.

Part-time small farm numbers have not changed much in recent years. About as many part-time operators and their families are entering as are leaving that category. Rural amenities, psychic benefits of the farm way of life, and tax advantages appear to compensate for low direct monetary rewards, suggesting that such farms are near a social equilibrium. The small farm with a full-time, non-aged operator once dominated farm numbers but has nearly vanished. Operators of such farms have expanded their operations, become part-time operators, exited farming, or retired. Assuming acceptance of my thesis that small farms remain in farming because they can realize tax advantages and finance consumption for their preferred way of life out of off-farm income, it follows that the economies of size curve in Figure 5.1 is consistent with an economic equilibrium apparent in only modest changes in numbers of small farms.

A growing body of research using other methodologies supports results in Figure 5.1. Studies of economies of size estimated from farm types specializing in various enterprises give results similar to the pattern in the figure. So called "engineering studies" of a hypothetical cost-minimizing farming resource-enterprise unit show patterns similar to that in Figure 5.1

but economies of size are not as pronounced (see OTA; Richardson, Smith, and Knutson; Helmers, El-Osta, and Azzam).[1]

Farm Prices. The substantial decline in *commodity terms of trade* apparent in Figure 5.2 would appear to be inconsistent with the above conclusion that commercial farms with sales of $100,000 or more per year have covered all costs and even increased real net income over time. Commodity terms of trade as measured by the parity ratio (the ratio of prices received by farmers for crops and livestock to prices paid by farmers for inputs) have been halved since 1910-14 -- a standard base period. Some have interpreted this to mean that farmers are paid half of a fair price, are underpaid for resources, and are predestined to chronic low returns. That interpretation is incorrect.

The parity ratio measures terms of trade for *commodities*. Because farmers commit *resources* and not products to the production process, what counts is factor or *resource terms of trade*. In 1989 farmers produced 3.2 units of output for the same volume (real cost) of resources producing 1.0 unit of output in 1910-14 (multifactor productivity data from Council of Economic Advisors, p. 396). That means they required only 1/3.2 or 31 percent as much price to cover all costs in 1989 as they did in 1910-14. But commodity terms of trade were 55 percent of the 1910-14 level in 1989. Real or factor terms of trade thus were 3.2(55) = 177 in 1989 or 77 percent higher than in 1910-14 (see Figure 5.2). Productivity gains have benefitted farmers' economic position mightily.

Government commodity program payments, greater farm size, and off-farm earnings of farm people have improved the economic position of farmers much more than indicated by factor terms of trade alone. Even those persons displaced from farming by labor-saving technology have made substantial economic gains on average for themselves and the nation (Perry, Schreiner, and Tweeten).

Rates of Return. Rates of return on resources of reasonably well managed commercial farms have averaged at least as high as returns on alternative investments. Real rates of return typically average approximately 10-15

---

[1] An advantage of the positivistic cost curve such as in Figure 5.1 is that actual ratios of economic costs to revenues indicate "what is" rather than "what ought to be", include some market as well as production economies of size, and record some of the transportation inefficiencies of small farms (some fuel and vehicle commuting costs for shopping, recreation, etc. are picked up in surveys). A disadvantage is that management quality and other controls are not held constant. The so-called "engineering studies" attempt to correct the latter shortcoming.

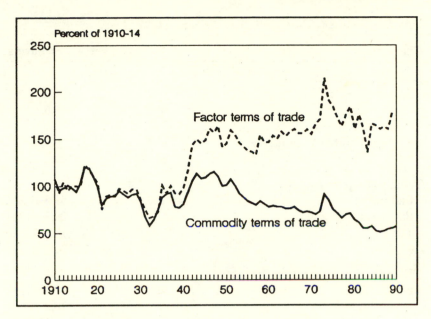

Figure 5.2. Commodity and Multifactor Terms of Trade.
Source: USDA (April 1990) and Council of Economic Advisors.

percent of equity on farms with sales of $250,000 or more, 5-10 percent on farms with sales of $100,000 to $250,000, and average negative on small farms (see Tweeten, 1988). Even larger farms experienced negative returns in the mid-1980s, however, and capital losses from falling land prices were massive.

Low returns in the mid-1980s manifest a phase of the perennial economic instability problem rather than a nonexistent chronic low rate of return on resources of commercial farms. Negative rates of return on small farms reflects their inability to achieve economies of size. Studies (Tweeten, 1988; 1989b, Ch. 4) examining in depth the question of farm returns conclude that *commercial* farmers are unlikely to experience chronically low rates of return on resources with or without government commodity supports.

Other Characteristics of Farms. Table 5.4 presents data from the 1987 Census of Agriculture showing legal organization, tenure, and off-farm employment of farm operators. Most farms are sole proprietorships (87.2 percent in 1987). Only 0.3 percent of all farms were corporations other than family-held in 1987, the same percentage as in 1982. Arbitrarily classifying industrial-type corporate and partnership farms as well as farms hiring more than half of their labor as nonfamily types, then family farms account for about 95 percent of all farms and 53 percent of all production (Tweeten, 1984, p. 8). Large corporate farms are prominent among fruit and vegetable farms in California, Florida, and Texas, and among large-scale livestock operations.

Table 5.4. Selected Characteristics of Farms, 1987.

Characteristic	Percent of Farms
Legal Organization	
Sole proprietorship	87.2
Partnership	9.6
Corporate, family	2.9
Corporate, other than family	0.3
	100.0
Tenure of Operator	
Full owner	59.3
Part owner	29.2
Tenant	11.5
	100.0
Off-Farm Employment of Operators	
None	43.1
1 - 99 days	10.2
100 - 199 days	9.1
200+ days	37.6
	100.0

Source: Census of Agriculture (Bureau of the Census).

Nearly three out of five farm operators are full owners (Table 5.4). Only one out of eight farmers is a full tenant. The trend in recent decades has been toward part-ownership, especially among commercial farmers. Part-owner farms average nearly twice as much area per farm as other farms. Part-owners operate only 29 percent of all farms but 54 percent of farmland. Full-ownership is especially prevalent on small farms. Part-owner farm families enjoy the advantages of security and an investment outlet of an owned homestead portion plus the economies of size achieved with minimal capital requirements by renting land.

The proportion of farmland owned by nonfarmers remained unchanged at 36 percent in the years covered by the 1978, 1982, and 1987 censuses of agriculture. About half of this land is owned by retired farm operators or their spouses. Thus approximately one-fifth of farmland is not owned by present or past farm operators or their spouses. Farm families control most farm real estate assets.

Several highlights are noted from enterprise receipt data by sales class (see Appendix Table 5.1):

1. Large farms predominate in production of fruits, vegetables, and horticultural crops and cattle and calves.

2. Medium and small family farms are prominent in production of grains, hogs, and dairy.
3. Rural residences emphasize production of tobacco, forages (hay, silage, pasture etc.), and cattle and calves.
4. Government supported crops, livestock, and livestock products are concentrated on small and medium size farms. Grains, cotton, dairy, and sheep and lamb production supported by commodity programs accounted for 23 percent of production on large farms and 27 percent of production on small farms but for 55 percent of production on farms with sales of $10,000 to $250,000 in 1987.
5. Overall, only 38 percent of farm output, as measured by market value in 1987, potentially was covered by commodity programs. Many operators particularly on small and large farms did not participate in programs so the actual portion of output covered by programs was less than indicated above.
6. Cattle and calf operations are the most numerous type of farm for every size classification. Cash grain types of farms are also very frequent among medium and small size farms.

Other notable features of American farms are:

1. Females were the operators of 6 percent of all farms in 1987. That number substantially underestimates the role of women on farming decisions. On family farms, major decisions often are made jointly and coequally by husband and wife although the husband is listed as the sole operator.
2. Blacks were operators of only 2 percent of all farms in 1987. Their share of commercial farm operators was even less.
3. The traditional family farm structure is for the operator and family to reside on the farm. However, 21 percent of farm operators listed nonfarm residence in 1987.
4. The family farm is not threatened by foreign ownership. Corrected for shares that Americans own in foreign firms buying land in the United States, less than 1 percent of the nation's farmland is foreign owned. Foreign ownership is much higher in some localities. This ac-counts in part for what appears to be an irrational fear by some Americans of foreign takeover of food production.
5. Excess farm production capacity is defined as production-equivalent removed from the market by government programs of acreage diversion, net stock accumulation, and subsidized exports. It is production in excess of what markets will clear at politically acceptable prices. That excess capacity averaged approximately 8 percent of farm output at prices of the mid-1980s, and dropped to a low level by 1991. Excess farm labor, once over 40 percent of farm labor, also dropped

to a low level. This means that disequilibrium, measured by resources and output in excess of those remaining in a well-functioning market, is now minimal. That conclusion should not be interpreted to mean that adequate food and fiber supplies are threatened by future shortages of farm laborers and operators. Truly outstanding management and entrepreneurship have been and always will be in short supply, but no special measures are needed to draw new operators into farming. The market and generous parents along with public programs of general and vocational education will ensure a plentiful supply of operators in the 21st century. Growing up on a farm is an extremely useful apprenticeship for a farm operator. However, some of the most innovative and successful farm operators in Ohio were not raised on farms. Perhaps that freed them from traditions that limited their thinking. The point is that the future supply of farm operators is not restricted to persons raised on farms.

The above indicators suggest that family farm operators control most decisions on farms although decisions increasingly are shared with spouses, bankers, bureaucrats, and a host of other participants in agriculture. Recent data are not available, but extrapolation from the 1970s suggests that vertical integration accounts for about 10 percent of all farms (see Tweeten, 1984, p. 17 for sources). Vertical integration combines two or more major components of the input supply-farm-product marketing stages in one firm. An example is the integrated poultry firm engaged in producing chicks and feed, and supplying these to contracting growers who for a flat fee per pound of gain raise broilers with their labor and housing, and who then turn the broilers back to the integrator for slaughter and processing. Vertical coordination, prominent for years in production of broilers, is rapidly advancing in beef and pork production. Grower-farmers are not coerced to sign production contracts; most are eager participants -- queues are often long. Growers can become independent producers if contracts are unsatisfactory. The freedom of entry and exit, alternatives, and incentives required to maintain grower participation minimizes opportunity for exploitation by contractors even though contracting firms are large relative to grower firms.

Environment and Natural Resources
Farmland irrigated fell by 1.6 million hectares from 1978 to 1987. Irrigated area will continue to drop in the Southern High Plains of Texas and Oklahoma and in parts of California as water supplies are depleted. The latter will be caused in part by growing urban demand and by declining federal subsidies to irrigation. Area in crops such as cotton, alfalfa (for dairy production), and rice with low value per unit of irrigation water will be curtailed to provide water for urban areas.

Extensive analysis indicates environmental problems of agriculture are manageable and are neither the basis for panic nor complacency (see Tweeten, 1992). Principal environmental problems are soil erosion; air, water, and food contamination by pathogens and toxic or carcinogenic chemicals; and limits to energy, phosphate, and other natural resources. The most serious environmental problem of agriculture is soil erosion. Several studies indicate that continuation of past erosion trends will reduce American agricultural productivity approximately 5 percent in a century. Improved technology can more than offset this loss but at a cost in research and education. Approximately 120 million hectares of cropland are lost to urban and other nonfarm development purposes each year (CAST). The rate of shift has fallen with slowing population growth and income growth.

Farm Numbers

The above perspective prepares us for scrutiny of the viability of family farms. Farm numbers declined from 2.2 million in 1982 to 2.1 million in 1987, an annual rate of 1.4 percent (Table 5.5). The extreme financial stress of the period raised the rate; pressures to break up farms on paper to avoid government program payment limitations reduced the rate. The rate of decline in farm numbers has been slowing for some time in part because the pace of technological change has slackened and because small farms with full-time operators, once the largest single category of farm operators, have nearly completed their adjustment. No technology on the horizon poses anywhere near the operator-displacement capacity of the tractor and its complements.

In 1987, 495,816 farm operators were between 55 and 64 years of age. That means that approximately 50,000 farm operators can be expected to retire or die each year for the next decade. The drop in farm numbers by only 31,000 per year from 1982 to 1987 meant that many new operators entered farming. In fact, both entry and exit were large. Gale and

Table 5.5. Farm Numbers and Shares, 1982 and 1987.

	Value of Sales ($1,000)				
	Large	**Medium**	**Small**	**Rural Residences**	
Item	$250 & Over	$100 to $250	$10 to $100	Less than $10	**Total**
1982	86,468	215,912	840,583	1,096,337	2,240,976
(% of total)	(3.9)	(9.6)	(37.5)	(49.0)	(100.0)
1987	93,171	202,550	763,852	1,028,186	2,087,759
(% of total)	(4.5)	(9.7)	(36.6)	(49.2)	(100.0)

Source: Census of Agriculture (Bureau of the Census).

Henderson (p. 5) estimate that 75,373 farmers entered annually while 106,017 farmers exited annually in the 1982-87 period.

U.S. agricultural census data for 1982 and 1987 in Table 4 evidence the "dual structure" and "disappearing middle" frequently mentioned in previous literature. That is, a few large farms account for most output, and small, mostly part-time, farms dominate farm numbers. The small and middle-size groups comprised of farms too small to reap all economies of size and too large to permit full-time off-farm jobs for operators continued to be marginalized. However, this "disappearing middle" group declined in numbers only a little faster than other farms from 1982 to 1987. Small farms defined as those with sales of $10,000 to $100,000 per year decreased from 38 percent of all farms in 1982 to 37 percent of all farms in 1987. The share of rural residence farms (sales of less than $10,000) held steady at 49 percent of all farms. The decline in full-time small farms was offset by gains in part-time small farms to maintain shares. Large farms (sales of $250,000 and over) increased share from 3.9 to 4.5 percent of all farms. Medium farms (sales of $100,000 to $250,000) declined in numbers but slightly increased share. In short, the farm size structure is changing but at a glacial pace. The great farm-urban exodus of the 1940s, 1950s, and 1960s has slowed to a trickle.

At issue is how a family farm economic unit with its massive capital requirements can be refinanced from generation to generation. The $1 million of assets required for an economic farming unit preclude ownership with full equity by retirement, once an attainable goal. Even a (say) 25 percent equity of $250,000 required to own an economic farming unit is beyond reach of most would-be operators. Several strategies and compromises to circumvent such constraints and form economic units will continue to be successful in the future:

Assistance from Parents. Without generous mothers and fathers, the family farm as we have known it would last one generation. We will continue to have generous parents passing their farming skills and assets to their sons and daughters, ensuring survival of the family farm.

Leasing. The traditional tenure "ladder" for an operator progressed without concessional financing from hired worker to tenant to owner. Capital requirements are too large for that ladder to work anymore. But operators will continue to use leasing of equipment, rental of land, and custom hiring of machinery and tasks to reduce capital requirements for an economic unit.

Off-farm Earnings. Many farm families will continue to earn substantial income from off-farm sources. An efficient, economic size unit requires full-time commitment of the operator to the farm, but a spouse may find off-farm work feasible.

Management consultants, computerized information systems, and public extension services can help. These are but a few strategies for growth and survival; ingenious families will come up with many more.

Conclusion

The family farm is not an endangered species. It will remain the backbone of agriculture for generations to come, although in declining numbers. It is economically viable as measured by income, net worth, and rate of return.

Agriculture will continue to adapt to changing circumstances, and could adapt to the absence of commodity programs and trade restrictions after a transition period. Problems of economic instability, soil erosion, poverty on small farms, and some loss of family farms over time are real. These problems will not be resolved without a major restructuring of public policy as noted in the next section.

What Is the Impact of Technology, Public Policies, and Other Forces on Farm Structure?

The discussion of forces explaining future changes in structure must be brief because the list is long and the space is short. Fortunately, the literature reporting analysis of these topics is considerable.

1. *Technology*. The most important force behind structural change is technology (see Batte and Schnitkey; Tweeten, 1984). Major labor-saving innovations such as the tractor and its complements produced massive changes in farm size and numbers. The automobile, by allowing part-time farmers to commute to nonfarm jobs, retained many families on farms who otherwise would have moved to jobs and residences in urban areas.

   Large four-wheel-drive tractors have been adopted slowly by farmers. Major new technologies such as growth hormones are mostly output-increasing rather than heavily scale-biased, labor-saving technologies that would cause major structural change. The declining impact of technology on structure is apparent in the relatively modest reduction in future farm numbers projected in Chapter 7 by Stanton.

2. *Off-farm income opportunities*. Off-farm income of farm people grew massively from 1940 to 1965, then leveled off as a proportion of farm income. To my knowledge, no one has explained why this trend toward dependence on off-farm income plateaued so quickly after climbing so rapidly.

   At any rate, off-farm income ensures the future of the family farm if one is willing to include in the definition those farms whose residents make most of their income from off-farm sources.

3. *Relative earnings*. Other things equal, more rapid growth in labor returns in the nonfarm than in the farm sector draws people from farm to nonfarm employment. The low income elasticity of demand for farm ingredients in food and the higher productivity gains in agriculture compared to the nonfarm sector have speeded out-migration.

Relative earnings will have less impact on farming adjustments in the future. The reason is slower growth of real per capita earnings in the nonfarm economy and slower growth in farm labor-saving technology.

Populist activists have proposed bans on new technology (e.g. growth hormones), trade restrictions, limits to firm size, and other market distortions to raise income of farmers relative to income of nonfarmers. Such distortions lower national income. And because of strong tendencies towards equilibrium in agriculture, nonfarm income ultimately determines farm income. The paradox is that efforts to raise farm income in the short run lower farm income in the long run.

4. *Agribusiness structure and performance.* Populists have blamed agribusiness firms for farm financial failure and family farm demise. Bankers, the grain trade, the Trilateral Commission, the futures market, and transnational corporations have been targeted. However, economists have found little evidence to link agribusiness structure to loss of family farms (Tweeten, 1988 and 1989b, ch. 8; Hudson and Mintert).

5. *Public policies.* Public policies have been intensively analyzed as causes of structural change in agriculture. One reason is because public policy is viewed as an instrumental variable capable of manipulation by the political process.

  a. *Commodity programs.* Commodity programs have been faulted for damaging the environment: encouraging monoculture and discouraging rotations containing forage legumes, encouraging synthetic fertilizer and pesticide application and discouraging biological sources of fertility and pest control, and of encouraging excess resource use to produce for government surplus stocks and subsidized exports while discouraging environmentally benign low input sustainable production systems. Commodity programs also encourage conversion of land to conserving uses and on the whole probably are environmentally neutral. Flaws could be corrected, but changes in environmental provisions will have little impact on the size and number of farms.

  After considerable empirical analysis and review of a number of previous studies, I (Tweeten, 1990) conclude that government commodity programs have had a small net impact on farm size and numbers. However, some economists (see Cochrane) feel strongly that commodity programs have diminished farm numbers. In contrast, many farmers feel that commodity programs are essential to preserve family farms. Commodity programs could be redesigned to save small family farms. Direct, decoupled income transfers could be the sole commodity program and could be targeted to farms chosen to survive.

b. *Taxes*.   Before federal tax reform in 1986, most economists concluded that taxes were structured (unintentionally) to reduce farm numbers, increase size, and speed corporate-industrial encroachment into farming. Since the 1986 reform to remove the most unfavorable features, taxes have not been a significant issue in the farm structure debate (see Durst; Helmers *et al.*).

c. *Monetary-fiscal policy*. American agriculture was severely buffeted by macroeconomic policies favoring low real interest and exchange rates in the 1970s and high real interest and exchange rates in the 1980s (Tweeten, December 1988).   These policies brought unsustainable expansion of exports, individual farm assets, and farming industry plant and equipment in the 1970s.   Opposite trends prevailed in the 1980s. Large farms (because they were more heavily leveraged with debt than other farms, had high capital-labor ratios, and depended mainly on the farm for their livelihood) were especially disadvantaged by ill-advised full-employment federal deficit policies of the 1980s. Although the share of large farms in all farm numbers held firm in the 1982-87 period, the share likely would have increased with sound macroeconomic policies.

d. *Credit and finance*. The Farmers Home Administration, a federal lender, and federal programs to assist the cooperative Farm Credit System saved many farms from financial failure in the 1980s. These agencies and policies also contributed to excessive expansion and financial leveraging in the 1970s that in turn contributed to the financial crisis in the 1980s. Searching questions have been raised regarding the wisdom of providing public incentives for undercapitalized marginal young operators to enter farming, the resulting high public costs of "bailouts," mismanagement of public credit, and subsidizing credit to speculators (plungers), incompetent operators, and to crop farms that the market says need to be in grass or trees. The injustice had been noted of rewarding the imprudent with loan writeoffs while providing no benefits for the prudent operator who managed wisely, avoided undue risk, and labored long and sacrificed much to repay debts. Major credit reforms have been made. The emerging credit structure of agriculture appears to be adequate to meet future needs (see Duncan; Barry and Gustafson).

e. *Natural resource and environmental policies*. Census of Agriculture and other data do not indicate that small farms are more beneficial than large farms (remember, most large farms are family farms) for environmental or natural resource use (see Tweeten, 1983; CAST). Large studies indicate that medium- and large-farm operators conserve soil better than do small-farm operators (see Tweeten,

1984). Compared to small farms, farms with sales of $250,000 or more in 1987 used considerably less commercial fertilizer, pesticides, petroleum fuel, and electricity per dollar of net farm output (Bureau of the Census, 1988; Tweeten, 1992).

Laws written nearly a century ago to restrict federally subsidized irrigation water to family-size farms were not enforced. The federal government has heavily subsidized water to farms of all types and sizes. In affected areas, farm structure is more tilted to large farms than would have occurred with legislated restrictions enforced.

Commodity programs have become more environmentally oriented. They also attempt to further restrict subsidies received by large farms. If legislated provisions are fully enforced, the result could be federal conservation features bypassing large farms. Such farms will not participate in commodity programs.

f. *Transportation and infrastructure*. The public has invested heavily in transportation infrastructure.   While this has facilitated commercial buy-sell activities which especially characterize larger farms, it also has made many small farms attractive for families who can commute from farm residences to jobs, recreation, schooling, and other activities in town.   Nearly all rural infrastructure (roads, utilities, etc.) and services (e.g., mail, school bus, etc.) are subsidized, encouraging small part-time farms -- sometimes called rural residences of urban people. The net effect on structure of these policies, if continued, is to ensure that small part-time farms will be a part of the rural landscape. If these farms are deemed to be family farms, the family farm is secure for the long run. But some commercial farmers resent "urban sprawl" into the countryside by city workers enticed by subsidies to reside on small acreages.

g. *Trade*. International trade policies heavily influence and are heavily influenced by agriculture.   Protectionist policies have preserved some peanut, tobacco, sugar beet, sugarcane, sheep, and dairy farms that would not have survived rigors of a more open world trade market. Less distorted international trade and less government commodity program intervention would raise national income but many less efficient farmers would not survive. At issue is whether benefits of more open trade would offset adjustment costs of displaced farm families.

Farm Structure: Does It Make a Difference?

Many Americans treasure the family farm because, compared to the larger industrial-type farm, it is perceived to provide a higher quality of life, to take better care of the environment, to practice energy conservation, and to be more committed to national ideals such as democracy. Many of these perceptions do not stand scrutiny.

Professor Paarlberg concludes that farm people have lost their uniqueness. There is no evidence that family farmers are more committed to democratic or other ideals than other people. Divorce, crime, and suicide rates on farms and in rural areas are approaching those of urban areas, and, in world perspective, nations with highest proportions of people on farms have the least democracy.

Feelings of well-being are no higher on family farms than on other farms or among nonfarmers (Coughenour and Tweeten). Farm people especially enjoy their work and amenities including self-employment, rural living, and open spaces. But the economic pressures of farming offset. Compared to nonfarmers, farmers on the whole do not have a higher quality of life or well-being. Suburbs, where most Americans live today, offer quality of life advantages at least as great as found in farming.

Public programs to save family farms are not cost-effective means to preserve rural communities. Only 8 percent of the U.S. rural population is employed in farming (Saupe and Carlin; Carlin, 1988). The economic base of most rural communities is not farming. Three times as many basic jobs in nonmetropolitan counties are in manufacturing as in agriculture, forestry, and fisheries (Tweeten, 1982, p. 176). Only 17 percent of the nation's 3,069 counties are farming dependent, defined as counties deriving at least 20 percent of their income from farming (see Reimund and Brooks, pp. 14, 14, 15). Most are located in the Great Plains. Thus if society wishes to preserve rural communities, it will have to rely on other than farm commodity programs.

Rural counties with a farm economic base on average have higher per capita incomes than rural counties with an economic base from other sources such as manufacturing, lumbering, higher education, recreation, or retirement centers. New investment will have a higher payoff in these latter industries than in an already oversized farm industry. Thus based on equity or efficiency, public policy might well focus on improving the economic foundations of nonfarm-based rural counties.

In the field of politics, perceptions are often reality. American farmers undoubtedly will continue to receive favored treatment by Congress because of the widespread belief that the family farm is an endangered species which must be preserved by commodity programs for the good of the nation. The public perception that food supplies would be threatened and the large industrial-type corporations would take over farming in the absence of government commodity programs is not supported by reality.

A 1984 study (Tweeten, p. 49) reviewed previous studies and summarized the relationship between farm size and rural communities. Compared to a system of large farms, the assumed system of small farms (sales of $20,000 to $40,000 per year) would support nearly seven times as many farm families and social activity that depends on farm population. The study then went on to conclude that

> In strictly economic terms, however, the gain to rural communities from a system of small farms is more than offset by higher food and other commodity costs to consumers due to the lower economic efficiency of small farms. Consumers would pay an estimated 14 percent more for food under a system of only small farms than under the actual farm structure in 1981. A system of even smaller farms might provide more stimulus to rural communities but at higher social costs in terms of lost exports and high food prices.
>
> In short, consumers pay more for food, but rural communities are favored with a superior social and economic base under a system of small farms. Such a system would require considerable off-farm employment to supplement limited income per unit of farm sources.

The most important determinant of farm well-being is income, not farm size. Small farms are "beautiful" primarily for those having substantial off-farm income. Small farms in poverty are not supportive of social vitality in rural communities. Middle-class families make for a more socially viable rural community than does a system of very large farms populated by upper class and lower (laborer) class families (Lobao).

Such thinking can cause much mischief. It is easy to be caught in the trap of a policy which assumes that the only "good" people are middle-class full-time owner-operator families. Not everyone can be a successful farm owner-operator. Some must start as hired workers, renters, or part-owners. Some critics view sectoralism (farm or rural people are superior to other people) to be as objectionable as racism or sexism.

Simply improving incomes of rural people will not necessarily preserve rural communities. Recent studies by David Henderson find that higher incomes of rural people cause spending to decline in small rural communities and to rise in more distant, larger towns and cities. Improved transportation has enabled rural people with higher income to exercise their preference to journey to larger communities with greater shopping options.

In short, society faces difficulty decisions that need to be resolved through the political process. The following quote is instructive (Tweeten, 1984, p. 53):

> The benefits of having a dominant moderate-size family farm structure must be balanced against the costs of adjusting from the current structure: many small farms would need to be consolidated and a few large farms would need to be broken up. Because each family and farming situation is unique, it is not clear that public policy could do a good job in determining which farms should be restrained in growth to benefit society.

Conclusions

Characteristics of farms provide the following answers to questions posed in the text.

1. The family farm is a remarkably resilient institution and will be around for generations, although in diminishing numbers. Major structural adjustments have been completed, and no technology looms on the horizon that threatens economic viability of most family farms.

2. Major public policies designed to preserve family farms kept many farms in business that otherwise would have failed in the financial stress years of the 1980s. On the whole over the long run, however, there is no basis to conclude that fewer family farms would exist today in the absence of farm commodity programs since 1933.

3. Empirical evidence indicates that medium to large size family farms are most consistent with economic, social, and environmental objectives. Small farms take less care of the soil and use more chemicals, energy, and other inputs per unit of output.

4. Rural communities are served best by a system of medium size family farms. However, a public policy to preserve such farms is not a cost-effective way to preserve rural communities. On the contrary, much can be said for a pluralistic public policy that utilizes the best opportunities for people to be farm workers, renters, owner-operators, or part-time farmers. In allocating market (non-public) goods and resources, there is no evidence that governments are superior to markets. Past public interventions such as price support and supply control policies have generated sizable national income losses while having little long-term impact on farm structure.

5. Problems of agriculture include environmental degradation and economic instability. Poverty remains a problem on full-time small farms. These problems can be targeted cost-effectively by soil conservation, commodity buffer stock, and income maintenance (welfare) programs rather than by commodity or structure policies.

6. American agriculture and the nation would benefit mightily from multilateral reductions in trade and other market distortions. Part of the reason is because American agriculture holds a global comparative advantage in grain and livestock production. It lacks comparative advantage in sugar cane and sugar beet production.

7. The uniqueness of farmers has eroded over time; no objective evidence indicates that farm people are superior to nonfarm people. The public might well choose through the political process to preserve small farms but it will do so out of intangible goals such as preserving a prized heritage rather than out of objective evidence that such farms best serve tangible economic, social, or environmental goals.

8. Adequate-size, reasonably well managed family farms are as efficient as large corporate industrial-type farms. While neither economies of size studies nor historic trends indicate consistent advantage of family-size versus large farmers, the appropriate farm structure depends on unique circumstances such as commodity, location, technology, operator

skills, and a host of other factors difficult to measure. Analysts are not good at singling out socially or economically preferred farms for special subsidies. There is no evidence to indicate that officials and bureaucrats in government are better than markets at deciding what size of farm to favor through public policy in serving the nation's well being.

References

Barry, Peter and C. Gustafson. Forthcoming. Alternative methods of farm finance and their impacts on structure. In Arne Hallam, ed., book on farm structure in press.

Batte, Marvin and Gary Schnitkey. 1990. Emerging technologies and their impact on American agriculture. Pp. 145-162 in Arne Hallam, ed.

Bureau of the Census. November 1989. *1987 Census of Agriculture: United States Summary and State Data.* AC87-A-51. Washington, DC: U.S. Government Printing Office.

Bureau of the Census. 1989. *Statistical Abstract of the United States.* Washington, DC: U.S. Government Printing Office.

Carlin, Thomas. 1988. Strong communities - strong farms: What is the connection? Pp. 177-190 in Lindon Robison, ed.

Carlin, Thomas and Sara Mazie, eds. June 1990. *The U.S. Farm Sector Entering the 1990s: Twelfth Annual Report on the Structure of Family Farms.* Agricultural Information Bulletin 587. Washington, DC: ERS, U.S. Department of Agriculture.

CAST. June 1988. *Long-term Viability of U.S. Agriculture.* Report No. 114. Ames, IA: Council of Agricultural Science and Technology.

Cochrane, Willard. 1986. The need to rethink agricultural policy. Ch. 17 in Joseph Molnar, ed.

Coughenour, C. Milton and Luther Tweeten. 1986. Quality of life perceptions and farm structure. Ch. 5 in Joseph Molnar, ed.

Council of Economic Advisors. 1991. *Economic Report of the President.* Washington, DC: U.S. Government Printing Office.

Duncan, Douglas. June 1990. Farm credit conditions and policy. Pp. 33-40 in Thomas Carlin and Sara Mazie, eds.

Durst, Ron. June 1990. Farm income tax policy. Pp. 29-32 in Thomas Carlin and Sara Mazie, eds.

Gale, Fred and David Henderson. February 1991. Estimating entry and exit of U.S. farms. Staff Report. Washington, DC: ARED, ERS, U.S. Department of Agriculture.

Goldschmidt, Walter. 1947. *As You Sow.* New York: Harcourt, Brace, and Co.

Hallam, Arne, ed. 1989 and 1990 issues. *Determinants of Size and Structure of American Agriculture.* (Proceedings of NC-181 Committee on Farm Size and Structure.) Ames: Department of Economics, Iowa State University.

Helmers, Glenn, Hisham El-Osta, and Azzeddine Azzam. Forthcoming. Economies of size in multi-output farms. In Arne Hallam, ed., book on farm structure in press.

Henderson, David, Luther Tweeten, and Mike Woods. 1992. A multicommunity approach to community impacts. *Journal of Community Development* Vol. 23, No. 1.

Hudson, Mike and James Mintert. Forthcoming. Impact of changes in input supply and output processing industries on farm structure. In Arne Hallam, ed., book on farm structure in press.

Lobao, Linda. 1990. *Locality and Inequality*. Albany: State University of New York Press.

Molnar, Joseph, ed. 1986. *Agricultural Change*. Boulder, CO: Westview Press.

OTA. March 1986. Analysis of size economies and comparative advantage in crop production in various areas of the United States. Appendix D in *Technology, Public Policy, and the Changing Structure of American Agriculture*. Washington, DC: Office of Technology Assessment, Congress of the United States.

Paarlberg, Don. December 1978. Agriculture loses its uniqueness. *American Journal of Agricultural Economics* 60:769-776.

Perry, Janet, Dean Schreiner, and Luther Tweeten. January 1991. Analysis of the characteristics of farmers who have curtailed or ceased farming in Oklahoma. Research Report P-919. Stillwater: Agricultural Experiment Station, Oklahoma State University.

Reimund, Donn and Nora Brooks. June 1990. The structure and status of the farm sector. Pp. 7-16 in Thomas Carlin and Sara Mazie, eds., *The U.S. Farming Sector Entering the 1990s*. Agricultural Information Bulletin 587. Washington, DC: ERS, U.S. Department of Agriculture.

Richardson, James, Edward Smith, and Ronald Knutson. December 1988. Who benefits from farm programs: Size and structure issues? Pp. 143-156 in Lindon Robison, ed.

Robison, Lindon, ed. December 1988. *Determinants of Farm Size and Structure*. (Proceedings of program sponsored by NC-181 Committee on Determinants of Farm Size and Structure held in San Antonio, Texas.) Michigan Agricultural Experiment Station Journal Article No. 12899. East Lansing: Department of Agricultural Economics, Michigan State University.

Saupe, Bill and Tom Carlin. Forthcoming. Structural change in agriculture and its effect on rural communities and rural life. In Arne Hallam, ed., book on farm structure in press.

Stanton, B.F. and K.D. Olson. 1990. The impacts of structural change and the future of American agriculture. Pp. 261-290 in Arne Hallam, ed.

Sumner, Daniel. 1985. Farm programs and structural issues. Pp. 283-320 in Bruce Gardner, ed., *U.S. Agricultural Policy: The 1985 Farm Legislation*. Washington, DC: American Enterprise Institute.

Tweeten, Luther. 1982. Employment. Ch. 17 in Don Dillman and Daryl Hobbs, eds., *Rural Society in the U.S.* Boulder, CO: Westview Press.

Tweeten, Luther. March 4, 1983. The economics of small farms. *Science* 219:1037-1041.

Tweeten, Luther. 1984. *Causes and Consequences of Structural Change in the Farming Industry*. NPR Report No. 207. Washington, DC: National Planning Association.

Tweeten, Luther. December 1988. World trade, exchange rates, and comparative advantage. Pp. 165-176 in Lindon Robison, ed.

Tweeten, Luther. 1988. Are farmers predestined to earn chronically low rates of return on resources in the absence of government support programs? Pp. 113-126 in Ray Goldberg, ed., *Research in Domestic and International Agribusiness Management*. Vol. 9. Greenwich, CN: JAI Press.

Tweeten, Luther. 1989a. Adjustments in agriculture and its infrastructure in the 1990s. Ch. 6 in *Positioning Agriculture for the 1990s: A New Decade of Change*. FAC Report No. 7 and NPA Report No. 238. Washington, DC: National Planning Association.

Tweeten, Luther. 1989b. *Farm Policy Analysis*. Boulder, CO: Westview Press.

Tweeten, Luther. 1990. Government commodity program impacts on farm numbers. Pp. 123-154 in Arne Hallam, ed.

Tweeten, Luther. 1992. The economics of an environmentally sound agriculture. Pp. 39-83 in Ray Goldberg, ed., *Research in Domestic and International Agribusiness Management*. Vol. 10. Greenwich, CN: JAI Press.

U.S. Department of Agriculture. April 1990. Economic indicators of the farm sector: Production and efficiency statistics, 1988. ECIFS 8-5. Washington, DC: Economic Research Service, USDA.

U.S. Department of Agriculture. January 1991. *Economic Indicators of the Farm Sector: National Financial Summary, 1989*. ECIFS 9-2. Washington, DC: Economic Research Service, USDA.

APPENDIX

Appendix Table 5.1. Legal Organization, Tenure, Off-farm Employment, and Enterprise Shares by Sales Class of Farms, U.S., 1987.

Item	Large $250 & Over	Medium $100 to $250	Small $10 to $100	Rural Residences Less than $10	Total
Legal Organization	(Percent of Farms in Legal Organization Class)				
Sole proprietorship	54.8	76.5	86.4	92.8	87.2
Partnership	23.0	15.7	11.0	6.2	9.6
Corporate, family held	19.8	7.3	2.4	0.9	2.9
Corporate, other than family	2.4	0.5	0.2	0.1	0.3
	100.0	100.0	100.0	100.0	100.0
Tenure of Operator	(Percent of Farms in Tenure Class)				
Full owner	32.2	27.0	47.1	77.2	59.3
Part owner	54.7	58.1	37.4	15.1	29.2
Tenant	13.0	14.9	15.5	7.7	11.5
	100.0	100.0	100.0	100.0	100.0
Off-Farm Employment of Operator	(Percent of Farms in Off-Farm Work Category)				
None	77.4	73.1	50.3	29.1	43.1
1 - 99 days	9.5	13.3	12.8	7.8	10.2
100 - 199 days	3.7	4.6	9.6	10.1	9.1
200+ days	9.4	9.0	27.3	53.0	37.6
	100.0	100.0	100.0	100.0	100.0
Commodity	(Percent of Receipts by Enterprise)				
Grains	10.3	32.1	35.5	17.9	20.8
Cotton	3.5	3.5	2.0	0.5	3.1
Tobacco	0.4	1.4	2.8	6.3	1.3
Hay, silage, & seed	1.3	1.6	3.1	8.2	1.9
Vegetables, fruits, & nursery	18.3	6.7	6.7	6.2	12.9
Other crops	4.4	2.5	1.5	0.5	3.4
Poultry & eggs	14.3	6.1	1.4	0.5	9.4
Dairy	8.8	18.5	13.2	0.5	11.8
Cattle & calves	30.4	16.3	24.4	49.5	26.3
Hogs	6.2	10.1	7.5	4.1	7.3
Other livestock	2.0	1.1	1.9	5.8	1.9
	100.0	100.0	100.0	100.0	100.0
Hectares per Farm	1,039	450	193	53	187

Source: Census of Agriculture (Bureau of the Census).

6

Sustainable Food and Agricultural Policies: A U.S. Perspective

Arne Hallam and Selahattin Dibooglu

Introduction

Sustainable Systems

The 1980s saw a rebirth of interest in sustainable agricultural systems (Harwood; NRC). While soil conservation has been discussed for years, and pollution control, at least in detail, since the 1960s and 1970s, the interest in recent years has been more holistic and systems oriented. The concerns raised by Carson's *Silent Spring*, which led to more pesticide regulation in the 1960s and 1970s, brought about a more fundamental rethinking of the food production and distribution system in the 1980s. The idea of sustainable agriculture became a buzzword for popular discussion groups and research projects. While definitions of "sustainable" varied, most parties agreed on the need for systems that were in some sense regenerative or that could maintain production and consumption levels without large amounts of outside input.

Most discussions of sustainability have been directed towards agricultural production. Issues related to sustainable production practices might be termed physical sustainability. While physical sustainability of a particular production practice is necessary to obtain sustainable food consumption, physical and biologic sustainability is not sufficient to ensure a safe and stable supply of food. A second type of sustainability is related to the economic system and might be termed economic sustainability. A physical system that can be sustained but does not return sufficient profit to entice entrepreneurs to choose or maintain it is not a stable system of food production. Thus economic sustainability is also necessary for sustainable food consumption.

In the parlance of the economic growth literature, a sustainable economic system is one that is capable of either constant or growing output per capita over the long run. While conservation of resources may allow a constant output stream, technical change is required for long-run output growth.

Economic ecologists (Daly) have argued that the second law of thermodynamics (that some physical systems move toward disequilibrium) prevents the long-run steady state of standard growth theory. That is, the long-term rate of economic growth is zero or negative and is not the positive constant of standard growth theory. Others (Young) have argued that such physical laws do not necessarily hold for economic systems. Some key issues in defining sustainable economic systems are the social discount rate, the actual time horizon used, and the ability of technological change to outweigh the law of entropy. The latter holds that there is economically unrecoverable leakage of energy and nutrients from any system which must be offset by technological change to maintain or increase productivity.

On a broader and perhaps more important spectrum, sustainable food consumption depends on the sustainability and stability of the political and social system in which the economic system rests. In a macroeconomic context, a sustainable system not only has stable output but has sustainable employment and income so that demand is sufficient to provide full utilization of resources. In a social context, a sustainable system provides the institutions that educate and train workers so that productivity increases.

Consider, for example, the current food production system for corn in the state of Iowa. Farm structure in this sector is characterized by many medium sized farms operated by families who live in rural areas near small rural communities. The sustainability of this food production system depends not only on the sustainability of the biological processes but on the sustainability of this structure and size of farms, on the sustainability of the rural communities that support the individuals who own and operate these farms, on the political sustainability of the current government policies which provide a subsidy in the form of target prices to these farms, and on the social acceptability of the use of chemicals on these farms at levels that may affect groundwater.

If any of these factors change over time, the sustainability of the food supplies emanating from these farms may be in jeopardy. For example, suppose that the economic system evolves in such a way that raises inequality and reduces purchasing power of society. Less income will reduce the demand for food. The result may be more hunger with no basic change in the physical integrity of the production system. On the other hand, technology may improve productivity of farm resources, freeing farm people for nonfarm jobs and reducing food prices. As nonfarm jobs are available, increased buying power raises income of society including per capita income of farmers. Poverty and hunger will decline. Thus a sustainable food policy must take into account the biological, economic, political, and social systems in which it operates. While food production seems resilient in the face of incremental structural change, over time such changes can have significant impacts.

Aggregate Versus Individual Sustainability

Economic systems and sustainability can be studied at both the individual and aggregate level. Most discussions of sustainability have related to individual production processes. Aggregate sustainability is related to supply and demand balances and pricing. If the economic system provides incentives such that the total quantity of food consumed is stable or growing over time, then the system might be termed sustainable. Individual sustainability, on the other hand, has to do with stable consumption and production by the individual. If an individual can maintain an adequate diet over time, then it might be said that this person has sustainable food consumption.

The aggregate system can be sustainable without guaranteeing sustainable consumption for an individual. Consider, for example, a change in income distribution such that total national food consumption is the same but person A starves to death. While some analysts are content with measuring aggregate food security, others with a more humanistic view of welfare concern themselves with poverty indices and individual food consumption. If income is not distributed in an "appropriate" manner, demand may fall, investment may decline, or (perhaps more radically) the disadvantaged may revolt. Alternatively, in a somewhat affluent democratic society such as the United States, the social conscience may be pricked and social reform will take place. If individuals are not on sustainable paths, the social system may not have the inherent fabric to hold together and sustain the system.

A dynamic economy shifting resources to where returns are highest will inevitably leave some individuals worse off even as the national economy grows. Change is not costless. The American economy has sometimes experienced business cycles causing change without growth -- a policy causing food insecurity that could have been reduced by sound monetary and fiscal policy.

The next section of the chapter discusses food security in the United States in historical perspective. This is followed by a section discussing the current research on sustainable production systems. The next two sections discuss the sustainability of the current agricultural structure and its relation to food security. Another section integrates the material on sustainable production and sustainable systems. The last section draws conclusions and suggests areas for further discussion.

A Historical Perspective on Food Security in the United States

Food Production, Consumption, and Security Prior to 1900

Self-sufficiency characterized much of American agriculture in the two and half centuries which followed the early settlements. Most American farmers in this period raised produce primarily for at-home consumption, although some produce was exchanged at local shops for sugar, salt, and other articles. Everything else from clothing to furniture, soap, and candles was produced on the farm. By the mid-1800s, manufacturing activities started to move from the farm to become independent industries. This was part of the transition from a self-sufficient subsistence to a commercial agriculture.

The food sector was much affected by this development. Slaughtering and meat packing; flour milling; butter, cheese, and dairy products; and the canning of fruits and vegetables previously confined to the farm began to organize as separate industries.

The expansion of agriculture was unprecedented after the Civil War ended in 1865. Of particular importance was the expansion of the markets, both domestic and foreign. The tremendous growth in non-agricultural population in the US and the industrial expansion of Britain and other European nations created an unparalleled demand for food and fiber. Emergence of cheap means of transportation permitted areas of production to be connected to distant consumption centers.

The increase in the acreage of cultivated land, specialization in production, and the widespread substitution of machines for human labor had a significant effect on farm output. Total farm output increased by some 53 percent between 1870 and 1880, and 135 percent between 1870 and 1900. During the period 1866-1900, the production of wheat increased four times, the production of corn some three and half times, and the production of barley some six and half times. The number of cattle on farms doubled between 1867 and 1900 and the number of hogs increased by about 50 percent (Cochrane, pp. 91-92). Of the farm products grown in the United States after 1860, cereals were the most important and in 1899 they constituted half of the total value of all crops raised in this country (Edwards).

Foreign markets were important in absorbing this agricultural output. The export of wheat increased from 35 million bushels in 1867-1871 to 197 million bushels in 1897-1901. Corn exports were 10 million bushels in 1867-1871 and then they rose to 193 million bushels in 1897-1901. The export of beef and beef products increased from 55 million pounds to 637 million pounds while pork and pork product exports increased from 128 million pounds to 1,528 million pounds in this period (Nourse).

Agricultural production did not always adjust quickly to changes in demand, prices, costs, and returns to the factors of production. Prices received by farmers for their products declined irregularly but continuously from the Civil War to the mid-1890s. The price of wheat fell from $1.14 per bushel in 1871 to $0.64 per bushel in 1884 and to 49 cents per bushel in 1894. The trend in the price of corn was similar. A bushel of corn, traded for 49 cents in 1870, received only 21 cents in 1896. The change in livestock prices was not so dramatic but followed the same downward trend (Nourse).

While productivity gains allowed farming to remain generally profitable, geographic and temporal concentrations of low farm income were frequent as the sector did not adjust quickly enough to the new land levels, technology, and demand patterns. Prairie fires, hail, drought, grasshoppers, and other forces of nature had adverse repercussions on the rural welfare. As Professor Cochrane put it "destitution was widespread on the central plains frontier in the 1870s; hunger and outright starvation were not uncommon" (Cochrane).

Some farmers responded to these developments by organizing and acting collectively in populist movements to influence government policies. The first major farm organization, the Grange, arose out of the Patrons of Husbandry established in 1867. Other movements that followed were the Greenback Movement, Farmers' Alliances, and the Populist Party whose candidate for president polled six and half million votes in 1896 (Edwards, pp. 256-265). The success of these attempts was limited, though some actions were taken by state and local governments and the army to help farmers. During this period, the system of agricultural production and distribution adjusted to changes in other sectors of the economy. While the resultant disequilibrium induced some movement towards a new equilibrium, the major impact was to create institutions and social movements designed to slow or ease change.

Food Production, Consumption, and Security 1900-1945

By 1897, agriculture started to recover from the depression of the mid-1890s. Farm prices continued to increase steadily until World War I when they rose sharply in response to the great increase in foreign demand for foodstuffs. Population growth also contributed to the price increase. Demand for cropland and the price of farmland increased dramatically. With the recovery of European agriculture after World War I, export demand for American products fell. With farm recession beginning in 1920, landowners were not able to make their land payments. As the domestic terms of trade turned against farmers, many went bankrupt. By the 1930s, the Great Depression began for the whole economy.

With stagnant markets and deepening depression, farmers sought help from the government. The Farm Block first became a force during this period and numerous remedies for the problem were proposed. Many early attempts to legislate farm relief failed. The first political success was the Agricultural Marketing Act of 1929, which was enacted to (but failed to) control crop surpluses. The Agricultural Adjustment Act of 1933 was the first substantive effort to deal with excessive farm production capacity and the low level of agricultural income. The Act of 1936 emphasized the need for conservation of soils and a continuing flow of income to agriculture. The Agricultural Adjustment Act of 1938 initiated more comprehensive and permanent measures for agricultural production and income. It included, among other things, an amendment to the soil conservation part of the 1936 Act, modified the marketing quota system, made arrangements with regard to freight rates, and introduced crop insurance (Benedict, pp. 276-384; Davis, pp. 312-323). The acts passed in the 1930s also contained provisions for price supports. Farm commodity legislation is discussed in detail elsewhere (Tweeten, chs. 11, 12).

The fluctuating foreign demand for farm products was the basic destabilizing factor in this period. The extraordinary foreign demand during and after World War I reached a peak in 1919 ($4.1 billion) and then declined persistently throughout the 1920s and 1930s to only $517 million in current value in 1940, the level of the 1880s. The Smoot-Hawley Tariff of 1930, designed to protect American farmers from foreign competition, closed foreign demand. The tariff was ill-advised because countries that could not export to America could not afford to import. During World War II, demand rose, leading to the recovery of the farm sector.

An examination of agricultural trade in this period reveals interesting patterns. First, between 1925 and 1941 the United States was a net importer of foodstuffs. Although a negative trade balance for raw food was prevalent over most of the early 20th century, during the early years in this period processed food exports helped to offset this deficit. But in the 1930s the United States was a net importer of processed food. The total trade deficit for food in 1930 was $225 million in 1913 prices, and had reached $665 million by 1936. The food trade deficit declined thereafter and by 1942 the United States had again become a net food exporter (Figure 6.1). Secondly, the United States had a domestic agricultural/food surplus during this period. This can be explained in part by price developments. There is a close association between prices and food trade deficits (Figure 6.2). This is because the foreign demand for foodstuffs was responsive to price and the United States did not enjoy the price advantage it had in the nineteenth century before other sources of supply had emerged in South America, Canada, and Australia. The American price disadvantage was closely related to protectionist trade policies of the 1930s and the domestic policies which supported prices and cut production in agriculture.

In response to the surplus of farm products and widespread unemployment and poverty, the first Food Stamp Plan and School Lunch Program were initiated in 1939. According to the Food Stamp Plan, low-income families could spend a small share of their income to acquire food stamps of much greater value -- enough to purchase an adequate diet.

Per capita food consumption remained steady during this period. The per capita food consumption index (1937-39 = 100) was 96 in 1913 and slightly above 100 by 1923-1931. It declined during 1932-36 due to the depression but started to recover during 1936-45 and had reached 115 by 1945. The per capita food production index (1937-39 = 100), on the other hand, mostly fluctuated between 100 and 110 during 1909-1940 and then moved sharply upward after 1940. Per capita calorie consumption decreased materially over this period, declining from 3,590 in 1897-1901 to 3,377 in 1925, and to 3,200 from 1935 to 1939. Several factors may have affected this trend. These factors include the mechanization of production, a relative decrease in agricultural population whose calorie requirement is relatively high, reductions in hours of work, improved heating of buildings, improved transportation

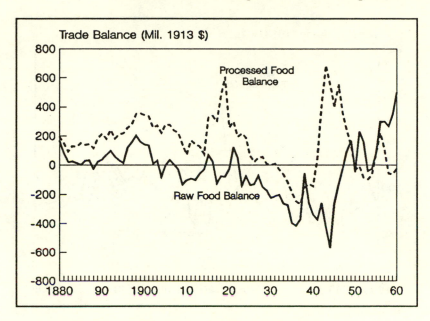

Figure 6.1. U.S. Foodstuffs Trade Balance, 1901-1960.
Source: Adapted by the authors from U.S. government data.

systems, a decrease in the average age of the population, and probably a shift toward fruits and vegetables which are low in calories (Barger and Landsberg, pp. 155-157).

Major changes took place in the production system in agriculture. Productivity increased dramatically as mechanization advanced. The number of gasoline tractors in operation on farms increased from 4,000 in 1911 to 246,000 in 1920 and to 920,000 in 1930. Other technological developments such as chemical fertilizers, plant and animal breeding, and disease control also increased agricultural productivity.

The system seemed primed to produce more than adequate food supplies to meet aggregate consumption targets. The questions were whether such surpluses could be managed in a way to ensure adequate returns to the sector, and also to help alleviate urban poverty. And although the system experienced significant technical change during this period, the underlying farm structure was relatively stable.

Food Production, Consumption, and Security After 1945

World War II was a revival period for U.S. agriculture. It strengthened domestic and foreign demand for agricultural products and increased employment in war-related industries. Between 1940 and 1946, farmers' income rose 236 percent. This trend continued until the Korean War when farm income begin to decline slightly until the sharp increase in 1972. This increase in

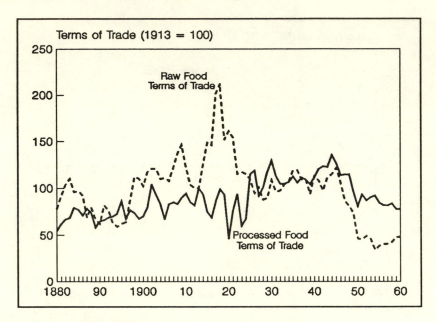

Figure 6.2. Terms of Trade, Foodstuffs, 1901-1960.
Source: Adapted by the authors from U.S. government data.

farm income helped farmers acquire new technologies and the post-war period witnessed a complete transformation of agriculture. This transformation not only included mechanization and the use of science in agricultural practices, but changed the structure of agriculture. The consequences were dramatic in that yield per acre for wheat increased from 17.3 per bushel in 1945 to 31.8 bushels in 1970. Corn yields per acre more than doubled between 1945 and 1970. The farm output index (1977=100) increased from 58 in 1945 to 84 in 1970 and reached 110 in 1987. This increase in production/output was due to productivity increases as well as intensive input use. The index of chemical input use increased about six times between 1945 and 1970.

These developments created enormous agricultural surpluses. The government has continued to support agriculture through various measures, including commodity programs on one hand while trying to vent surpluses through Public Law 480 and domestic food stamps on the other. At the same time, there were 39.5 million people (22.4 percent of the total population) living below the official poverty line in 1959. Although this number declined in the sixties and seventies, there were still 31.9 million people (13 percent of population) below the poverty level in 1988. Human resource development through education and training; a moral renaissance apparent in lower rates of family disintegration, drug use, crime, and dysfunctional work habits; and more rapid adjustment to economic incentives by agricultural producers, industry, and urban workers could help to reduce poverty problems. Some individuals inevitably will be left behind because they are physically or mentally unable to participate in the economy or draw on family or other assets. For them, a social safety net of food stamps and other welfare is essential.

In a historical context, the transformation from an agrarian economy to an industrial/post-industrial economy caused a change in the value system. These traditional values, be they the "protestant ethic" or "progressivism of the enlightenment", encompassed views which emphasized the virtues of work, material progress, and man's dominion over nature. These values have undergone changes in recent decades partly due to the civil rights, anti-war, and environmental movements of the 1960s. Growth as a goal in itself came under serious questioning as people recognized that scientific and technological advances have costs in compromise of culture and the natural environment. As knowledge of the delicate nature of the ecological system spread, people demanded wide-ranging measures to protect the environment. Nuclear power and genetic manipulation are not being received with the enthusiasm they would have received 30 years ago. This has led some authors to suggest that a new ethic or life-style is emerging -- a move toward "voluntary simplicity", an effort to live life within a new balance between inner and outer growth (Hamrin).

As for agricultural development, the increasing awareness of the impact of modern technologies on the environment became evident when pesticides were traced in food chains and crop nutrients began to accumulate in streams and in underground aquifers. The energy shortage of the early 1970s was another significant factor in reminding people of the limited nature of the resources. Due to these and other reasons, agricultural development directions have come under serious debate and analysis. New directions include the following: the interrelatedness of all parts of the farming system, the importance of the many biological balances in the system, and the need to maximize desired biological relationships in the system while minimizing the use of material and practices that disrupt these relationships (Harwood).

Changes in the agricultural production process during the inter-war years led to even larger changes in productivity and the social system of agriculture following World War II. The changes in the structure of agriculture that have occurred in the last 30 years are due in large measure to changes in technology. Most importantly, food abundance has allowed society to become more sensitized to issues related to the environment, animal rights, and poverty. These changes in social perceptions could have major impacts on the structure of agriculture in the years ahead.

Current Issues in Sustainable Agricultural Production

The ability of agriculture to sustain output growth indefinitely depends on wise use of natural and other resources, and technological progress. These are "internal aspects of sustainability". It is also very important that agricultural practices maintain an environment favorable to humans and other species. Environmental effects of agricultural production can be called "external aspects of sustainability". These are captured in the following statement: "Sustainable agriculture should involve the successful management of resources for agriculture to satisfy changing human needs while maintaining or enhancing the natural resource base and avoiding environmental degradation" (TAC). The law of entropy noted earlier that it is not possible to maintain a natural resource base. But application of science and knowledge can raise output even if natural resources leak from a more useful to less useful position in the system.

Internal Aspects of Sustainability

An adequate land base is necessary for sustainable agricultural production. Two threats that affect the availability and efficiency of this base are soil loss due to non-agricultural uses, and soil erosion. Every hour between 1967 and 1977, about 320 acres of U.S. agricultural land was converted to nonfarm uses and one third of this land had the capability to be used as cropland. This means paving a one-mile wide strip from New York to California every year (Sampson). Conversion of farmland to other uses has slowed since 1977 and is often a regional as opposed to national problem.

Soil erosion is still a serious problem in the U.S. despite decades of state and federal conservation efforts. It affects crops by reducing the depth of the topsoil and thereby affecting the availability of soil nutrients, the capacity of the soil to supply water, and the infiltration of water and air into the soil. These effects vary with soil type, climate, topography, type of crop, and farming practices. The damage caused by soil erosion can be on-farm (productivity loss), as well as off-farm. Sediment from soil erosion and water runoff carry along agricultural chemicals and dissolved minerals. Erosion caused by wind reduces air quality. Although there is a considerable debate over estimating the losses, it is recognized that wind and water erosion cause serious damage which is more severe in certain areas than others. For example, the National Research Council estimates that wind and water erode between 2.7 and 3.1 billion tons of topsoil from U.S. cropland each year. This is roughly equivalent to removing one inch of topsoil from 20 million acres each year.

Estimates of this soil erosion on productivity vary due to assumptions made and techniques used. If technology does not change and other inputs are not adjusted, soil erosion can lead to significant losses in productivity. Sampson estimates that the equivalent of 25-62 million acres of cropland could be lost in the next 50 years due to reduced productivity. Crosson used cross-section data from the 1982 National Resource Inventory to estimate the effect of topsoil depth and erosion on crop yields. He projected yield declines of 3-5 percent over a fifty year period starting in 1982. Pierce *et al.* use a productivity impact model to estimate yield losses due to soil erosion in the

Midwest. They found yield losses of closer to 2-3 percent over a 50 year period, but their model assumes producers will increase fertilizer as erosion proceeds. Alt and Putman using the Erosion Impact Productivity Calculator (EPIC) developed at USDA's Temple Texas facility found yield losses of 3 percent over a 100 year period. As with the model described by Pierce, EPIC adjusts fertilizer as soil erodes. Thus the lower yields of 3 percent would require 1.5 percent more nitrogen, 4.4 percent more phosphorous, and 7.4 percent more lime. In all studies impacts are much larger on poorer quality soils or soils with less topsoil depth. If erosion eventually moves large quantities of land to poorer classifications, the productivity impacts will be higher. Technological change can, of course, compensate for erosion. A panel of experts (English *et al.*) assembled in 1982 predicted crop yield increases due to technological change far exceeding the losses presented above. The issue is then one of technology being able to continue to improve faster than resources are depleted. If productivity loss from soil erosion is 5 percent per century, then today's annual productivity gains (from technology) of 1.5 percent annually offset a century of erosion in just three years.

Water induced soil erosion can be controlled at tolerable levels through a combination of conservation, cropping, and management practices. The use of conservation tillage practices has increased in the past decade. The extent of conservation will depend mostly on government policies and/or economic incentives associated with the adoption of conservation practices. Also, future losses due to erosion will depend on how many acres are planted in crops. To the extent that more marginal lands are brought into production, erosion will be a more serious problem. To the extent that technology increases yields faster than demand for output expands, fewer acres will be cropped and erosion will be a less serious problem.

One difference between a natural system and an agricultural system is that in the agricultural system some nutrients are removed from the system as output and they are replaced by nutrients from commercial fertilizers. The viability of the agricultural system in the long run depends on minimization of losses from erosion, leaching, and denitrification, as well as additional sources of nutrients including biologically fixed nitrogen, commercial fertilizers, and recycled wastes. Currently in the United States, off-farm nutrient sources are the major components of the nutrient budget. Based on a study conducted in 1987, Miller and Larson reported that commercial fertilizers accounted for 70 percent of nitrogen, 69 percent of phosphorus, and 51 percent of potassium additions to cropland soil. The remaining nutrients were from manure and crop residues.

Farmers choose nutrient sources based on availability, cost, and compatibility with other production activities. For instance, one should not expect nutrients to come from manure or legumes in predominantly cash grain producing areas since this would require livestock to consume the hay and produce the manure for this system.

The sustainability of commercial fertilizer supplies depends upon the reserve of raw materials and the energy required for manufacturing and distribution. For example, the raw material for nitrogen is abundant but its production is energy intensive and hence is susceptible to any energy shortage. (For a summary of reserves of nutrients and petroleum, see Tweeten, pp. 280, 281.) Future agricultural systems may depend more on biological nitrogen fixation, manure, and other wastes.

External Aspects of Sustainability

The viability of agricultural production in the long run also depends on the minimization of adverse consequences that some agricultural practices have on natural resources and the environment. Agriculture is the largest source of nonpoint water pollution, which accounts for about half of all water pollution. Surface water damage from agriculture is estimated to be between $2 and $16 billion each year (NRC). Runoff from precipitation and irrigation carries sediment, minerals, nutrients, pesticides, and other agricultural chemicals into rivers, streams, lakes, and other reservoirs. Sediment deposition and nutrient loading are the major sources of pollutants. Among the nutrients, nitrogen reaches surface water via runoff and percolation because it is relatively soluble, whereas phosphorus is mostly attached to sediment because it is relatively insoluble. Commercial fertilizers are the major suppliers of nitrogen and phosphorus. Animal waste ranks second. It is recognized that the effects of erosion on water sources are greater than its potential effects on farming productivity.

The principal effects of these pollutants are declining aquatic plant and animal populations, a decline in the recreational use of water, and an increase in the costs associated with cleaning reservoirs and water treatment facilities. Some pesticides and herbicides are not effectively removed from drinking water by conventional treatment facilities and they represent potential health risks. Other concerns include high levels of pesticide residues found in the tissues of birds, fish, and other aquatic life and uptake by crops of soil pesticides which can contaminate foods.

The extent of drinking water contamination by nitrates and pesticides is only beginning to become known. USDA (NRC) has estimated that 1,437 counties have potential problems with nitrate or pesticide pollution. A recent EPA study of 1,347 wells found that more than 50 percent contained nitrates. While levels in most were low and nitrogen occurs naturally in groundwater, some individual areas had concentrations above the acceptable level. Only 1.2 percent of urban wells and 2.4 percent of rural wells contained nitrogen concentrations above levels considered to be safe by the Environmental Protection Agency. Groundwater pollution tends to be seasonal with low average concentrations, but very high concentrations during key periods. High levels are particularly dangerous for elderly individuals and infants.

Sustainable Production and Sustainable Systems

While the internal aspects of sustainability relate directly to the physical production process, external aspects may involve the social and political system as well. In extreme cases, externalities may so harm the outside environment that feedback effects on the production process are of major concern. An example might be severe erosion such that downstream lakes and reservoirs fill with silt, back up, and cause damage upstream. In an indirect way, pollution may make an area undesirable, and cause firms and workers to move away. A more indirect but currently important aspect of externalities is social consciousness. If a production process is particularly obnoxious and forms a rallying point for popular opinion, society may no longer allow the process to continue, thus making the system unsustainable. The current public concern with pollution and environmental damage may make some current practices unsustainable politically even if they are sustainable from a technical and purely economic viewpoint.

Food Security and
Sustainable Agricultural Production

Trade and Food Security

While the United States has historically been the world's largest exporter of farm products, the 1970s witnessed a dramatic expansion in agricultural exports due to rising foreign demand and a depreciating U.S. dollar. Agricultural exports almost tripled between 1971 and 1981, making agricultural trade a significant narrower of the trade deficit. With a strong dollar, agricultural exports fell in the first half of the 1980s. Though exports started to recover after 1986, they were short of the 1981 record level in 1989.

This volatility of demand, supply, and price levels has raised concerns for some (Koppel) about the economic viability of agricultural producers, the ecological sustainability of the resource base, and the nutritional status of low income consumers. However, these are not threatened by volatility except in marginal cases.

Unstable international markets are due to weather, business cycles, barriers to trade, and lack of truly international futures markets (Johnson; Schuh; Thompson). Part of the instability is due to market failure, and the appropriate solution is more open markets, not more insulation from the world. Buffer stocks, perhaps some of them internationally coordinated, also hold promise.

The effect of international trade on natural resources is important. The export boom of the 1970s led some to argue that the U.S. was exporting "its soil" as rising foreign demand induced the cultivation of marginal cropland. Indeed, some 20 million acres of pasture, range land, and idle land (4.8 percent of total cropland acreage) was converted to cropland between 1975 and 1981.[1] This led legislators to include some provisions in 1985 Food Security Act slowing soil erosion and conversion of fragile soils and wetlands into cropland.

Purchasing Power and Food Security

Aggregate food security is not an issue in the short or medium run in the United States, since chronic surpluses have characterized US agriculture for many decades. This cannot be said for individual food security. Because individual food security ultimately concerns the individual or the family unit, its principal determinant is purchasing power or income adjusted for what the income can buy. Therefore, individual food security is mostly a problem of poverty. Reducing poverty requires human resource development, jobs, intact (two-parent) families, and other measures.

Poverty in the United States received attention in the 1960s when nearly one quarter of the population was living below the official poverty level. The poverty level was reduced in the 1960s and 1970s to 11 percent by 1980. The trend reversed in 1980s and by 1984 the poverty level had reached 15.2 percent. It has been declining slightly since then and was 13.1 in 1988.

Like the poverty issue it is related to, the hunger issue received public attention in late 1960s and reemerged in the 1980s. Numerous groups and organizations conducted hunger studies in mid-1980s and found that the problem was becoming more widespread (e.g., U.S. Conference of Mayors; U.S. General Accounting Office; Physicians Task Force on Hunger in America). Among the factors that affected this development were cuts in social program benefits such as medical assistance and unemployment insurance.

The government has dealt with this problem through federal food assistance programs such as the Food Stamp Program, Special Supplemental Food Program for Women, Infants, and Children, and several nutrition assistance programs for children. These programs can provide "food money" to purchase a nutritious diet by those with inadequate buying power. Some people choose to spend "food money" for other necessities or for non-essentials. Thus, food security relates to job security, individual decisions, and preferences as well as to food cost.

---

[1] In the first half of the 1980s, almost the opposite occurred, reversing the trend in commodity exports, harvested cropland, and intensity of use leading to a decline in land values.

Sustainable Food Supplies and
a Sustainable Production System

Farm Structure and Rural Communities

The assertion that the structure of agriculture is closely related to the rural community and its quality of life led many to explore the characteristics of this relationship. Carlin and Saupe noted that structural change in farming is only one of a set of factors that determine the nature of rural communities. Proximity to larger urban centers, the adequacy of transportation and communication systems, the presence of mineral and forest sources, recreational attributes of the area, a restructuring of the retail sector, government initiatives for community economic development, and the original settlement patterns and cultural beliefs are all important in influencing rural community characteristics. For most rural Americans and communities, agriculture is no longer the economic base.

Many studies of the effects of farm structure on rural community viability are along the lines of the classical Goldschmidt study. That latter study focused on two similar California towns that differ in the structural characteristics of their farming: Arvin, dominated by large scale farms and hired labor and Dinuba, characterized by mid-size owner-operated farms. The study found that Dinuba enjoyed higher standards of living with better public services, better schools, and higher participation in community institutions. Although numerous studies note the limitations of the Goldschmidt study and some draw contradictory conclusions, much empirical evidence does support his hypothesis that large scale and/or hired labor farming is related to worse socioeconomic conditions (and mid-size, operator family labor farming is related to better conditions) through the following impacts:

- a decline in or smaller local population,
- lower incomes for certain segments of the population such as hired laborers,
- increase in income inequality or increase in poverty,
- lower standards of living,
- lower numbers or quality of community services,
- less democratic political participation,
- lower community social participation and initiative,
- decreased retail trade and fewer and less diverse retail outlets,
- environmental pollution and depletion of natural resources,
- greater unemployment (Lobao; see also for references).

The Small Farm Viability Project studied the towns that were subject to Goldschmidt's study three decades later and found that the disparity in quality of life and civic participation remains today, and economic and social gaps had become greater. While these two cases should not be generalized, they point out some of the potential problems of an agriculture characterized by large firms who hire primarily unskilled labor.

More crucial than these findings is the mechanism through which these characteristics are generated. A key concept is the uneven character of capital accumulation in agriculture. As Buttel (1983) indicates, some farmers are more successful in accumulating capital so that the process results in increasing stratification or differentiation among farmers; larger more successful and aggressive farmers out-compete and purchase the land of their neighbors. As production becomes concentrated on larger farms, productivity and national income rise, and the number of farms and the size of the farm labor force decrease. Also, the number of hired laborers and managers decrease although at a slower rate than the number of owner-operators. As farm numbers and the size of the workforce decrease, some must leave the community for better jobs elsewhere unless nonfarm employment opportunities can be secured in the same area. And because outmigration results in a decline in population, economic and social institutions dependent on this population base decline. Public service costs rise per capita. Over time, of course, the economy will adjust to these changes and reach a new equilibrium.

The current structure of agriculture is dominated by family farms where the majority of labor, management, and equity capital are provided by the operator and his/her immediate family. If this structure can continue in an efficient manner, many of the problems addressed above can be mitigated. A number of proposals have been advocated (Paarlberg) to prevent the decline of rural communities. Most, such as farm commodity program payment limitations, progressive taxes on real estate, industry location incentives, or jobs programs would require government intervention and political cooperation not usually forthcoming from large and small business operations and populist rural institutions. Americans may not like to see the number of farm and rural residents decrease, but government measures to stop such changes have not had a good record of success. Part of the reason is that costs are high either in taxpayer outlays or foregone national economic growth.

Conclusions

This chapter has discussed aspects of the U.S. agricultural production system and some implications for food security and sustainability. Although productivity and production quantity of American agriculture is unmatched, future progress of American agriculture depends on wise use of the resource base, increased productivity through science and industry, and smooth transition to external shocks. Increasing emphasis on soil conservation, regulation of pesticide use, and promising new technology such as bioengineering give basis for optimism but not for complacency about sustainable physical output growth.

In a broad context, the previous sections have painted a guardedly optimistic picture about the sustainability of aggregate agricultural production in the United States. Most studies support the notion that with proper husbandry, technical advances will compensate for deterioration in soil quality.

The effects of soil erosion, nitrate and pesticide contamination, and food residues are of continuing concern and are being monitored. As society puts more restrictions (either through quotas or taxes) on input use to protect the environment, farm yield increases will be restrained. While the overall effects of such limitations may be positive from society's viewpoint, continued food abundance will depend on significant technical advances.

Agriculture in the U.S. is characterized by many small farms with minimal production, significant numbers of medium and large farms producing a large portion of the output, and a small number of very large farms in specific industries which also produce large quantities of output. Operators choose to produce based on their expected returns in agriculture compared to their opportunities elsewhere. The monetary return on small farms is low. Many small farms are in operation because the owners derive benefits from rural living, closeness to nature, and enjoyment of growing crops and livestock, and tax advantages. While such factors are probably of less importance for larger commercial farms, they also play a role.

Although the current food production system in the United States provides aggregate food security and seems to be sustainable in a physical and probably economic sense, the system does not provide food security for every individual or family. Individual food security is more related to income and purchasing power than it is to the system of food production, especially in an advanced industrial society such as the United States. While arguments about food for people and individual food self-sufficiency may make some sense in a primarily agrarian society, the U.S. economy has long since moved beyond any practical or efficient way to food subsistence for every family. The seeming paradox of food surplus with hunger does not go away, however. Labor and other markets need to be improved and human resources developed. Potentially beneficial programs include improved schooling, vocational training, on-the-job training, job relocation assistance, better welfare programs for the truly disadvantaged, and short-term food assistance.

Many criticize a system which provides riches for some and allows hunger for others. Such contradictions can not be avoided in a free society but they can be minimized through appropriate programs.

References

Alt, K. and J. Putman. 1987. Soil erosion dramatic in places, but not a serious threat to productivity. In *Agricultural Outlook*. AO-129. Washington, DC: ERS, U.S. Department of Agriculture.

Barger, H. and Hans H. Landsberg. 1942. *American Agriculture, 1899-1939: A Study of Output, Employment, and Productivity.* New York: National Bureau of Economic Research, Inc.

Benedict, Murray R. 1953. *Farm Policies of the United States, 1790-1950: A Study of Their Origins and Development.* New York: The Twentieth Century Fund.

Buttel, F.H. 1983. Farm structure and rural development. Pp. 103-124 in D. E. Brewster, W. D. Rasmussen, and G. Youngberg, eds., *Farms in Transition.* Ames: Iowa State University Press.

Carlin, Thomas A. and William E. Saupe 1990. Structural change in agriculture and its relationship to rural communities and rural life. Pp. 103-121 in A. Hallam, ed., *Determinants of Farm Size and Farm Structure.* Proceedings of the Program Sponsored by the NC-181 Committee on Determinants of Farm Size and Structure in North Central Areas of The United States, held in Albuquerque, NM.

Carson, R. 1962. *Silent Spring.* Boston: Houghton Mifflin.

Cochrane, Willard W. 1979. *The Development of American Agriculture: A Historical Analysis.* Minneapolis: University of Minnesota Press.

Crosson, P.R. 1986. Soil erosion and policy issues. In T. Phipps, P.R. Crosson, and K.A. Price, eds., *Agriculture and the Environment.* Washington, DC: Resources for the Future.

Daly, Herman E., ed. 1980. *Economics, Ecology, Ethics: Essays Toward a Steady-State Economy.* San Francisco: W. H. Freeman and Company.

Daly, Herman E., ed. 1973. *Toward a Steady-State Economy.* San Francisco: W. E. Freeman and Company.

Davis, Chester C. 1940. The development of agricultural policy since the end of the World War. In *Farmers in A Changing World, USDA Yearbook of Agriculture, 1940.*

Denison, E.F. 1985. *Trends in American Economic Growth, 1929-1982.* Washington, DC: The Brookings Institute.

Edwards, Everett E. 1940. American agriculture -- The first 300 hundred years. In *Farmers in A Changing World, USDA Yearbook of Agriculture, 1940.*

English, B.C., J.A. Maetzold, B.R. Holding, and E.O. Heady. 1984. *Future Agricultural Technology and Resource Conservation.* Ames: Iowa State University Press.

Environmental Protection Agency. 1990. *National Pesticide Survey: Summary Results.* Washington, DC: Office of Water and Office of Pesticides and Toxic Substances, EPA.

Fischer, S. 1988. Symposium on the slowdown in productivity growth. *Journal of Economic Perspectives* 2:3-8

Goldschmidt, Walter. 1946. *Small Businesses and the Community: A study in Central Valley of California on Effects of Scale of Farm Operation.* Report to the Special Committee to Study Problems of American Small Business, United States Senate, December 23.

Hamrin, Robert. 1981. The road to qualitative growth. Pp. 115-152 in H. Cleveland, ed., *The Management of Sustainable Growth*. New York: Pergamon Press.

Harwood, Richard R. 1990. A history of sustainable agriculture. Pp. 3-19 in C. A. Edwards *et al.*, eds., *Sustainable Agricultural Systems*. Ankeny, IA: Soil and Water Conservation Society.

Johnson, D.G. 1975. World agriculture, commodity policy, and price variability. *American Journal of Agricultural Economics* 57:823-828.

Koppel, Bruce. 1984. International trade and American food security. Pp. 359-396 in L. Busch and W. B. Lacy, eds., *Food Security in the United States*. Boulder, CO: Westview Press.

Lobao, Linda M. 1990. *Locality and Inequality: Farm and Industry Structure and Socioeconomic Conditions*. Albany: State University of New York Press.

Mankiw, N.G. and D. Romer, eds. 1991. *New Keynesian Economics, Vol. I, Vol. II*. Cambridge: MIT Press.

Miller, Fred P. and William A. Larson. 1990. Lower input effects on soil productivity and nutrient cycling. Pp. 549-568 in C.A. Edwards *et al.*, eds., *Sustainable Agricultural Systems*. Ankeny, IA: Soil and Water Conservation Society.

Nourse, Edwin G. 1924. *American Agriculture and the European Market*. New York: McGraw Hill.

National Research Council (NRC). 1989. *Alternative Agriculture*. A Report prepared by Committee on the Role of Alternative Farming Methods in Modern Production Agriculture, Board on Agriculture, National Research Council. Washington, DC: National Academy Press.

Paarlberg, Don. 1980. *Farm and Food Policy: Issues of the 1980s*. Lincoln: University of Nebraska Press.

Physicians Task Force on Hunger in America. 1985. *Hunger in America: The Growing Epidemic*. Middletown, CN: Wesleyan University Press.

Pierce, F.J., R.H. Dowdy, W.E. Larson, and W.A.P. Graham. 1984. Soil productivity in the cornbelt: An assessment of erosions long-term effects. *Journal of Soil and Water Conservation* 39:131-136.

Sampson, Neil. 1984. America's agricultural land: Basis for food security? Pp. 11-26 in L. Busch and W. B. Lacy, eds., *Food Security in the United States*. Boulder, CO: Westview Press.

Schuh, G. Edward. 1983. The role of the markets and governments in the world food economy. Pp. 277-301 in D.G. Johnson and G.E. Schuh, eds., *The Role of Markets in the World Food Economy*. Boulder, CO: Westview Press.

Small Farm Viability Project. 1977. *The Family Farm in California: Report of the Small Farm Viability Project*. Sacramento, CA: Small Farm Viability Project.

Technical Advisory Committee (TAC). 1988. Sustainable agricultural production: Implications for international agricultural research. Consultative Group on International Agricultural Research, Washington, DC.

Thompson, Robert L. 1983. The role of trade in food security and agricultural development. Pp. 227-257 in D.G. Johnson and G.E. Schuh, eds., *The Role of Markets in the World Food Economy*. Boulder, CO: Westview Press.

Tweeten, Luther. 1989. *Farm Policy Analysis*. Boulder, CO: Westview Press.

U.S. Conference of Mayors. 1983. *Hunger in American Cities*. Washington, DC.

U.S. General Accounting Office. 1983. *Public and Private Efforts to Feed America's Poor*. Washington, DC.

Young, J.P. 1991. Is the entropy law relevant to the economics of natural resource scarcity? *JEEM* 21:169-179.

7

Structural Change in American Agriculture into the Next Century
Bernard F. Stanton

The current structure of farming in the United States is a reflection of several historic forces: the land distribution systems that were used as the country expanded, opportunities for employment outside of agriculture, access to new technology for production, and the availability of markets both within and outside the country. In the 18th and 19th centuries agricultural production was a major component of gross national product in most states and communities. The land could be tilled only by a combination of human and animal power. Individual families provided the labor force on most farms, except for the plantations of the Old South. These too were broken into smaller units after the Civil War in the 1860s. The immigrants to the "new world" settled the Midwest and West as freeholders. Land was their capital; most rural communities were dominated by small, independent farmers.

The number of farms and land in farms continued to increase into the early years of the 20th century (Table 7.1). Land in farms doubled between 1850 and 1890. Another 300 million acres were added by 1920. Interestingly, in this period of rapid expansion, average farm size held relatively constant. Power for farming continued to come from oxen, horses, and mules and the strong arms and backs of farm families. Farm numbers reached a peak in the first half of the 20th century and held fairly steady until after World War II.

Industrialization of Agriculture

New technology in the form of machinery and equipment allowing the substitution of capital for labor began to appear in the 19th century. The full impact of that technology was harnessed in the mid-twentieth century when gasoline engines and electricity became available along with mechanization and the results of agricultural science. Farm numbers were cut in half in the

Table 7.1. U.S. Farm Numbers and Land in Farms.

Year	Number of Farms (Millions)	Land in Farms (Million Acres)	Average Farm Size (Acres)
1850	1.4	294	203
1869	2.0	407	199
1870	2.7	408	153
1880	4.0	536	138
1890	4.6	623	137
1900	5.7	839	146
1910	6.4	879	138
1920	6.4	956	148
1930	6.3	987	157
1940	6.1	1,061	174
1950	5.4	1,161	216
1954	4.8	1,158	242
1959	3.7	1,124	303
1964	3.2	1,110	352
1969	2.7	1,063	389
1974	2.3	1,017	440
1978	2.3	1,015	449
1982	2.2	987	440
1987	2.1	964	462

Source: Bureau of the Census.

20 years between 1950 and 1969.   This tremendous change in such a short span of time came about from an unusual combination of circumstances: (1) a backlog of technology was applied that had been developed in the 1920s and 1930s but delayed by economic depression; (2) the upheaval of World War II introduced new ideas and new skills into rural areas; (3) electricity and all-weather roads had come to nearly all parts of the country; and (4) good jobs were available for "surplus" labor freed by farm mechanization.

Structural change continued in the 1970s and 1980s. The striking loss in farm numbers between 1950 and 1969 could never occur again because relatively few people earn their living from farming resources. It takes additional information to recognize and interpret the structural change occurring at the end of the 20th century and not readily evident in the aggregates in Table 7.1. Land in farms has been falling slowly since the peak in 1950 and will continue to fall slowly into the next century. Cropland harvested is more stable but it too is trending downward in the aggregate (Figure 7.1).

Exit of land from agriculture occurs for two primary reasons. (1) Land is converted to a "higher" use associated with our increasingly urbanized society; returns from farmland cannot compete with returns from its use for houses, industry, or parkland. (2) Land is converted to a "lower" use such as forestry, recreation, or open space; in this case, farms with less productive resources (land) are unable to compete effectively in national or international markets. Important areas of farmland in the Eastern United States, that were hewn out of the wilderness with an axe and the aid of oxen, have reverted to the forest from which it was drawn. When the horse was replaced by the tractor, small rocky fields close to markets could no longer support a family in competition with more productive agricultural resources. In the West, many crop farms once in grass have returned to grass. That process continues today in every part of the country as poorer resources are forced out of farming.

Examination of Structural Change

In this report, structural change will be considered in terms of: (1) the number and size distribution of farms measured by land area and output, (2) tenure patterns and ownership of farm resources, (3) forms of business organization, and (4) control of production decisions and markets for products. It is important to recognize that the farm business and the farm

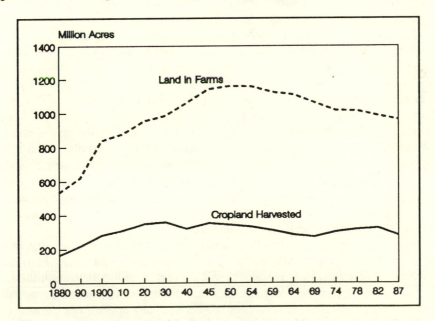

Figure 7.1. U.S. Land in Farms and Cropland Harvested, Census Data.
Source: Bureau of the Census.

household can be thought of as separable entities in a modern industrialized world. In the 19th century, the welfare of the two were tightly interwoven. What was best for the farm was best for the farm household and vice versa. Now at the end of the 20th century, this is much less the case. The welfare of the farm household may take precedence in decision making where multiple wage-earner families are often the rule and where farming is but one source of family income.

Distribution of Farms by Land Area

During the first half of the 20th century, the size distribution of farms remained surprisingly constant (Table 7.2). The majority were between 50 and 260 acres in size. Relatively few had more than 260 acres and most of these included large areas of pasture. Small farms of less than 50 acres have been an important component of total numbers throughout the century. Many of these have always been part-time units. In the first half of the century, the contribution to family living of these units from livestock, gardens, and a few cash crops was much more important than in the last two decades.

The increasing importance of larger units by land area is evident from 1950 onward. In the census years 1978 and 1987, farm numbers remained quite stable as did the component of farms with 260 acres or more (31-32 percent). As farm numbers declined, the actual number of larger farms remained quite steady and the number with 1,000 acres or more became more and more important in the total.

Improved perspective on the distribution of farms by land area is provided in Table 7.3. The percent of all land in farms in 20-year intervals is distributed by size class. The percentage of all farmland operated in units of 50 acres or less has always been small and now amounts to only about 1 percent of the total. The medium-sized farms (50-259 acres) include a substantial proportion of the total in any of the census years. Their proportion of land area has declined in each 20-year period, with the smallest change between 1969 and 1987. Farms with 1,000 acres or more have made up more than half of the farmland since 1969 and this size class continues to grow. With mechanization, large tractors, and increased technical skills, economies of size in crop farming have not yet been slowed by risk and management problems.

Tenure Patterns and Ownership of Resources

The U.S. Census has classified farms throughout the 20th century into three important groups: full owners, part owners, and tenants. *Full owners* operate only the land they own and report no rented land in their operations. *Part owners* have farms made up of land that they own and operate as well as rented land. *Tenants* do not own any of the land they operate but have their working capital in such items as livestock and machinery.

Table 7.2. Percent of U.S. Farms by Size Class.

Year	Number of Farms	Size Class, Acres in Farms		
		Small Under 50	**Medium** 50-259	**Large** 260 & Over
	(1,000)	(Percent of Total)		
1900	5,737	33.7	57.1	9.2
1910	6,362	35.4	54.8	9.7
1920	6,448	35.7	53.6	10.7
1930	6,289	37.5	51.5	11.0
1940	6,097	37.5	50.6	11.9
1950	5,382	36.5	49.0	14.5
1959	3,711	28.5	49.7	21.8
1969	2,730	23.2	48.0	28.8
1978	2,258	24.0	44.0	32.0
1987	2,088	28.5	40.0	31.5

Source: Bureau of the Census.

Table 7.3. Percent of U.S. Land in Farms by Size Class (Percent of Land in Farms).

Acres per Farm	1910	1930	1950	1969	1987
Small					
Under 50	6.2	5.7	3.6	1.3	1.2
Medium					
50 - 179	35.1	28.3	19.4	10.2	7.0
180 - 259	12.0	11.2	9.1	6.2	4.3
Subtotal (under 260)	(53.3)	(45.2)	(32.1)	(17.7)	(12.5)
Large					
260 - 499	18.2	15.8	14.4	14.0	10.7
500 - 999	9.5	11.0	10.9	13.9	14.4
1,000 & over	19.0	28.0	42.6	54.4	62.4
Subtotal (over 260)	(46.7)	(54.8)	(67.9)	(82.3)	(87.5)
Land in farms (Mil.)	879	987	1,161	1,063	964

Source: Bureau of the Census.

Tenancy was an important issue in American public policy in the first half of the 20th century. The number of tenants was large and the plight of the sharecropper was an item of wide social concern. A combination of New

Deal programs, the end of the Great Depression, and the availability of good nonfarm jobs after World War II brought an end to major concerns about tenancy. The number of tenants and their importance as users of U.S. farmland decreased rapidly between 1930 and 1960 (Figure 7.2).

As tenancy decreased in importance, part ownership became the dominant form of organization in commercial agriculture. Capital requirements in agriculture are large. Increasingly, farmers recognized that higher returns could be obtained from their own limited capital by investing in working capital rather than buying additional farmland. Renting part of the land they operate is now a normal practice in nearly all parts of the country. Full owners (1,239,000) outnumbered part owners (609,000) and tenants (240,000) by a wide margin in 1987. But more than half of the land is operated by part owners. They have been increasingly dominant since the 1960s.

Will the trends of the 1970s and 1980s continue into the 21st century? Further reductions in the importance of full owners seem likely, particularly in terms of *cropland* farmed. It may well be that a relatively large number of units, designated as farms, will continue to be operated primarily as residences and recreation areas by individuals whose primary source of family income comes from off-farm sources. These residential farms, producing less than $10,000 of agricultural products, are unimportant in terms of national agricultural output (less than 3 percent in 1987). Yet they remain important in terms of numbers, land area (not cropland), and local political interest. The remaining full-owner farms, either operated part-time or full-time, are likely to decrease as part-owner businesses become increasingly dominant.

In the 21st century, tenancy may expand among beginning farmers as a means of getting access to agricultural capital. Some of the most productive agricultural lands in the country are seen as safe havens for capital and a way to spread risk in a financial portfolio. If economies of size continue to be important, the proportion of rented land in commercial agriculture may continue to grow.

Business Organization

Information on forms of business organization have been reported in census reports beginning in 1969 and for succeeding years. Sole proprietorships were the expected norm in the 18th and 19th centuries. There was little thought of formalizing business arrangements, in most cases, until the second half of this century. More widespread use of incorporating small businesses has come with differential tax treatments, increased risk of personal liability, and the general use of formal business arrangements in other sectors.

Sole proprietorship accounted for more than 90 percent of total farm businesses in 1969 and 86.7 percent in 1987. Corporations have become more common especially in larger, more complex farm businesses. In 1987 they accounted for 25.6 percent of aggregate sales, up from 14.2 percent in 1969

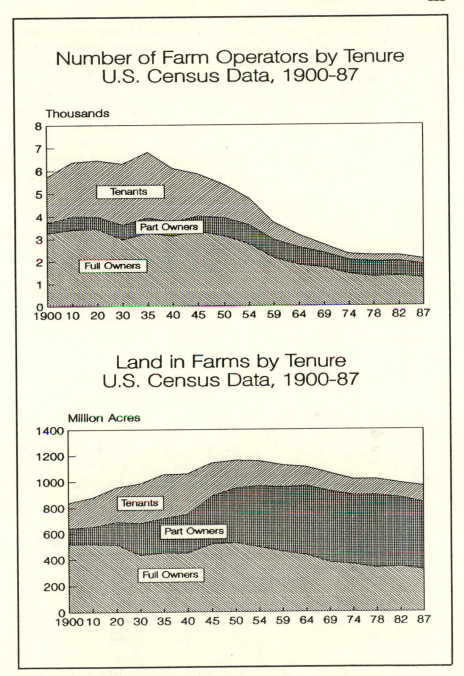

Figure 7.2. U.S. Land Tenure Patterns.

(Table 7.4). Partnerships are also an important form of business organization accounting for about one-sixth of aggregate sales in each of the census years.

Foreign ownership of agricultural land and corporate ownership of agriculture particularly has been a concern in the Corn Belt and Great Plains states. The Agricultural Foreign Investment Disclosure Act of 1978 (AFIDA) was in part enacted as a response to these concerns. Each year foreign owners of agricultural land are required to report such ownership to the Secretary of Agriculture and an annual report is issued. At the end of 1989, foreign persons or entities owned slightly less than 1 percent of the farm and forest land in the country. Corporations accounted for 81 percent of this

Table 7.4. Type of U.S. Business Organization (Number of Farms).

Type of Business Organization	1969	1978	1987
Sole proprietorship (individual or family)	2,477,031	1,965,860	1,809,324
Partnership	221,535	232,538	199,559
Corporation	21,513	50,231	66,969
All others	10,070	9,146	11,907
Total	2,730,250	2,257,775	2,087,759
Type of Corporation Family-held:			
10 or less stockholders	19,716[a]	43,138	59,599
10 or more stockholders	1,797[a]	1,275	1,172
Other than family-held:			
10 or less stockholders	[a]	4,688	5,379
10 or more stockholders	[a]	1,130	819
Total	21,513	50,231	66,969
Percent of Total Value of Sales	67.8	61.6	56.3
Sole proprietorship	17.4	16.1	17.1
Partnership	14.2	21.7	25.6
Corporation	0.6	0.6	1.0
Other			
Total	100.0	100.0	100.0

Source: Bureau of the Census.
[a]Not classified in 1969 except by number of shareholders.

total. Between 1981 and 1989, foreign ownership remained remarkably steady. Most of this land is in the South and West except for large forest holdings in Maine (DeBraal).

Will corporations become more important in future decades? The advantages of incorporation for many single proprietors are not yet strong enough to expect that all commercial farms are likely to take this step. Sole proprietorships, even for relatively large businesses in terms of output, are likely to continue to be the norm. Incorporated businesses that are family held are likely to grow in number and share of farm output.

Very few agribusiness corporations have been actively and directly involved in agricultural production. They are increasingly involved in contracting for production, providing inputs to producers, establishing specific practices to follow, and determining harvest dates and procedures. This degree of control over production decisions and the supply of large amounts of operating capital raises questions about the position of contracting farmers relative to giant integrators and marketing organizations. One of the important structural issues of the next century may well be market access and control by producers of perishable products like meat, milk, fruits, and vegetables.

Size Distribution Based on Gross Sales

The most commonly used method of analyzing the structure of farming since 1950 has been study of frequency distributions based on gross sales of agricultural products. This has the advantage of examining the gross output of all types of farms based on a common measure used by all types of business, that is, gross sales. At any one point in time, this provides a good picture of the relative proportions of the total of small, medium, and large farms. Problems arise when one tries to examine changes in structure through time, however. Changes in price levels are difficult to account for in the distributions. Moreover, as new technology is adopted, productivity in various enterprises changes along with relative prices for output so that comparisons between periods are made more difficult. Thus, comparisons over time need careful adjustment and interpretation to see underlying shifts by size classes.

Some of the inherent problems of interpretation are suggested in the distribution based on gross sales in the agricultural census in each of the last three decades (Table 7.5). In 1969, the minimum sales required to qualify as a farm were $250. In 1978, that minimum had been increased to $1,000. Prices nearly doubled between 1969 and 1978. A farm that had sold $50,000 of agricultural products in 1969 was equivalent to one that sold $100,000 in 1978. One way to put 1969 on an approximate 1978 base in terms of prices is simply to shift comparable size classes forward. Thus, the 390,425 farms in the $5,000-9,999 class in 1969 are placed in the $10,000-19,999 class on a 1978 base. The size distributions for 1969 on a 1978 base and those for 1978, 1982, and 1987 are somewhat more comparable as shown in Table 7.6.

Changes in prices received by farmers between 1978 and 1987, while important, were much less dramatic than the changes experienced between 1969 and 1978. Rough comparisons over this time span with 1969 corrected to 1978 prices is possible.

1. Farm numbers decreased modestly over this 18-year span, about 10 percent after a reduction recognizing the change in definition is taken into account.
2. About 60 percent of all the units were residential or part-time farms where family income came primarily from off-farm sources. Change over time in the farms with sales of $20,000 or less was modest; stability was the general rule.

Table 7.5. Distribution of U.S. Farm Numbers by Sales Class (Number of Farms).

Description	1969	1978	1987
Producer price index, farm products (1967=100)	109.1	212.5	230.1
Prices received by farmers (1977=100)	59	115	126
Value of Farm Products Sold			
$500,000 or more	4,079	17,973	32,023
$200,000 - 499,999	12,608	62,645	61,148
$100,000 - 199,999	35,308	141,050	202,550
$40,000 - 99,999	169,695	360,093	287,587
	(221,690)	(581,761)	(583,308)
$20,000 - 39,999			
$10,000 - 19,999	330,992	299,175	225,671
	395,472	299,215	250,594
$5,000 - 9,999			
$2,500 - 4,999	390,425	314,088	274,972
Under $2,500	395,104	300,699	262,918
	994,456	460,535	490,296
Abnormal			
	2,111	2,302	---
Total	2,730,250	2,257,775	2,087,759

Source: Bureau of the Census.

Table 7.6. U.S. Farm Numbers by Sales Class (Number of Farms).

Sales Class	1969 in 1987 Prices	1978	1982	1987
Index of Prices Rec'd by Farmers (1977=100)	(59) 118	115	133	126
Under $5,000	686,176	761,234	814,535	753,214
$5,000 - 19,999	748,347	613,303	540,809	525,566
Subtotal	1,434,523	1,374,537	1,355,344	1,278,788
	(60.2%)	(60.9%)	(60.5%)	(61.3%)
$20,000 - 39,999	395,472	299,175	248,825	225,671
	(16.6%)	(13.3%)	(11.1%)	(10.8%)
$40,000 - 99,999	396,697	360,093	332,751	287,587
	(16.6%)	(16.0%)	(14.9%)	(13.8%)
$100,000 - 249,999	103,990	165,493	215,912	202,550
$250,000 - 499,999	40,460	38,202	58,668	61,148
$500,000 and Over	11,535	17,973	27,800	32,023
Subtotal	155,985	221,668	302,380	295,721
	(6.6%)	(9.8%)	(13.5%)	(14.2%)
Total	2,384,788[a]	2,255,473[b]	2,239,300[b]	2,087,759

Source: Olson and Stanton.
[a]Reduced from 2,730,250 to account for all farms with sales of $500 or less in 1989 because of definition change.
[b]Totals adjusted downward by unclassified abnormal farms.

3. Important decreases in absolute and percentage terms occurred in the two size classes with sales of $20,000-39,999 and $40,000-99,999. The decrease in numbers for the $20,000-39,999 class was most dramatic, about 170,000 farms. Some of these dropped out of farming, others moved into higher sales classes.
4. In the three classes with sales of $100,000 or more, there were important increases in each of the census years. More of national production is being concentrated in these larger units.
5. The number of farms with sales of $40,000 or more has remained surprisingly constant at roughly 600,000 farms. There has been an important shift upward in the distribution; less in the $40,000-99,999 class and more in the other three. There is more stability in numbers for these larger farms than most recognize.

Total Value of Sales by Sales Class

Further perspective on recent changes in structure are provided when aggregate sales by size class are considered instead of farm numbers alone (Table 7.7). The changes in the percentage shares of each of the three groups in the total may be as important to consider as the absolute numbers. (Some distortion from inflation remains for 1978, 1982, and 1989 in Table 7.6 because over that period prices received by farmers increased in the aggregate by 9.1 percent.) In a span of nine years, aggregate sales by farms with $40,000 of sales or less decreased from 15.7 to 9.9 percent of the total. Perhaps of greater significance is the decreasing percentage of farms with sales of $40,000-99,999, which went from 21.4 to 13.8 percent of total number of farms. This group of farms includes both part-time and full-time operations. In nearly all cases, farm income is an important component of family income. The shrinking importance of this group, almost 300,000 farms, is of concern to many, particularly those concerned with the "survival of the family farm" (Tweeten, 1984).

Farms with sales of $100,000 or more accounted for 76.3 percent of sales in 1987. This increase from 62.9 percent in nine years results from more than the small (9.1 percent) increase in prices received. Some of the increase, in both farm numbers and the aggregate percentage, results from family farms moving up into the $100,000 or more classes. Other farms, already within these groups, continue to grow in size.

The most important change between 1978 and 1987 was the increase in the percentage of the aggregate from farms with sales of $500,000 or more -- from 27.7 percent to 38.2 percent of the total. The number of farms in this class increased substantially (Table 7.6) in percentage terms but still only numbered 32,023. In terms of structural change in the future, the relative importance of these largest farms is of substantial significance.

Table 7.7. Total Value of Sales by Size Class (Percent of Total).

Sales Class	1978	1982	1987
$500,000 and over	27.7	32.5	38.2
$250,000 - 499,999	12.0	15.1	15.2
$100,000 - 249,999	23.2	25.0	22.9
Subtotal	62.9	72.6	76.3
$40,000 - 99,999	21.4	16.5	13.8
$20,000 - 39,999	8.0	5.4	4.8
Under $20,000	7.7	5.5	5.1
Subtotal	15.7	10.9	9.9
Total	100.0	100.0	100.0
Aggregate sales ($ Bil.)	$106.8[a]	$131.6[a]	$136.0[a]

Source: Bureau of the Census.
[a]Reduced by aggregate sales from abnormal farms.

Size Distribution from FCRS Data

The Economic Research Service (ERS), United States Department of Agriculture, provides annual data on U.S. farms by size and numbers. These data are constructed using Census statistics, the Farm Costs and Returns Survey (FCRS), and other annual survey data collected by the National Agricultural Statistics Service. Estimates of size distribution for net value-added per farm in 1989 have been constructed for the 11,836 farms in the FCRS from which national estimates are developed. Net value-added is calculated as gross farm income adjusted for changes in inventory less all cash expenses except cash wages, rent, interest, and taxes. Depreciation is deducted as well. The procedure used to calculate net value-added can be interpreted as the return to all labor, capital, land, and management used in the business regardless of source.

There is substantial similarity between the size distribution for gross sales in the ERS estimates for 1989 and those from the Census in 1987. One should expect the distribution of net value-added to be somewhat different (Table 7.8). Net value-added seeks to measure net contributions to the national economy from farm operations. That is, it subtracts from the value of all output that part which did not originate on the farm from productive activity. Purchased inputs from other farms or from other businesses are deducted from the value of output whether sold or inventoried. In this sense, it is an important measure of size, describing what has been added to value as a result of farm production.

In Table 7.8, 20 percent of farms (those with net value-added of $40,000 or more) account for almost 97 percent of total value-added. Thus, a little

Table 7.8. Size Distribution of Farms, United States, 1989 (Percent of Total).

Size Class	Percent of All Farms By:		Percent of a National Total For:	
	Gross Sales[a]	Net Value-Added	Gross Sales[a]	Net Value-Added
$500,000 and over	1.8	1.0	38.0	35.2
$250,000 - 499,999	3.4	1.7	15.9	15.6
$100,000 - 249,999	9.7	6.7	21.6	28.0
$40,000 - 99,999	14.0	10.6	13.7	18.0
$20,000 - 39,999	12.4	9.1	5.4	7.1
$10,000 - 19,999	11.8	7.5	2.6	2.9
$5,000 - 9,999	12.1	7.3	1.6	1.4
$0 - 4,999	34.8	21.3	1.2	1.0
-$1 - -4,999		23.3		-1.2
-$5,000 - -9,999		5.7		-1.1
-$10,000 - -19,999		3.0		-1.1
Less than -$20,000	____	2.8	____	-5.8
Total[b]	100.0	100.0	100.0	100.0

[a]Source: USDA.
[b]ERS estimates a total of 2,171,000 farms in 1989.

over 430,000 farms provide most of the value-added for the sector. The net value-added series also calls attention to a component of farms that does not add to the productivity of the sector in any given year. The relatively large number of farms with net value-added between + $5,000 and -$5,000 is instructive, paralleling closely the number of farms with gross sales of $10,000 or less.

Projections by Sales Class to the Year 2000

Nearly all projections are based on some kind of trend analysis, whether relatively simple or mathematically sophisticated.   Markov projections, improved by additional variables in logit or probit models, have given some acceptable results (Olson and Stanton). Unless one has access to individual farm data, can recognize problems of exit and entry systematically in some manner, and can correct for price level changes over time, it is difficult to project distributions which do not reflect the personal interpretations of data by the analyst. Subjective judgment in handling the evidence is commonly a part of the analysis.

One approach is to observe the changes in distribution over a recent time period after adjusting for shifts in numbers because of price level. Percentage changes in each size class are calculated and roughly similar percentage changes are projected into the future for a span of years. This assumes that the same forces which led to change in the earlier time span will continue to affect size distribution in the future. Such a procedure is followed in Table 7.9. The period between 1978 and 1987 experienced five good years before a major agricultural depression hit, particularly in the Corn Belt and Great Plains. Land prices fell dramatically between 1982 and 1987. Many agricultural lending institutions and farmers faced very difficult financial situations. Evidence of change in size distribution over the whole period was less than one might have expected given the depressed five-year period.

The percentage changes observed in this period of good income followed by substantial farm stress (Table 7.9) were rounded and extended for the 13-year period, 1987-2000 (Table 7.10). This could be considered a conservative, direct extrapolation of trend using the full range of the 1978-87 experience. Further reductions in farm numbers are forecast for the three classes with sales of less than $100,000 (1987 prices). The net reduction in farm numbers is 230,000. This modest reduction occurs because the increase in numbers in each of the three size classes with sales over $100,000 (62,000 farms) does not offset losses of small farms. Aggregate sales from these larger farms more than compensates for the reductions in the three smaller size classes so that output expands.

A second projection in Table 7.10 was made using the rates of percentage change observed for each of the size classes between 1982 and 1987, the period of major farm stress. The percentage changes in numbers for each class were extended for the longer period with appropriate rounding. This projection can be thought of as a more drastic scenario of continued rapid change under unfavorable conditions for small, full-time farms.

Comparison with OTA Projections

One of the more widely publicized projections of the size distribution of farms to the year 2000 in the United States was prepared by the Office of Technology Assessment (OTA), U.S. Congress (1986). That distribution is compared with the two projections based on trends from recent censuses (Table 7.11). The major differences between the OTA numbers and the ones just presented are in the estimates of farms with sales under $20,000. The OTA projections assumed a much more rapid rate of exit from this group than has occurred or seems likely to occur.

Projections for Farms with Sales of $40,000 or More

Much interest in projecting size distributions of farms focuses on the upper end of these distributions where most of agricultural production occurs. In

Table 7.9. Number of Farms by Sales Class, United States, 1987 Base, 1978 Base, 1978 and 1987 Census (Number of Farms).

Sales Class	Actual 1978	9.1% Net Adjustments for Prices	1978 Census on 1987 Base	Actual 1987	Percent Change
Residential & Part-Time					
Under $20,000	1,375,000	-27,000	1,348,000	1,279,000	-5.4
$20,000 - 39,999	299,000	-3,000	296,000	226,000	-31.0
Small Commercial					
$40,000 - 99,999	360,000	-5,000	355,000	288,000	-23.3
Large Commercial					
$100,000 - 249,999	165,000	+17,000	182,000	202,000	+11.0
$250,000 - 499,999	38,000	+13,000	51,000	61,000	+19.6
$500,000 and over	18,000	+5,000	23,000	32,000	+39.1
Total	2,255,000[a]		2,255,000	2,088,000[a]	-9.1

Source: Olson and Stanton.
[a]Reduced by number of unclassified "abnormal" farms.

Table 7.10. Projected[a] Number of Farms by Sales Class, United States, 1987 Prices, 1987 and 2000 (Number of Farms).

Sales Class	Actual Distribution 1987	Projection from 1978-87 Trend		Projection from 1982-87 Trend	
		Trend Percent Change (1978-87)	Projection for 2000	Percent Change Based on 1982-87 Rates	Projection for 2000
Residential & Part-Time					
Under $20,000	1,279,000	-10	1,154,000	-15	1,083,000
$20,000 - 39,999	226,000	-36	145,000	-25	169,000
Small Commercial					
$40,000 - 99,999	288,000	-30	202,000	-36	184,000
Large Commercial					
$100,000 - 249,999	202,000	+14	230,000	-18	166,000
$250,000 - 499,999	61,000	+27	77,000	+9	66,000
$500,000 and over	32,000	+55	50,000	+38	44,000
Total	2,088,000	-11	1,858,000	-18	1,712,000

Source: Olson and Stanton.
[a]Projections based on trends between 1978 and 1987.

Table 7.12, only farms with sales of $40,000 on a 1987 base are considered. An additional class of farms with sales of $1,000,000 or more is included because of their increasing importance in aggregate sales. Data for this size group were published for the first time in the 1987 Census.

Each of the projections has some common elements. For all projections, (1) the class with sales of $40,000-99,999 decreases substantially compared to the 1987 census base, (2) the total number of farms decreases but at different rates, and (3) the number of farms with sales of $500,000 or more increases substantially in percentage terms. The results for farms with sales of $100,000-249,999 are widely variant with one suggesting modest increases in numbers and one implying very large reductions. All of these results project a continuing shift of output to farms in the larger size classes.

Major Forces Affecting Structural Change Beyond Trend

While the complex of past forces which brought about change in size distributions is fundamental to any set of projections, other major forces must be recognized, at least in a qualitative sense. Among such forces are:

1. Political stability.
2. Rates of growth or recession in the general economy.
3. Availability of new technology or lack of it.
4. Government intervention and protectionism.
5. Environmental issues and food safety.

Political stability is often taken for granted. In those countries where this is not the case, one should recognize that this single factor can be overriding in major structural change. One need only think of events in the 20th century in Japan, Russia, and China to recognize the importance of political upheaval on agriculture, land ownership, and the distribution of resources.

What happens in the general economy affects agriculture and vice versa. Recession generally slows down rates of change; growth tends to speed it up. Attitudes and expectations about the future are also important.

New technology generally speeds structural change. If biotechnology makes major breakthroughs in crop or livestock production, this will affect the size distribution of farms in the associated sectors of agriculture.

Government intervention, in most cases, is intended to protect some components of agriculture from the ups and downs of market forces. This provides somewhat greater stability, but also establishes some limits to rates of change. Many analysts see this as size neutral in the long run (Sumner). I think it slows down rates of change.

Table 7.11. Alternative Projections of Size Distribution of Farms, United States, 2000.

Size Class	1987 Census	Number of Farms in Year 2000		
		OTA Projection from 1982 Base	Trend 1982-87 Change (Table 7.10)	Trend 1978-87 Change (Table 7.10)
Under $20,000	1,279,000	638,000	1,083,000	1,154,000
$20,000 - 39,999	226,000	363,000	169,000	145,000
$40,000 - 99,999	288,000		184,000	202,000
$100,000 - 249,999	202,000	75,000[a]	166,000	230,000
$250,000 - 499,999	61,000	125,000[a]	66,000	77,000
$500,000 and over	32,000	50,000	44,000	50,000
Total	2,088,000	1,251,000	1,712,000	1,858,000

Source: Olson and Stanton.
[a]OTA used $100,000 - 199,999 and $200,000 - 499,999 as the size classifications; proportionately, these could be reallocated to 100,000 farms in each of the census classes.

Table 7.12. Alternative Projections for Year 2000 of Size Distribution of Larger Farms, United States, 1987 Base.

Size Class 1987 Prices	Actual 1987 Census Base	Projected 1978-87 Trend Base	Projected 1982-87 Trend Base	Projected Adjusted OTA 1982 Base
		(Number of Farms)		
$40,000 - 99,999	288,000	202,000	184,000	203,000
$100,000 - 249,999	202,000	230,000	166,000	100,000[a]
$250,000 - 499,999	61,000	77,000	66,000	100,000[a]
$500,000 - 999,999	21,000	33,000	29,000	33,000
$1,000,000 and Over	11,000	17,000	15,000	17,000
Total	583,000	559,000	460,000	453,000

Source: Olson and Stanton.

[a]Adjustments made in these classes.

In the richer countries of the world, public interest in the environment is increasing. Food safety is a major concern. Concentration of production of high-value crops or livestock in one location is likely to command public attention. Questions about point pollution and the need for investment to reduce possibilities of potential damage to the environment are likely on larger farms. Food safety and environmental considerations will have some impact on the ways in which increases in firm growth are accomplished. It is difficult to establish whether these issues will speed up or slow down firm growth in the long run.

Concluding Observations

This brief review of change in the structure of farming in the United States has concentrated on the processes of agricultural development with emphasis on rates of change which occurred in the 1970s and 1980s. Never again is there likely to be as much structural change as occurred between 1950 and 1969. In that span of 20 years, half of U.S. farms were lost, and industrialized agriculture became the norm. The availability of nonfarm jobs and of labor-saving technology in farming along with pressure and willingness of farm people to take nonfarm jobs allowed this quiet revolution to occur.

In the 1970s and 1980s, rates of change in terms of numbers of farms were much more modest. Less obvious but perhaps of equal importance has been the increasing proportion of total output accounted for by the relatively small number of farms with sales of $500,000 or more. By most commercial standards, these are "small" businesses and hardly worthy of special attention. Nevertheless, the somewhat romantic idea of maintaining an agricultural system where the norm remains a set of independent, small, family-operated farms persists both within segments of agriculture and the minds of many in society at large. Belief in the primacy of small farms operated primarily by family labor dies hard (Tweeten, 1984; Knutson *et al.*).

I contend that "family" farms are likely to continue to dominate in the 21st century in the United States. The old definition, however, will have to be reworked to accommodate the core businesses that will produce most of U.S. agricultural production. Most of these "family" farms will be operated as family corporations or formal partnerships, whatever is best to minimize personal liability and taxes. Part of the real estate operated will be owned and part rented. Capital will come from some family members actively involved in the business and some family members who work outside farming. Hired labor will provide much more than half the labor force. Key employees will have the opportunity to buy into the business. Such farms will operate much like other small businesses outside farming in rural communities. Public interest in farm operations, however, will be much greater than for other small businesses because the land base is large and public consciousness of environmental impacts remains high. Public nostalgia for a bucolic countryside dominated by small farms may remain, but production will come primarily from these modern "family" farms organized to compete in a service-oriented, industrialized setting.

References

Ahearn, Mary. September 1986. Financial well-being of farm operators and their households. Agricultural Economics Report No. 563. Washington, DC: Economic Research Service, USDA.

Bureau of the Census. 1900, 1930, 1950, 1969, 1978, 1982, and 1987. *Censuses of Agriculture*. Volume II, General Reports. Washington, DC: U.S. Government Printing Office.

Carlin, Thomas and Sara Mazie, eds. June 1990. The U.S. farm sector entering the 1990s: Twelfth annual report on the structure of family farms. Agricultural Information Bulletin No. 587. Washington, DC: Economic Research Service, USDA.

Cochrane, W.W. 1979. *The Development of American Agriculture -- A Historical Analyses*. University of Minnesota Press.

DeBraal, J. Peter. May 1990. Foreign ownership of U.S. agricultural land through December 31, 1989. Staff Report No. AGES9026. Washington, DC: Economic Research Service, USDA.

Economics, Statistics, and Cooperative Service (ESCS). November 1979. *Structure Issues of American Agriculture*. Agricultural Economics Report No. 438. Washington, DC: ESCS, United States Department of Agriculture.

Hallam, J. Arne, ed. December 1990. *Determinants of Farm Size and Structure*. Proceedings of NC-181 Committee. Ames: Iowa State University.

Hanson, G.D., B.F. Stanton, and M.C. Ahearn. January 1989. Alternative measures of farm output to classify farms by size. Technical Bulletin No. 1749. Washington, DC: Economic Research Service, USDA.

Harrington, David and Thomas Carlin. April 1987. The U.S. farm sector: How is it weathering the 1980s? Agricultural Information Bulletin No. 506. Washington, DC: Economic Research Service, USDA.

Knutson, R.D., J.B. Penn, and W.T. Boehm. 1990. *Agricultural and Food Policy*. 2nd edition. Englewood Cliffs, NJ: Prentice-Hall.

Office of Technology Assessment. March 1986. *Technology, Public Policy, and the Changing Structure of American Agriculture*. Washington, DC: U.S. Congress.

Olson, K.D. and B.F. Stanton. 1992. Projections of structural change and the future of American agriculture. In Hallam, J. Arne, ed., *The Changing Size and Structure of Americas Farms*. Boulder, CO: Westview Press.

Robinson, K.L. 1989. *Farm and Food Policies and Their Consequences*. Englewood Cliffs, NJ: Prentice-Hall.

Robison, L.J., ed. December 1988. Determinants of farm size and structure. Agricultural Experiment Station Journal Article No. 12899. East Lansing: Michigan State University.

Stanton, B.F. April 1990. Changes in farm size and structure in American agriculture in the twentieth century. Agricultural Economics Staff Paper No. 90-8. Ithaca, NY: Cornell University.

Sumner, Daniel. 1985. Farm programs and structural issues. In B.L. Gardner, ed., *U.S. Agricultural Policy: The 1985 Farm Legislation*. Washington, DC: American Enterprise Institute.

Tweeten, Luther. 1984. Causes and consequences of structural change in the farming industry. NPA Report No. 207. Washington, DC: National Planning Association.

Tweeten, Luther. 1989. *Farm Policy Analysis*. Boulder, CO: Westview Press.

USDA. January 1991. Economic indicators of the farm sector: National financial summary, 1989. ECIFS 9-2. Washington, DC: Economic Research Service, USDA.

8

Food Consumption in Japan
Masaru Morishima, Yoshihisa Aita,
and Mitsuhiro Nakagawa

Long-Term Trends in Food Consumption

Calorie Supply

Long-term trends in the daily per capita calorie supply in Japan fall roughly into two periods with World War II as the dividing line. Daily per capita calorie supply almost leveled off for many years, but after World War II it increased dramatically (see Figure 8.1).

Before World War II, Japan grew most of its own food and the volume of food imports was low. However, it imported rice from Taiwan and Korea, sugar from Taiwan, and soybeans from mainland China. From 1911 to 1915, Japan annually imported 647,000 metric tons (MT) of grain, including 526,000 MT of rice. The volume of imported grains was about 6 percent of the total supply. Domestic agricultural production consisted mainly of rice, wheat, tubers, legumes, and vegetables. These commodities, supplemented by some seafood, formed Japan's traditional diet.

The daily per capita calorie supply reached a prewar peak in the five years from 1925 to 1929 and then decreased slightly thereafter. Starchy foods were the major source of calories. Their proportion of the total calorie supply was 85 percent from 1911 to 1915, 82 percent from 1921 to 1925, and 75 percent from 1935 to 1939. The most important of the starchy foods was rice, with its proportion of the total calorie supply about 60 percent.

After Japan went to war with China in 1937 and entered World War II in 1941, the workforce and production resources declined. Consequently, agricultural production began to decrease. Between 1935-39 and 1941-45, rice production decreased by 1.3 million MT to 8.5 million MT and wheat production decreased by 190,000 MT to 2.8 million MT. When World War II ended in 1945, rice production was at 5.9 million MT and wheat production at 2.2 million MT.

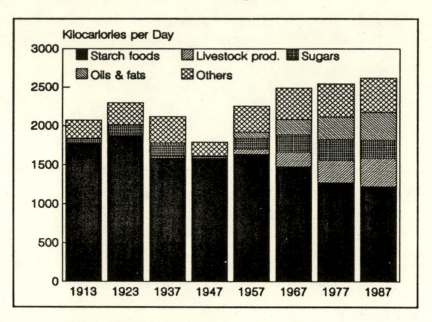

Figure 8.1. Per Capita Calorie Supply.
Sources: *The Current Situation of the Nation's Food*, Japan Society for the
Promotion of Science; *The Prewar and Postwar Food Situation*,
Headquarters for Economic Stability; and *Food Balance Sheet*,
Ministry of Agriculture, Forestry, and Fisheries, various issues.

The decline in domestic production and imports during the war period
caused food consumption in Japan to decline significantly and by the end of
World War II it had reached a crisis level. After World War II, agricultural
production began to increase. However, the level of the country's nutrition
continued to worsen as a result of the sharp population increase caused by an
influx of returnees from overseas and the first baby boom. The daily per
capita calorie supply was 1,791 kilocalories from 1946 to 1950, or 15 percent
less than in the five years from 1935 to 1939.

The daily per capita supply recovered to prewar levels around 1960, and
thereafter increased steadily during the high economic growth period. The
daily per capita calorie supply increased 12 percent from 2,291 kilocalories in
1960 to 2,569 kilocalories in 1973, after which, mainly due to the first oil crisis,
it stayed below the 1973 level until 1983. In the latter half of the 1980s, it
increased to around 2,600 kilocalories.

The proportion of starchy foods to the total calorie supply decreased from
73 percent to 47 percent between the 1955-1959 period and the 1985-1989
period. However, the proportion of livestock products and fats to the total
calorie supply increased steadily. Meat and fishery products, which amounted
to 27.5 and 86.8 kilocalories respectively in 1960, increased to 177.8 kilo-

calories and 133.2 kilocalories in 1989. In recent years, consumption of fishery products has reached a saturation point, while meat consumption is still increasing after a saturation period around 1980. Sugar intake reached a peak of 294.9 kilocalories in 1973 and then decreased to 220.7 kilocalories in 1989.

Composition of Nutrients

The daily per capita protein supply was 67.7 grams from 1921 to 1925, and then decreased steadily during the war period (see Figure 8.2). After World War II, the daily per capita protein supply was 43.4 grams from 1946 to 1950, and recovered to the prewar level around 1950. Since then, it has increased continually and was 86.6 grams from 1985 to 1989.

In contrast to western countries, the protein supply in Japan comes mainly from vegetable sources. For example, the proportion of vegetable protein to total protein was 95 percent from 1911 to 1915. In particular, the proportion of vegetable protein from rice was 44.6 percent. However, the proportion of animal protein to total protein increased steadily, except between 1946 and 1950, and was 51.5 percent between 1985 and 1989.

The protein supply in Japan is also highly dependent on fishery products. The proportion of seafood protein to the total protein supply has remained at around 20 percent since the five years from 1955 to 1959. Because the growth rate of livestock product consumption was higher than that of seafood

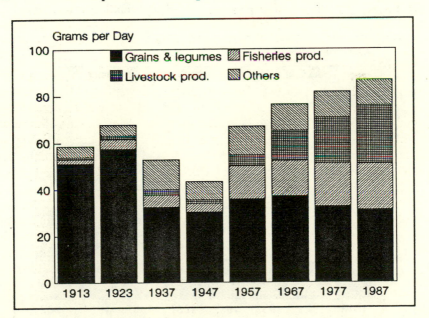

Figure 8.2. Per Capita Protein Supply.
Sources: See Figure 8.1 sources.

consumption, the proportion of livestock protein in the total protein supply began to exceed that of seafood protein from 1975 to 1979. At present, the ratio of livestock protein to seafood protein is 5 to 4.

After World War II, oil and fat consumption increased very rapidly (see Figure 8.3). The daily per capita oil and fat supply was 82 grams from 1985 to 1989, or 4.7 times higher than that in the 1951-1954 period. A rapid increase in livestock product and fat consumption has caused a drastic change in Japan's food consumption patterns.

As previously mentioned, a major characteristic of Japan's food consumption is that, compared with western countries, the proportion of starchy foods in the total calorie supply is high although it has been steadily decreasing. Among western countries, the proportion of starchy foods to total calorie supply is relatively high in Italy and Spain. In 1989 the proportion of starchy foods in the total calorie supply in Japan was 47 percent, almost the same level as that of Italy in 1965.

Food Consumption Expenditures

Engel's coefficients are often used to observe the characteristics of food consumption expenditures. It is generally recognized that Engel's coefficient, which is the proportional ratio of food consumption expenditures to total household expenditures, decreases as income increases. Nakayama confirmed that Engel's coefficient in Japan was relatively small for its economic

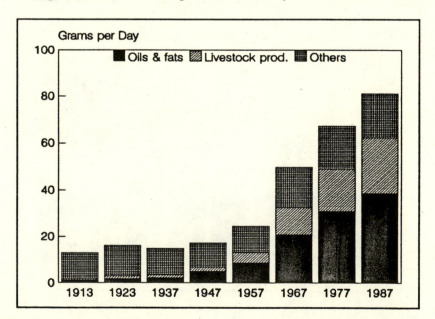

Figure 8.3. Per Capita Fat Supply.
Sources: See Figure 8.1 sources.

progress, reflecting a high proportion of starchy food consumption. Namiki later reconfirmed this finding.

According to the Household Expenditure Surveys[1], Engel's coefficient decreased from 38.7 percent in 1963 to 25.3 percent in 1989 (see Figure 8.4). During the first oil crisis, Engel's coefficient showed an exceptional increase from 31.9 percent in 1973 to 32.6 percent in 1974.

Engel's coefficient also decreases as consumer income increases. For example, in 1989 Engel's coefficient was 30.0 percent in the lowest of the five income groups classified, while it was 21.8 percent in the highest income group.

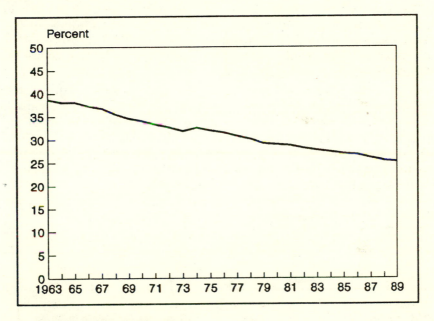

Figure 8.4. Engel's Coefficient.
Source: *Household Expenditure Survey*, Prime Minister's Office, various issues.

---

[1] The Household Expenditure Survey investigates the household expenses of consumers, excluding farmers, fishermen, and single households, and accumulates the data by region, occupation, and personal income level. This survey started in 1916. After World War II, it was reorganized as the Consumer Price Survey in 1946, and then revised to its present form in 1962. The sample numbered about 2,700 households in 1989, which were determined according to the results of the 1985 census. The households investigated are changed every 6 months.

Despite the obvious effects of income differences on Engel's coefficient, the effects of urbanization are not as clear. In 1989 the average Engel's coefficient in large cities was 25.9 percent, while in small towns it was 25.0 percent. Some effects of regional differences were recognized. For example, Engel's coefficients in the Tohoku, Hokuriku, and Kinki regions were around 26 percent, while they were around 24 percent in the Hokkaido, Kanto, and Chugoku regions in 1989.

As is the case for food items, expenditures on food away from home are increasing. The proportion of food away from home to total expenditures increased from 9.3 percent in 1970 to 12.7 percent in 1980, and to 15.6 percent in 1989 (see Table 8.1). Expenditures on cakes and processed foods also are increasing while, on the other hand, expenditures on grains are decreasing. Food consumption has come to depend more on outside food services.

Sasaki and Saegusa investigated food consumption by using Leser type and Powell type complete demand analyses. The estimated income elasticities during the 1958-1968 period were as follows: -0.58 to -0.60 for rice, 1.46 to 1.57 for meat, 1.40 to 1.41 for milk and eggs, 1.35 to 1.42 for fruits, and 1.25 to 1.29 for food away from home. In those years, expenditures on milk and eggs, fruits, and food away from home were projected to increase as personal income increased. As for price elasticities, the figures for elasticities varied slightly according to the estimated demand system. Compared with non-food items, in general the demands for foods were price inelastic.

Table 8.1. Food Consumption Expenditures by Household.

	1970		1980		1989	
	Yen/ Month	%	Yen/ Month	%	Yen/ Month	%
Grains	4,576	16.9	9,196	13.7	9,185	12.1
Fishery prod.	3,041	11.2	9,682	14.5	10,270	13.5
Meat	2,783	10.3	7,533	11.3	7,608	10.0
Milk & eggs	2,080	7.7	3,639	5.4	3,613	4.8
Vegetables	2,843	10.5	8,591	12.8	9,370	12.4
Fruits	1,713	6.3	3,367	5.0	3,503	4.6
Oils & fats	1,299	4.8	2,837	4.2	2,945	3.9
Cakes	1,548	5.7	4,168	6.2	5,121	6.8
Processed foods	2,110	7.8	3,877	5.8	5,875	7.7
Beverages	1,239	4.6	2,515	3.8	2,812	3.7
Liquor	1,337	4.9	3,054	4.6	3,690	4.9
Food away from home	2,523	9.3	8,467	12.7	11,858	15.6
Total	27,092	100.0	66,923	100.0	75,849	100.0

Source: *Household Expenditure Survey.*

Sawada investigated food demand by using a classified complete demand analysis during the 1963-1981 period. The estimated income elasticities were as follows: -0.73 for rice, 1.78 for fishery products, 1.93 for beef, 1.69 for chicken, 1.88 for processed meat, 1.56 for fresh fruits, and 1.82 for food away from home. The estimated price elasticities of demand were as follows: -0.26 for rice, -0.16 for milk, -0.19 for eggs, -0.04 for cakes and beverages, -1.74 for beef, -1.19 for pork, -1.30 for chicken, -1.96 for processed foods, and -1.31 for food away from home.

Japanese Diet Guidelines and Current Food Consumption

Japanese-Style Diet

In recent years, Japanese diets have been generally recognized as balanced from a nutritional viewpoint with a relatively high proportion of carbohydrates and low proportion of fats. As a result of the balanced diet, the occurrence of circulatory diseases is relatively low. It is difficult to prove the relationship between diet and health but longevity statistics provide clues. According to a 1989 annual report on population, average lifespans in Japan were 75.5 years for males and 81.3 years for females, both of which were the longest in the world (see Figure 8.5).

With the health of the people and domestic agriculture in mind, the government began to recommend a "Japanese-style diet" and promote its diffusion in the 1980s. The protein, fat, and carbohydrate ratio (PFC ratio) is usually used to evaluate the proper balance in the diet. The PFC ratio measures the proportion of protein, fat, and carbohydrate in the total calorie supply. A balanced PFC ratio for Japan is considered to be 12-13 percent protein, 20-30 percent fat, and 57-68 percent carbohydrates (see Figure 8.6).

From a viewpoint of nutrition, western people eat too much fat at present, while the Japanese previously ate relatively too many carbohydrates. After World War II, the Japanese diet became balanced as a result of westernization of food consumption. However, it is not certain whether the present balanced diet will be maintained in the future.

East Asian countries share many common characteristics regarding agricultural production and food consumption, but at the same time there are some differences. In 1984 the PFC ratio in Japan was 12.8:28.0:59.2 in 1984, while it was 11.7:34.9:56.2 in Taiwan, and 12.2:17.4:70.4 in Korea. Compared with the Japanese, the Taiwanese eat more fats and Koreans eat more carbohydrates.

According to a 1989 food balance sheet, the PFC ratio in Japan was 13.4:28.4:58.2, which was within the appropriate balance range. After changing drastically from that in earlier decades, the PFC ratio in Japan now seems to be stable. However, there is the possibility that the PFC ratio in Japan may change gradually as a result of the adoption of foreign-style eating habits.

148

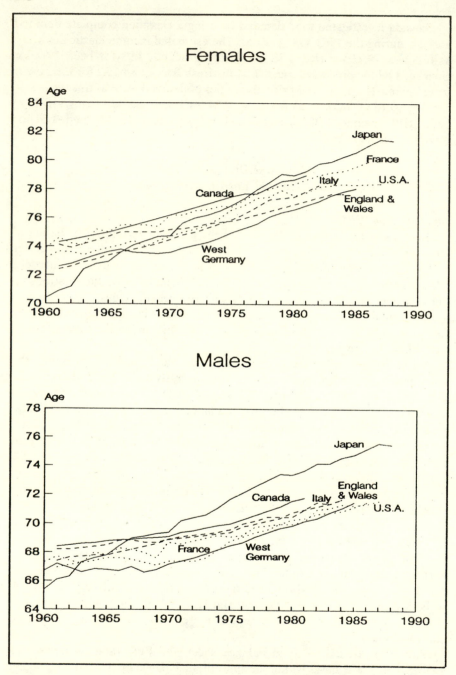

Figure 8.5. An International Comparison of Average Lifespans.
Source: *Lifespan Tables*, Ministry of Health and Welfare.

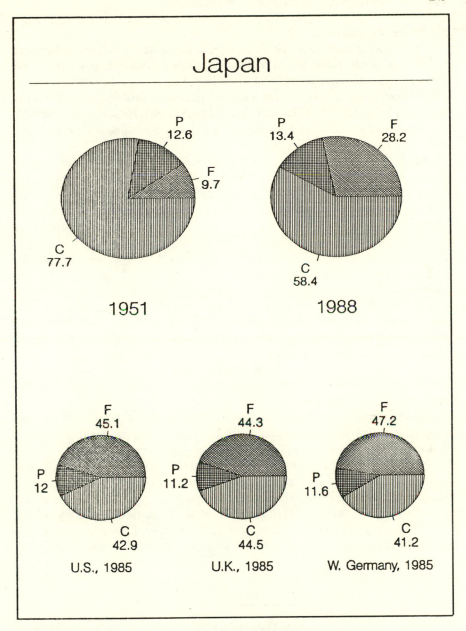

Figure 8.6. An International Comparison of Protein P, Fat F, and Carbohydrate C Proportions.
Source: Changes in Japan's food consumption, *Japan's Agricultural Review*, Vol. 19, Ministry of Agriculture, Forestry, and Fisheries.

Nutritional Problems

Despite a Japanese diet that on average is nutritionally balanced, there are some nutritional problems in individual cases. According to the 1988 Survey on the Nation's Nutritional Situation[2], the average Japanese received 2,057 kilocalories in total energy and 79.2 grams of protein daily, while the necessary levels were 2,019 kilocalories and 66.5 grams, respectively. The only element lacking in the diet was calcium, which was 80 milligrams short of the necessary level of 604 milligrams.

There were few differences in nutritional intake between high income groups and low income groups. The people in the highest income group consumed 184 kilocalories more energy and 11.3 grams more protein than those in the lowest income group. However, except for calcium, people in every income group got sufficient nutrition. There were also few differences in nutritive intake among regions.

On the other hand, the Japanese diet significantly changes according to age and marital status. From a viewpoint of nutritional intake, the most unbalanced situation appears among unmarried individuals. In particular, single persons in their twenties consumed only 1,913 kilocalories in total energy compared to the necessary level of 2,368 kilocalories. They also lacked 1 gram of protein, 200 milligrams of calcium, and a little vitamin B2.

Demographic Factors

Age

Present food consumption in Japan is affected not only by price and income but also by demographic factors. Age is the most representative demographic factor affecting food consumption (see Figure 8.7).

In Surveys on the Nation's Nutritional Situation, except for single households the age of the consumer cannot be identified. Only the age of the household head can be identified both in household expenditure surveys and in surveys on the nation's nutritional situation. Classified by the age of the household head, in general, the per capita food expenditures are the largest in the 60-64 year old class and smallest in the 30-34 year old class. Per capita

---

[2] The Survey on the Nation's Nutritional Situation, compiled by the Ministry of Health and Welfare, investigates the nutritional intake of 6,000 households, including farmers, for a total of 20,000 household members, which are chosen by random sampling methods. The data, which include information on diet and physique, are analyzed by region, occupation, and personal income. The survey is carried out on three consecutive days in November.

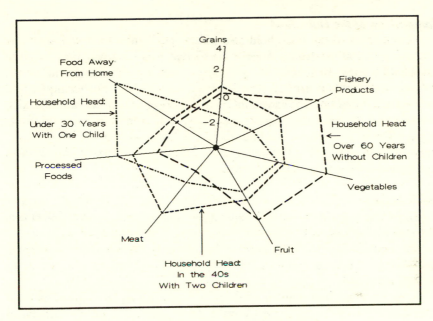

Figure 8.7. Food Consumption Patterns by Lifestage.
Source: An Agricultural White Paper, Ministry of Agriculture, Forestry, and Fisheries.

total consumption expenditures are the largest in the 50-54 year old class and smallest in the 35-39 year old class. As for the Engel's coefficient, those in the over 65 year old class, in the 35-39 year old class, and in the 40-44 year old class are relatively high, while those in the younger generations and in the 50s are relatively low.

The per capita consumption expenditures on grains, vegetables, and fishery products are relatively high for the older generation, and that of meat in the 45-54 year old class. The per capita consumption expenditures on dairy products are high for those 34 and under.

The per capita expenditures on processed foods are highest for those 24 and under, but also are high among seniors. The per capita expenditures on food away from home are high in the under-30 age groups and for those in their 40s with young children.

Because food consumption by age cannot be identified directly, Morishima estimated it by using a regression analysis of the individual data sheets from a household expenditures survey. He found that rice consumption increased slightly among the younger age groups, mainly due to school lunch programs, even though overall consumption of rice has been steadily decreasing.

Composition of the Household

Composition of the household also affects per capita food consumption. According to 1989 statistics, Engel's coefficient was relatively high in large household groups. In general, the per capita consumption of grains and meat in large households is greater than in small households. For example, in a three-person household the consumption of fishery products, vegetables, fruits, processed foods, beverages, liquors, and food away from home was relatively large, while in a seven-person household the consumption of grains, meat, dairy products, fats, and cakes was relatively large. Three-person households tend to use more external food services.

Labor Force

According to a 1989 household expenditures survey, Engel's coefficient was 27.1 percent in blue collar worker households, 23.0 percent in white collar worker households, and 30.3 percent in privately owned businesspersons' households. These differences were, of course, related to differences in household income.

In recent years, the number of married women who have jobs has been increasing. According to a 1989 household expenditures survey, compared with households in which there is one breadwinner, households where both husband and wife work consume relatively large quantities of grains, fishery products, meat, processed foods, liquors, and food away from home (Aita). In particular, in households in which both spouses work outside the consumption of food away from home was 28 percent larger than in households in which just one spouse works. However, in recent years, these differences have been narrowing.

Food Consumption Trends and Development of the Food Industry

Overview of the Food Industry

According to household expenditures surveys, the proportion of grains in total food consumption decreased by half during the 1965-85 period. On the other hand, the ratio of food away from home to total food consumption doubled. The proportion of processed foods in the total food consumption remained relatively high, between 44.0 percent and 46.8 percent. In recent years, processed foods and food away from home markedly improved their positions in total food consumption.

The food industry mainly consists of food processing industries, wholesale and retail stores, and restaurants. According to Onodera, the food industry in Japan: (1) accounts for about 10 percent of the total economy in terms of production value, (2) has many types of businesses, (3) is dominated by small- to medium-sized enterprises which together comprise 99 percent of all food industry firms, and (4) is deeply related to the regional economy.

The annual growth rate of the food processing industry was 6.9 percent and that of restaurants was 5.4 percent during the 1980-85 period, as opposed to 4.1 percent for industry in general. These growth rates also exceeded the 4.3 percent annual growth rate of agribusinesses as a whole. However, in recent years, these growth rates have slowed due to stagnation of food consumption. In 1985 the food processing industry and restaurants accounted for 5.2 percent and 2.2 percent of the total GDP and 36.0 percent and 15.5 percent of agribusinesses, respectively.

In the food processing industry, production of processed foods and ready-to-eat dishes has increased remarkably, reflecting diversification of demand. Due to the strong yen, imports of processed and semi-processed food products are also on the rise. Moreover, the number of food companies investing overseas is increasing. The number of large-sized restaurants is increasing. To reduce production costs and ensure a wide variety of foods, many restaurants are depending more on food imports.

Domestic Production and Imports

In past years, food consumption patterns reflected regional production conditions, and a unique food culture developed in each region. However, as transportation and storage techniques improved, people could enjoy all kinds of foods, some produced in remote places.

As for Japan's food self-sufficiency rate, the total self-sufficiency rate declined from 98 percent in 1960 to 68 percent in 1989. During the same period, the calorie-based food self-sufficiency rate declined from 79 percent to 48 percent, and the grain self-sufficiency rate declined from 82 percent to 30 percent.

Breaking down this decline in food self-sufficiency, we find that an increase in bread and meat consumption led to much greater imports of wheat, barley, and feed grains. Corresponding to the increase in consumption of livestock products, the domestic production of livestock rose but at a slower rate than imports of meat, which made remarkable gains. During the 1960-89 period, domestic production of meat increased from 576,000 MT to 3,565 thousand MT while imports of meat increased from 41,000 MT to 1,514 thousand MT, lowering the self-sufficiency rate of meat from 93 percent to 72 percent. Self-sufficiency rates of vegetables and fruits declined from 100 percent to 92 percent and 100 percent to 67 percent, respectively. Due to the strong yen, imports of vegetables and fruits increased rapidly in recent years.

Although food demand increased dramatically, farmland area decreased from 6.004 million hectares to 5.279 million hectares during the 1965-89 period, while the utilization ratio of cropland harvested to farmland declined from 123.8 percent to 103.3 percent. In response to expanding consumption, production of livestock products and some fruits was stepped up, However, on the whole, Japanese food consumption came to depend more on overseas farmland. It is estimated that farmland would have to increase fourfold to meet food demand without imports (Kaneda).

Using input-output data, Kuroda estimated value-added of industries supplying food (see Table 8.2). He confirmed that, although food consumption expenditures increased, the value-added of agriculture and fisheries decreased during the 1970-1980 period. On the other hand, the value-added of the food processing industry, restaurants, distribution industry, and other industries increased during the same period. The value-added of overseas agricultural products also increased during the same period, except in 1975.

Conclusions

Food consumption in Japan recovered from the difficult situation at the end of the World War II when it was hard to obtain food. As the general economy developed, food consumption steadily increased until it has reached an unprecedented high level. The changes in food consumption during this period could be called westernization, diversification, and maturity. The major changes in food consumption were summarized as follows: a decrease in starchy foods and increases in livestock products, oils and fats, processed foods, and food away from home.

A turning point in food consumption in Japan occurred immediately after the first oil crisis in 1973. As the general economy shifted gears from rapid growth to stable growth, food consumption also reached a saturation point. In the 1980s, from the viewpoint of nutrition, the traditional Japanese-style diet began to be reconsidered in a favorable light.

Food consumption in Japan is saturated in terms of its calorie base. It maintains the characteristics of a traditional Japanese-style diet, including a high proportion of rice, vegetables, legumes, and fish compared with the western diet. However, it is not certain that recent trends in food consumption in Japan will continue in the future, especially in light of the strong yen.

In general, food consumption in Japan is not significantly affected by personal income and regional factors. On the average, food consumption in Japan seems to have reached an appropriate standard, although some nutritional problems persist in individual cases such as single households.

References

Aita, Yoshihisa. 1987. Syokuseikatsu no henka to kako syokuhin gaisyoku no syohi douko (Changes in Diet and Trends in Consumption of Processed Foods and Food Away from Home). In Namiki Masayoshi, ed., *Nihon no Syokuhin Sangyo II: Keiei Keizai (Food Industry in Japan II: Management and Economy)*.

Table 8.2. Induced Value Added by Food Consumption.

	1970		1975		1980	
	Million Yen	%	Million Yen	%	Million Yen	%
Agriculture and fisheries	7,444,707	28.7	7,244,042	22.7	6,656,550	18.2
Crop	5,437,875	21.0	5,228,500	16.4	4,643,696	12.7
Livestock	494,187	1.9	457,985	1.4	594,021	1.6
Fisheries	1,512,645	5.8	1,557,557	4.9	1,418,833	3.9
Food processing	4,303,927	16.6	6,505,226	20.3	7,454,342	20.4
Restaurants	3,640,404	14.0	4,937,825	15.4	5,478,640	15.0
Distribution and retailing	1,798,079	6.9	2,578,737	8.1	3,143,428	8.6
Other industries	3,983,508	15.4	5,184,736	16.2	6,354,260	17.4
Overseas	4,740,663	18.3	5,517,738	17.3	7,494,940	20.5
Imports	3,099,934	12.0	3,410,144	10.7	4,944,344	13.5
Total	25,911,288	100.0	31,968,304	100.0	36,582,160	100.0

Source: Adapted from Kuroda, 1988.

Kanada, Norikazu. 1991. Nihon no yusyutunyu ni taikasareta tochi sigen ryou no Kenkyu (A study on the land resources substituting for export and import in Japan). Master's Thesis. University of Tokyo.

Kuroda, Natsuki. June 1988. Syokuryo shohi ni yotte yuuhatsu sareru fukakachi no sangyo kousei (Composition of Induced Value Added by Food Consumption). *Nougyou Kyoudou Kumiai (Agricultural Cooperative)*.

Morishima, Masaru. 1986. Sedai-betsu no kome juyou bunseki (Rice consumption analysis by age group). In Sakiura Seiji, ed., *Kome no Keizai Bunseki (Economic Analysis on Rice)*.

Nakayama, Seiki. 1964. *Syokuryo no Keizaigaku (Economics on Food)*.

Namiki, Masayoshi. 1973. Engel keisuu no kokusaiteki hyojyunka (International comparison of Engel's coefficients). *Nogyou Sougou Kenkyu (Quarterly Journal of Agricultural Economy)*, Vol. 27, No. 4.

Onodera, Yoshiyuki. 1990. Syokuhin kougyou no keiei keizai kouzou (Structure of management and economy in food industry). In Kato Yuzuru, ed., *Shokuhin Sangyo Keizai Ron (Economics on Food Industry)*.

Sasaki, Kouzou and Saegusa Yoshiharu. 1972. Senkei sisyutsu taikei ni okeru shokuryo jyuyou kansuu (Food demand functions in linear expenditure systems). *Nougyou Keizai Kenkyu (Japanese Journal of Rural Economics)*, Vol. 44, No.1.

Sawada, Manabu. 1984. Kaisouteki juyou taikei to shokuryo juyou bunseki (A hierarchical model of demand for food in Japan). *Nougyou Keizai Kenkyu (Japanese Journal of Rural Economics)*, Vol. 56, No. 3.

9

Factors of Growth in Japanese Food Industries: 1980-1988
Natsuki Fujita

Introduction

It is often noted that Japanese agricultural policies have been against consumers. Thus, demand side analysis has become more and more important, especially assessment of the effects of the yen's recent appreciation. For such purposes, examination of household food expenditures is indispensable.

Table 9.1 summarizes the changes in Japanese household food expenditures for the period 1980-1988. According to the table, household food expenditures increased from 30,993 to 36,630 million yen and total household expenditures increased from 138,585 to 178,399 million yen. As a result, the proportion spent on food decreased from 22 to 21 percent.

The share of the components also changed. The shares of restaurants, beverages, meat and dairy products, and processed fish increased while those of other crops, livestock, miscellaneous food, cigarettes, fisheries, and grain milling decreased. The proportion spent on food away from home (FAFH) has trended upward.

Much of the previous literature on FAFH has focused on the "causes" of the trend in the proportion spent on FAFH. Whether it was qualitative or quantitative, the changes in income, relative prices, and tastes have been key issues in the framework of microeconomics (Egaitsu and Tokoyama). On the other hand, the "effects" of such a trend have largely been neglected by agricultural economists. Although several studies have been done in the framework of input-output (I-O) analysis, the effects of the changes in the components and size of household food expenditures have not been explicitly identified (Onodera; Ueji and Oguchi).

With this in mind and in order to assess the effects of such a trend, this research will propose a new decomposition method in the framework of an

Table 9.1. Structure of Household Expenditures, 1980 Prices (Million Yen).

	1980		1988	
	Value	Percent	Value	Percent
Restaurants	6,937	22	9,866	27
Rice & wheat	0	0	0	0
Other crops	2,550	8	2,684	7
Livestock	383	1	449	1
Fisheries	1,180	4	1,125	3
Grain milling	2,755	9	2,539	7
Meat & dairy prod.	3,247	10	4,008	11
Processed fish	2,172	7	2,898	8
Misc. food	6,558	21	7,160	20
Beverages	3,083	10	3,907	11
Cigarettes	2,129	7	1,995	5
		100		100
Food total	30,993	22	36,630	21
Non-food total	107,592	78	141,769	79
Grand total	138,585	100	178,399	100

NOTE: Calculated from SNA Input-Output Table for each year.

input-output model. It will then be applied to the most recent set of I-O tables for the 1980s.

Methodology

I-O Model

In the framework of an I-O model, the following balance equation can be derived:

$$X_t + M_t = A_t X_t + F_t + E_t \qquad (1)$$

where t, X, M, F, E, and A denote time period t, and vectors of output, import, domestic final demand, export, and an import coefficient matrix, respectively. When imports are assumed to be a function of total demand, M can be written as follows:

$$M_t = (I - U_t)(A_t X_t + F_t) \qquad (2)$$

where U denotes a diagonal matrix of self-sufficiency ratios.

Then, by assuming X and M are endogenous variables, the following solution can be derived:

$$X_t = R_t(U_t F_t + E_t) \tag{3}$$

where $R = (I-UA)^{-1}$ is a domestic Leontief inverse matrix.

Syrquin's Decomposition

Several decomposition methods have been proposed in the framework of I-O models (Chenery; Bulmer-Thomas; Torii and Fukasaku). Among them, Syrquin's method, which as developed from Chenery's method, is useful to assess the role of import substitution.

First, by using (3), the output at period $t+1$ can be written as follows:

$$X_{t+1} = R_{t+1}(U_{t+1} F_{t+1} + E_{t+1}) \tag{4}$$

Then, by using (3) and (4), it is possible to solve for the increase in output in terms of increases in internal and external demands and changes in two sets of parameters:

$$\Delta X = R_t U_t \Delta F + R_t \Delta E + R_t \Delta U Y_{t+1} + R_t U_t \Delta A X_{t+1} \tag{5}$$

where Δ denotes the differences of variables and parameters and Y is a vector of total domestic demand.

The right hand side four terms of (5) can be interpreted as follows:

(a) Domestic Final Demand Expansion Effect (DF): The ith element of the first term captures the effect of the expansion of domestic final demand in all sectors on the output growth of sector i.

(b) Export Expansion Effect (EF): The ith element of the second term captures the effect of exports in all sectors on the output growth of sector i.

(c) Import Substitution Effect (IS): The ith element of the third term captures the effect of the changes in self-sufficiency ratios in all sectors on the output growth of sector i.

(d) Technological Change Effect (TC): The ith element of the third term captures the effect of the changes in technological coefficients in all sectors on the output growth of sector i.

This method has been applied mainly to manufacturing sectors of developing countries because the performance of export-led (or import substitution) development strategies can be quantitatively evaluated (Fujita and James). However, this method is also useful for the analysis of some aspects of agricultural growth (Fujita; Lee).

Modification

As mentioned previously, the proportion spent on FAFH increased significantly in the 1980s. However, the conventional method is not suitable for such analysis. For this reason, the following decomposition of F is necessary:

$$F = SH + N + D \tag{6}$$

where S is a vector of the shares in household food expenditures, H is total household food expenditures, N is a vector of non-food expenditures, and D is a vector of the other domestic final demand. (In other words, $SH + N$ makes a vector of household expenditures.) Then, the first term of (5) can be modified as

$$R_t U_t \Delta F = R_t U_t S_t \Delta H + R_t U_t \Delta S H_{t+1}$$
$$+ R_t U_t \Delta N + R_t U_t \Delta D \tag{7}$$

because $\Delta F = \Delta S H_{t+1} + S_t \Delta H + \Delta N + \Delta D$.

The first term captures the effects induced by changes in total household food expenditures. Because total household food expenditures generally increase year after year, this effect (HFT) is expected to be positive. The second term captures the effects induced by changes in the shares of household food expenditures. Needless to say, this effect (HFS) is expected to be positive for FAFH. The third and fourth terms capture the effects induced by changes in household non-food expenditures and in other domestic final demand such as inventories. We call these effects HN and ODF, respectively.

Finally, HFS of sector i captures the effects induced by the changes not only in the share of sector i but also in the shares of the other sectors. For example, HFS of meat and dairy products is created by changes not only in the shares of meat and dairy products but also in the shares of the other food sectors such as restaurants. Thus, in order to capture the source of HFS, the following decomposition is useful:

$$R_t U_t \Delta S H_{t+1} = R_t U_t (\Delta s_1 \ 0 \ 0 \ 0)' H_{t+1}$$
$$+ \ldots\ldots\ldots\ldots\ldots \tag{8}$$
$$\ldots\ldots\ldots\ldots\ldots$$
$$+ R_t U_t (0 \ 0 \ 0 \ \Delta s_n)' H_{t+1}$$

where $S' = (s_1 \ldots s_n)$. The jth element (e.g. meat and dairy products) of the ith term (e.g. restaurants) indicates the effects induced by the change in sector i's share on sector j's output growth. The other effects can be decomposed in the same way (Fujita).

Some Empirical Results

The proposed decomposition method was applied to the I-O tables for 1980, 1985, and 1988. These tables are for competitive imports and evaluated in 1980 prices. The results are summarized in Tables 9.2 and 9.3 where the figures are normalized so that HFT becomes 100.

Factors of Growth
Growing Sectors
Restaurants: This is the only sector where the effect on expansion of outputs arising from changes in household food shares (HFS) was larger than the effect from changes in household food expenditure totals (HFT). In other words, share expansion played an important role for the growth of this sector. The effect induced by changes in household non-food expenditures (HN) was generally expected to be small for food industries. However, this was the only sector whose HN was larger than 50 percent of HFT. The contribution of technological change (TC) was also relatively large. These findings suggest the importance of the role played by "social expenses" (Kousai-hi) paid by the private companies.

Other crops: The import substitution effect (IS) was negative and offset more than 70 percent of HFT. HFS was also negative. However, output increased because other factors (especially TC) were positive.

Meat and dairy products: IS was negative and offset more than 95 percent of HFT. However, output increased because all other factors (especially, HFS, ODF, and TC) were positive.

Processed fish: IS was negative and completely offset HFT. However, output increased because most of the other factors (especially HFS) were positive.

Table 9.2. Factors of Growth, 1980-1988 (Effect on Percent of Household Expenditure Effect).

Sector Name	ΔX	HFT	HFS	HN	ODF	EE	IS	TC
Restaurants	405	100	129	59	56	27	-20	54
Rice & wheat	-4	100	-94	11	50	-3	-14	-54
Other crops	84	100	-45	19	20	7	-71	53
Livestock	118	100	25	23	22	10	-84	22
Fisheries	-14	100	-18	16	32	-1	-97	-46
Grain milling	-22	100	-111	8	28	-1	-11	-36
Meat & dairy prod.	131	100	34	14	35	6	-97	38
Processed fish	100	100	80	8	53	-16	-138	13
Misc. food	98	100	-27	11	14	4	-55	52
Beverages	139	100	60	17	14	2	-32	-22
Cigarettes	-107	100	-134	5	-39	3	-32	-11

NOTE: Calculated from SNA Input-Output Table for each year.

Table 9.3. Factors of Growth in Demand for Output ΔX by Time Periods (Effect as Percent of Household Expenditure Effect).

Sector Name	ΔX	HFT	HFS	HN	ODF	EE	IS	TC
			(a)	1980-1985				
Restaurants	511	100	178	46	38	32	3	114
Rice & wheat	141	100	-72	9	175	-5	-2	-64
Other crops	65	100	-55	15	2	13	-62	52
Livestock	101	100	11	17	-4	17	-40	0
Fisheries	-4	100	-54	14	27	7	-27	-71
Grain milling	1	100	-81	7	16	-2	-7	-33
Meat & dairy prod.	141	100	24	11	21	9	-31	7
Processed fish	163	100	62	8	47	2	-53	-2
Misc. food	114	100	-21	9	20	7	-46	45
Beverages	42	100	-25	16	24	4	0	-77
Cigarettes	-82	100	-79	4	-95	3	-10	-5
			(b)	1985-1988				
Restaurants	171	100	14	76	80	13	-55	-57
Rice & wheat	-625	100	-87	160	-362	14	-82	-368
Other crops	127	100	-22	29	50	-2	-82	53
Livestock	146	100	50	26	58	0	-151	65
Fisheries	-38	100	57	23	42	-18	-240	-2
Grain milling	-72	100	-180	11	55	0	-15	-42
Meat & dairy prod.	110	100	49	18	58	0	-208	93
Processed fish	-15	100	101	10	60	-49	-277	39
Misc. food	73	100	-37	17	0	-1	-67	60
Beverages	344	100	236	18	-9	-4	-94	98
Cigarettes	-172	100	-249	8	73	3	-82	-26

NOTE: Calculated from SNA Input-Output Table for each year.

Miscellaneous food: IS was negative and offset more than 55 percent of HFT. HFS was also negative. However, output increased because other factors (especially TC) were positive.

Beverages: Both IS and TC were negative. However, they offset only 55 percent of HFT. In addition, HFS was positive and the size was almost 60 percent of HFT. As a result, output increased.

Stagnating Sectors

Rice and wheat: HFS was negative and offset more than 90 percent of HFT. TC and IS were also negative. As a result, output decreased.

Fisheries: IS was negative and offset more than 95 percent of HFT. TC was also negative and offset more than 45 percent of HFT. As a result, output decreased.

Grain milling: HFS was negative and offset HFT. TC was also negative. The other factors were relatively small. As a result, output decreased.

Cigarettes: HFS was negative and completely offset HFT. Most of the other factors were also negative. As a result, output decreased.

The Effects of the Recent Appreciation of the Yen

The Japanese yen had appreciated slowly until 1985. However, the pace accelerated between 1985 and 1988. A rising yen encourages imports and discourages exports. The results (substitution and income effects) of appreciation can be examined by comparing the factors of growth for 1980-1985 and 1985-1988 (Table 9.3).

1. The number of stagnating sectors increased from two (fisheries and cigarettes) to five (rice and wheat, fisheries, grain milling, processed fish, and cigarettes).
2. HFS of fisheries and beverages changed from negative to positive. Thus, their qualities might be upgraded.
3. EE of many sectors (especially fisheries and processed fish) changed from positive to negative.
4. The size of negative IS significantly increased in most sectors. IS of restaurants changed from positive to negative.
5. The role of TC became favorable for output growth in many sectors. However, TC of restaurants changed from positive to negative.

The Effects of the Changes in the Demand for Restaurants

As previously mentioned, HFS of each sector captures the effects induced by changes not only in the share of household expenditures for that sector but also in the shares of other sectors. Thus, in order to clarify the source of HFS, the method of equation (7) was proposed. The sources of the other effects can be also clarified in the same way. By using this method, it is possible to distinguish the effects of changes in demand for restaurants from those of other sectors. The results are summarized in Table 9.4.

First, HFT of restaurants induced demand for 105 million yen of miscellaneous food and 107 million yen of beverages. Second, HFS of restaurants induced demand for 55 million yen of rice and wheat, 59 million yen of other crops, 61 million yen of fisheries, 61 million yen of meat and dairy products, 139 million yen of miscellaneous food, and 142 million yen of beverages. Finally, TC of restaurants increased demand for 299 million yen of other crops, 52 million yen of livestock, 464 million yen of miscellaneous food, and 108 million yen of meat and dairy products. On the other hand, TC of restaurants decreased demand for 83 million yen of fisheries, 58 million yen of grain milling, and 97 million yen of beverages.

Table 9.4. Effects of the Increase in Demands by Restaurants (Million Yen).

Sector Name	ΔX	HFT	HFS	HN	ODF	EE	IS	TC
Restaurants	5,369	1,301	1,720	0	0	10	-181	464
Rice & wheat	-27	41	55	0	0	0	-6	-43
Other crops	532	44	59	0	0	0	-6	299
Livestock	527	36	47	0	0	0	-5	52
Fisheries	-56	46	61	0	0	0	-6	-83
Grain milling	-137	38	50	0	0	0	-5	-58
Meat & dairy prod.	816	47	61	0	0	0	-6	108
Processed fish	374	25	33	0	0	0	-3	40
Misc. food	1,658	105	139	0	0	1	-15	464
Beverages	925	107	142	0	0	1	-15	-97
Cigarettes	-411	0	0	0	0	0	0	1

NOTE: Calculated from SNA Input-Output Table for each year.

Summary and Conclusion

To analyze the effects of the changes in the structure of household food expenditures, this research proposed a new decomposition method. It was applied to the Japanese I-O tables for 1980, 1985, and 1988. The results can be summarized as follows:

1. Growing sectors were restaurants, "other crops," livestock, meat and dairy products, processed fish, miscellaneous food, and beverages. In general, the increase in total household expenditures was the most influential growth factor. Thus, growth patterns contrasted sharply with the export-led type of U.S. growth patterns (Lee). In Japan, the increase in the share of household food expenditures contributed to the growth of restaurants, processed fish, and beverages. Technological change was important for the growth of other crops and miscellaneous food.

2. Stagnating sectors were rice and wheat, fisheries, grain milling, and cigarettes. The falling share of household food expenditures was the main factor for the stagnation of rice and wheat, grain milling, and cigarettes. On the other hand, the decrease in self-sufficiency ratio was the most influential factor for the decline in fisheries.

3. The recent appreciation of the yen made imported food cheaper. As a result, self-sufficiency ratios decreased in most sectors. The positive effects induced by the increase in total household food expenditures were largely offset by such negative effects.

4. The recent appreciation of the yen increased real income. As a result, restaurants, livestock, fisheries, meat and dairy products, processed fish, and beverages increased their shares of household food expenditures.

5. The increase in household expenditures for restaurants contributed greatly to most food sectors except cigarettes. Technological changes in restaurants also contributed to the output growth for other crops, miscellaneous food, and meat and dairy products.

References

Bulmer-Thomas, V. 1982. *Input-Output Analysis in Developing Countries*. New York: John Wiley & Sons.

Chenery, H.B. 1960. Factors of growth: 1950-1960. *American Economic Review*.

Egaitsu, F. and H. Tokoyama. 1990. Change in life style and food consumption structure. In Y. Kato, ed., *Economics of Food Industries*. Norin-Tokei Kyokai.

Fujita, N. 1986. Factors of growth in agricultural sectors: 1960-1980. *Journal of Rural Economics* 57(1):12-21.

Fujita, N. and W.E. James. 1990. Export-oriented growth of output and employment in Taiwan and Korea, 1973/74-1983/84. *Weltwirtschaftliches Archiv*, Band 126, Heft 4, pp.737-753.

Lee, C. 1990. Growth and change in the structure of the U.S. agricultural economy, 1972-1982: An input-output perspective. *Economic Systems Research* 2(3):303-311.

Ministry of Agriculture, Forestry, and Fisheries. 1990. *Economic Analysis of Food Industries*. Norin-Tokei Kyoka.

Onodera, Y. 1985. *Japanese Agri-business*. Norin-Tokei Kyokai.

Syrquin, M. 1976. Sources of industrial growth and change: An alternative measure. Paper presented at European Meetings of the Econometric Society, Helsinki.

Torii, Y. and K. Fukasaku. 1984. Economic development and changes in linkage structure: An input-output analysis of the Republic of Korea and Japan. *Proceedings of the Seventh International Conference on Input-Output Techniques*, New York, pp. 333-363.

Ueji, T. and C. Oguchi. 1989. The effects of an increase in the eating out expenditure on agricultural and food industrial production -- A food demand analysis by input-output tables. *Journal of Rural Problems* 25(1):10-18.

APPENDIX

Natsuki Fujita

This research intensively utilized I-O tables. The following official I-O tables are now available in Japan.

General Management Agency (GMA)
I-O Tables in Current Prices
    1951 1960 1965 1970 1975 1980 1985

I-O Tables in Constant Prices
    1960-1965-1970 in 1970 prices
    1965-1970-1975 in 1975 prices
    1970-1975-1980 in 1980 prices
    1975-1980-1985 in 1985 prices

Economic Planning Agency (EPA)
SNA I-O Tables in Current Prices
    1980 1985 1986 1987 1988 1989

SNA I-O Tables in Constant Prices
    1980-1985-1986-1987-1980 in 1980 prices
    1980-1985-1986-1987-1988-1989 in 1985 prices

Ministry of International Trade and Industry (MITI)
Extension I-O Tables in Current Prices
    1976 1977 1978 1979 1981 1982 1983 1984 1986 1987

The sector classification of EPA's SNA I-O tables are highly aggregated. However, since they are relatively new and evaluated in constant prices, this research utilized them.

10

American Food System Structure and Consumption[1]

Benjamin Senauer, Elaine Asp, and Jean Kinsey

The food system links farmers and consumers by producing, transporting, storing, and transforming basic commodities into food products and services. Some analysts would include industries that supply inputs to farmers and marketers as part of that system. By any measure, the U.S. food system is a huge industry. The total food and fiber system accounted for about 15 percent of the value-added in the U.S. economy in 1988 and about one of every six jobs (U.S. Dept. of Commerce, 1990, p. 637). The farm value of food products sold in 1988 was $97 billion and the final sales of the food marketing system to consumers reached about $638 billion (USDA, Aug. 1989, p. 1).

This enormous industry is increasingly consumer, as opposed to producer, driven. The emphasis is shifting from production to marketing (Pierson and Allen). The basis of successful marketing is understanding the ultimate customer, in this case the American food consumer. In this environment, the consumer is setting the agenda for the food industry and the most successful firms have acquired a consumer-focused marketing orientation. The major attributes that consumers are looking for in food products are quality, taste, convenience, nutrition, wholesomeness, and value (Borra).

A knowledge of major consumer trends and an understanding of their marketing implications has become crucial in the food industry. This chapter

---

[1]This chapter draws directly on the authors' new book titled, *Food Trends and the Changing Consumer*. The material in this chapter is used with the permission of the book publisher, Eagan Press, 3340 Pilot Knob Road, Eagan, Minnesota 55121, U.S.A.

outlines major food and demographic trends and their significance to the U.S. food industry. The first section examines trends in the American diet. The second section discusses major demographic trends and some of their effects on food consumption. The third provides a brief overview of the structure of various sectors of the food industry and discusses some of the impacts of current consumer trends. The final section briefly relates U.S. trends to global food consumption patterns.

Trends in the American Diet

This section explores long-run trends in food consumption patterns, current recommendations for a healthy diet, and recent trends in eating behavior in the United States.

Long-Run Trends in Food Consumption

A saturation level has been reached for the total *quantity* of food consumed in affluent societies such as the United States. When incomes allow the purchase of more food than the human body needs, the rate of growth in food consumption declines and the quantity consumed stabilizes. Evidence of food saturation comes from looking at the stability of calories in the food supply.[2] In 1987, 3,500 Calories per day were available in the food supply, compared to 3,400 Calories in 1910, and a low of 3,100 in 1957 (Hiemstra; Putnam).

Meat, poultry, and fish consumption is depicted in Figure 10.1. The increase in poultry (80 percent of which is chicken), the rise and fall of beef, and the long-run stability of pork consumption can be readily observed. By 1989, poultry consumption per person surpassed beef by 16 pounds and pork by 22 pounds. Measures are in retail weight for red meat and ready-to-cook weight for poultry. On a boneless, trimmed weight basis, 1989 consumption of poultry was 4.5 pounds per capita less than beef and 18 pounds per capita more than pork. However it is measured, poultry consumption is expected to continue upward at the expense of red meat.

Relative prices of various animal products have a strong influence on the relative amounts consumed of individual animal products.[3] However, with

---

[2] A Calorie equals one kilocalorie.

[3] This chapter gives little attention to the effect of prices on food demand, not because price effects are not important. One chapter in our book is devoted to the impact of traditional economic factors, income and prices, on food demand.

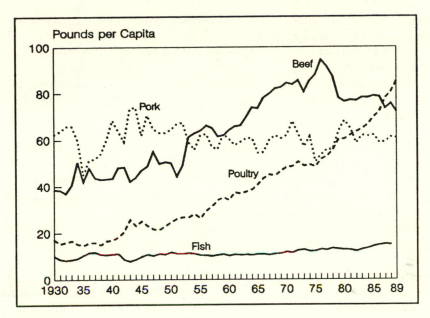

Figure 10.1. U.S. Per Capita Consumption of Beef, Pork, Poultry, and Fish, 1930-1989.
Source: Hiemstra; Putnam, 1989a and 1990a.

affluence, consumers respond less to retail food prices and the demand for the various forms of animal protein becomes more sensitive to demographic factors and health concerns. For example, the consumption of fish increased 42 percent between 1967 and 1988 while its price increased 418 percent, more than twice as much as the increase in the price of red meat and almost three times as much as the increase in the price of poultry. This indicates a shift in consumers' preferences. Likewise, egg consumption declined in the face of almost flat egg prices (Putnam).

For dairy products, the quantity of whole fluid milk consumed fell, while lowfat milks (including lowfat, skim, buttermilk, and lowfat yogurt) increased. Total fluid milk consumption fell over 100 pounds per person between 1950 and 1987, and by that time, lowfat milk consumption was 115 pounds per capita compared to 110 pounds of whole milk (Smith *et al.*). Changes in the demand for fluid milk may be partially attributed to consumers' concern for the high fat and calorie content of whole milk, but it can also be attributed to the decreased number of children in the population. On the other hand, consumption of cheese has increased even though most cheese is high in fat.

Americans have steadily increased their overall consumption of fats and oils, while substituting vegetable oil for animal fat. In 1952, vegetable oils overtook animal fats and have climbed at a rate of 3.5 percent per year since, pushing up total fat consumption by 1.2 percent per year. For every one pound decline in animal fat consumption since 1950, vegetable oils consumption increased 2.8 pounds. Soybean oil has the largest share of the vegetable oil market (70 percent), with corn oil next at 7.7 percent (USDA, April 1990).

The fall in crop product consumption since the 1940s is due mostly to a decline in flour and cereal products (from 300 pounds per capita annually in 1909 to 172 pounds per capita in 1988), and in the consumption of fresh fruits (from 123 pounds per capita in 1909 to 94 pounds in 1988) (Hiemstra; Putnam). Between 1967 and 1987, consumption of breakfast cereals increased 44 percent to 14.1 pounds per capita, accounting for a substantial part of recent increases in the consumption of cereals and grains (Smith and Yonkers).

Fruit consumption has increased since 1970, but Americans annually consumed much more fresh fruit prior to 1950 than since. This is a surprise to many, in light of the recent popularity of fresh produce. It can be explained partly by the demise of home grown and home processed fruit during the first half of the century. Even with a large increase in frozen fruit products (especially juice), there was a sharp decline in total fruit consumption between 1947 and 1963, with a modest increase since. Fruit juices, 79 percent of which was orange juice, comprised 42 percent of all fruit consumption (by weight) in 1981, an increase from 12 percent in 1950. In terms of fresh fruit consumption, apples, bananas, and oranges dominate.

Vegetables, in contrast to fruit, have increased in American diets. There has been a 42 percent increase in the consumption of fresh vegetables since 1970, including a 400 percent increase in broccoli consumption to 3.5 pounds per capita annually, and a 257 percent increase in cauliflower consumption to 2.5 pounds per capita (United Fresh Fruit and Vegetable Association). As with fruits, the most common reasons for increasing fresh vegetable consumption are concerns with health and nutrition. About 18 percent of fresh produce was imported in 1986, with an 80 percent increase in imported vegetables since 1977.

In spite of health and diet concerns, Americans continue to like sweets. The increase in all types of sweeteners is phenomenal, up 25 percent between 1966 and 1987 to 152 pounds per capita per year. The composition of this increase is important. Refined cane and beet sugar consumption has declined since 1972, while corn sweeteners and non-caloric sweetener consumption increased. In 1987, 42 percent of all sugars and sweeteners were from refined sugar, 45 percent from corn sweetener and 13 percent from a non-caloric source. The rise in total sweeteners is connected to the rise in the consumption of soft drinks, almost all of which are now sweetened with either corn sweetener or a non-caloric sweetener.

The shift in beverage consumption is an interesting trend. Coffee consumption peaked in 1946 at 20 pounds per capita, falling back to its 1914 level of a little over 9 pounds in 1977, and then rising and holding steady at about 10-11 pounds per capita (Hiemstra; Putnam). Tea consumption has remained unchanged and juice consumption increased slightly. Soft drink consumption increased notably from less than 20 gallons per capita annually in 1966 to over 30 gallons in 1987. The substitution of soft drinks for milk and coffee are thought to be related to concerns about being overweight, to their snappy taste, and to advertising. Although alcoholic beverage consumption rose between 1966 and 1982, its consumption has declined since.

Figure 10.2 shows the rise in percent of food expenditures on food away from home and the fall in food at home since 1966. The grocery business must compete vigorously for the consumer's food dollar. Furthermore, as take-out-to-eat (TOTE) food increases in importance, the distinction between at-home and away-from-home food expenditures becomes blurred and less significant, since food for "off-premise use" (usually at home) may be fully cooked away from home and purchased in a restaurant or a grocery store.

Diet and Health

In the past 20 years, a veritable flood of research and a massive number of reports have been produced documenting connections between diet and health. New dietary recommendations reflect a shift from concern about preventing diseases associated with nutritional deficiencies to an emphasis on the contributions of nutrition to enhancing health and decreasing the risks of chronic diseases. These reports were stimulated by the 1977 U.S. Senate

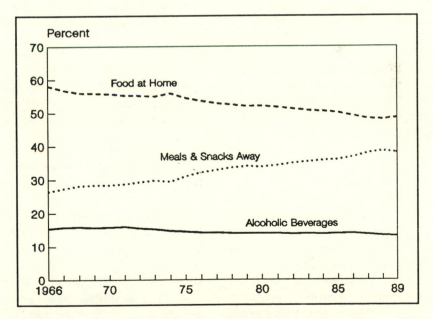

Figure 10.2. Percent of Total U.S. Food Expenditures: Food at Home, Meals & Snacks Away from Home, and Alcoholic Beverages, 1966-1989.
Sources: Hiemstra; Putnam, 1989a and 1990a.

Select Committee on Nutrition and Human Needs which defined a set of Dietary Goals for the United States. The various guidelines, set forth by organizations such as the Surgeon General, the National Research Council, and the American Heart Association, all recommend reduced consumption of fat, generally to 30 percent or less of total calories with saturated fat less than 10 percent of calories. Most recommend that cholesterol consumption be reduced, usually to 300 mg/day or less. The consumption of complex carbohydrates, found in fruits, vegetables, and whole grains, should be increased generally to 50 percent or more of total calories. They recommend that consumers eat a wide variety of foods. The consumption of both refined sugar and sodium (salt) should be decreased and alcohol consumed in moderation, if at all. Interestingly, a traditional Japanese diet would largely be in line with these recommendations for a healthy diet, except for being high in sodium (salt).

Consumers send conflicting messages concerning food and health concerns, but in general, diets seem to be moving in the direction of the dietary recommendations. Americans now consume about 36 percent of their calories in the form of fat, which is down from 41 percent in 1977-78. Consumers have cut down on many old staples like eggs and whole milk, yet indulge in gourmet ice cream and brie cheese. They eat oatmeal for breakfast, hamburgers and french fries for lunch, and work out at gyms before dinner. The young (age 18-29) are the most contradictory, endorsing healthy food and exercising vigorously in many cases, but eating more snack food and exercising less often than older people on average (Mueller).

Current Trends in Eating Behavior

Ten trends in consumer attitudes and behavior were identified for the Food Marketing Institute in 1987 by futurist Faith Popcorn (Iggers). They are consistent with the observations of many others and show promise of continuing for some time to come. They are:

1. A desire for *premium quality* products and a willingness to pay more to obtain them. This is reflected in the increased demand for gourmet foods.
2. A trend towards *adventure* expresses itself in a desire for variety, for example, new tastes and new foods. However, this is adventure that involves little real risk. Consumers increasingly want more *variety and diversity* in their diets.
3. A trend towards *indulgence* is consistent with the trend toward quality, adventure, and individualism. It is an attitude that says "I deserve it" and "I want gratification now."
4. An *individualistic* lifestyle allows consumers to make statements about who they are and what they believe through their choices of food and

other consumer products. Increasingly, individuals in the household are choosing their own food, independently of other members.

5. A trend towards *cocooning* (staying at home) reflects a desire to protect oneself from the hassles of public appearances and uncertainties of social interactions. Cocooning means a higher demand for TOTE food, frozen foods, and home delivered foods.

6. At home or away, people will *graze* more (eating small, frequent snacks) and eat fewer full, sit down meals.

7. In the 1970s and 1980s, physical fitness was the craze. That has matured into a trend towards *wellness* which includes, for many, an increased concern for good nutrition and food safety.

8. An increased need to manage one's time has and will lead to a great demand for *convenience* in foods and other goods and services.

9. Consistent with a quest for quality and convenience, consumers are increasingly *intolerant* of unsafe, poorly constructed, and over-priced products. This relates to the importance of quality and value as food attributes.

10. The 1990s will see a return of the *ethics and culture of the 1930s to 1950s*. A search for moral stability will lead consumers to seek value in those things that will endure (Fisher). The environmental concern over fast-food packaging was seen as an attack on a "...throw-away, fast-food lifestyle" as much as a concern with solid waste buildup (Holusha).

Demographic Trends

Demographic, cultural, and economic diversity are increasing in the United States. More and more people display different ethnic back-grounds, lifestyles, and tastes than ever before. According to Tim Hammonds and Judith Kozacik, Senior Vice President and Vice President for Research at the Food Marketing Institute, "Tastes and preferences for food products are rooted in the fundamental forces of demographics and lifestyles. They move slowly and powerfully" (Hammonds and Kozacik).

Population Growth

Population growth is slowing down. In 1990, the U.S. population of 250 million people was growing at half the rate it was in the middle of the twentieth century. An average growth rate of 1.3 percent per year led the total population to increase 80 percent over the 30 years prior to 1980. Population is expected to increase by only 15 percent in the 30 years following 1980 and the growth rate is expected to be less than 0.2 percent per year. Growth rates in the U.S. are quite uneven across ethnic groups. Non-Hispanic whites increased at a rate of 0.5 percent in 1990. Hispanics and other races (except blacks) increased at a rate of 2.7 percent and blacks at a rate of 1.5 percent. By 2010, these rates are estimated to be 0.15 percent for whites, 1.8 percent for Hispanics and 1.1 percent for blacks (Spencer).

Population growth has traditionally depended upon fertility rates, but future population growth in the U.S. will depend mainly on declining mortality, continued immigration, and the fertility of non-white women. The demand for specific foods will depend less on population growth and more on the diversity of consumers' preferences.

Ethnic Diversity

The faces and places of immigration have changed dramatically over the past century. By 1986, Europeans comprised less than 15 percent of immigrants; 41 percent were Asian and 37 percent were Latin American. These new immigrants moved primarily into the South, West, and Mid-Atlantic states (Batson). Ethnic diversity is increasing the diversity of the types of consumer goods demanded. Ethnic diversity creates market niches. For example, some Hispanics prefer high-fat milk.

Various ethnic groups not only increase the diversity of foods demanded, they also introduce new foods into the American diet by selling them to the larger population. Americans are becoming more cosmopolitan eaters. At the same time some ethnic groups are adopting more traditional American foods like hamburgers and french fries, other Americans are adopting ethnic foods such as egg rolls and tacos.

Regional Shifts

The population continues to shift to the South and West. The South gained 16 percent and the West gained 21 percent between 1980 and 1990. These regions are expected to grow by another 11 percent and 13 percent, respectively, by 2000. Migration from rural to urban centers continues. Almost half of the people in the U.S. live in metropolitan areas of 1 million or more (U.S. Dept. of Commerce, Sept. 30, 1988). Mobility helps to introduce a variety of food preferences across the country, but differences in food tastes persist between regions. Urbanization increases the number of meals eaten away from home, estimated to be at least 50 percent of all meals in urban centers (National Restaurant Association).

Household Composition

Household composition is the foundation of demographic trends. Its major components are household size, age distribution, and marital status. The general trend in American households has been towards smaller, older households with fewer married couples and fewer children. The average number of people per *household* was down to 2.6 by 1988 due to a growing number of singles and a decline in fertility. The average number of people per *family* was down to 3.2 due to fewer children and an increase in single parent families. Married couples declined as a percent of families from 87 percent in 1970 to 80 percent by 1987. The percent of families that were married couples with children declined from 50 percent to 38 percent (U.S. Dept. of Commerce, 1990).

Over half of all U.S. households had only one or two members in 1990. Smaller household size increases per capita food expenditures, because economies of scale cannot be realized in food purchasing and preparation. Small households increase the demand for food away from home, TOTE food, conveniently prepared food, and food that can be purchased in small portions. Single persons spend up to 50 percent of their food budget on food away from home (Lubin).

Single parent families accounted for almost one-half of the increase in the number of families during the eighties. Four out of five single parent families were headed by women who had been divorced, widowed, or who had children outside of marriage. The percent of households that looked like the traditional stereotype -- a married couple with two or more children under age 18 and a wife not in the labor force -- dropped from 23 percent in 1955 to 7 percent by 1987 (Rich).

Age

The baby boom lasted from 1946 to 1964 with the birth rate peaking in 1957 at 25.3 births per 1,000 population (U.S. Dept. of Commerce, 1988). Baby boomers were age 26 through 44 in 1990 and they will swell the ranks of older middle-age households (ages 46 through 63) until 2010, when they will begin to swell the ranks of the retired population. The nation's median age was 30 in 1980, 32 in 1990, and will be over 40 by 2030.

Increased life expectancies have created a growing population of elderly people. For example, less than 12 percent survived to age 80 in 1900 while 50 percent are expected to do so by 2000 (O'Reilly). Age affects food consumption because caloric and nutritional needs change as people age. Food preferences also change with income and experience. Households headed by persons age 55-64 spent about 10 percent more on food than the average household while those over age 65 spent about 12 percent less. On a per capita basis though, elderly households under age 75 spent 14 percent more than the average household, mostly due to the small household size which requires larger food outlays per person (Lazer and Shaw).

Education

The major trends in education are an increasing number of high school and college educated people over the age of 25 along with a disparity in educational achievement between whites and non-whites. Overall, completion of at least four years of high school increased from 24 percent of the population in 1940 to 76 percent in 1986. Among blacks, that percentage was about 51 percent; among Hispanics, 44 percent. One-fifth of adults had completed college in 1988, compared to 5 percent in 1940. The rate for whites was 21 percent, compared to 33 percent for Asians, 11 percent for blacks, and 10 percent for Hispanics (U.S. Dept. of Commerce, Dec. 2, 1987; April 8, 1988).

A continuing disparity in education and concomitant incomes means that there will be a persistent group of food consumers who are poor. They will be mostly non-white or single parent households and, at the extreme, the homeless. These consumers are very sensitive to prices and will be purchasing lower cost food and fewer services.

Income Trends

A popular perception is that real household incomes in the United States are not growing, that the rich are getting richer and the poor are getting poorer, that the large middle class mass market is diminishing, and that an underclass of permanently unemployable persons has developed. Considerable evidence supports this perception. Aggregate income statistics such as per capita personal disposal income, median family income, and individual wage earnings reveal much the same picture -- rising incomes until about 1973 and basically stagnation thereafter (Levy, 1987). In terms of income distribution, the poorest 20 percent of households received 5.6 percent of all household income in 1969, a year in which the richest 20 percent received 40.6 percent. By 1989, the richest 20 percent of households received 46.8 percent of aggregate household income (U.S. Dept. of Commerce, Sept. 26, 1990).

A mixed picture of income trends has developed. More families are entering the low and high income brackets, that is, those below $10,000 and over $50,000 per year (Levy, 1988). The loss of many middle-income (blue-collar) jobs, the type held by many males with little education, led to thousands of displaced workers whose family incomes declined dramatically as a result. On the other hand, dual earner families at all levels of income have improved their spending power relative to single earner families.

Labor Force Participation

The greatest change in the labor force over the past two decades has been an increase in the percent of married women working outside the home. The labor force participation rates of men and women are converging. Those of single men and women are very close at all ages below 65. Almost 70 percent of married women in prime childbearing years (age 20-44) were in the labor force in 1988 (U.S. Dept. of Commerce, 1990). In spite of their maternal roles, over half of mothers with children under age 6 and over 70 percent of those with children ages 6 to 17 were in the labor force in 1988.

As labor participation has increased, one of the primary ways of cutting household work has been to spend less time in the kitchen (Burros, Feb. 24, 1988). Microwave ovens have helped as have convenience foods, take-out food, fast food, and home delivered food. Since 86 percent of employed women still do most of the cooking and 91 percent do most of the shopping, they are looking for ways to feed themselves and their families quickly. Most spend less than a half hour preparing an evening meal; 20 percent spend less than 15 minutes (Burros, Feb. 27, 1988).

The Food Industry

One of the things that makes an impression on foreigners who visit the United States for the first time are American supermarkets. They are amazed by the abundance, variety, and quality of foods which most Americans take for granted. Boris Yeltsin, the well-known Russian politician, after his first trip to the United States remarked: "Their supermarkets have 30,000 food items. You can't imagine it" (Porubcansky). Some aspects of the U.S. food industry can perhaps be criticized but, overall, it is a marvel of efficiency and responsiveness to the consumer unmatched in most other countries in the world.

Figures 10.3 and 10.4 show the value added to the domestic economy and the employment generated by the various major sectors in the total food and fiber system. By presenting the data for both 1975 and 1988, the growth of the various sectors can be compared. Value-added measures the net contribution of an economic sector to the national economy and is determined by subtracting the value of the inputs used by a sector from the market value of

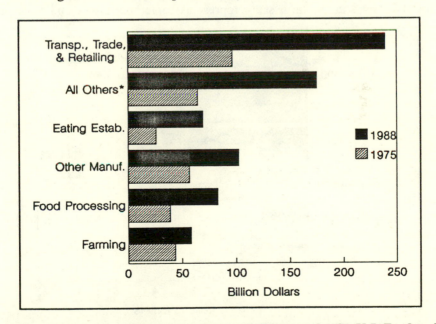

Figure 10.3. Valued Added to the Domestic Economy by the U.S. Food and Fiber System, 1975 and 1988.
*Includes other services, mining, and forestry.
Source: U.S. Dept. of Commerce, 1990, p. 637.

the final goods and services produced. Value-added in the food and fiber system has steadily risen over time and totaled $727 billion in 1988. However, its relative contribution to the national economy has gradually declined, as other parts of the economy have grown more rapidly. In 1975, for example, the food and fiber system accounted for 20.4 percent of the total value-added in the economy, 5.5 percentage points more than in 1988 (U.S. Dept. of Commerce, 1990, p. 637).

Figure 10.3 shows that the largest and fastest growing sector in terms of value-added was transportation, trade, and retailing. Farming grew the least between 1975 and 1988.

The food and fiber system provided jobs to 19.6 million workers in 1988 and 20.2 million in 1975. As shown in Figure 10.4, the largest generator of jobs is the transportation, trade, and retailing sector of the industry. With increasing productivity, employment in the first three sectors -- farming, processing, and other manufacturing -- declined between 1975 and 1988 even as their output and value-added rose.

The distribution of consumer food expenditures between the marketing system and farmers has been shifting. The farm value share of total consumer expenditures for domestic foods, 41 percent in 1950, declined to 33 percent by 1965 and was only 25 percent in 1988 (Dunham, p. 39). Some might conclude that this trend in the farm share represents something unfair and perhaps

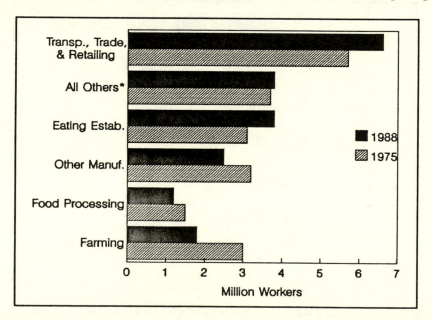

Figure 10.4. Employment in the U.S. Food and Fiber System, 1975 and 1988.
*Includes other services, mining, and forestry.
Source: U.S. Department of Commerce, 1990, p. 637.

even a little suspicious. However, the basic explanation is simple. Consumers have demanded more convenient, and hence more highly processed food products, and have shifted to eating more food away from home. Therefore, more and more of the value and the costs of the final retail-level products are added after the basic commodities leave the farm. In addition, food marketing costs have risen more rapidly than farm-level costs, particularly because of increased labor costs (Kohls and Uhl, p. 185).

Other chapters will be covering the structure of farming and the food-away-from-home market in the United States. Therefore, the remainder of this section will focus on food processing and manufacturing, foodwholesaling, and food store retailing. We will also introduce some of the implications of the earlier food and consumer trends for these sectors of the U.S. food industry.

Food Processing and Manufacturing

Sales by the food processing and manufacturing industries were an estimated $340 billion in 1988 (USDA, 1989). There are two major segments of the food processing industry (Kohls and Uhl). One is a dominant core of a few very large firms which produce popular brands and have the major share of industry sales and the second is a competitive fringe of a large number of small firms which produce less popular brands and have a small share of industry sales. The food processing industry is becoming more and more concentrated with mergers and acquisitions creating fewer, larger, and highly diversified firms.

Food processors are becoming consumer-oriented as they respond to consumer demands. For example, Hormel, a large meat processor, was trying to sell "to a consumer who no longer existed" before realizing that consumers wanted convenience and prepared foods rather than fresh meat that had to be cooked for a meal (Marcotty). Processors increasingly target specific consumer groups with line extensions of successful products which are developed to please particular consumers' preferences and needs (Schiller). About 12,000 new grocery products were introduced in 1989, including about 9,200 new food products of which 1 to 10 percent were expected to succeed and only 8 to 9 percent were actually new or "significant" (Gorman; USDA, 1989; Friedman, p. 9D).

The microwave oven has opened new product categories for food manufacturers. New food product introductions for the microwave oven reached almost 1,000 in 1989, about 10 percent of new product introductions (Lingle; Dornblaser). In the future, improving the quality of microwave food will be extremely important for consumer acceptance. Product formulations for a growing number of microwave foods now include the use of specialized ingredients and the addition of flavors to duplicate flavors in conventionally-cooked foods. There is also an increasing use of active packaging such as susceptors to direct power to the crusts of products to make them brown and crisp.

Technological and institutional changes in the food industry can be attributed, at least in part, to "induced innovation" (Hayami and Ruttan). The theory of induced innovation says that technical innovations may result from a change in the relative prices of inputs to the production process and/or to shifts in consumer demand that change the ratio of product prices to costs of production. For example, because refined sugar has been more expensive than corn sweetener, soft drink producers have found ways to use corn sweetener to achieve the same flavor. This technological innovation was induced by a change in relative input costs.

The food industry is responding to changes in consumer attitudes and tastes with innovations in product characteristics. Consistent with long-term preferences for good health, many consumers want food with less fat and cholesterol. Some are willing to pay more for lower fat and cholesterol food. Consequently, many processors have stopped using animal fats or saturated vegetable fats such as palm and coconut oils. Fast food chains have cut down the fat in their hamburgers, started to use vegetable oils to fry foods, reduced the fat in milk shakes, and added salad entrees (Hume). The race has been on to develop fat-free ingredients which function like fats in food products. By mid-1990, some 150 new fat-free food products had been introduced including everything from Kraft's nonfat salad dressings to McDonald's muffins.

Consumer concerns about the impact of packaging on the environment are starting to induce innovation in the amount and type of packaging used for food. About 12 percent of the total solid waste now comes from food packaging (Dziezak). Trash generated by the fast food industry is being viewed as a major environmental problem.

The automation of food processing plants should significantly increase their efficiency in the future with "mega-factories" designed with "multiple product, flexible lines." (Gorman, p. 17). Automation can be viewed as an "induced innovation" in response to rising labor costs. For example, just-in-time inventory control, a Japanese method of materials requirement planning, is now being introduced into some segments of the U.S. food industry (*Baking and Snack Systems*). This method is based on market turnover. Products are produced just in time to replace those sold rather than on a schedule based on processing economies. The traditional U.S. method was to produce products in large runs off assembly lines, then hold the products in inventory until needed.

Food Wholesaling

The food wholesaling industry had sales of $417 billion in 1988 (USDA, 1989). Of this total, merchant wholesaler sales were the largest at $240 billion or 58 percent, manufacturers' sales branches were at $101 billion or 24 percent, and agents' and brokers' sales were $75 billion or 18 percent. Merchant wholesalers purchase and take ownership of the products.

Major changes in food wholesaling occurred during the 1980s as a result of mergers and acquisitions and the accompanying increase in aggregate concentration (Epps; USDA, 1989). The acquisition of local and regional distributors by large wholesalers is expected to continue. Increasingly, these firms will supply the financial and managerial services needed by independent retailers.

Electronic ordering is increasing the efficiency of wholesalers by enabling retailers to place orders directly using computers. Direct store delivery, which involves transporting products directly from producers or processors to retailers, is another development that increases efficiency in distribution. To minimize losses from product failures in the supermarket, wholesalers are charging "flop fees" to remove products from the warehouse when they have not met a minimum sales goal within three months (Therrien).

Food Store Retailing

The last step in the food marketing chain is the retailer who markets the food to individual consumers. Final sales by the food marketing system to consumers reached $638 billion in 1988 (USDA, 1989). Food retailing today includes two main segments: food stores and food service. Grocery food sales were $254 billion in 1988, with another $100 billion in sales of nonfood products. Food service sales were $210 billion. The distinction between these two markets is diminishing, however, with many food stores now including delicatessens and restaurants and many food service establishments offering take-out services and home delivery. In fact, TOTE food is the fastest growing market segment with sales predicted to grow at about 15 percent per year (Kiplinger Agriculture Letter).

It may be helpful to define the major components of the food store segment of food retailing. A food store can be either a grocery store or a specialized food store. Grocery stores are classified as supermarkets, convenience stores, or superettes (USDA, 1989). The average size of a conventional supermarket is 22,500 square feet. They carry about 12,000 items and in 1988 they had 42.8 percent of supermarket sales. The superstore, which is the format that often develops when conventional supermarkets are expanded and upgraded, ranges in size from 55,000 to 65,000 square feet in area. Superstores had over 30 percent of supermarket sales in 1988 (Heller; USDA, 1989).

Superwarehouse stores, warehouse stores, and limited assortment stores are called "no frills" stores because they stock and shelve products in case lots, offer low prices and few services, and have lower labor costs. For example, customers pack their own groceries and store personnel handle the products as little as possible (Heller; Williamson; USDA, 1989). Hypermarkets, which combine an economy supermarket and a discount department store, are the largest of the supermarkets (Heller; USDA, 1989). They range from 100,000 to more than 200,000 square feet in area.

The trend toward fewer food stores is resulting in greater average sales per store and substantial increases in the number of items stocked (Kohls and Uhl). New stores are getting bigger, averaging 43,830 square feet in 1986 compared to 29,056 in 1976 (Hamel). Large stores stock more nonfood items and have more flexibility in merchandising and ordering. In the future, more stores will use scanner and demographic data to tailor store inventories to the clientele of individual neighborhoods.

Customers increasingly demand service and choices in the supermarket. Working women have less time to shop and cook. Convenience for the consumer is one of the major goals of food retailing. Convenience has two components, ease of purchase and ease of preparation, both of which are important in the products and services offered by food retailers (Hammonds and Kozacik).

Retail food stores employed over 3 million workers in 1988 (USDA, 1989). Increases in the number of employees will continue because more food preparation and services must be provided by retailers in order to market more fresh and prepared foods. Consequently, labor productivity has been decreasing in food retailing even though several labor-saving technologies are being introduced.

In 1988, about 60 percent of grocery store sales went through optical scanning systems (USDA, 1989; Hamel). The advantages of scanners include faster checkouts and fewer errors. Scanning data and computer technology make it feasible for retailers to calculate direct product profitability for each item in a food store (Food Marketing Institute). Direct product profitability could develop into an important management tool. It involves calculation of the profitability of each item in a supermarket based on labor, space, inventory, transportation, and any other costs associated with the item. Because of the shortage of retail shelf space, supermarkets carefully control how much space they will give a product, and "they're demanding a growing list of fees and discounts to do so" (Schiller, p. 62).

Global Food Trends

Eating patterns around the world seem to be moving in directions that will make them increasingly similar across countries in the future. As incomes rise during economic development, typically the proportion of calories coming from cereals and starchy foods declines and the proportion from vegetable oils, fats, sugar, meat and other animal products rises. Although rice is still the major staple of the Japanese diet, per capita rice consumption is declining and meat consumption is increasing (OECD).

In the U.S. and Western Europe, the proportion of food from animal sources is leveling out. The U.S. trend of declining beef and increasing poultry consumption has also been observed in England (British Ministry of Agriculture). More generally, over the past 20 years the consumption of dairy products, sugar, potatoes, and grains has declined across Europe while meat held steady and vegetable consumption increased (Frank).

The globalization of food consumption patterns is occurring along two tracks. First, basic food commodities available and eaten in rich and poor countries are becoming more alike. Concerns regarding food safety and quality and environmental integrity are also spreading around the world, though more rapidly in advanced, well fed nations. Simultaneously, more diverse food preferences are developing within countries and a greater variety of foods is being purchased by individuals. International trade, telecommunications, travel, and an increasingly international media are fostering the homogenization of food consumption patterns and concerns across countries and the diversification of food preferences within countries. These food trends are occurring in the context of the more general globalization of world economies and mass culture (Lambert).

Furthermore, many of the same underlying demographic trends discussed in this paper are occurring elsewhere and pushing consumption patterns in similar directions. Rising incomes, shifting relative prices, aging populations, and women entering the labor force are widespread phenomena. Imports and exports of not just agricultural commodities but also of value-added food products can be expected to increase. Food is increasingly becoming a global business.

References

American Heart Association Nutrition Committee. 1988. *Dietary Guidelines for Healthy American Adults: A Statement for Physicians and Health Professionals*. Washington, DC: American Heart Association.

American Heart Association Nutrition Committee. 1990. What does just-in-time really mean? *Baking and Snack Systems* 12(6):18.

Batson, L. December 7, 1987. The new immigrants. *Minneapolis Star Tribune*.

Borra, S.T. November 3, 1988. A healthy diet with animal product options: What the food marketer and consumer are doing. Paper presented at the *Intercollegiate Nutrition Consortium FAN Forum*, University of Minnesota, St. Paul. Washington, DC: Food Marketing Institute.

British Ministry of Agriculture, Fisheries, and Food. 1989. Household food consumption and expenditure, 1988: Annual report of the National Food Survey Committee. London: British Ministry of Agriculture, Fisheries, and Food.

Burros, M. February 24, 1988. Women: Out of the house but not out of the kitchen. *New York Times*.

Burros, M. February 27, 1988. It's still women's work. *New York Times*.

Dornblaser, L. 1990. Take the 'F' train. *Prepared Foods New Products Annual* 159(8):70-74.

Dunham, D. July 1989. *Food Cost Review 1988.* Ag. Econ. Report No. 615. Washington, DC: Economic Research Service, U.S. Department of Agriculture.

Dziezak, J.D. 1990. Packaging waste management. *Food Technology* 44(7):98-101.

Epps, W. 1989. Food wholesaling. *National Food Review* 12(2):25-32.

Fisher, A.B. January 29, 1990. What consumers want in the 1990s. *Fortune,* pp.108-112.

Food Marketing Institute. 1984. Productivity. *1984 Food Marketing Facts.* Washington, DC: Food Marketing Institute.

Frank, J.D. March 1987. European community consumers food consumption and expenditure patterns. Bradford, England: Food Policy Research, University of Bradford.

Friedman, M. 1990. Twenty-five years and 98,900 new products later. *Prepared Foods New Products Annual* 159(8):23-25.

Gorman, B. 1990. New products for a new century. *Prepared Foods New Products Annual* 159(8):16-18; 47-52.

Hamel, R. 1989. Food fight. *American Demographics* 11(3):37-39, 60.

Hammonds, T.M. and J. Kozacik. 1988. Consumer preferences and the American farmer. *Forum for Applied Research and Public Policy* Summer:49-54.

Hayami, Y. and V.W. Ruttan. 1985. *Agricultural Development.* Baltimore, MD: Johns Hopkins University Press.

Heller, W.H. December 1986. A new look at store formats. *Prog. Grocer.,* pp.29-34.

Hiemstra, S.J. 1968. Food consumption, prices and expenditures. Ag. Econ. Report No. 138. Washington DC: Economic Research Service, U.S. Department of Agriculture.

Holusha, J. November 2, 1990. McDonalds announces end to foam packaging. *Minneapolis Star Tribune,* p.1A.

Hume, S. July 2, 1990. Fast food faces wary public. *Advertising Age.*

Iggers, J. May 9, 1987. Food marketers are told of emerging consumer trends. *Minneapolis Star Tribune.*

Kiplinger Agriculture Letter. October 7, 1988.

Kohls, R.L. and J.N. Uhl. 1990. *Marketing of Agricultural Products.* New York, NY: MacMillan.

Lambert, C. January-February 1990. Global spin. *Harvard Magazine,* pp.17-30.

Lazer and E.H. Shaw. September 1987. How older Americans spend their money. *American Demographics,* pp.36-41.

Levy, F. 1987. *Dollars and Dreams: The Changing American Income Distribution*. New York, NY: Russell Sage Foundation.

Levy, F. 1988. Incomes, families, and living standards. Pp. 108-153 in M. Baily *et al.*, eds., *American Living Standards: Threats and Challenges*. Washington, DC: The Brookings Institute.

Lingle, R. 1990. Packaging reminiscences: the year in review. *Prepared Foods New Prod. Ann.* 159(8):55-61.

Lubin, J.S. May 28, 1986. Rise in never-marrieds affects social customs and buying patterns. *Wall Street Journal*.

Marcotty, J. May 7, 1990. Survivor Hormel carving a new niche. *Minneapolis Star Tribune*, p.1D.

Mueller, W. 1989. Are Americans eating better? *American Demographics* 11(Feb):30-33.

National Restaurant Association. 1978. *N.R.A. Report* 21:1.

National Research Council Committee on Diet and Health. 1989. *Diet and Health*. Washington, DC: National Academy Press.

O'Reilly, B. September 25, 1989. New truths about staying healthy. *Fortune*, pp. 57-66.

Organization for Economic Cooperation and Development. 1986. *Food Consumption Statistics, 1973-1982*. Paris: OECD.

Pierson, T.R. and J.W. Allen. November 29, 1988. Directions in food marketing: Responding to consumers of tomorrow. Paper presented at the *Annual Agricultural Outlook Conference*. Washington, DC: U.S. Department of Agriculture.

Porubcansky, M.J. September 24, 1989. Yeltsin gives life in the U.S. rave reviews. *St. Paul Pioneer Press*, p.2A.

Putnam, J.J. 1990. Food consumption, prices and expenditures, 1967-88. Stat. Bul. No. 804. Washington, DC: Economic Research Service, U.S. Department of Agriculture.

Rich, S. July 26, 1987. Hyping the family's decline. *Washington Post*.

Schiller, Z. August 28, 1989. Stalking the new consumer: As markets fracture, P and G, and others sharpen micro marketing. *Business Week*, pp.54-62.

Smith, B.J. and R.D. Yonkers. February 1990. The importance of cereal to fluid milk consumption. Marketing Research Report 8, AE&RS 211. University Park: Pennsylvania State University.

Smith, B.J., R.O. Herrmann, and R.H. Warland. February 1990. Milk consumption and consumer concerns about fat, cholesterol, and calories. Marketing Research Report 7, AE&RS 210. University Park: Pennsylvania State University.

Spencer, G. 1986. Projections of the Hispanic population: 1983 to 2080. *Current Population Reports*. Series P-25, No. 995. Washington, DC: U.S. Government Printing Office.

Therrien, L. August 7, 1989. Want shelf space at the supermarket? Ante up. *Business Week*, pp. 60-61.

U.S. Department of Agriculture. April 1990. *Oil Crops, Situation, and Outlook Report.* OCS-25. Washington, DC: Economic Research Service, USDA.

U.S. Department of Agriculture. August 1989. *Food Marketing Review, 1988.* Ag. Econ. Report No. 614. Washington, DC: Economic Research Service, USDA.

U.S. Department of Commerce. 1990. *Statistical Abstract of the United States, 1990.* 110th Edition. Washington, DC: U.S. Govt. Printing Office.

U.S. Department of Commerce. September 30, 1988. *News.* CB88-157. Washington, DC: Bureau of the Census, USDC.

U.S. Department of Commerce. April 8, 1988. *News.* CB88-59. Washington, DC: Bureau of the Census, USDC.

U.S. Department of Commerce. December 2, 1987. *News.* CB87-188. Washington, DC: Bureau of the Census, USDC.

U.S. Department of Commerce. 1987. *Statistical Abstract of the United States, 1989.* 109th Edition. Washington, DC: U.S. Government Printing Office.

U.S. Department of Commerce. September 26, 1990. *News.* CB90-171. Washington, DC: Bureau of the Census, USDC.

U.S. Department of Health and Human Services. 1988. *The Surgeon General's Report on Nutrition and Health.* DHHS (PHS) Publ. No. 88-50210. Washington, DC: U.S. Government Printing Office.

U.S. Senate Select Committee on Nutrition and Human Needs. 1977. *Dietary Goals for the United States.* 2nd Edition. Washington, DC: U.S. Government Printing Office.

United States Fresh Fruit and Vegetable Association. 1988. *The Produce Industry Fact Book.* Alexandria, VA: United States Fresh Fruit and Vegetable Association.

Williamson, T.H. 1987. Superwarehouse markets: What they are, how they operate, why they succeed. *Cereal Foods World* 32(6):431-432.

11

American Food-Away-From-Home Consumption
Dorothy Z. Price, Stephen J. Hiemstra,
Vicki A. McCracken, and David W. Price

Introduction

In this chapter, the present status of American food-away-from-home consumption will first be discussed, available data sources will be reviewed, and research will be summarized. This will be followed by a discussion of the food service industry in the U.S. Finally, brief comments will be made in regard to the future of these issues.

Present Status of
Food-Away-From-Home Consumption

Total food expenditures in the U.S. increased 68 percent between 1980 and 1989, from $306.2 billion to $515.6 billion (Table 11.1). At the same time, disposable income increased 94 percent. As a result, the percentage of income spent for food declined from 16.0 to 13.8 percent. Between 1965 and 1988, real spending for food at home rose 29 percent, while spending for meals and snacks away from home increased 87 percent.

The proportion of total food expenditures for food obtained and eaten away from home has gradually increased over time (Figure 11.1). For example, in 1963 it was about 30 percent, but by 1987 it had increased to 44.5 percent. This increase has been attributed to higher disposable incomes and to the growing number of households without children. One may conjecture that changes in lifestyles have also contributed to the increase.

The demographics of eating away from home shows a sensitivity to both income and age of the household head (Table 11.2). The most notable effect is the low level of expenditures by retired persons. This effect is prominent at all income levels. Expenditures are high for households with heads less than 25 years of age. This may be due to the large number of single-person

Table 11.1. Food Expenditures in Relation to Disposable Income, 1970-89 (Billion Dollars).

Year	Food at Home	Food Away from Home	Total Food	Disposable Income
1970	77.5	39.6	117.1	715.6
1980	185.6	120.5	306.2	1,918.0
1987	254.1	203.9	457.9	3,194.7
1988	266.2	219.6	485.8	3,479.2
1989	243.8	230.8	515.6	3,725.3

Source: Food expenditure data from ERS, USDA; income data from National Income Accounts, Department of Commerce (Manchester).

households and the accompanying lack of children in these households. In addition, expenditures for food-away-from-home are higher for households with heads over 45-65 years than for households with heads 25-44 years of age.

However, about 40 percent of people aged 25-44 eat dinner out or buy a take-out meal one or two times per week; this is more than any other age group. The fact that they eat out often but have lower expenditures may

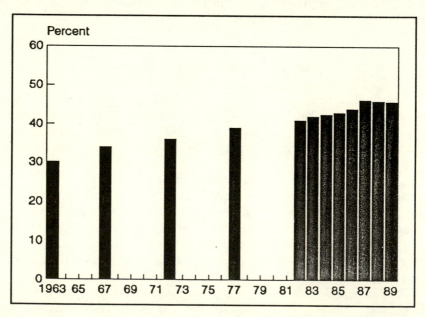

Figure 11.1. Food Expenditures Away From Home as Percent of Total Food Expenditures.
Source: Economic Research Seminar, 1990b.

Table 11.2. Per Capita Consumer Expenditures for Food-away-from-home by Age and Income.

Age of Household Head	Annual Household Income (Dollars)						
	Less than 5,000	5,000 to 9,999	10,000 to 14,999	15,000 to 19,999	20,000 to 29,999	30,000 to 39,999	40,000 and Over
(Years)	(Dollars)						
Less than 25	754	576	608	826	758	900	898
25 - 34	345	201	384	474	579	612	899
35 - 44	303	258	311	398	514	623	856
45 - 54	384	237	380	455	621	688	1,026
55 - 64	283	414	466	493	673	848	1,028
65 - 74	277	388	476	523	701	747	1,069
75 +	183	270	479	462	466	656	823

Source: Bureau of Statistics, Consumer Expenditure Survey, 1988; National Restaurant Assn.

relate to food being purchased at fast food establishments -- a tendency prevalent in households with children.

Several studies have focused on food-away-from-home consumption at different income levels. One study based on the 1985 Continuing Survey of Food Intakes by Individuals (CSFII) conducted by the U.S. Department of Agriculture's Human Nutrition Information Service (HNIS) looked at women between the ages of 19 and 50 using four consecutive days of dietary information. (The sample included 220 low income, 364 middle income, and 384 high income women). Overall, there was more away-from-home consumption as income increased, with 19 percent having food or drink away from home each of the four days and 12 percent having no food-away-from-home consumption during this time period (Table 11.3). In general, it is obvious that people in the U.S. are involved in away-from-home food consumption, regardless of income level.

Consumers in the United States have become increasingly aware of and concerned about the amounts of fat, cholesterol, sugar, sodium, and fiber in their food diet. Also of concern is the availability of certain vitamins and minerals in the foods they consume. This trend toward increased nutritional interest is supported by the actions of food producers, processors, and eating establishments who currently devote a substantial portion of their advertising budget to stress the nutritional quality of their food products, with the goal of selling their products to consumers. In addition, in the past several years, concerns about food safety have intensified.

Coupled with the increased nutritional and food safety concerns of consumers are other socioeconomic and demographic trends which directly impact the quantity of food consumed and the quality, variety, and source of

Table 11.3. Prevalence of Eating Away from Home by Women, 1985-86 (Percent of Individuals).

	Number of Days Food Away Reported				
	0	1	2	3	4
All Women	12	20	23	26	19
Income Group					
Low	24	27	23	21	5
Middle	14	17	27	24	19
High	5	14	21	32	28

Source: Family Economics Review, No. 1, 1988.

foods in the diets of U.S. consumers. In particular, average household size has been falling (down from 3.33 persons in 1960 to 2.63 in 1990); the percentage of the population in the older age categories has been increasing, with those 65 years of age and older constituting 13 percent of the population in 1990; and nontraditional household types, particularly single-person and single-parent households, have been growing in numbers (U.S. Department of Commerce, 1990). Also important is the trend toward multiple-wage-earner households. In 1960, 31 percent of married women (with spouses present) were working outside of the home but by 1987 this figure had increased to about 56 percent (U.S. Department of Commerce, 1988). The location of residence and racial and ethnic mix of the population, as well as per capita income, have been changing.

These changes have been accompanied by alterations in food eating patterns, including not only what foods they eat but also when, where, and with whom this food is eaten (Reese and Mickle). The food service market (eating out) has been growing more rapidly than the off-premise food market (at home), with the fast-food industry experiencing the greatest growth. Eating out accounted for 45 percent of all food dollars in 1989, up from 24 percent in 1954. In terms of quantity, the share of food quantities eaten out is considerably less than the share of total dollars, 32 percent in 1989 and 22 percent in 1954. This difference (between dollar and quantity shares) is due to the higher margins in the food service market (Manchester, 1991).

This substitution of expenditures on food-away-from-home (FAFH) for food at home (FAH) reflects an increased demand for marketing services that reduce preparation and consumption time associated with eating and directly affects the marketing channels and institutions with which producers, food processors, shippers, and commodity specialists must deal (O'Rourke). Traditionally, a small number of food items accounted for the majority of food purchases away from home. In recent years, this has changed toward more variety in the foods obtained from the FAFH sector. Within the FAH market, a large number of convenience foods have appeared, such as canned and frozen entrees, vegetables, and salads; ready-to-eat desserts; and ready-to-use fresh fruits and vegetables. Hence certain individuals and households demanding this time savings component of food preparation may be substituting consumption of convenience foods at home for eating out. These changes in the structure of the food sector will likely continue to impact the marketing, distribution, retailing, and food service systems as well as the nutritional status of the consumer. Identifying and understanding the motivating factors affecting consumer behavior is the key to rapid and efficient adjustments to changing consumer demands on the food system.

Food-away-from-home is extremely varied with respect to cost, quality, and services provided. It varies from meals eaten at restaurants with complete table service to fast food establishments with no table service. Forty-two percent of the food and drink sales in 1988 was at restaurants while 29 percent was at fast food establishments (Table 11.4). Other eating places are quite varied. They include cafeterias, vending machines, bars and taverns, and institutional food service.

There are a number of reasons for eating away from home. Haines *et al.*'s list of reasons for eating out includes: (1) it is fun, (2) people are too busy

Table 11.4. Estimated Food and Drink Sales, 1988.

	Sales	
Type of Establishment	($1,000)	(Percent)
Restaurants, lunchrooms, lodging places, retail host restaurants	89,065,557	42.2
Limited-menu restaurants, refreshment places (fast-food)	61,397,191	29.1
Bars and taverns	8,899,046	4.2
Cafeterias	3,960,224	1.9
Caterers	2,689,131	1.3
Recreation and sports	2,367,322	1.1
Vending and non-store retailers	4,937,911	2.3
Ice cream, frozen custard stands	1,894,213	0.9
Food contractors	12,071,146	5.7
Institutional foodservice[1]	23,562,999	11.2
Total	210,844,740	99.9

Source: Adapted from National Restaurant Association, "Restaurants USA," December 1990, p. 18.
[1]Business, educational, governmental, or institutional organizations that operate their own food services.

to prepare a meal, and (3) eating out accompanies doing something else, such as the business luncheon. Economists have emphasized the convenience aspect and have used household production theory as a framework for their analyses. With the microwave oven and frozen entrees, the convenience aspect can be obtained at home. Home delivery also provides convenience similar to that obtained in restaurants. Thus, it is important to consider other factors when attempting to explain why people eat out.

One factor which is important in explaining why consumers choose to eat out is the different atmosphere provided by a restaurant. Consumers derive utility from eating at places outside the home. The type of atmosphere desired varies with such factors as age, sex, and social class. Young children may prefer the atmosphere provided by many of the fast food outlets. A working class male may prefer the atmosphere of the local cafe, while the professional may prefer a more "elegant" atmosphere.

Other people who eat away from home include workers who eat lunch out as a convenience. The brown bag lunch prepared from home food supplies would be an important substitute. Consumers eat out frequently while traveling. The substitutes for this are limited. Many birthdays, anniversaries, etc. are celebrated by eating out. An elegant meal at home or at a friend's home may be a substitute. The type of atmosphere and service desired depends on the purpose of eating out.

Another dimension of the food-away-from-home market is ethnic food. The most popular ethnic foods in the U.S. are Chinese, Italian, and Mexican. A National Restaurant Association study reports that 78 percent of the U.S. population have tried Chinese food at restaurants, 76 percent have tried Italian, and 74 percent have tried Mexican food. Only 36 percent have tried Japanese food. This study reports that interest in ethnic food is increasing. Between 1986 and 1989 the traffic in Asian restaurants increased by 12 percent, as compared to a 6 percent increase for the industry as a whole.

The type of meal eaten away from home also has important implications for demand analysis. The 1988 NPD CREST Annual Household Report shows that breakfast accounted for only 9.4 percent of restaurant traffic but that this is increasing. Traffic for lunch and dinner was 36 and 41 percent, respectively, of total traffic. The study also showed that the five most important breakfast items were eggs, breakfast sandwiches, pancakes/waffles, sausage, and bacon.

The foods eaten away from home differ from those eaten at home. The individual intake portion of the USDA's Nationwide Food Consumption Survey lists quantities of total and away-from-home consumption. The percent consumed away from home varies by product (Table 11.5). Many beverages, seafood, white potatoes, and frozen desserts have the largest proportions consumed away from home. Most fruits and vegetables, cheese, eggs, milk, cereals, and pasta have the lowest. It should be noted that away-from-home

Table 11.5. Quantity of Selected Foods Consumed Away from Home in the Western Region of the U.S. (Percent).

Food Item	Percent Away from Home
Soft drinks	33.1
Alcoholic beverages	27.9
Mixtures (mainly meat)	26.9
Seafood	25.0
White potatoes	22.6
Frozen desserts, cream	21.7
Mixtures (mainly grain)	20.0
Beef	19.3
Sugars, sweets	19.2
Coffee	18.6
Bakery products (other than bread, rolls, and biscuits)	18.4
Fats and oils	16.7
Poultry	16.7
Other vegetables	16.3
Bread, rolls, biscuits	15.8
Franks, luncheon meats, sausage	14.3
Legumes, nuts, seeds	13.8
Pork	12.5
Dark green vegetables	12.5
Fluid milk	12.2
Tea	12.1
Tomatoes	11.1
Cheese	10.5
Eggs	10.3
Non-citrus fruit juice	8.0
Citrus fruit juice	7.0
Cereals, pasta	5.9

Source: USDA 1977-78 NFCS Food and Nutrient Intake: Individuals in Four Regions.

cheese and pasta consumption may actually be much higher since these products are included in the "mixtures" food categories.

Table 11.6 indicates the types of foods eaten away from home by income level. Meats, carbonated soft drinks, and alcoholic beverages are relatively high while milk is infrequently consumed away from home regardless of income level.

The different away-from-home diet has two major implications when compared to the at-home diet. First, producers of products that are consumed in low proportions away from home are concerned with the demand for their products. Second, the nutritional quality of the away-from-home diet is in question. The USDA Nationwide Food Consumption Survey also lists the intake of nutrients for total and away-from-home consumption. The percent of nutrients from away-from-home consumption is shown in Table 11.7. The nutritional quality of the diet is often measured as the intake of a particular nutrient in relation to the intake of total energy. These data show the away-from-home diet to be higher in fat and lower in vitamins and minerals than the at-home diet.

Studies by Bunch, Haines *et al.*, and Enns and Guenther also show the nutritional quality of the diet to be lower for food-away-from-home than for at-home food. These and other nutritional concerns such as high cholesterol in the away-from-home diet have led the away-from-home food industry to examine the nutritional content of its food.

Table 11.6. Contributions of Food Obtained and Eaten Away from Home to Total Food Intake (Percent of Intake).

Food Item	Income		
	Low	Middle	High
Meat, poultry, and fish	20	29	38
Meat mixtures	22	32	41
Beef	19	24	32
Poultry	22	29	41
Milk and milk products	12	13	17
Fluid milk	8	6	9
Vegetables	16	26	32
Fruits	11	12	18
Grain products	12	23	30
Grain mixtures	10	27	34
Beverages	21	30	37
Coffee	14	22	47
Carbonated soft drinks	36	41	47
Alcoholic beverages	34	38	49

Source: Family Economics Review, No. 1, 1988.

Table 11.7. Nutrients Consumed in Food-away-from-home: Western Region of the U.S. (Percent).

Nutrient	Percent Away From Home
Fat	18.1
Total energy	17.9
Protein	17.5
Carbohydrates	17.5
Phosphorous	16.7
Niacin	16.6
Iron	15.9
Vitamin B12	15.9
Magnesium	15.8
Calcium	15.6
Riboflavin	15.4
Vitamin B6	15.3
Thiamin	15.1
Vitamin A	12.4
Vitamin C	12.4

Source: Adapted from National Restaurant Association, "Restaurants USA," December 1990, p. 18.

Available Data Sources

A wide variety of data series have been designed, developed, and maintained by public and private sources (Raunikar and Huang, Chapter 2). Most of these data series were not developed with demand analysis in mind, particularly not for food away-from-home (FAFH) demand analysis. Also, demand analysts are often more concerned with their theoretical models and estimation techniques than with their data, although data are equally important to their results (Manchester, 1990). The focus in this section is on the data that are available and used by economists in FAFH studies.

Food demand analysis is based on either time-series or cross-section data or a combination of time-series and cross-section data (panel data). Time-series data are usually of an aggregate nature (e.g., total value for the United States) and are collected regularly at various time intervals (e.g., annual or by quarters), while cross-section data typically refers to observations on individual units such as individuals or households at approximately a single-point in time. Household consumer panel data usually consist of detailed cross-section information about individual or household characteristics, collected at multiple points over time. A true panel is one in which the group of households or individuals is followed over time (except for replacements as dropouts occur). Some surveys, however, have a prearranged rotation of households or individuals in and out of the panel. Data used in demand analysis can be further categorized by whether it was collected by a public agency (e.g., government or university) or by a private firm. The most frequently used data type in FAFH studies is from a public data system and is either cross-section or panel data. However, other types are used as can be seen in the following discussion of specific data sources.

Three major food expenditures time series data sets include measures of annual aggregate U.S. FAFH expenditures (Manchester, 1990). The first series, total expenditures, is available from the U.S. Department of Agriculture's Economic Research Service (ERS). Total expenditures cover all human food, both purchased (with money or food stamps) and in-kind (donated, home-produced, and sportfish and game). This data series includes annual data back to 1889. The second series, personal consumption expenditures, is available from U.S. Department of Commerce's Bureau of Economic Analysis (BEA). Personal expenditures for food includes expenditures paid out of personal income for human food, pet food, animal feed, and ice. This series includes food stamps and food produced and consumed on the same farm and includes data back to 1929. The third data series, constructed from the Continuing Consumer Expenditures Survey (CCES), is available from the U.S. Department of Labor's Bureau of Labor Statistics (BLS). The CCES includes only human food purchased by families and individuals with money or food stamps. Home production, donations, and gifts and consumption by military families are excluded. These data have been available only since 1980. The CCES will be discussed further later because it and earlier versions (i.e. the CES) are also frequently in cross-sectional type analyses.

Data on actual ingestion of and expenditures on FAFH are available only from periodic surveys of households and individuals. Most economic-based FAFH analyses have utilized data from national consumer surveys conducted either by the U.S. Department of Agriculture or the U.S. Department of Labor's BLS. The U.S. Department of Agriculture conducts a National Food Consumption Survey (NFCS) every 10 years with the most recent one conducted in 1987-88. Earlier versions had been used in a number of the FAFH studies discussed later in this paper. These surveys are designed to describe food consumption behavior and to assess the nutritional content of the U.S. diet, but are not specifically for demand analysis. The survey is a multistage area probability sample of the defined population, namely, private households in the 48 contiguous states and individuals in those households. Households and individuals of all income levels (basic survey) and with incomes consistent with eligibility for the Food Stamp Program (low-income survey) are usually surveyed. Information is collected concerning food used from home food supplies (and a measure of the number of and expenditures on meals consumed away from home) during one week by the entire household and food ingested by individual household members at home and away from home for three consecutive days. Household and individual socioeconomic and demographic information is also collected. Since 1985, continuous surveys of food intakes (CSFII, 1985 and 1986) for subgroups of U.S. individual households have been conducted on a more frequent basis. Their primary purpose is to provide timely information on diets of population groups of concern (e.g., women 19-50 years of age and their children 1-5 years) and to provide the basis for assessing "usual" diets by measuring food intakes of respondents from six 24-hour recalls collected at about 2-month intervals. The intake information includes food ingested at home and away from home. Similar CSFIIs are being conducted annually from 1989 to 1996.

The BLS Consumer Expenditures Surveys (CES), conducted at about 10-year intervals between 1888 and 1979, are another group of household surveys with national coverage used in FAFH analyses. The 1972-73 CES was the last of the large-scale periodic surveys. The main purpose of the CES was to obtain expenditure information on various goods and services in order to develop appropriate weights for the Consumer Price Index. In 1979, continuous CES (CCES) were initiated on a smaller group of households (with a pre-arranged rotation of households in and out of the panel). Data for the CES and CCES are obtained from a national probability sample of households designed to represent the civilian noninstitutionalized population and a portion of the institutionalized population (e.g., students in college dormitories). Both the CES and the CCES consist of two parts, an interview recall survey and a diary record survey, each with a different data collection technique and sample. Detailed household socio-economic and demographic information is also collected. The CES and CCES provide comprehensive data on all spending categories (food and nonfood), but do not provide as much detail for individual food products as do the NFCS surveys. The focus of the CES and CCES is on expenditure rather than quantity used. One category of expenditures is for FAFH. This variable has been used in a number of FAFH analyses. Manchester (1990) provides a detailed discussion of the differences in the NFCS and CES measures of FAFH consumption and expenditures.

Consumer panel data that contain information used in FAFH analyses are also collected by a number of other public (state universities) and private groups (Raunikar and Huang, Chapter 2). The Survey Research Center in the Institute of Social Research of the University of Michigan maintains a Panel Study of Income Dynamics (PSID) which contains a variety of economic information, including a measure of expenditures on FAFH. This panel includes approximately 5,000-7,000 households that have been interviewed about attitudes, behavior, and economic status annually since 1968. The size of the panel changes as the original households dissolve and as new households form.

National Purchase Diary Research (NPDR) is a private market research firm that maintains household panels and supplies (on a fee basis) data to individual firms desiring information on specific product markets.   One specialized panel of NPDR funded by the food service industry is known as CREST (Consumer Reports on Eating Share Trends).   This survey is designed to track expenditures in the commercial segment of the food service industry and includes information by type and classification of restaurant and by meal or snack period.   Approximately 10,000 families and 2,800 non-family households representing demographic patterns in the United States are selected to participate in the survey.   Households record every meal and snack experience during a particular two-week period for each of the four quarters of the year.   Detailed entries are required for meals eaten or purchased away from home in establishments such as restaurants, hotels and motels, fast-food/drive-in places, delicatessens, refreshment stand carryouts, coffee shops, donut shops, ice cream shops, or eating places inside variety stores or other retail stores.   Information is not collected on meals eaten at schools, hospitals, colleges, or other institutional feeding places.   Socio-economic and demographic information on the households is also collected.   One advantage of the CREST data is the vast detail.   A problem, however, in population representation, is a lower response rate and higher attrition of certain types of households (e.g., black, single-person, and low-income households).   The CREST data are also limited by failure to contain information on food-at-home (FAH) expenditures or foods consumed at school and other institutional feeding places (Raunikar and Huang, Chapter 2).   Another limitation of the CREST data for academic researchers is their cost.

Summary of Research

Numerous studies relate various socio-economic and demographic variables to total at-home food expenditures and expenditures on (and consumption of) various groups of foods and specific commodities. (These are discussed in detail in another paper.) These studies show income and household size and composition to be important variables affecting at-home food decisions. Other variables typically found to affect at-home food consumption are: region of the United States, city size, food stamp program participation, education of the homemaker or other household head, assets, family life cycle, and season of the year. Other researchers have estimated the relationship between many of the same socio-economic and demographic variables and household intake of selected nutrients from foods consumed at home (e.g., Adrian and Daniel), others have analyzed the demand for FAH based on the characteristics of the products (e.g., Ladd and Suvannunt; Prato and Bagali; Gorman; Pudney, 1976, 1978, 1981a, 1981b; and Boyle, Gorman, and Pudney), and still others have taken a hedonic approach to analyzing the demand for FAH (e.g., LaFrance, Hagar, Lenz, and Kim). These and other studies provide a framework within which to specify at-home food consumption models. They are not, however, as useful in specifying models which differentiate between at-home and away-from-home consumption.

Much of the literature recognizing the importance of FAFH has been descriptive rather than analytically economic (e.g., LeBovit; Manchester; Rogers and Green; Van Dress). Another related group of studies focuses more on the food service industry itself with respect to structure, reasons for growth, consumer attitudes, and the like. These studies provide background information for the final section of this chapter on the food service industry.

Other studies have looked at FAFH expenditures as a single aggregate category within the context of consumer eating habits (e.g., Houthakker and Taylor; Lee and Phillips; Raunikar; Salathe; Smallwood and Blaylock; Smallwood, Baylock, and Zellner; Haidacher *et al.*; Huang and Raunikar; Lee and Brown). In the work of Huang and Raunikar, total household income was decomposed into discretionary income and consigned income (defined as the fixed portion of disposable income over which the household has no control for adjustments). They found that consigned income had a negative influence on household food expenditures, with the influence being stronger for FAFH than for FAH, and concluded that as consigned income increased there was a tendency to substitute FAH expenditures for FAFH expenditures.

In the study by Lee and Brown, the emphasis was on the household's decision of whether to eat out and the factors affecting consequent away-from-home and at-home food expenditures. Lee and Brown's statistical model accounted for the interrelated decisions for food consumption at home and away from home. They found that the decision to eat away from home was positively affected by income while the amount spent on FAFH was affected by income (positively) but only at higher levels of income. Food expenditures at home were also affected by income only at higher income levels and if the household also had consumed FAFH. If the household had not consumed FAFH, then FAH expenditures were positively affected by income at all income levels. These results point out the importance of simultaneously modelling at-home and away-from-home food decisions.

Another related group of studies has also treated FAFH expenditures as a single aggregate category but within the broader context of total consumer market good expenditures (e.g., Mann; Lamm; Ketkar and Cho; Goddard, 1983; and Chern and Lee). Chern and Lee used a complete demand system methodology to analyze FAH and FAFH expenditure decisions along with other nondurable goods and services and durable goods decisions. They used both parametric and nonparametric analyses to address the validity of particular groupings of goods and their implied demand structure. In light of conflicting results from these analyses, they concluded that the estimation results from a one-stage budgeting model are more dependable than from a model that assumes a two-stage decision process.

Two other studies dealing with FAFH expenditures within the context of other aggregate expenditures decisions were conducted by Demousis and

Wohlgenant and Soberon-Ferrer and Dardis. Demousis and Wohlgenant considered aggregate FAFH decisions within the broad context of total consumer expenditures allocation and labor supply decisions. Soberon-Ferrer and Dardis investigated factors influencing household expenditures for services in the United States, with their dependent variables being total household service expenditures and expenditures on major service categories such as child care, clothing care, domestic services, personal care, and FAFH.

Recent economic literature has stressed the importance of viewing the household as both a producing and consuming unit. This "household production theory" stresses the importance of accounting for time constraints in the household's decision process. A number of studies of the FAFH market have drawn upon this theory to develop models for empirical analyses. Prochaska and Schrimper concluded that the value of the homemaker's time, as well as household size and the presence of small children, were important factors affecting food consumption reflected through the number of household meals consumed out and total household expenditures on FAFH. Prochaska and Schrimper used the employed homemaker's (the female adult in the household) market wage rate and an exogenously estimated wage rate for the nonemployed homemaker as the measure of the household's value of time. While their procedure of imputing wages for nonemployed homemakers has been criticized, they laid the foundation for other, more sophisticated studies of the FAFH market.

Redman, closely following the work of Prochaska and Schrimper, found that household income had a positive effect on FAFH expenditures while household size had a negative effect. In contrast to other studies, Redman's model failed to establish a significant relationship between FAFH expenditures and the household time variable (a simple employment dummy variable) in a sample that included both married and unmarried females. Kinsey also analyzed the effect of labor-force participation of wives on FAFH expenditures. Based on the observation that the average wage rate of full-time and part-time working wives was nearly the same but their labor force time varied greatly, her empirical model included a dummy variable which differentiated full-time working wives from other wives. Contrary to the hypothesis of household production theory, Kinsey found that income earned by full-time working wives did not increase the household's marginal propensity to consume FAFH, but income from other sources did. Her results indicated, however, that income earned by part-time working wives increased the household's marginal propensity to consume FAFH.

Other studies have used a similar dummy variable to quantify the value of time in FAFH demand or expenditure models with varying degrees of success (e.g., Ortiz, MacDonald, Ackerman, and Goebel; Derrick, Dardis, and Lehfeld; Goebel and Hennon; Kolodosky; and Yang, 1988). Yang's sample referred to a select portion of the U.S. population, namely low income women 19-50 years old and their children 1-5 years old. Yang's results were generally similar (in terms of the direction of the relationships) to those obtained from studies of the general U.S. population. In particular, household income and education level and employment status of the homemaker had a positive impact on FAFH expenditures, while food stamp participation and the presence of young children had a negative impact on eating out.

Fletcher and McCracken and Brandt (1987 and 1990) accounted for the value of time for the household in their FAFH models by a potential wage estimated using the Heckman two-step procedure. These studies confirm the positive relationship between total household expenditures on FAFH and household time value as suggested by household production theory, after controlling for the effect of income, household size and composition, and other household variables.

In summary, these studies of total household expenditures on FAFH have typically included variables measuring characteristics of the individual homemaker head such as age, education level, race or ethnic group, employment status, and value of time; variables measuring household characteristics such as income (total and disaggregated by source of income), food stamp participation, and household size and composition; and variables measuring location of residence of the household, such as urbanization and region. The results of the various studies differ in certain respects, but there are many similarities. Many of the dissimilarities are likely the result of the different data sets (and subsets of the data) and the different estimation procedures, as well as the different empirical measures of the theoretical variables used in the models.

Kinsey hypothesized that "households with two full-time workers...might frequent limited-menu, family-type, or fast-food restaurants, ... or substitute food that can be prepared quickly at home" (p. 18). Her data did not allow her to investigate this link between household time and FAFH expenditures at different types of eating places or purchase of convenience food for consumption at home. The conclusions of Capps, Tedford, and Havlicek support Kinsey's latter hypothesis concerning convenience foods. Concerning the former hypothesis, McCracken and Brandt (1987 and 1990) and Haines (1983) analyzed the importance of socio-economic and demographic factors on expenditures on FAFH in different types of food facilities: full-service restaurants, fast-food establishments, and other commercial facilities (e.g., school or work cafeterias). McCracken and Brandt hypothesized that the increased value of household time would increase expenditures at fast-food facilities more than at time-intensive full-service restaurants. Their results confirm their hypothesis, indicating that the value of time had a stronger effect on fast-food expenditures than on restaurant expenditures. The value of the homemaker's time was more important than household income in determining fast-food expenditures.

Limited research focuses on consumption of or expenditures on specific commodities away from home. McCracken (1984) and McCracken and

Brandt (1986) used probit analysis to identify factors that affected the probability that a household consumed items in major food groups (dairy products, meat/meat products, egg/egg mixtures, grain products, fruits, and vegetables) while eating out. Not only were there substantial differences in the frequency in which these products were consumed in the FAFH market, the results suggest regional, race, and/or age differences in these demand relationships. McCracken also conducted a detailed analysis of consumer demand for specific commodities away from home, including meat (1986), seafood (1987), and potatoes (1990). Smith related various characteristics of individuals (including taste and preference factors) to the likelihood of drinking milk away from home relative to drinking milk at home.

A new data source being developed at Purdue University makes use of input-output data to trace expenditures for food-away-from-home back to the individual food processing industries from which it originated. This methodology will be used to measure impacts on agricultural commodity groups from changes in food-away-from-home expenditures from 1977 to 1985.

Ries, Kline, and Weaver recently analyzed the effect of eating out at commercial establishments on nutritional adequacy by examining the frequency of eating out, the nutritive value of FAH and FAFH, and the nutritional adequacy of the individual. Despite their finding that the nutrient density of FAFH was lower than FAH, they concluded that for the typical individual the frequency of eating out was low enough not to significantly influence dietary adequacy. They did recognize that there might be adequacy problems with selected nutrients for some types of individuals.

Growth and Maturity
of Foodservice Industry

Over the past several decades, the foodservice industry has been the most dynamic sector of the retail food business. It has tended to increase in size about in proportion with consumer incomes, even though the overall demand for food tends to increase at a much slower rate than income, in response to Engel's Law. As a result, food for use at home has absorbed the entire decline relative to income. Recent years, however, have witnessed a slowdown in growth of demand for food-away-from-home.

Spending increases for total food -- up 68 percent since 1980 -- are due to a faster rate of increase for foodservice than for food purchased for use at home (Manchester, 1991). Foodservice increased a total of 92 percent in comparison with 53 percent for food at home. These trends, which have persisted for many years, resulted in foodservice accounting for 45 percent of total food spending in 1989, up from 39 percent in 1980 and only 34 percent in 1970. These trends have also resulted in food at home dropping as a share of income at the same time as foodservice nearly maintained its share of income (Table 11.8) implying an income elasticity of nearly 1.0.

Table 11.8. Spending Increases for Food at Home and Foodservice (Percent of Income).

Year	Food at Home	Foodservice
1970	10.8	5.5
1980	9.7	6.3
1987	8.0	6.4
1988	7.7	6.3
1989	7.6	6.2

Source: Manchester, 1991.

However, this situation reversed slightly in the most recent year of the comparison. In 1989, foodservice spending increased only 5.1 percent compared with 7.0 percent for food at home. The previous year, foodservice had increased 7.9 percent in comparison with 4.8 percent for food at home. Disposable personal income gains also declined. Foodservice slipped in relation to total food spending from 45.2 percent of the total in 1988 to 44.8 in 1989. It is not certain at this time whether the slowdown in foodservice was due to a downward shift in demand or to cyclical factors. It was not caused by relative prices; prices for food at home increased faster than for foodservice (6.6 vs. 4.7 percent).

While spending for food-away-from-home recently has accounted for about 45 percent of total spending for food, the share of U.S. total food produced and marketed for away from home use was only about 32 percent (Manchester, 1991). The farm value of a consumer's dollar was 30 percent at retail food stores in 1987, compared with 17 percent at foodservice establishments (ERS, 1988). (This percentage remained unchanged through 1990.) The value of foodservice alone accounts for about 60 percent of the foodservice dollar. Further, only about 83 percent of food spending goes for U.S. farm foods. The balance of food spending goes for imported foods and foods, such as seafood, that do not originate on U.S. farms.

The 1989 slowdown in foodservice appears to have continued into 1990 and become more noticeable in view of the slowdown in the general economy. The industry slowdown has affected the large fast food chains as well as table service restaurants. Many of the fast food operations recently have reduced their prices quite substantially in an attempt to increase market share. Some analysts regard the fast food segment of the industry as an advanced indicator of trends in the general economy.

Structure of the Foodservice Industry

The foodservice industry is characterized by a large number of relatively small companies, many of which operate multiple units, many of those being franchised. However, the industry is becoming more concentrated, due primarily to horizontal expansion to larger firms. The structure of the industry from the demand side of the industry differs substantially from its supply side which faces concentrated food distributors and some factor markets.

Franchising

Franchising among restaurants provides a unique industry alternative for food retailing or other food industries and it has implications for the assessment of industry concentration.   Franchising involves shared management and financing on the basis of a contractual agreement rather than ownership. Franchises are long-term relationships which have been used extensively to facilitate growth and expansion in the foodservice industry with relatively little financial obligation.

Franchised restaurant operations accounted for $76.5 billion in sales in 1990, up about 11 percent from a year earlier and nearly three times the $27.9 billion in 1980 (Bureau of Industrial Economics and International Franchise Association).   Franchising is the most rapidly expanding segment of the industry, accounting for over 43 percent of total sales of eating places in 1988. Franchised operations tend to be larger establishments than their independent counterparts, so the dollar impacts are greater than the number of operations would suggest.

About 71 percent of franchised operations were franchisee owned and 29 percent were company owned in 1990. The ownership question is of interest for many reasons, including its effect on the usual measurement of industry concentration. Concentration ratios, which often are used as one method of assessing the nature of competition in an industry, typically are computed only on the basis of owned operations and therefore completely exclude franchising as a method of concentrating management and operational control.

Market Concentration

There were some 731,724 foodservice establishments in the U.S. in 1988, of which about 490,383 were separate, commercial eating and drinking places (Table 11.9). The balance was composed of noncommercial operations or complementary units of commercial establishments, such as hotels, hospitals, schools, or department stores. The number of companies with paid employees totaled only 191,798 in 1988, due to the large number both of multi-unit operations and independents with no paid employees.

National concentration of sales into fewer firms has been growing significantly in the foodservice industry, even with no regard for the impacts of franchising on the concentration of management. In 1987, 8.1 percent of the businesses were owned by the four largest firms, up from 4.5 percent 10 years earlier. The 20 largest firms had 17.0 percent of the businesses in 1987, compared with 12.4 percent a decade earlier (Bureau of the Census).

Table 11.9. Foodservice Establishments by Industry Segment in 1982, 1985, and 1988 (Number).

Industry Segment	1982	1985	1988[1]
Commercial			
Separate eating places	122,851	125,502	125,042
Restaurants, lunchrooms	117,119	124,809	127,930
Fast-food outlets	61,029	5,388	4,312
Cafeterias	300,999	255,699	257,284
Total			
Lodging places	24,448	22,613	26,252
Retail hosts	57,578	56,005	54,008
Recreation, entertainment	34,093	34,910	36,660
Separate drinking places	44,478	40,642	37,113
Commercial feeding total	410,155	409,869	411,317
Noncommercial			
Education	91,300	89,424	89,692
Elementary, secondary	3,280	3,299	3,511
Colleges, universities	2,966	3,076	3,240
Other education	97,546	95,799	96,443
Total			
Military services			
Troop feeding	1,387	1,290	1,217
Clubs, exchanges	2,431	1,980	1,904
Total	3,818	3,270	3,121
Plants, office buildings	15,414	15,963	17,250
Hospitals	6,915	6,835	6,772
Care facilities	26,817	29,711	31,945
Vending	3,608	3,535	3,453
Transportation	664	640	594
Associations	19,272	19,450	19,070
Correctional facilities	7,031	7,204	7,282
Child day-care centers	70,679	88,410	96,918
Elderly feeding programs	13,246	14,068	20,000
Other	16,159	17,101	17,767
Noncommercial feeding total	281,169	301,986	320,461
Total	691,324	711,855	731,724

Source: National Agricultural Statistics Service.
[1]Preliminary.

Based on systemwide sales (which includes franchised operations), the top 4 firms accounted for about 15.3 percent of national total eating place sales in 1980, compared with 18.9 percent in 1987. The largest 20 firms accounted for about 31 percent of systemwide sales in 1980, compared with 35 percent in 1987 (Narayanan). While concentration in foodservice has been growing significantly, the level of concentration is still much less than in other segments of the food industry, unless one includes franchised operations. On that basis, concentration is comparable with that in food retailing but less than that in wholesaling and in many food processing or manufacturing industries (Table 11.10).

Separate wholesale industry data are not available for foodservice distributors and wholesale clubs which market to the foodservice industry, but they are believed to be more concentrated than for the general line wholesalers noted above.

These data relate to total national markets for food. However, the relevant market for the demand side of the foodservice business is more likely to be local than national. Concentration of sales is expected to be much higher in local markets. About three-fourths of the customers of fast food operations typically are believed to be willing to drive no more than about three miles, or 10 minutes, to obtain service. Table service restaurants draw customers from a larger radius but seldom from more than 10 or 20 miles. In both cases, the relevant market is quite small.

Horizontal and conglomerate concentration has been increasing significantly, both through mergers and internal growth. Sizable recent mergers include Grand Metropolitan acquiring Burger King (as a part of Pillsbury, $4.9 billion) and Coniston Partners acquiring Denny's (as a part of TW Services, $1.7 billion). However, Grand Met divested Bennigan's ($500 million) and Steak and Ale ($200 million). There were some 75 major foodservice mergers in 1988 as tabulated by ERS/USDA (1990b) compared with 77 in 1987 and 81 in 1986. Pepsico's acquisition of Kentucky Fried Chicken, Taco Bell, and Pizza Hut epitomizes recent concentration. However, the leader in fast food, McDonald's, has focused on internal growth.

Table 11.10. Four-Firm Concentration, 1987 (Percent).

Firm Type	Concentration
Foodservice (owned)	8.1
Foodservice (systemwide)	18.9
Retail food industry	17.1
General line food wholesaling	26.0
Food processing (avg. for 25 industries)	39.8

Source: ERS, 1990b.

Vertical concentration of the foodservice industry backward into their sources of supply is relatively uncommon. Almost all foodservice companies purchase through foodservice distributors which are separate operations. Denny's is one of the few sizable exceptions; it has its own vertically integrated foodservice distribution.

Factor Markets

The food supply side of the foodservice market is much more concentrated than the demand side. Some large foodservice operations are serviced from a single national distributor, which may deliver from local or regional warehouses. However, purchases may be made centrally using common specifications, particularly for company-owned stores. Franchisers are legally precluded from requiring their franchisees to purchase products from them. However, food specifications may be closely specified and favorable purchasing arrangements based on systemwide product purchases may be offered to franchisees on a voluntary basis.

Some of the other factor markets servicing the foodservice industry, such as television advertising services, are largely national or regional in scope. Economies of scale for television advertising are used to great advantage by many of the large foodservice companies. They rank among the top advertisers among all food industries in the country. Restaurants spent $1.4 billion on advertising in nine different media in 1988. This figure compares with $760 million for all food stores and $6.0 billion for all food processing. The top five advertisers in the foodservice industry spent nearly $1.0 billion of the above $1.4 billion industry total, and 90 percent of it was spent on television advertising (ERS, 1990b).

The other major factor market, that for labor, is largely local, particularly for hourly employees. The foodservice industry is by far the largest employer of human resources in the food industry. Eating and drinking places, which account for only about two-thirds of total foodservice sales, employed 6.6 million people in 1988. Comparisons with other food industries are shown in Table 11.11.

Table 11.11. Foodservice Industry Employment, 1988 (Number of Employees).

Industry Segment	Number of Employees
Retail food stores	3.2
Food wholesaling	0.8
Food processing	1.6

Source: Bureau of Labor Statistics, 1991b.

Foodservice employment has increased sharply over time, up from 4.6 million in 1980 and 2.6 million in 1970 for eating and drinking places alone. Labor productivity in the foodservice industry has been decreasing; therefore, growth of industry output has required a greater proportionate increase in the number of employees. The labor productivity index for eating and drinking places, which measures output per man-hour, dropped 9 percent between 1977 and 1988 and another 1.7 percent in 1989 (Bureau of Labor Statistics, 1991a). The National Restaurant Association (1986), in its assessment of the labor shortage facing the industry, projected a shortfall of 1 million workers by 1995.

The last decade has brought many changes to the foodservice industry which may be due in part to the maturing of a young industry. Growth rates have slowed but remain positive, labor productivity has decreased, costs and labor demands are increasing, and, the structure of the industry is changing as it struggles to make adjustments to the new environment and remain profitable. A study by the National Restaurant Association (1988) using focus groups points to increasing concentration by way of mergers and acquisitions leading to even stronger competition facing the industry by the year 2000.

The nature of the market for foodservice tends to be local and characterized by franchising, of which two-thirds is franchisee-owned. From a national perspective, in terms of ownership, the market appears to be less concentrated than most other parts of the food industry. But, in terms of management and operations, concentration is similar to that of food retailing and general-line wholesaling. However, the foodservice industry faces food distributors and food processors who are more concentrated.

The foodservice industry is a major market for many factors, including food, labor, and advertising services. It accounts for over two-fifths of all food expenditures. However, this industry buys only about one-fourth of the volume of food sales by U.S. producers. Marketing cost margins dominate farm ingredient costs in foodservice as well as food sales.

Consumers face a wide variety of products and market segments within the overall foodservice industry. The industry is highly competitive; new independent entrants face a life expectancy measured in months. However, economists term the market *monopolistically competitive* because of the market power found within selected market segments and local geographic areas.

Conclusions and Implications

Food consumption away from home in the U.S. represents a significant share of the consumer dollar. This percentage increased over a number of years, but appears to have remained at a plateau since the mid-1980s. This plateau, however, has not resulted in a stagnant condition. The industry has been going through a number of structural changes, sharply increasing the concentration of business into fewer hands. A variety of other trends have also emerged, such as:

1. Increased interest in nutritional aspects, by both consumers and the industry.
2. Greater emphasis on meals previously seen as less important, such as breakfast away from home.
3. Greater demand for fast-foods, particularly by households including children.
4. A move toward more use of take-out foods from restaurants.

A study from *Restaurants USA* showed that while restaurant sales for dinners grew about 18 percent between 1982 and 1985, the customer traffic for take-out dinners doubled. The take-out market share was 35 percent in 1991. Much of this increase appears to be due to time constraints faced by many dual-career couples and families who are demanding greater convenience.

In 1988, the National Restaurant Association formed a Delphi panel of foodservice experts to predict changes which would occur in the industry by the year 2000. The two most likely developments identified were: (1) lower calorie menu items will be commonplace and (2) nutrition concerns will be critical to menu development in all types of foodservice. Menu offerings were predicted to include more fish; more wholesome, fresh, natural foods; more lower fat/cholesterol items; more poultry; more lower salt dishes; and more lower fat beef dishes. Menu items will include less sauces, less game, and less beef. (However, it should be noted that there is an increase in farm-raised game). Other most likely developments are interesting from the perspective of predicting future demand and nutritional issues. They were that: (1) genetic engineering will enhance the food supply with products such as leaner beef and lower cholesterol eggs, (2) flavors and natural enhancement will be more important, (3) richer flavors will be achieved without the addition of fats and salt, and (4) aquaculture will be a major source of fish supply. In fact, some of these trends are already beginning to occur.

A final issue increasingly complicates any discussion or analysis of food-away-from-home consumption: the concept of "food-away-from-home" is becoming blurred. As grocery stores move toward providing more partially and fully prepared foods and as restaurants sell "take-out" food for consumption at home, it is difficult to distinguish between meals purchased at restaurants to be eaten at home and meals, perhaps completely prepared, purchased at grocery stores and eaten at home. Are either of these to be considered as food-away-from-home?

References

Adrian, J. and R. Daniel. February 1976. Impact of socio-economic factors on consumption of selected food nutrients in the United States. *American Journal of Agricultural Economics* 58:31-38.

Boyle, J.R., W.M. Gorman, and S.E. Pudney. 1977. The demand for related goods: A progress report. In M. Intriligator, ed., *Frontiers of Quantitative Economics*, Vol. IIIA. Amsterdam: North Holland.

Bunch, K.L. 1984. Look away from home and the quality of diet. *National Food Review*, pp. 14-16.

Bureau of the Census, U.S. Department of Commerce. Various issues. *Census of Retail Trade*. Washington, DC: U.S. Government Printing Office.

Bureau of the Census, U.S. Department of Commerce. 1990. *Statistical Abstract of the United States*. Washington, DC: U.S. Government Printing Office.

Bureau of Industrial Economics. 1986. *Franchising in the Economy*. Washington, DC: U.S. Department of Commerce.

Bureau of Labor Statistics. November 28, 1991. Productivity by industry: 1989. (News release.) Washington, DC: U.S. Department of Labor.

Bureau of Labor Statistics. July 1991. Private Communication.

Capps, O., Jr., J.R. Tedford, and J. Havlicek, Jr. 1985. Household demand for convenience and non-convenience foods. *American Journal of Agricultural Economics* 67:862-869.

Chern, W.S. and J. Lee. 1989. Nonparametric and parametric analyses of demand for food at home and away from home. Unpublished manuscript. Columbus: Department of Agricultural Economics and Rural Sociology, The Ohio State University.

Demousis, M.P. and M.K. Wohlgenant. April 1981. Food consumption and household time: A test of the weak separability hypothesis. Unpublished manuscript.

Derrick, F.W., R. Dardis, and A. Lehfeld. 1982. The impact of demographic variables on expenditures for food-away-from-home. *Journal of the Northeastern Agricultural Economics Council* 11:1-11.

Economic Research Service. 1990a. *Food Consumption, Prices, and Expenditures, 1967-88*. Statistics Bulletin No. 804. Washington, DC: U.S. Department of Agriculture.

Economic Research Service. 1990b. *Food Marketing Review, 1989-90*. Agricultural Economics Report No. 639. Washington, DC: U.S. Department of Agriculture.

Economic Research Service. 1988. *Food Cost Review, 1987*. Agricultural Economics Report No. 596. Washington, DC: U.S. Department of Agriculture.

Enns, C. and P. Guenther. 1988. Women's food and nutrient intakes away from home, 1985. *Family Economics Review*, pp. 9-12.

Fletcher, S. M. 1981. Economic implications of changing household food expenditure patterns. Unpublished Ph.D. Thesis. Raleigh: North Carolina State University.

Goddard, D. 1983. An analysis of Canadian aggregate demand for food at home and away from home. *Canadian Journal of Agricultural Economics* 31:289-317.

Goebel, K.P. and Hennon, C.B. 1983. Mother's time on meal preparation, expenditures for meals away from home, and shared meals: Effects of mother's employment and age of young child. *Home Economics Research Journal* 12:170-188.

Gordon, E. 1991. Asian update. *Restaurant USA* 11:40-42.

Gordon, E. 1989. Slowdown in breakfast traffic continues. *Restaurant USA* 9:39-40.

Gorman, W.M. 1980. A possible procedure for analyzing quality differentials in the egg market. *Review of Economic Studies* 47:843-856.

Hagar, C.J. 1985. Demand for nutrient and nonnutrient components in household purchases of red meat, poultry, and fish products using a Hedonic approach. Unpublished Ph.D. dissertation. Raleigh: North Carolina State University.

Haidacher, R.C., J.A. Craven, K.S. Huang, D.M. Smallwood, and J.R. Blaylock. 1982. *Consumer Demand for Red Meats, Poultry, and Fish*. AGES 820818. Washington, DC: National Economics Division, ERS, USDA.

Haines, P.S. 1983. Away from home food consumption practices and nutrient intakes of young adults. *Proceedings of the 29th Annual Conference of American Council in Consumer Interests*, pp. 5-9.

Haines, P.S., B.M. Popkin, D.K. Guilkey, and D.W. Hungerford. 1989. Eating out: Who and where. *Proceedings of 1989 Agricultural Outlook Conference*, Washington, D.C.

Houthakker, H.S. and L.D. Taylor. 1970. *Consumer Demand in the United States: Analyses and Projections*. Cambridge, MA: Harvard University Press.

Huang, C.L. and R. Raunikar. 1985. Effect of consigned income on food expenditures. *Canadian Journal of Agricultural Economics* 33:315-329.

International Franchise Association Educational Foundation. 1988-1990. *Franchising in the Economy*. Washington, D.C.

Ketkar, S.L. and W. Cho. 1982. Demographic factors and the pattern of household expenditures in the United States. *Atlantic Economics Journal* 10:16-27.

Kinsey, J. 1983. Working wives and the marginal propensity to consume food-away-from-home. *American Journal of Agricultural Economics* 65:10-19.

Kim, J.S. 1990. An econometric analysis of meat prices: A Hedonics approach. Unpublished Ph.D. dissertation. Pullman: Washington State University.

Kolodinsky, J. 1987. Female labor force participation and expenditures in food-away-from-home. In V. Hampton, ed., *Proceedings of the 33rd Annual Conference of the American Council on Consumer Interests*, pp. 175-180.

Ladd, G.W. and V. Suvannunt. August 1976. A model of consumer goods characteristics. *American Journal of Agricultural Economics* 58:504-510.

LaFrance, J.T. 1983. The economics of nutrient content and consumer demand for food. Unpublished Ph.D. dissertation. Berkeley: University of California.

Lamm, R.M., 1982. "The Demand for Food Consumed at Home and Away from Home," *Agricultural Economics Research*, 34, pp. 15-20, July.

LeBovit, C. 1967. Expenditures for food-away-from-home. *National Food Situation* 152:36-38.

Lee, J.Y. and M.C. Brown. 1986. Food expenditures at home and away from home in the United States--A switching regression analysis. *Review of Economics and Statistics* 68:142-147.

Lee, F.Y. and K.E. Phillips. 1971. Differences in consumption patterns of farm and nonfarm households in the United States. *American Journal of Agricultural Economics* 53:573-582.

Lenz, J.E. 1989. A retail-level Hedonic analysis of milk component values. Unpublished Ph.D. dissertation. Pullman: Washington State University.

Manchester, A.C. 1987. Developing an integrated information system for the food sector. Agricultural Economic Report No. 575. Washington, DC: U.S. Government Printing Office.

Manchester, A.C. 1990. Data for food demand analysis: Availability, characteristics, and options. Agricultural Economic Report No. 613. Washington, DC: U.S. Government Printing Office.

Manchester, A.C. 1991. U.S. food spending and income--Changes through the years. Agricultural Information Bulletin No. 618. Washington, DC: U.S. Government Printing Office.

Mann, J.S. 1980. An allocation model for consumer expenditures. *Agricultural Economic Research* 32:12-24.

McCracken, V.A. 1984. An econometric analysis of the away-from-home food market. Unpublished Ph.D. thesis. West Lafayette, IN: Purdue University.

McCracken, V.A. 1989. The importance of demographic variables on the probability of consuming meat away from home. In R.C. Buse, ed., *The Economics of Meat Demand*. Published proceedings of the Conference in the Economics of Meat Demand, October 20-21, 1986.

McCracken, V.A. 1987. Consumer demand for seafood-away-from-home. *Proceedings of Symposium on Markets for Seafood and Aquacultural Products*, August 1987.

McCracken, V.A. 1990. Consumer demand for potatoes: At home and away from home. *Journal of Consumer Studies and Home Economics* 14:147-163.

McCracken, V.A. and J.A. Brandt. 1990. Measurement of household time value and its impact on the demand for food-away-from-home. *Home Economics Research Journal* 18:267-285.

McCracken, V. A. and J. A. Brandt. 1987. Household consumption of food-away-from-home: Total expenditure and by type of food facility. *American Journal of Agricultural Economics* 69:274-284.

McCracken, V. A. and J. A. Brandt. 1986. *Analysis of Economic and Socio-Demographic Factors Affecting the Consumption of Food-away-from-home*. Agricultural Experiment Station Bulletin No. 480. West Lafayette, IN: Purdue University.

Michalski, Nancy. 1990. Consumer expenditures for food-away-from-home increased in 1988. *Restaurants USA* 10:40-42.

Narayanan, H. 1989. Structure and performance of the commercial U.S. food service industry. Unpublished M.S. thesis. West Lafayette, IN: RHI Department, Purdue University.

National Agricultural Statistics Service. 1989. *Agricultural Statistics, 1989*. Washington, DC: NASS, U.S. Department of Agriculture.

National Restaurant Association. 1986. *Foodservice and the Labor Shortage*. Washington, DC: National Restaurant Association.

National Restaurant Association. 1988. *Foodservice Industry 2000*. Washington, DC: National Restaurant Association.

Nutrition Monitoring Division, HNIS, USDA. 1985. Food and nutrient intakes: Individuals in four regions, 1977-78. *Nationwide Food Consumption Survey 1977-78*. Report No. I-3. Washington, DC: United States Department of Agriculture.

O'Rouke, A.D. 1981. *The Changing Market for Food-away-from-home and Its Implications for Washington Producers and Processors*. Agricultural Research Center Bulletin No. 0894. Pullman: Washington State University.

Ortiz, B., M. MacDonald, N. Ackerman, and K. Goebel. 1981. The effects of homemakers' employment on meal preparation time, meals at home, and meals away from home. *Home Economics Research Journal* 9:200-206.

Prato, A.A. and J.N. Bagali. May 1976. Nutrition and non-nutrition components of demand for food items. *American Journal of Agricultural Economics* 58:216-221.

Prochaska, F.J. and R.A. Schrimper. 1973. Opportunity cost of time and other socioeconomic effects on away-from-home food consumption. *American Journal of Agricultural Economics* 55:595-603.

Pudney, S.E. 1976. The demand for related goods: Estimation and testing of a characteristics model. Discussion Paper No. B5. LSE Econometrics Programme.

Pudney, S.E. 1978. Instrumental variable estimation of a characteristics model: Some preliminary results. Discussion Paper No. B9. LSE Econometrics Programme.

Pudney, S.E. 1981a. An empirical method of approximating the separable structure of consumer preferences. *Review of Economic Studies* 48:561-677.

Pudney, S.E. 1981b. Instrumental variable estimation of a characteristics model of demand. *Review of Economic Studies* 48:417-433.

Raunikar, R. October 1977. *Summary of Food Purchases and Prices, Griffin, Georgia, April-June 1976 with Previous Periods.* Experiment Station Research Report No. 258. Georgia State.

Raunikar, R. and C.L. Huang. 1987. *Food Demand Analysis.* Ames: Iowa State University Press.

Redman, B.J. 1980. The impact of women's time allocation on expenditure for meals away from home and prepared foods. *American Journal of Agricultural Economics* 62:234-237.

Reese, R.B. and S.J. Mickle. 1982. Where to eat -- at home or away. In Jack Hayes, ed., *Food -- Farm to Table.* Washington, DC: 1982 Yearbook of Agriculture, USDA.

Ries, C.P., K. Kline, and S. Weaver. 1987. Impact of commercial eating on nutrient adequacy. *Journal of American Dietetics Association* 87:463-468.

Rogers, D.S. and H.L. Green. April 1978. Changes in consumer good expenditure patterns: What are the implications for a retailer's strategy? *Journal of Marketing*, pp. 14-19.

Salathe, Larry E. 1979. An empirical comparison of functional forms for Engel relationships. *Agricultural Economics Research* 31:10-15.

Soberon-Ferrer, H. and R. Dardis. 1991. Determinants of household expenditures for services. *Journal of Consumer Research* 17:385-397.

Smallwood, D. and J. Blaylock. 1981. *Impact of Household Size and Income on Food Spending Patterns.* ESCS Technical Bulletin No. 1650. Washington, DC: U.S. Government Printing Office.

Smallwood, D., J. Blaylock, and J. Zellner. Spring 1981. Factors affecting food choice. *National Food Review*, pp. 20-22.

Smith, B. February 1990. The effect of away-from-home-eating in the consumption of fluid milk. AE&RS 217, Marketing Research Report 9. University Park: Department of Agricultural Economics and Rural Sociology, The Pennsylvania State University.

Tedford, J.R., O. Capps, Jr., and J. Havlicek, Jr. April 1984. Regional equivalence scales for convenience foods. *Journal of Northeastern Agricultural Economics Council* 13:33-39.

Tyrrell, T. and T. Mount. 1982. A nonlinear expenditure system using a linear logic specification. *American Journal of Agricultural Economics* 64:539-546.

U.S. Department of Commerce. Various issues. *Current Population Reports: Population Characteristics.* Series P-20. Washington, DC: U.S. Government Printing Office.

U.S. Department of Commerce. Various issues. *Current Population Reports: Population Estimates and Projections.* Series P-25. Washington, DC: U.S. Government Printing Office.

VanDress, M.G. 1980. Fast food industry growth. *National Food Review* 9:35-37.

Yang, H.W. 1988. Expenditures on food-away-from-home by U.S. low-income households - 1985/86. Unpublished M.S. thesis. College Park: University of Maryland.

Yang, H.W. 1987. Taking to take-out. *American Demographics*, pp. 13-14.

Yang, H.W. 1990. Spending for food. *Family Economics Review*, p.26.

Yang, H.W. 1990. Eating place highlights. *Restaurant USA* 10:17-18.

12

Japanese Consumer Demand
*Michio Kanai, Yutaka Sawada,
and Manabu Sawada*

Databases

Introduction

Most Japanese food demand studies have been based on official databases. One reason for this is that the official databases are quite informative (we think they are among the best in the world) and easy to access. Second, non-official data are difficult and expensive to collect. Non-official data are used to supplement official data only when necessary. Third, scanner data have become very popular. Many supermarkets, convenience stores, department stores, and other stores use scanners to read bar codes attached to commodities being sold. Scanner data provide point-of-purchase information about customer purchases. Data typically include the bar code, price, time of purchase, and even the customer's sex and approximate age (the latter two data are added by the salesclerk). However, scanner data are usually store secrets and are very difficult to access.[1] In the next section we will discuss the major official databases.

---

[1] Recently, some Japanese companies began selling scanner data to U.S. companies. For example, Nihon Keizai Shimbun, Inc., publisher of a leading daily economic newspaper, sells scanner data through a technical connection with Information Resources, Inc., a U.S. company. As of June 1, 1992 it began selling scanner data gathered daily from 60 stores representing 33 store chains and about 4,300 households in three districts.

Official Databases

Seven official databases relate to Japanese consumer demand. These official databases are published in Japanese, however, some English explanations are added to the FIES, NSFIE, and CC. The databases are:

1. The *Food Balance Sheet (Shokuryo Jukyu Hyo)* (FBS) which is provided by the Minister's Secretariat of the Ministry of Agriculture, Forestry, and Fisheries (MAFF).
2. The *Annual Report on the Family Income and Expenditure Survey (Kakei Chosa Nempo)* (FIES) which is provided by the Statistical Bureau of the Management and Coordination Agency (MCA).
3. The *National Survey of Family Income and Expenditure (Zenkoku Shohi Jittai Chosa)* (NSFIE) which is also provided by MCA.
4. The *Statistics on Living Expenditures of Farm Household (Noka Seikeihi Chosa)* (SLEFH) which are provided by the Statistics and Information Department of MAFF.
5. The *National Nutrition Survey (Kokumin Eiyo Chosa)* (NNS) which is provided by the Ministry of Health and Welfare (MHW).
6. The *Input-Output Tables (Sangyo Renkan Hyo)* which are jointly provided by MCA, the Economic Planning Agency (EPA), and the nine Ministries.
7. The *Census of Commerce (Shogyo Tokei Hyo)* (CC) which is provided by the Ministry's Secretariat of the Ministry of International Trade and Industry (MITI).

In the following sections we will comment on the above databases concerning food demand and food away from home.

Food Demand

1. The *Food Balance Sheet* is published annually by MAFF. It is estimated by a formula devised by the Foreign Agriculture Organization (FAO). The calculation period is the Japanese fiscal year (FY) which runs from April 1 to March 31.
2. The *Family Income and Expenditure Survey* is published annually by MCA. This survey provides data on income and expenditures for all non-agricultural households of two or more members. It is based on the calendar year records of approximately 8,000 households. Its commodity classification consists of about 650 items including food. Most of the items have both expenditure and quantity data.
3. The *National Survey of Family Income and Expenditure* (NSFIE) has been performed every five years since 1959 by MCA. It provides more detailed information than the FIES. In addition, the sample size is far larger than the FIES. For example, the NSFIE surveyed 54,000 households in 1984 compared to about 8,000 households surveyed by

the FIES. In addition, it includes one-person households whereas the FIES does not. The NSFIE has also included all categories of agricultural households since 1984. The only exceptions have been in 1974 and 1979 when the surveys included agricultural households except "those households whose head engaged exclusively or mainly in agriculture". The NSFIE covers a 1-3 month period per annual survey.

4. The *Statistics on Living Expenditures of Farm Households* (SLEFH) is a part of the *Farm Household Economy Survey* (FHES) compiled by MAFF. The FHES is based on the Japanese fiscal year and is published annually. The SLEFH surveys agricultural households and gives similar statistics to the FIES which surveys non-agricultural households. SLEFH's sample size is around 11,000 households. It also published the *Statistics on Farmers' Nutrition* as an Appendix until 1988.

5. The *National Nutrition Survey* is published annually by MHW. Its sample size is about 6,000 households consisting of nearly 20,000 persons and including both agricultural and non-agricultural households. The dietary intake survey is based on a three-day survey conducted in November.

Food Away From Home (FAFH)

1. Food away from home data are rather limited in the FIES, NSFIE, and SLEFH surveys. In the FIES, FAFH data are divided into only four categories: noodles, other meals, drinks and cakes, and lunch provided at school. In 1980, however, the number of categories was increased to those shown in Table 12.1. In the NSFIE, eating out is divided into only two categories: general meals and school lunch. The SLEFH has the same categories as the NSFIE except it has a category for community cooking. The SLEFH had a category for community cooking until 1972 but the amount had become so small that it was included in the school lunch category beginning in 1973.

2. The NNS began its *Food Away From Home Survey* in 1971. It began as a five-day survey but in 1976 was reduced to a three-day survey. Food categories were: noodles, sushi, domburi-mono, curried rice, pasta, sandwiches, other Japanese meals, and other western meals. In 1986, the categories "lunch at office" and "lunch at school" were added.

3. The *I-O Tables* have been compiled every five years since 1955 through cooperation of various Agencies and Ministries after independent EPA and MITI trial surveys in 1951 (see item 6 under Official Databases above). Special *I-O Tables* stressing agriculture, forestry, and fisheries (and food industries) have been calculated by MAFF in recent years.

4. The *Census of Commerce* (CC) has been conducted every two or three years since 1952. Although eating and drinking places have been categorized somewhat differently each year, they were categorized as shown in Table 12.2 in 1988.

Table 12.1. FIES Categories, 1980.

Category	Number
Eating out	390 ~ 399, 39X
General meals	390 ~ 399
Japanese noodles	390
Chinese noodles	391
Other noodles	392
"Sushi"	393
Chinese & other Japanese meals	394
Western meals	395
Other meals	396
Unclassifiable	399
Drinking	398
Other refreshment	397
School lunch	39X

Source: MCA, FIES.

Methodology

Introduction

Many Japanese demand studies used databases presented in the previous sections. The FIES was used frequently with appropriate consumer price indexes in time-series as well as in cross-section analyses. The NSFIE was used mainly in cross-section analyses. Otherwise, the FBS was most often used for simple analyses such as estimating macro food trends or discussing the levels of food self sufficiency, but not for demand analyses. The FBS is a highly aggregated database and it is difficult to construct price indexes or find price indexes corresponding to the quantity series.

Demand Models

In this review, we concentrated on some of the most recent studies on the Japanese demand system by reviewing the literature of the past 10 years or so. Unless otherwise indicated, the data in the studies reviewed here use consumption data such as the FIES, NSFIE, and MCA's *Annual Report on Consumer Price Index* (ARCPI).

Single Equation Approach

Time Series Analysis. In the 1950s, 1960s, and 1970s, Aita reviewed demand studies using analysis based on the single equation approach which focuses on individual food commodities. Generalized Box-Cox was applied by Kusakari (1982) using annual per capita data for milk for 1963-1975. The

Table 12.2. Eating and Drinking Places Categories, 1988.

Number	Category
59	General eating and drinking places
591	Eating places
5911	Eating places, not elsewhere classified
5912	Japanese restaurants
5913	Western restaurants
5914	Chinese and oriental restaurants
592	Noodle shops
5921	Noodle shops
593	"Sushi" shops
5931	"Sushi" shops
594	Coffee shops
5941	Coffee shops
599	Miscellaneous general eating and drinking places
60	Other eating and drinking places
601	Special Japanese restaurants "Ryotei"
6011	Special Japanese restaurants "Ryotei"
602	Bars, cabarets, and night clubs
6021	Bars, cabarets, and night clubs
603	Public taverns and beer halls

Source: MITI, CC.

estimation method used was Iterative Maximum Likelihood Estimation (IMLE). His results suggest that the Box-Cox model is superior to double log, linear, and semi-log models.

The Houthakker-Taylor dynamic demand model was applied to beef by Monma using national annual and monthly per capita data for 1959-1976 and regional annual data for 1963-1976. The estimation method used was IMLE. He estimated the response of beef consumption to habit formation, short- and long-run price, and regional differences.

Cross-Section Analysis. Morishima and Hirao used the individual household data of the FIES in their studies. Morishima explained rice consumption by age for 1973, 1976, and 1980. The estimation method used was OLS without a constant term. His results suggest that for the group below 18 years of age, rice consumption increased slightly during the study period; for the age group 19-39 years old, it decreased significantly; and for the age group of more than 40 years of age, it decreased initially but then has been increasing.

Hirao used multivariate analysis to estimate food consumption patterns from 1973 and 1982 data. He analyzed the relationship between consumption patterns and household characteristics (household head's age and occupation, yearly income, family composition, etc.).

Demand System Approach

Food demand system analyses in Japan have been mostly of time series type except for the analysis done by M. Sawada (1985; 1989a, b). In terms of the data used, all studies used the FIES and NSFIE, except for Mori and Lin and Kusakari (1991). Typical estimates are presented in Table 12.3.

Linear Expenditure System (LES). Sasaki and Saegusa (1972; 1973), and then Sasaki (1976a) himself, estimated Leser, Powell, and Approximate Powell systems using annual per capita data for several food groups and one non-food group for the two decades after 1958. Other foods in the studies included dried foods and processed foods, condiments, and beverages. The price data were taken from MCA's ARCPI.

M. Sawada (1989a, b) estimated a modified extended linear expenditure system for 1976-1983 using the FIES, and for 1979 using the NSFIS for four (FIES) and nine (NSFIS) food groups and one non-food group along with some demographic variables.

The Rotterdam Model. Sasaki (1973, 1976b) analyzed changes in the value shares of food demand using a Rotterdam model. The parameters used in the study were from the Sasaki and Saegusa (1973) and Sasaki (1976a) studies. His results suggest that the income effect is more important than the price effect.

Y. Sawada (1980a) estimated a Rotterdam subsystem for meat (beef, pork, chicken, and fish) using annual per capita data for 1956-1970. His study, using unit price, suggests that beef and pork are mutually strong substitutes. He (1980b, 1982) also estimated a Rotterdam model using per capita data for 1956-1975 for eight (eleven) food groups and one non-food group.

Sasaki (1990) estimated a large Rotterdam model using per capita data for 1963-1985 and a household model for 16 food groups and one non-food group. He examined the time trend effect by including a constant term.

Almost Ideal Demand System (AIDS). M. Sawada (1980) estimated an AIDS for the same data used by Y. Sawada (1980b). He also estimated an AIDS for evaluating the impact of changes in income (expenditures) distribution on the aggregate food consumption patterns within a complete demand system framework. This system included seven food groups and one non-food group and was for 1964-1979.

Mori and Lin used quarterly market series data from the second quarter of 1978 to the first quarter of 1988 to estimate an LA/AIDS for meat.

Table 12.3. Comparison of Food Demand Elasticity in Japan.

Author(s)	Commodity	Evaluated Period	Elasticity Own-Price	Elasticity Expend-iture
Sasaki & Saegusa (1972)	Rice	Sample mean 1958 - 1968	-0.52	-0.61
	Other cereals		-0.60	0.34
	Fish		-0.60	0.44
	Meat		-0.64	1.46
	Milk & eggs		-0.63	1.40
(Leser)	Vegetables		-0.61	0.48
	Fruits		-0.62	1.35
	Food away from home		-0.63	1.22
	Others		-0.63	0.80
	Food		-0.61	0.61
	Non-food		-1.00	1.25
	Rice		0.33	-0.58
	Other cereals		-0.19	0.38
	Fish		0.07	-0.14
	Meat		-0.76	1.57
	Milk & eggs		-0.69	1.41
(Powell)	Vegetables		0.08	-0.15
	Fruits		-0.69	1.42
	Food away from home		-0.62	1.26
	Others		-0.47	0.86
	Food		-0.41	0.54
	Non-food		-0.92	1.29
Sasaki (1976a)	Rice	Sample mean 1956 - 1970	0.33	-0.51
	Other cereals		-0.13	0.18
	Fish		-0.16	0.28
	Meat		-0.80	1.43
	Milk		-0.89	1.61
	Dairy products		-0.82	1.49
	Eggs		-0.64	1.16
	Milk & eggs		-0.77	1.38
(Approximate Powell)	Vegetables		-0.17	0.30
	Fruits		-0.74	1.33
	Food away from home		-0.80	1.44
	Others		-0.50	0.81
	Food		-0.49	0.60
	Non-food		-0.93	1.25
M. Sawada (1980)	Cereals	Sample mean 1956 - 1975	---	-1.19
	Fish		-0.28	0.44
	Meat		-0.62	1.43
	Milk & eggs		-1.22	0.84
	Vegetables		-0.08	0.18
	Fruits		-1.02	1.13

Table 12.3 cont.

Author(s)	Commodity	Evaluated Period	Elasticity	
			Own-Price	Expend-iture
M. Sawada	Food away from home	Sample mean	---	2.39
(cont.)	Others	1956 - 1975	-0.52	0.77
	Nonfood		-0.48	1.29
Y. Sawada	Beef	Sample mean	-1.38	1.09
(1980)	Pork	1956 - 1970	-1.81	1.02
	Chicken		-2.18	1.64
	Fish		-0.27	0.24
Y. Sawada	Rice	Sample mean	-0.14	-0.46
(1982)	Other cereals	1956 - 1975	-0.86	0.57
	Fish		-0.58	0.51
	Meat		-0.89	1.61
	Milk		-0.79	1.16
	Dairy products		-1.09	0.50
	Eggs		-1.36	0.49
	Vegetables		-0.46	0.52
	Fruits		-1.04	1.30
	Food away from home		-0.70	1.50
	Others		-0.52	0.66
	Non-food		-0.28	1.23
M. Sawada	Cereals	1975	-0.90	-0.96
(1983)	Fish		-1.13	1.08
	Meat		-0.98	1.60
	Milk & eggs		0.57	-0.02
	Vegetables & Fruits		-0.55	0.78
	Food away from home		-1.52	1.25
	Processed food		-0.72	-0.01
	Non-food		-0.93	1.19
M. Sawada	Rice	Sample mean	-0.26	-0.73
(1984)	Other cereals	1963 - 1981	-0.03	0.37
	Fish		-1.04	1.78
	Beef		-1.74	1.93
	Pork		-1.19	1.12
	Chicken		-1.30	1.69
	Meat products		-0.84	1.88
	Milk		-0.16	0.82
	Eggs		-0.19	0.74
	Fresh vegetables		-0.49	0.75
	Fresh fruits		-1.06	1.56
	Cooked food		-1.96	0.92
	Oils & fats		-0.70	0.23
	Other processed food		-0.54	0.26

Table 12.3 cont.

Author(s)	Commodity	Evaluated Period	Own-Price	Expend-iture
			\multicolumn{2}{c}{Elasticity}	
M. Sawada	Cakes, candies, & bev.	Sample mean	-0.04	1.08
(cont.)	Food away from home	1963 - 1981	-1.31	1.82
	Non-food		-0.96	1.07
M. Sawada	Cereals	Sample mean	-0.08	0.27
(1986a)	Fish & meat	1979	-0.15	0.40
	Vegetables, etc.		-0.11	0.36
	Cakes, fruits, & bev.			
	Food away from home		-0.30	1.00
	Non-food		-0.72	1.22
Mori & Lin	Dairy beef	Sample mean	-1.78	0.77
(1990)	Wagyu beef	1978 II -	-3.02	2.55
	Imported beef	1988 I	-0.95	1.81
	Pork		-0.41	0.54
	Chicken		-0.17	0.89
	Higher valued fresh/ frzn. fish		-0.74	1.50
	Processed fish		-0.34	0.29
	Lower valued fresh/ frzn. fish		-0.66	1.39
Sasaki	Rice	Sample mean	-0.14	-1.21
(1990)	Other cereals	1963 - 1985	-0.64	-0.31
	Fish		-0.51	0.55
	Beef		-1.38	0.54
	Pork		-1.40	1.70
	Chicken		-0.36	1.75
	Meat products		-0.21	1.54
	Fresh milk		-0.65	0.98
	Dairy products		-0.72	1.09
	Eggs		-0.69	1.35
	Vegetables		-0.38	0.54
	Fruits		-0.71	1.74
	Oils & fat		-0.47	1.14
	Other food		-1.10	0.41
	Beverages		-0.46	1.92
	Food away from home		-0.99	1.42
	Non-food		-0.96	1.15
Kusakari	Semi-controlled rice	Sample mean	-0.47	
(1991)	Gov't.-controlled rice class-1 and -2	1981.1 - 1988.12	-1.10	
	Gov't.-controlled rice below class-3		-0.92	

Other Models. M. Sawada (1984) estimated a two-level demand system using annual data for 1963-1981 for seven food groups and one non-food group. Five of the eight food groups were divided into more detailed food categories as follows: cereal included rice and other cereals; fish and meat included fish, beef, pork, chicken, and meat products; milk and eggs included milk and eggs; vegetables and fruits included fresh vegetables and fresh fruits; and processed food included cooked foods, fat and oil, and other processed foods. This system was constructed by assuming a two-stage budgeting process.

Kusakari (1991) estimated a modified Armington model using the MAFF Food Agency's aggregated data for 1981-1988 for the rice group which consists of three types: semi-controlled rice; class 1 and 2 combined government-controlled rice; and below class 3 of government-controlled rice.

Demand Forecasting Models

Whether a single equation approach or a demand system approach is adopted depends on the purpose of a study. There can be many criteria in evaluating a demand forecasting model. We think that the best criterion is average information inaccuracy (AII). At the same time, we must examine the fitness of the model not only within the sample period but also outside of it. Usually Japanese food demand system studies do not compare alternative demand systems.

Sasaki and Saegusa (1972, 1973) and Sasaki (1976a) himself tried to evaluate alternative LES models by using AII, the simple correlation of estimated and actual expenditures, and the ratio of estimated to actual quantities for an interpolation test. As an extrapolation test, this study used the ratio of estimated to actual quantities. All three of the LES models (Leser, Powell, and Approximate Powell) produced similar results based on the latter two tests. If AII is used, the Leser System is the best.

M. Sawada (1983) compared AIDS and the Powell system by using AII. He found AIDS to be superior.

Sasaki (1990) compared four Rotterdam models (per capita consumption with and without a constant term and household consumption with and without a constant term) by using AII for extrapolation as well as interpolation tests. He found the per capita model with a constant term to be superior.

M. Sawada (1991) examined, by non-parametric demand analysis, what food grouping is best suited to the preferences of Japanese consumers (separability in the utility function) using many of the past demand studies including his own estimates based on data for 1965-84. His results suggest: (1) that static demand systems can be applied to analyze per capita food consumption patterns, (2) that the weak separability can be applied for various food groups, and (3) the assumption of (block) additive preference has become inappropriate for static demand system analyses since 1975.

References

Aita, Y. 1982. Shokuryo Juyo Bunseki Kenkyu no Gaikan (Survey of food demand analysis). *Nogyo Sogo Kenkyu (Quarterly Journal of Agricultural Economics)* 36:83-102.

Hirao, M. 1988. Gyuniku Shohi no Pata-n Bunseki (The pattern analysis of beef consumption). Pp. 157-181 in Morishima, ed., *Gendai Gyuniku Keizai no Shomondai (Problems of Modern Beef Economy)*. Tokyo: Meibun Shobo.

Kusakari, H. 1982. Yudo Sentaku Moderu to Gyuniku Juyo kansu heno Tekiyo (Maximum likelihood model and its application to the demand function for milk). *Nogyo Keizai Kenkyu (Journal of Rural Economics)* 42:35-39.

Kusakari, H. 1991. Kome no Hinshitsubetsu Juyo to Yunyu Jiyuka (Rice demand by consideration of quality differentials and import liberalization). Pp. 146-174 in The Rice Policy Study Group, ed., *Kome Yunyu Jiyuka no Eikyo Yosoku (Forecast on the Impact of the Liberalization of Rice Import)*. Tokyo: Fumin Kyokai.

Monma, T. 1984. Gyuniku Shohi Juyo no Chiikisei (The regionality of consumer demand on beef). Pp. 44-80 in T. Monma, ed., *Gyuniku Jukyu Kozo to Shijo Taio (The Demand and Supply of Beef and Market Correspondence)*. Tokyo: Meibun Syobo.

Mori, H. and B.H. Lin. 1990. Japanese demand for beef by class: Results of the almost ideal demand system estimation and implications for trade liberalization. *Nogyo Keizai Kenkyu (Journal of Rural Economics)* 61:195-203.

Morishima, M. 1984. Sedaibetsu no Kome Juyo Bunseki (A rice demand analysis by the generation). Pp. 20-29 in S. Sakiura, ed., *Kome no Keizai Bunseki (Economic Analysis of Rice)*. Tokyo: Yokendo.

Saegusa, Y. and K. Sasaki. 1973. Shokuryo Juyo Bunseki to Senkei Shishutsu Taikei (Food demand analysis and linear expenditure analysis). *Nogyo Sogo Kenkyu (Quarterly Journal of Agricultural Economics)* 27:1-42.

Sasaki, K. 1973. Shokuryo Shishutsu Kosei no Hendo Bunseki (Variation analysis of food expenditure share). *Nogyo Keizai Kenkyu (Journal of Rural Economics)* 45:103-110.

Sasaki, K. 1976a. Shokuryo Juyo Bunseki to Senkei Shishutsu Taikei (2) (Food demand analysis and linear expenditure analysis (2)). *Nogyo Sogo Kenkyu (Quarterly Journal of Agricultural Economics)* 30:91-109.

Sasaki, K. 1976b. Shokuryo Shohi no Hendo Pata-n (Changing patterns of food consumption). *Nogyo Sogo Kenkyu (Quarterly Journal of Agricultural Economics)* 30:1-32.

Sasaki, K. 1990. Applications of per capita and aggregate household models of the Rotterdam system to Japanese food expenditure data. Discussion

Paper Series No.430. Institute of Socio-Economic Planning, University of Tsukuba.

Sasaki, K. and Y. Saegusa. 1972. Senkei Shishutsu Taikei ni okeru Shokuryo Juyo Kansu (Food demand functions in linear expenditure systems). *Nogyo Keizai Kenkyu (Journal of Rural Economics)* 44:20-29.

Sawada, M. 1980. Almost Ideal Demand System to Shokuryo Juyo Bunseki (Almost ideal demand system and food demand analysis). *Nokei Ronso (The Review of Agricultural Economics Hokkaido University)* 37:151-182.

Sawada, M. 1983. Soshishutsu Bunpu no Henka to Kakei Shokuryo Juyo (Changes in total expenditure distribution and aggregate food demand of household sector). *Nogyo Keizai Kenkyu (Journal of Rural Economics)* 54:185-195.

Sawada, M. 1984. Kaisoteki Juyo Taikei to Shokuryo Juyo Bunseki (A hierarchical model of demand for food in Japan). *Nogyo Keizai Kenkyu (Journal of Rural Economics)* 56:163-173.

Sawada, M. 1985. Shokuryo Juyo to Hinshitsu (Food demand and quality). Pp. 70-89 in S. Sakiura, ed., *Kezai Hatten to Nogyo Kaihatsu (Economic Development and Agricultural Development)*. Tokyo: Norin Toukei Kyoukai.

Sawada, M. 1986a. Gurupuwake sareta Kurosu-Sekushon Deta karano Juyo Taikei Suitei (On estimating demand system parameters from grouped cross-section data). Research Bulletin 14:373-379. Obihiro University of Agriculture and Veterinary Medicine.

Sawada, M. 1986b. Shokuryo Juyo to Kakaku, Setai zokusei - Juyo Taikei niyoru Sekkin (The effects of prices, income, and household characteristics on food demand -- A demand system approach). *Nogyo Keizai Kenkyu (Journal of Rural Economics)* 57:228-239.

Sawada, M. 1991. Shohisha Senko no kozo ni kansuru Nonparametorikku Juyo Bunseki (Nonparametric demand analysis of the structure of consumer preferences). *Nogyo Keizai Kenkyu (Journal of Rural Economics)* 63:1-10.

Sawada, Y. 1980a. Nikurui Juyo ni okeru Daitai Kankei no Keisoku (Estimation of substitution relations on meat demand). *Nogyo Keizai Kenkyu (Journal of Rural Economics)* 52:101-109.

Sawada, Y. 1980b. Shokuryo Juyo Taikei no Keisoku (Estimation of food demand system). *Hokusei Ronsyu (Hokusei Review)* 18:147-161.

Sawada, Y. 1982. Shokuryo Juyo Kozo no Bunseki (Analysis of food demand structure). Pp. 115-126 in M. Morishima and M. Akino, eds., *Nogyo Kaihatsu no Riron to Jissho (The Theory and Practice of Agricultural Development)*. Tokyo: Yokendo.

13

Sources of
U.S. Food Consumption Data[1]
Rueben C. Buse, David Eastwood
and Thomas I. Wahl

Introduction

A wide variety of data sets can be used for consumer demand analysis. These data sets can be categorized as cross-sectional versus time-series and experimental versus nonexperimental. Nonexperimental cross-sections and time-series are most frequently used in applied food demand analysis. Most of the nonexperimental data employed are surveys of households (cross-sectional or panel), historical data series (time series), or information on the store purchases by individuals (scan data). There are no publicly available experimental data sets useful for estimating food demand.[2]

Data sources can also be classified as public or private. Public data sets are usually generated by government agencies such as the United States Department of Agriculture (USDA) or the Bureau of Labor Statistics

---

[1] An expanded version of this chapter is available from the authors. The longer version includes a discussion of relevant methodological issues, more detail on the data sets, and a review of relevant demand studies.

[2] The rural income maintenance experiment and the New Jersey graduated work incentive experiment conducted by the Institute for Research on Poverty at the University of Wisconsin used the experimental approach to measure the impact of income support programs on work incentives. The data contain expenditures on housing, durables, clothing, health, and a 24-hour recall of food intake (Bawden).

(BLS) and are readily available at low cost. Private data sets are usually generated by firms for profit and are now difficult and expensive to acquire.

In nearly all cases, the data were not designed to be used for demand analysis. Thus, it is important to describe the available data sets as well as to understand the characteristics of the different types of data. The first section discusses the characteristics of various types of data. The following five sections discuss sources for various data and systems currently used for demand analysis. The final section discusses some of the pragmatic issues of which users should be aware.

Types of Data

Assuming utility maximization, demand theory leads to a series of demand equations that relate quantity (Q) (or expenditures) to price (P), income (I), and other variable (Z) influencing the level of Q.[3] To estimate the system of demand equations data on the variables, Q, P, I, and Z are needed. These data can be time-series, cross-sectional, pooled time-series and cross-sectional, panel, or scan.

Time-Series Data

Time-series data measure the variables during successive time periods. The periodicity can be daily, weekly, monthly, quarterly, annual, or longer. The data on quantity and prices are generally aggregate market data (i.e., total quantity moving through a market in a specific time period) at the corresponding prevailing prices and may be measured at various levels including farm, central market, processor, wholesaler, or retailer.[4] The most readily available market data series are those collected and published by public agencies such as USDA. Other independent variables that can affect quantities consumed include trends, changes in population distribution, and binary variables to account for the description of market structure.

Cross-Sectional Data

An alternative approach to estimate the demand system is to observe a set of consumers in one period and to relate differences in the quantity consumed to differences in the levels of independent variables across observed units. Cross-sectional data are usually generated by a survey on consumption or expenditure during a given period and generally do not include price. Prices are assumed to be constant, and homogeneity across individuals is assumed.

---

[3] For details on alternative demand systems see Johnson *et al*.

[4] For more details on the aggregation problem see Intriligator, pp. 233ff.

Sociodemographic factors, such as age of head, number of persons in the unit, marital arrangement, wealth, and measures of expected income are included to account for known differences between survey units.   BLS consumer expenditure surveys and USDA household food consumption surveys are examples of cross-sectional data.

Pooled Time-Series and Cross-Sectional Data

Occasionally time-series and cross-sectional data series are merged to create a time series of cross-sections or a cross-section of time-series. These pooled data sets utilize the strengths of both types of data and use information from both to estimate a demand system. This method can be used to reduce multicollinearity problems in time-series data.

Panel Data

Panel data are pooled cross-sectional and time-series observations on the same consuming unit over several periods. Panel data are superior for studying individual behavior but are expensive to obtain and generally are designed for other research objectives. Attrition is a major problem with a panel. In practice, "pseudo panels" that do not attempt to maintain the individual units over time are used most frequently.

The oldest nationwide household panel is the Market Research Corporation of America (MRCA) panel begun in 1939. The most recent public panel data set is the BLS Consumer Expenditure Survey which is a pseudo-panel begun in 1980.

Store panels, which are continuous data from a sample of retail stores were developed because of the high cost of household panels. An example is the A.C. Nielson data on retail sales of food chains which audits store sales every 60 days to obtain information on product sales during the last 30 days.

Scan Data

Scan data are relatively new and has been rarely used for demand analysis.[5] These data are the byproduct of a computer scanning special product codes that identify each product. The Universal Product Codes (UPC) are 12-digit numbers. The first six digits identify specific manufactures and the last six identify specific products.

The UPC bar code is read by a scanner. The information is transmitted to a computer that uses the information much like a cash register. The

---

[5] See Capps for a review of recent literature on using scan data in demand analysis.

scan data can be stored to provide point of sale information about consumers' purchases.

Scan data are much more detailed than other types of demand data and typically include the product code, price, and time of purchase for individual products. Scan data for food retailers result in very large data sets that can be aggregated across stores, products, and/or time to obtain more traditional measures.

Time-Series Data

Nearly all time-series data used for food demand analysis are collected by USDA and BLS as byproducts of their responsibilities. The counterpart of food quantity Q needed to estimate a demand system is disappearance data.

Disappearance data are comprehensive measures of the consumption and utilization of domestically produced food and measure domestic market supply for a given period, usually annual. Food disappearance quantities are calculated as a residuals from total estimated production adjusted for stock changes, imports, exports, nonfood, and nonmarket uses.[6] The residuals are converted from primary commodity weights to retail weights using estimated conversion factors.[7] The estimated retail weight is divided by population to obtain per capita disappearance or consumption. Because total disappearance is measured, both at-home and away-from-home consumption are included. The data are published regularly in USDA's *Agricultural Statistics* and *Food Consumption, Prices, and Expenditures*.[8]

Prices

Prices are published for several levels in the marketing channel. State and national farm level prices are reported in *Agricultural Prices*. This report is based upon a survey of prices paid to farmers. The Agricultural Marketing Service also reports prices by grade and variety at designated central wholesale markets. BLS reports wholesale prices for many products, both individually and by product group, monthly in the *Survey of Current Business*.

---

[6] For details on the procedures see USDA (1988). Rauniker and Huang describe disappearance data as "...estimated as a residual balance from estimated total commodity production, stock changes, imports and exports balances, and nonfood and nonmarket supply dispositions."

[7] For an example of the problems in deriving retail weights, see Nelson and Duewer's discussion for red meat.

[8] As an example see USDA (1987).

A Consumer Price Index (CPI), a Consumer Price Index for Urban consumers (CPI-U), and another for Wage earners (CPI-W) are published monthly and annually by the BLS. The CPI-U has been published since 1978 and in a broad index that covers all urban residents. The CPI-W has been published for over 50 years and covers urban hourly wage earners and clerical workers in the civilian noninstitutional population.

Income

Per capita disposable income, which is frequently used as an income series, is published annually and quarterly by the U.S. Department of Commerce in *The Survey of Current Business*. A more detailed estimate of annual per capita income for individuals and families is published by the Bureau of the Census. Specific estimates are included for different regions, ethnic groups, occupations, household types, and ages on a national basis.

Major Cross-Section Data

This section describes the design and information in recent surveys that are useful to analyze U.S. food demand. Information on how to obtain machine readable data can be obtained from the National Technical Information Service of the U.S. Department of Commerce, the Division of Consumer Expenditure Surveys of the Bureau of Labor Statistics (BLS), or the U. S. Department of Agriculture.

BLS Consumer Expenditure Surveys (CES/I, CES/D)

The Bureau of Labor Statistics conducts consumer expenditure surveys that include detailed information on the expenditure, income, and financial status of a representative sample of U.S. households. The surveys have been conducted intermittently since 1888 and continuously since 1980.[9] The methodology and scope of the surveys have changed over the period.

Beginning in 1972-73, two separate surveys were conducted. One is based upon interviews (CES/I) and the other on diaries (CES/D). The CES/I was designed to obtain detailed information on 60 to 70 percent of household expenditures and aggregate information on another 20-25 percent of expenditures. The CES/D was designed to obtain information on the subgroups of the aggregates and the remaining expenditures.[10]

Sample Design. The sample design of surveys prior to 1960-61 varied but generally concentrated on urban areas. The 1960-61 survey included both

---

[9] For a detailed history of the early surveys, see Carlson.
[10] See U.S. BLS Bulletin No. 1992.

urban and rural areas. The 1972-73 and later surveys sampled all urban, rural, farm, and nonfarm households.

Data. All surveys collected expenditure data as well as information on socioeconomic characteristics with the more recent surveys including a wider variety of information. The CES/I includes detailed expenditure data for more than 3,500 different items, detailed inventory and characteristics data for major durable goods, and minor appliances, assets, and income.

The CES/D includes information on broad categories such as food, household, housekeeping, and personal care supplies. Each of the broad categories may contain up to several thousand individual items. The BLS data surveys do not include explicit price information because constant prices across the time frame are assumed.[11]

USDA Nationwide Food Consumption Surveys (NFCS)

The USDA has conducted nationwide food consumption surveys about every 10 years since the 1930s. The early surveys include only information on household food use, primarily in the spring, while the later ones also include food consumed away from home and during all seasons. The 1965-66, and 1977-78, and 1987-88 surveys also include food intake by individuals.

Sample Design. The NFCS use a national sample to represent U.S. population in the lower 48 states, although at times selected subpopulations have been emphasized. The 1955 survey was a self-weighing probability sample of the 48 states. The 1965-66 sample was similar to the 1955 design but included a supplementary farm sample. The 1977-78 survey sample was representative of households in the 48 coterminous states and included several supplementary samples.[12]

Data. The NFCS was designed to obtain information on the home food consumption of the members of the sampled household rather than expenditures. The NFCS include varying levels of detail. All include information on income, family size and composition, and the quantity and source of food consumed. Each survey also contained unique sets of questions. In general the more recent surveys provide more socioeconomic and food intake detail.

The 1977-78 NFCS provides information on the types and amount of food used from home supplies by the entire household at home during the previous

---

[11] See Capps and Havlicek or Capps, Spittle, and Finn.
[12] See USDA, 1982.

seven days as well as individual intake records for each household member.[13] The intake records, based upon a diary, detail the kind and quantities of food consumed at home and away from home.

The sociodemographic characteristics include information on income, household size and composition, race, religion, urbanization, general food shopping practices, number of meals and snacks, dwelling type, level of education and employment status of the heads of household, and the sex and age of each household member.

The National Health and Nutrition Examination Survey (NHANES)

The National Center for Health Statistics (NCHS) of the Department of Health and Human Services has been collecting statistics on a wide range of health issues for more than 20 years. The objectives of the NHANES are to measure the health and nutrition status of the U.S. population, to monitor and describe health and nutritional conditions, and to provide information on the prevalence of diseases. In addition they provide normative measures of U.S. population characteristics such as weight and height over time. Although the primary purpose of the NHANES is to collect data on the health of the population, it also contains information on individual food intake. In some respects it is an alternative source of food intake data similar to the NFCS.[14] The NHANES emphasis is health and nutrition, consequently the economic details on income and food expenditure information are very limited.

The National Center for Health Statistics conducted its first nationwide health examination survey in 1960-62 on adults 18 to 74 years old. During the 1960s two additional surveys were conducted on children 6-11 years old and adolescents 12-17 years old. The second survey was initiated in 1971. It included new information on food consumption and on the nutritional status of individuals. Nutritional status was assessed through a complete medical history, questions on diet, body measurements, a physical examination, and other medical tests. This survey, called the National Health and Nutrition Examination Survey (NHANES-I), was carried out from 1971 to 1974. It

---

[13] Home supplies include food and beverages used at home whether eaten at home, carried from home in packaged meals, thrown away, or fed to pets. Excluded food included commercial pet food, household food fed to animals raised for commercial purposes, food that was given away for use outside the home and food consumed at restaurants, fastfood outlets, roadside stands, and meals at other homes.

[14] See the report of the Coordinating Committee on Evaluation of Food Consumption Surveys for a discussion of the similarities and differences between the NHANES and NFCS and Swan for a comparison of findings.

sampled the U.S. population 1 to 74 years old. NHANES-II, conducted between 1976-80, extended the surveyed population to infants six months of age or older.

In 1982-84 NCHS conducted the Hispanic Health and Nutrition Examination Survey (HHANES). The survey sample was limited to areas with a large Hispanic population. It surveyed persons of Mexican-American, Puerto Rican, and Cuban ancestry living in the southwestern U.S., the New York City area, and Dade County, Florida. NCHS is currently working on NHANES-III.

Sample Design. Monitoring changes across time requires comparability across the survey and consistent design and implementation. NHANES-I is a probability sample of the U.S. civilian, noninstitutionalized population of all 50 states aged 1 to 74 years. The sample was stratified by broad geographical regions and by socioeconomic characteristics within regions. It included very detailed health examinations for the population between 25 and 74 years of age. In NHANES-II the sample was expanded to include persons between 6 months and 74 years. Because preschool children (six months to five years), the aged (60 to 74 years old), and the poor (persons below the poverty line as defined by the U.S. Census Bureau) were assumed to have more malnutrition problems, they were oversampled. NHANES-I included about 20,750 individuals and NHANES-II approximately 21,000 individuals.

Data. For each participant, the NHANES recorded data on family relationships, sex, age, and race of family members; housing characteristics; occupation, income, and educational level of each household member; and participation in the food stamp, school breakfast, and school lunch programs. Dietary information included a recall of food intake for the preceding 24 hours, usual food consumption during the preceding three months, diets, medications, and vitamin and mineral supplements. Medical data included body measurements, allergies, and the results of a series of clinical assays of blood and urine.

Food consumption included estimated portion sizes of all foods and beverages consumed in the previous 24 hours, the time of day the food was eaten and its source (home, school, restaurant, or other). For each food the quantity consumed and its nutrients, fats, vitamins, and minerals were also recorded. The consumption data were reported by food (about 4,800 food items). The frequency of consuming 18 groups of foods in terms of never, daily, weekly, or less than once weekly, the type and frequency of alcohol consumption, and the use of salt, special diets, and commonly prescribed medications were also obtained. The NHANES included no explicit prices or sufficient data to calculate implicit prices.

Panel Data

The following is a description of the design, operation, and data of those panel data sets considered useful for analyzing the food demand of U.S. households or individuals. They include data on either food consumption or expenditures by households or food intake by individuals. Generally, the food intake data can be aggregated to a household level.

Continuing Survey of Food Intake by Individuals (CSFII)

The CSFII is a yearly nationwide survey of the food and nutritional intake of selected groups of individuals in the 48 states. The first was conducted in 1985 and 1986. It is one component of the Federal National Nutrition Monitoring System. The CSFII provides annual updates and details of diet adequacy of selected subgroups of the population and timely indications of dietary changes in the sample populations. It is designed to complement the larger NFCS conducted every 10 years (the most recent is for 1987-88).[15] The CSFII was discontinued in 1987 and 1988 and begun again in 1989 and is to be conducted every year through 1996. It collects three consecutive days of dietary information.

The primary focus of the early CSFII's was on households containing women 19 to 50 years of age and their children 1-5 years of age. This group has been referred to as the "Core Monitoring Group.". It was selected because previous surveys showed that women of child- bearing age and their young children were more likely than other groups to have diets deficient in certain nutrients. Other age and sex groups were also included but with less frequency. From 1989 through 1996 the CSFII will collect dietary information on men, women, and all children.

Sample Design. The CSFII is a stratified sample of households in the lower 48 states. The sampling procedures take into account geographic location, degree of urbanization, and the socioeconomic characteristics of areas. The sampling and screening procedures produce three separate samples, (1) women 19-50 years of age and their children 1-5 years old (the core monitoring group), (2) a sample comparable to (1) of low income women and their children, and (3) men 19 to 50 years old. The final sample of the 1985 CSFII included 1,342 households, providing information on 1,503 women, 550 children in the core monitoring group, a comparable low income sample

---

[15] Although the data can be compared with the 1977-78 NFCS, there are differences in data collection procedures, the food composition information, and the nutrient data base used to calculate nutrient intake. For details, see USDA, 1985.

of 2,120 women and 1,314 children, and 658 men in the third sample. Later surveys include similar sample sizes. The data are a "pseudo panel" in that each succeeding year a new panel of subjects in the same age-sex groups is selected. The survey design permits adding supplementary samples of other age-sex categories as funds and interest dictate.

Data. The pre-1989 CSFIIs collected data on the previous day's food intake of individuals. In 1985, men were surveyed once during the year while women and children were surveyed on six separate days over a one year period. The food intake information was converted into 28 dietary components plus energy. In contrast, the 1977-78 NFCS individual intake data were converted into 14 nutrients plus energy. From 1989 on the survey collects information on food ingested at home and away from home based on a one-day record plus a two-day recall.

Information included all food eaten by the individual either at home or away from home, the time of day it was consumed, the use of salt and fat, and the form in which the food was brought into the household (i.e., commercially frozen, canned, bottled, etc). Each woman in the sample also provided information on her age, race, whether pregnant or nursing, employment status, occupation, education, and her use of special diets, and vitamin and mineral supplements. Information on household characteristics included the previous year's before-tax income; participation in food programs; the male head of household's age, education, occupation, and employment status; household size; tenancy; usual amount spent on food; and each household member's sex, age, and relationship to the female head of the household.

The public use data tapes include information on the quantities and nutritional content of more than 4,500 different foods. Since the unit of observation is the individual, there is no price or expenditure information. The individual's data can be related to the person's household.

BLS Continuing Consumer Expenditure Surveys

In October 1979 BLS began a continuing survey of consumer expenditures. It continues up to the present and can be classified as a "pseudo panel" in that the sampled units are replaced periodically. It is patterned after the 1972-73 survey in that it consists of two separate samples and questionnaires. One is a diary survey in which the sampled unit is asked to complete a diary of expenditures for two consecutive 1-week periods. The other is a quarterly interview in which each sampled unit is visited by an interviewer once every three months over a 15 month period. The diary obtains data on frequently purchased items including food, personal care items, and household operations. The interview obtains expenditures on less frequently purchased items such as major appliances, autos, rent, and insurance premiums. The continuing CES is emerging as a very detailed time series of cross sections. Currently, data for 1980 through 1988 are available for analysis. In addition BLS plans to publish integrated data from the interview and diary.

Sample Design. The continuous interview visits 5,000 consumer units every three months over a 15 month period and then replaces them with a new household. The data from the last four visits are included in the data set. The diary sample is of 5,000 different consumer units visited twice in two consecutive one week periods. Because of budget cuts, rural consumer units were dropped in the 4th quarter of the 1981 survey and then resumed in the 4th quarter of 1983. Thus, published data for 1980-81 are only for urban households, although data tapes do contain rural observations for 1980 and part of 1981.

Data. The data in the continuing surveys are very similar to those the earlier BLS diary and interview, described above.

University of Michigan Income Dynamics Panel

Since 1968 the Survey Research Center of the Institute for Social Research at the University of Michigan has maintained a panel of almost 5,000 families. The purpose of the panel is to study the determinants of family income and their changes. The long-term study hopes to gain a better understanding of the dynamics of household economic behavior. Currently, there are almost 20 years of data available on the same families and their descendants. All new families formed by members of the original families are added to the sample. Each spring heads of the families are interviewed about attitudes, economic status, and economic behavior.

Sample Design. Initially, the sample was a representative cross section of about 3,000 families plus a subsample of 1,900 low income families. The combined sample could be weighted to be representative of the total U.S. population. The current sample size is over 6,500 families because of the procedure of adding new families that contain adult members of the original families.

Data. The data include information on income, employment, housing, auto ownership, food expenditures, transportation, education, marital status, family composition and background, and attitudes. Questions about topics of special interest are added from time to time. Household food stamp participation data are also available. The survey collects little information on food expenditures outside of global data on food consumed at home and away from home. Detail on food expenditures are unavailable on a regular basis, and no price information is in the data set. The data have been used for estimating aggregate food demand, incorporating regional food prices from the BLS CPI (Benus and Sapiro).

Retirement History Survey (LRHS)

The Social Security Administration initiated the Longitudinal Retirement History Study (LRHS) in 1969 (Ireland). It assembled information useful in studying the process of retirement and changes in such households over time. It investigated the reasons for early retirement and the changes in the economic and social characteristics of older persons as they approached and entered into retirement. To explore the factors most affecting the timing of retirement and the changes in life style and living standards in retirement, the survey design followed a sample of individuals aged 58-63 in 1969 for ten years. The individuals were reinterviewed in odd numbered years through 1979. It is a true panel.

Sample Design. The LRHS sample represented all persons born between 1905 and 1911 in the 50 states. The study began with a sample of pre-retirees who were then followed into retirement until ages 68-73. The initial sample included 11,153 persons. The study included men aged 58-63 and women of the same age in households without husbands. It did not include employment data on women who were living with husbands when the sample was selected because, to women in that age group at that time, the concept of retirement usually meant their husband's retirement, not their own.

Data. Information collected in the LRHS included basic demographic data, work history, health and living arrangements, leisure activities, spouse's work history, financial resources and assets, expenditures, family composition, household family and social activities, and retirement plans. The LRHS obtained information on the respondents' expenditures for the major budget items of food, shelter, transportation, and medical care. Expenditure data are also available for personal care, entertainment, dues, gifts, and contributions.[16]

The LRHS is a limited data base. It is a study of the living patterns of older American households but does not include an exhaustive list of their expenditures. Consequently, it is useful for limited demand analyses that focus on elderly households and does not require complete budget information. It also does not permit calculating or otherwise obtaining prices from the data set.

Special University Panels[17]

There are several consumer panels, operated by academic institutions, that contain very comprehensive information on food purchases. These panels cover various periods of time. More information can be obtained from the university that operated the panel. The University of Georgia operated a consumer panel in Griffin, Georgia between 1974 and 1981 and in Atlanta, Georgia for 1956-62 (Purcell and Raunikar). Detailed information on the purchase and use of food was collected by Michigan State University in East Lansing, Michigan (Quackenbush and Shaffer) and by North Carolina State

---

[16] For details see Social Security Administration.
[17] See Raunikar and Huang (1987b) pp. 41-42 for more details.

University in Raleigh, North Carolina during the late 1950s and early 1960s. The Puerto Rico Agricultural Experiment Station also conducted a continuous household panel for several years beginning in October 1978.

Private Panels

A number of panels of consumers and retail outlets are operated by marketing research firms. The information from the panels is summarized and sold as a proprietary product. Major panels are described below. For more details and addresses of the firms operating the panels, see Forker *et al.*

Chain Restaurant Eating Out Share Trend (CREST). CREST is operated by the National Purchase Diary Group (NPD). It collects data from a continuing panel of 10,000 families and 2,800 singles. All 12,800 households report on a quarterly basis, producing data that can be aggregated into away-from-home purchases for eight weeks of the year.

For each meal, information is recorded on each family member on the type of eating establishment, the meal eaten, day of the week, total cost, tip, and what foods were eaten. Socioeconomic and demographic information on the sample family includes its size and composition, race, income, education, hours of work for husband and wife, location of residence, and home ownership status.

CREST is probably the best current source of data on food consumed away from home. University researchers have purchased parts of the data for demand analysis to augment data from other areas (Folwell and Baritelle). Because the data are generated by the private sector, they are costly to obtain. The NPD Group also operates a number of other special purpose panels that could be useful for particular demand studies. The "Packaged Goods Diary Panel" provides information from two national panels of 6,500 households and 40 local panels of 1,000 households each. Panelists record their purchases over a month for all items that are listed in the Diary. The items vary from period to period depending upon client interest. It also operates special purpose "National Food Consumption Panels." These panels provide in-depth analysis on at-home food preparation and consumption patterns.

MRCA Panel. The MRCA panel is operated by the Market Research Corporation of America and is one of the oldest nationwide household panels. It is a nationwide sample of 7,500 households that records purchases of *selected* items in a weekly diary. The panel was chosen to represent different demographic and geographic classifications. The data can be projected to the national level by region and demographic groups. The data set is generally not available for public research but has been used for special demand studies (Boehm and Babb).

Products covered include food, beverages, health, beauty, and personal products. The specific products vary across time depending upon the interest of client firms. The purchase information in the diaries includes UPC codes, where purchased, and characteristics of the product such as brand, type, flavor. The data can be related to household socioeconomic information.

Mail Diary Panel (MDP). MDP reports information on a limited number of grocery, drugstore, and household items through monthly mail diaries from 5,000 households. The sample can be weighted to reflect national level data. The products included in the diaries change depending on MDP clients' product offerings.

Market Sales and Purchase Data

Several private firms provide continuous data on samples of retail stores. They track the sales or movement of food store products at the wholesale and retail levels. The information is sold to clients interested in the movement of particular products in specific market areas. The best known of these is SAMI.

SAMI (Selling Areas Marketing Incorporated). These data have been collected on product movement at the processor and wholesaler level for most food chains since 1966. The data are used to estimate volume movement across the United States. SAMI reports shipments from warehouses to retail stores for most major food chains in most metropolitan statistical areas (MSAs). The data cover 468 categories of goods incorporating more than 220,000 specific items. Manufactured dairy products, juices, and other foods that move through warehouses as part of the wholesaling process are included. The SAMI data do not include information on fresh meats, fruits, or vegetables because they do not pass through warehouses.

Other private firms also sell this type of data, but most sets are not very useful for demand analysis. They do not include most of the conditioning variables required to estimate reliable demand equations.

Scan Data

The detailed nature of scan data permits demand analyses for individual products at individual retail food outlets over time. Aggregation can take place across shoppers, products, stores, and/or time. Cross-sectional characteristics include comparisons among closely related products during the same time period. If a chain is involved, then this can be extended to cross-store comparisons and different prices. Time-series analyses of products also can be conducted, including models that contain dynamic adjustments. Some scan data systems enable analysts to relate individual shopper characteristics to food purchases.

Scan data represent individual product point-of-purchase information on the quantities sold and the prices paid by customers at retail food outlets. Most time-series and cross-sectional data contain aggregated food price and quantity records and may not reflect the tradeoffs that actually confront consumers in stores. Important substitutions within the individual components of the aggregates may exist that would not be seen in the cross-sectional or time-series data but are found in scan data. Scan data permit the estimation of elasticities for very close substitutes and complements.

Scan data represent actual sales, but they do not contain any information on the income and sociodemographic characteristics of the customers purchasing the products. Consequently, time-series analyses using scan data cannot account for changes in these important determinants of demand. Some researchers have argued that a store or group of stores represent a controlled experiment. Assuming the sociodemographic variables of store patrons are constant, once the consumer is in the store, the only constraint on behavior is the economic constraint of relative retail prices (Wisniewski). If true, store scan data are suitable for demand estimation.

Data Sources

In addition to individual store scan data, a number of private firms provide data on samples of retail stores. The information is sold to clients interested in the movement of particular products in specific market areas. The following are two well known such products.

Scantrack US. This is a product of the A.C. Nielsen Company. It records sales of selected products in a sample of 2,000 U.S. retail outlets via scanners. It also provides similar data in 23 other countries. The sample of stores is stratified by store type, size, service type, ownership, and income level of the area it serves. All items that have UPC codes are included in the data. The data are available on a weekly basis. The data can be combined with outside factors affecting sales such as weather conditions, unemployment rates, local pay schedules, government assistance, and the demographic characteristics of the market in which the sample outlet is located. It has been used for demand analysis on specific products such as orange and grapefruit juices (Brown and Lee).

Since 1989 A.C. Nielsen has been tracking household level food consumption via scanning equipment provided to 15,000 participants. Socioeconomic data on the households are gathered annually. Households are located in geographic areas served by the Scantrack stores. Through merging the purchases with the price files from the stores and with the socioeconomic information, it is possible to obtain data suitable for demand analyses.

Behaviorscan and Infoscan. Both data sets are produced by Information Resources Inc. (IRI). The former is drawn from a nationally representative sample of 3,000 grocery stores and is for fixed weight food items. Socioeconomic characteristics of the neighborhoods in which the stores are located are part of the record keeping. Behaviorscan tracks the purchases of 70,000 households located near a subset of the 3,000 stores. Participants complete a questionnaire and are given ID cards to be used at the stores.

The panels are designed to track consumption in response to promotional, pricing, and other merchandising campaigns. The Behaviorscan households are linked to cable television networks for testing promotion programs in a set of sample communities. Each participating household has a computerized ID card that is used to record purchases automatically by store scanners in those communities. Behaviorscan relates household characteristics to the scanner records of the sample household's purchases. Ten communities have been participating in the Behaviorscan system for up to eight years. There are 3,000 to 3,500 households in each of the communities. Infoscan tracks consumer purchases of UPC coded products sold in supermarkets. The unit of observation is the supermarket. The sample encompasses 2,000 stores in 53 different market areas.

For both Infoscan and Behaviorscan it is possible to recover information on individual items and prices. For Behaviorscan the purchase data can be linked with the socioeconomic characteristics of the sample households. For Infoscan the price and quantity data can be linked to market characteristics such as type of clientele and other socioeconomic characteristics of the market area.

The data for Infoscan are available since 1985 and for Behaviorscan since 1978. Behaviorscan and Infoscan offer the researcher the opportunity to combine accurate purchase data from store scanners with socioeconomic information of purchasing households. Obtaining data from IRI for research purposes outside of IRI is likely to be difficult and costly.

Pragmatic Issues with
Alternative Data Sources

Researchers using any of the data sets discussed above should be cognizant of the potential statistical problems and differences in the data series. All types of data are susceptible to statistical problems. Autocorrelation, multicollinearity, and structural change complicate the computations in time series. In cross sections the problems are more likely to be heteroscedasticity, measurement errors, and missing values. In panel data it is a combination of all the problems. The modest experience with scanner data in demand analysis to date has provided no literature on statistical problems peculiar to such data. Nevertheless, problems surely exist and will be appearing in the literature in the near future.

Researchers attempting to use more than one of the above data series -- even within the same major survey series -- must exercise great care. The data are oftentimes not as comparable as they might at first appear. For example, in the 1972-74 Bureau of Labor Statistics Consumer Expenditure Survey, students were not included or surveyed if living away from home in a dormitory. In the 1980-81 sample they are included as separate consuming units. Other well known examples include: when or if food purchased and consumed away from home is reported; butter is included in fats and oils in the 1977-78 USDA Household Food Consumption Survey and in dairy products in the recent BLS surveys; sales taxes can be included or excluded from the cost of the product; and the inclusion of one-person households varies across surveys and within surveys from one period to another. Probably the most troublesome variable is income. Both its definition and reference period depend upon the particular survey. In fact, the reference period for annual income varies from one sample household to the next in the most recent BLS surveys. In the 1977-78 NFCS, income data included the income of all household members ages 14 and older except roomers, boarders, and employees. In contrast, in the 1965 NFCS income data were recorded only for all related persons living in the household who were part of the family's finances.

The researcher should look for changes in the definition of demographic characteristics such as race and origin, employment status, and occupation across data sets. Researchers must carefully examine the definition of each variable *and* the sampling procedure before making comparisons.

Documentation for a data set is an absolute necessity but, by itself, is not sufficient if the data set is to be used properly. Complete documentation, particularly of survey data, are oftentimes lacking and may not correspond exactly with the data set in hand. Major consumer expenditure or consumption surveys usually provide documentation in the form of a codebook that lists the variables in the data file and assigned values. It is not unusual to find discrepancies between the published codes and those encountered in the data.

Finally, in spite of all the best efforts of the agency generating the data, there can still be problems with large or unusual data values that can seriously distort a statistical estimate. Very large expenditures are particularly troublesome. Should they be included or excluded? Two examples noted by Buse, and Buse and Johnson from the 1977-78 USDA/NFCS are $50,000 of welfare income and two-week purchases of 13.5 pounds of tea.

Even scan data, automatically recorded by sophisticated equipment, are subject to inaccuracies. Unrecorded sales, poorly trained checkers, bad labels, and incorrect UPC codes contaminate the data set (Lesser and Smith). The point is that the researcher must clearly decide what to do with such observations and to assess the implications for the ensuing analysis.

. . .The data are imperfect not by design, but because that is all there is. Empirical economists have over generations adopted the attitude that having bad data is better than having no data at all, that their task is to learn as much as is possible about how the world works from the unquestionably lousy data at hand. While it is useful to alert users to their various imperfections and pitfalls, the available economic statistics are our main window on economic behavior. In spite of the scratches and the persistent fogging, we cannot stop peering through it and trying to understand what is happening to us and to our environment, nor should we. The problematic quality of economic data presents a continuing challenge to econometricians. It should not cause us to despair, but we should not forget it either. [Griliches, p. 199].

References

Bawden, Lee. 1970. Income maintenance and the rural poor: An experimental approach. *American Journal of Agricultural Economics* 52:638-44.

Benus, J., J. Kmenta, and H. Sapiro. May 1976. The dynamics of household budget allocation to food Expenditure. *The Review of Economics and Statistics* 57:129-138.

Boehm, William T. and E.M. Babb. March 1975. *Household Consumption of Beverage Milk Products*. Purdue Agricultural Experiment Station Bulletin No. 75. West Lafayette, IN: Purdue University.

Brown, Mark G. and Jong-Ying Lee. 1986. Orange and grapefruit juice demand forecasts. In Oral Capps Jr. and Benjamin Senauer, eds., *Food Demand Analysis: Implications for Future Consumption*. Blacksburg, VA: Department of Agricultural Economics, VPI.

Buse, Rueben C. July 1979. Data problems in the BLS/CES Pu diary tape: The Wisconsin 1972-73 CES diary tape. Ag. Econ. Report No. 164. Madison: Department of Agricultural Economics, University of Wisconsin.

Buse, Rueben C. and A.C. Johnson Jr. 1986. Diagnosing a data base for demand analysis. In D. Peter Stonehouse, ed., *Demand Analysis and Policy Education*. Bulletin No. 197/1986. Ottawa, Canada: International Dairy Federation.

Capps, O., Jr. and J. Havlicek Jr. 1987. *Meat and Seafood Demand Patterns: A Comparison of the S_r-Branch Demand System and the Constant Elasticity of Demand System*. Agricultural Experiment Station Bulletin No. 81-2. Blacksburg, VA: VPI.

Capps, O., Jr., G.D. Spittle, and T. Finn. April 1981. *The Virginia Tech Version of the 1972-74 BLS Consumer Expenditure Diary Survey: Data Description and Data Inconsistencies*. Staff Paper SP-81-4. Blacksburg, VA: Department of Agricultural Economics, VPI.

Carlson, Michael D. December 1974. The 1972-73 consumer expenditure survey. *Monthly Labor Review*, pp. 16-23.

Coordinating Committee on Evaluation of Food Consumption Surveys. 1984. *National Survey Data on Food Consumption: Uses and Recommendations*. Washington, DC: National Academy Press.

Folwell, R.J. and J.L. Baritelle. 1978. *The U.S. Wine Market*. Washington DC: U.S. Government Printing Office.

Griliches, Zvi. 1985. Data and econometricians -- The uneasy alliance. *American Economic Review* 75:196-200.

Intriligator, Michael D. 1978. *Econometric Models, Techniques, and Applications*. Englewood Cliffs, NJ: Prentice-Hall.

Ireland, Lola M. November 1972. Retirement history study: Introduction. *Social Security Bulletin* 35:3-8.

Johnson, Stanley R., Zuhair A. Hassan, and Richard D. Green. 1984. *Demand Systems Estimation: Methods and Applications*. Ames: Iowa State University Press.

Lesser, William G. and Jonathan Smith. February 1986. The accuracy of supermarket scanning data: An initial investigation. *Journal of Food Distribution Research* 17:69-74.

Nelson, Kenneth E. and Lawrence A. Duewer. 1986. ERS's measures of red meat consumption. Paper presented at *A Symposium on the Demand For Red Meat*, Charleston, South Carolina, October 20-21.

Purcell, Joseph C. and Robert Raunikar. 1971. Price elasticities from panel data: Meat, poultry, and fish. *American Journal of Agricultural Economics* 53:216-221.

Quackenbush, G.G. and James D. Shaffer. 1960. Collecting food purchase data by consumer panel. Agricultural Experiment Station Technical Bulletin 279. East Lansing: Michigan State University.

Raunikar, Robert and Chung-Liang Huang. 1987a. Food expenditure patterns: Evidence from U.S. household data. Pp. 33-53 in Oral Capps Jr. and Benjamin Senauer, eds., *Food Demand Analysis: Problems, Issues, and Empirical Evidence*. Ames: Iowa State University Press.

Raunikar, Robert and Chung-Liang Huang, eds. 1987b. *Food Demand Analysis: Problems, Issues, and Empirical Evidence*. Ames: Iowa State University Press.

Social Security Administration. 1976. *1976 Almost 65: Baseline Data From the Retirement History Study*. Washington, DC: Office of Research and Statistics, U.S. Government Printing Office.

Swan, Patricia B. 1983. Food consumption by individuals in the United States: Two Major Surveys. *Annual Review of Nutrition* 3:413-432.

U.S. Bureau of Labor Statistics. 1981. *Consumer Expenditure Survey: Integrated Diary and Interview Survey Data, 1972-73*. Bulletin 1992. Washington, DC: U.S. Government Printing Office.

U.S. Department of Agriculture. 1982. *Food Consumption: Households in the United States, Spring 1977*. Report No. H-1. Washington, DC: U.S. Government Printing Office.

U.S. Department of Agriculture. 1985. *Nationwide Food Consumption Survey, Continuing Survey of Food Intakes by Individuals, Women 19-50 years, and Their Children 1-5 Years, 1 Day*. Report No. 85-1. Washington, DC: U.S. Government Printing Office.

U.S. Department of Agriculture. 1987. *Food Consumption, Prices, and Expenditures*. Statistical Bulletin No. 749. Washington, DC: U.S. Government Printing Office.

U.S. Department of Agriculture. 1988. *Major Statistical Series of the U.S. Department of Agriculture: How They are Constructed and Used.* Volume 5: Consumption and Utilization of Agricultural Products. Washington, DC: Government Printing Office.

Wisniewski, K. 1984. Statistical issues in using UPC scanner data. Proceedings of the *American Statistical Association, Business and Economic Statistics Section.* Washington, DC: American Statistical Association.

14

Food Demand Models for Forecasting
Wen S. Chern, Kuo S. Huang, and Hwang-Jaw Lee

Introduction

One of the main objectives of the joint U.S.-Japan research project is to assess future food demand and supply balance in the United States and Japan. This assessment would, in turn, shed some light on the future potential agricultural trade between the two countries. The time span is tentatively set for the year 2000 or perhaps more appropriately for the next 10 to 15 years. The reason for proposing a medium-term assessment is that any significant adjustment in agricultural structure takes many years. Also, food demand patterns are unlikely to dramatically change in the short run. Therefore, a longer term assessment would provide more useful information for designing appropriate policy instruments for various economic objectives in agricultural and trade development in the two countries.

The assessment of agricultural supply and demand in 2000 and beyond obviously requires some forecasts of supply and demand in the two countries. There can be, of course, quantitative and qualitative forecasts. A rigorous quantitative forecast would require modeling of supply and demand. The objectives of this chapter are to review and assess the state-of-the art in food demand modeling and to evaluate the usefulness of these models for forecasting food demand in the United States. Because consumer behavior of food consumption can be assessed by various demand elasticities such as price and income, the available estimates of these elasticities in the United States are presented in this chapter. The magnitudes and dispersion of these estimates suggest the degree of uncertainty in making food demand forecasts.

As pointed out by Senauer *et al.*, future food consumption patterns are likely to be affected by changing demographic variables and consumer's concerns about health, food safety, and nutritional quality. It is, therefore, important to assess the methodology for incorporating demographic variables and health concerns into food demand modeling. Any structural change in food demand would make the forecasting more difficult.

Issues Related to Food Definition and Commodity Aggregation

Farmers produce such agricultural products as soybeans, wheat, and cattle while consumers consume such food items as margarine, bread, and hamburger. The products produced by farmers and consumed by consumers are often quite different. Raw agricultural materials typically go through several stages of processing before they are finally consumed. Food demand analyses generally deal with the end-uses of agricultural products beyond the farm gate. On the other hand, typical supply analyses deal with farmers' decisions on output and factor substitutions inside the farm gate. Similarly, agricultural trade often involves raw agricultural materials (trade in processed food products has been increasing in recent years, and in the future processed products may provide consistent price and quantity data for supply and demand analysis). These differences in producers' raw products and consumers' end-use products make it difficult, in some cases, to reconcile the forecasts of agricultural supply and food demand, as they are often provided from separate models. The problems are clearly related to food definition and commodity aggregation.

The following example may put these problems in perspective. Consider the case of soybeans. In 1988, Japan imported 4,685,000 metric tons (MT) of soybeans which accounted for about 84 percent of its total supply. In the same year, Japan utilized 891,000 MT as food (for making soy sauce, tofu, etc.) and 3,687,000 MT for crushing into soybean oil and soybean meal. Soybean oil is used for making margarine, shortening, and cooking oils while soybean meal is used mostly as feed. In 1988, precisely 700,000 MT of soybean oil were consumed in Japan while 2,971,000 MT of soybean meal were consumed. That year, Japan also imported 587,000 MT of soybean meal. Therefore, in order to estimate the demand for soybeans in Japan, one has to consider all of these demand components. In fact, the demand for soybean meal is not consumer demand but is a derived input demand for livestock production. Among the food demand components, it is not entirely clear at which stage different demand components can best be modelled. Should we model demand for soybean oil separately from the demand for soybean products (such as tofu)? These methodological issues must be addressed to develop appropriate forecasts for soybeans, one of the most important agricultural products traded between the U.S. and Japan. In the remainder of this section, we will discuss additional issues that have important implications for demand modeling.

Consumer Demand vs. Demand for Farm Output

Demand relationships estimated at the retail level do not necessarily translate directly to the demand at the farm level. In a recent study, Wohlgenant developed a conceptual framework for estimating demand relationships for farm outputs, based on reduced form specifications for retail and farm prices. He then applied the model to a set of eight food commodities for which retail product and corresponding raw product data can be found. His empirical estimates indicated that the derived demand for farm products is more price elastic than retail demand. Despite the ability of his model to derive the farm level demand from the retail demand and the marketing input prices of food marketing, inconsistencies remain between retail demand and farm level demand. In the case of eggs, for example, the retail demand refers to the eggs directly purchased by consumers while the farm level demand includes also a substantial quantity of eggs consumed by food processors for making cakes, cookies, and other processed foods. What should be the retail price of eggs embodied in these processed products?

Price-quantity relationships depend not just on domestic but also on foreign demand. Few demand elasticity estimates incorporate foreign demand, but the impact on price of supply controls, for example, will be a function of exports as well as domestic use in open economies. An early (1967) estimate of aggregate U.S. farm output elasticity by Tweeten combined the domestic and export demand responses. When the elastic export demand was included with the highly inelastic domestic food demand (used to justify acreage controls to raise farming receipts), aggregate demand was found to be of unitary elasticity in the long run with exports included. This estimate, raising doubts whether acreage control increased farming receipts in the long run, indicated the policy prescriptions could be influenced by the way demand is estimated.

Food at Home vs. Food Away From Home

In 1989, American households spent, on average, 44 percent of their food expenditures on away-from-home meals and snacks, up from 34 percent in 1969 and 24 percent in 1949 (Manchester). In fact, the U.S. retail food industry has undergone dramatic structural changes over the last 20 years, with the fast food industry growing at a phenomenal rate. Despite this growing importance of the food-away-from-home component, data on away-from-home food consumption have been scarce. Consequently, most food demand analyses are based on quantity data obtained for at-home consumption, price data (such as CPI components) for at-home consumption, or both. Many studies treated food away from home as an aggregate group in a food demand system. How can we use the demand relationships estimated for food at home for predicting the total consumption of food commodities when their food-away-from-home consumption components are not adequately treated in the model? This important issue will be addressed by other participants in the symposium.

Alternative Demand Models

Many demand models are available to applied demand analysts. Usually there is a trade-off between sound theoretical properties and estimation complexity in developing each of these models. To provide information for selecting a proper model for forecasting food consumption, some well-known demand systems are reviewed here.

Conceptual Framework for Deriving Demand Models

A brief explanation of the duality properties of Marshallian demand is given here to demonstrate that all well-known demand systems are derived within a consistent framework of classical demand theory. Let q denote an n-coordinate column vector of quantities demanded for a "representative" consumer, p an n-coordinate vector of the corresponding prices, m = $p'q$ the consumer's income (or expenditure), and u(q) the utility function, assumed to be nondecreasing and quasi-concave in q. The primal function for maximizing consumer utility is the following Lagrangean function with multiplier π:

$$\underset{q,\pi}{Maximize}\quad L = u(q) - \pi(p'q - m). \tag{1}$$

Defining $u_i(q)$ as the marginal utility of the ith commodity, one can express the necessary conditions for an optimum as follows:

$$u_i(q) = \pi p_i \qquad i = 1,2,...,n \tag{2}$$

$$p'q = m. \tag{3}$$

A solution of the above n+1 equations gives an ordinary demand system, in which quantities are functions of prices and income:

$$q_i = f_i(p,m) \qquad i = 1,2,...,n. \tag{4}$$

Furthermore, multiplying by q_i in equation (2) and summing over n to satisfy the budget constraint, the Lagrangean multiplier becomes

$$\pi = \frac{\sum_j q_j u_j(q)}{m}. \tag{5}$$

Substituting (5) into (2) yields the following Hotelling-Wold identity (Hotelling; Wold) or an inverse demand system, in which prices are functions of quantities demanded and income, or

$$\frac{p_i}{m} = \frac{u_i(q)}{\Sigma_j q_j u_j(q)} \qquad i = 1,2,...,n. \tag{6}$$

As indicated by Hicks (p.83), the Marshallian demand has two functions: (a) it shows the quantities consumers will take at given prices, and (b) it shows the prices at which consumers will buy given quantities. The former function is represented by the ordinary demand system (4) and the latter function by the inverse demand system (6). This chapter reviews various forms of ordinary demand systems. However, readers may refer to Huang (1983, 1988, 1989, 1990, and 1991) for some recent developments in the inverse demand system research.

An ordinary demand system (4) also can be derived from an indirect utility function. Substituting the equilibrium quantity q_i from (4) into the utility function yields an indirect utility function, say v(p, m), which gives the maximized utility for specified values of prices and income. One may apply Roy's identity (1942) and obtain an ordinary demand system

$$q_i = \frac{-\partial v(p,m)/\partial p_i}{\partial v(p,m)/\partial m} \qquad i=1,2,...,n. \tag{7}$$

In addition, one can derive an ordinary demand system from a cost function. Inversion of an indirect utility function for the level of u that satisfies v(p, m) = u gives a cost function, say c(u, p) = m, which is defined as the minimum cost of attaining u at a price vector p. One may apply Shephard's lemma to derive a Hicksian (compensated) demand as a function of u and p:

$$\frac{\partial c(u,p)}{\partial p_i} = g_i(u,p). \qquad i = 1,2,...,n \tag{8}$$

Substituting the indirect utility into the Hicksian demand equation, one may obtain an ordinary demand system

$$q_i = h_i[v(p,m),p]. \tag{9}$$

The utility function is not known. Instead of assuming an arbitrary utility function, an alternative approach to derive a demand model is direct approximation of the conceptual demand model (4) and then incorporate parametric restrictions provided by classical demand theory. A summary of alternative routes in deriving an ordinary demand system is given in Figure 14.1; an arrow indicates the direction of derivation.

Demand Models Derived by Utility Function Approach

Because utility, indirect utility, and cost functions are interrelated with each other, all demand systems derived from these functions are classified under the utility function approach.

The Linear Expenditure System

Klein and Rubin suggested a form of consumer preference which is strongly or additively separable with a utility function expressed as

$$u = \Sigma_i \alpha_i \log(q_i - \delta_i) \tag{10}$$

where parameters are characterized by $1 > \alpha_i > 0$, $\Sigma_i \alpha_i = 1$, $\delta_i \geq 0$, and $q_i > \delta_i$. δ_i is interpreted as "subsistence" or "committed" quantities of ith goods. Their marginal utilities are thus derived as

$$\frac{\partial u}{\partial q_i} = \frac{\alpha_i}{(q_i - \delta_i)} \qquad i = 1, 2, ..., n. \tag{11}$$

By solving the necessary conditions for maximizing utility function subject to a budget constraint, a set of ordinary demand equations is obtained:

$$p_i q_i = p_i \delta_i + \alpha_i (m - \Sigma_j p_j \delta_j) \qquad i = 1, 2, ..., n. \tag{12}$$

This demand system called the "linear expenditure system" was developed by Stone and has been used extensively by applied economists. The demand system reflects the consumer's budget allocation process in which the committed expenditures ($p_i \delta_i$'s) are allocated first, leaving the remaining "supernumerary expenditure" ($m - \Sigma_j p_j \delta_j$) distributed over all commodities in the fixed proportions α_i.

The Indirect Translog Demand System

Christensen *et al.* approximated an indirect utility function by a quadratic form in the logarithms called "transcendental logarithmic indirect utility function" as

$$\log v = \alpha_0 + \Sigma_i \alpha_i \log r_i + .5 \Sigma_i \Sigma_j \beta_{ij} \log r_i \log r_j \tag{13}$$

where $\beta_{ij} = \beta_{ji}$, and r_i is a normalized price of ith commodity defined as p_i/m.

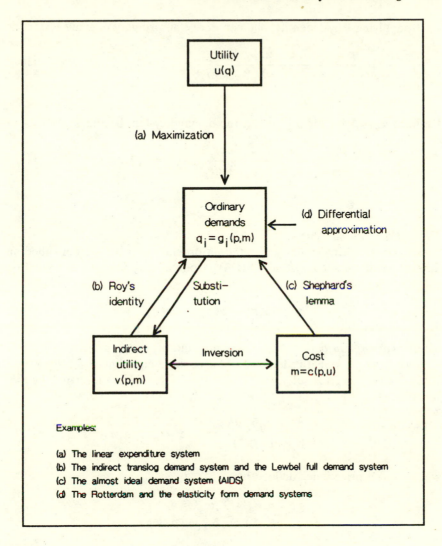

Figure 14.1. Modeling Ordinary Food Demand Systems.

A differentiation of the indirect utility function with respect to the normalized price and expenditure in logarithmic form is given respectively by

$$\frac{\partial \log v}{\partial \log r_i} = \alpha_i + \Sigma_j \beta_{ij} \log r_j \qquad i = 1, 2, \ldots, n \qquad (14)$$

and

$$\frac{\partial \log v}{\partial \log m} = -\Sigma_j (\alpha_j + \Sigma_k \beta_{jk} \log r_k). \qquad (15)$$

By applying Roy's identity, one can derive an ordinary demand system as

$$\frac{p_i q_i}{m} = \frac{\alpha_i + \Sigma_j \beta_{ij} \log r_j}{\Sigma_j (\alpha_j + \Sigma_k \beta_{jk} \log r_k)} \qquad i = 1,2,...,n. \qquad (16)$$

Defining $\alpha_m = \Sigma_j \alpha_j$, and $\beta_{mk} = \Sigma_j \beta_{jk}$, the demand system becomes

$$\frac{p_i q_i}{m} = \frac{\alpha_i + \Sigma_j \beta_{ij} \log r_j}{\alpha_m + \Sigma_k \beta_{mk} \log r_k} \qquad i = 1,2,...,n. \qquad (17)$$

The AIDS Demand System

Deaton and Muellbauer generated an ordinary demand system called an "almost ideal demand system (AIDS)" from a cost function. They first suggested a cost function

$$\log c(u,p) = a(p) + u b(p) \qquad (18)$$

where $a(p) = \alpha_0 + \Sigma_j \alpha_j \log p_j + .5 \Sigma_j \Sigma_k \gamma_{jk} \log p_j \log p_k$, and $b(p) = \beta_0 \Pi_j (p_j^{\beta j})$.

By applying Shephard's lemma, a budget share equation $\partial \log c / \partial \log p_i = w_i$, is obtained which gives, after substitution for u derived from inverting the cost function,

$$w_i = \alpha_0 + \Sigma_j \delta_{ij} \log p_j \\ + \beta_i \log(m/p^*) \qquad i = 1,2,...,n \qquad (19)$$

where p^* is a price index defined by

$$\log p^* = \alpha_0 + \Sigma_j \alpha_j \log p_j \\ + .5 \Sigma_j \Sigma_k \delta_{jk} \log p_j \log p_k \qquad (20)$$

and $\delta_{jk} = \delta_{kj} = .5(\gamma_{jk} + \gamma_{kj})$, $\Sigma_j \beta_j = \Sigma_j \delta_{jk} = \Sigma_j \delta_{kj} = 0$, $\Sigma_j \alpha_j = 1$ to confirm the theoretical properties of adding up, homogeneity, and symmetry. Deaton and Muellbauer further suggest simplifying the model by substituting the logarithm of the Stone price index given as $\Sigma_j w_j \log p_j$ for $\log p^*$ to allow for linear estimation.

The Lewbel Full Demand System

Recently, Lewbel proposed a general demand system that nests, as two special cases, the AIDS and the translog. He suggested the following indirect utility function v(p, m):

$$\log[v(p,m)] = \Sigma_i \, \beta_i \log p_i + \log[\delta + \Sigma_i \, \alpha_i \log p_i$$
$$+ .5 \, \Sigma_i \, \Sigma_j \, \gamma_{ij} \, \log p_i \, \log p_j \tag{21}$$
$$- \left(\Sigma_i \, \alpha_i + \Sigma_i \, \Sigma_j \, \gamma_{ij} \, \log p_j\right) \log m],$$

where

$$\Sigma_i \, \alpha_i = 1, \quad \Sigma_i \, \beta_i = 0,$$
$$\Sigma_i \Sigma_j \gamma_{ij} = 0, \quad and \quad \gamma_{ij} = \gamma_{ji} \; for \; all \; i,j. \tag{22}$$

By Roy's identity the demand system in expenditure-share form can be derived as

$$w_i = \frac{\{ \alpha_i + \Sigma_j \, \gamma_{ij} \log p_j + \beta_i(\delta + \Sigma_j \, \alpha_j \log p_j + .5 \, \Sigma_j \Sigma_k \gamma_{jk} \log p_j \, \log p_k) - [\Sigma_j \, \gamma_{ij} + \beta_i(1 + \Sigma_j \Sigma_k \gamma_{jk} \log p_k)] \log m \}}{(1 + \Sigma_j \Sigma_k \gamma_{jk} \log p_k).} \tag{23}$$

$$i = 1,2,...,n$$

The restrictions (22) altogether imply adding-up, homogeneity, and symmetry of the demand system (23). The interesting properties of (23) are that restrictions $\beta_i = 0$ for all i reduce the system to the exactly aggregable translog, whereas restrictions

$$\Sigma_j \gamma_{ij} = 0, \; for \; all \; i$$

lead to the AIDS. These restrictions can be tested to assess the adequacy and relative explanatory power of the AIDS and the translog.

Demand Models Derived by Differential Approximation Approach

Another approach to derive a demand system is by the direct approximation of a conceptual ordinary demand model (4), while the parametric constraints derived from classical demand theory are incorporated into the model. Following is a review of two typical examples: the Rotterdam and the elasticity form demand systems.

The Rotterdam Demand System

Theil and Barten proposed the Rotterdam model by approximating the conceptual demand model in a total differential form

$$dq_i = \Sigma_j(\partial q_i / \partial p_j)dp_j + (\partial q_i / \partial m)dm. \tag{24}$$

Multiplying both sides of the equation by p_i/m and using $w_i = p_iq_i/m$, one obtains a logarithmic differential form

$$w_i d(\log q_i) = \Sigma_j \, (p_i p_j / m)(\partial q_i / \partial p_j)d(\log p_j)$$
$$+ \, p_i(\partial q_i / \partial m)d(\log m). \tag{25}$$

Furthermore, by substituting the Slutsky equation for $\partial q_i / \partial p_j$ to express the quantity effects of price changes, one can rewrite the demand system as

$$w_i d(\log q_i) = p_i(\partial q_i / \partial m)d(\log m)$$
$$+ \Sigma_j(p_i p_j / m)[\pi h^{ij}$$
$$- (\pi / \pi_m)(\partial q_i / \partial m)(\partial q_j / \partial m) \tag{26}$$
$$- (\partial q_i / \partial m)q_j] \, d(\log p_j)$$

where π is the Lagrangean multiplier or the marginal utility of income of equation (2), π_m is $\partial \pi / \partial m$, and h^{ij} is the (i,j)th terms of the Slutsky substitution defined as the inverse of a matrix of the second order partials of u(q).
   To simplify the expression of the demand system, one may define $\mu_i = p_i \partial q_i / \partial m$ as the marginal value share of ith commodity, $\phi = (\pi/m)/\pi_m$ as the reciprocal of money flexibility, and $\mu_{ij} = p_i p_j \pi_m h^{ij}$ for satisfying $\Sigma_j \, \mu_{ij} = \mu_i$. Then the demand system (26) can be rewritten as

$$w_i d(\log q_i) = \mu_i [d(\log m) - \Sigma_j w_j d(\log p_j)]$$
$$+ \Sigma_j \phi(\mu_{ij} - \mu_i \mu_j)d(\log p_j). \tag{27}$$

A workable demand system is then defined as

$$w_i d(\log q_i) = \mu_i d(\log Q) + \Sigma_j \alpha_{ij} d(\log p_j) \tag{28}$$

where $\alpha_{ij} = \phi(\mu_{ij} - \mu_i\mu_j)$, and $d(log \, Q) = d(log \, m) - \Sigma_j w_j d(log \, p_j)$. This is the absolute price version of the Rotterdam model, in which the parametric restrictions are $\Sigma_i \, \mu_i = 1$, $\Sigma_j \, \alpha_{ij} = 0$, and $\alpha_{ij} = \alpha_{ji}$.
   One may further rearrange equation (27) and define a relative price version of the Rotterdam model as

$$w_i d(\log q_i) = \mu_i d(\log Q) + \Sigma_j \phi \mu_{ij} \, [d(\log p_j)$$
$$- \Sigma_k \mu_k d(\log p_k)] \tag{29}$$
$$= \mu_i d(\log Q) + \Sigma_j \beta_{ij} d(\log p_j - \log P)$$

where $\beta_{ij} = \phi \mu_{ij}$, and $log \, P = \Sigma_k \, \mu_k \, d(log \, p_k)$.

The Elasticity Form Demand System

The elasticity form demand system has been applied by Huang and Haidacher and Huang (1985). Similar to the Rotterdam model, the demand system is approximated by a total differential form

$$dq_i = \Sigma_j (\partial q_i / \partial p_j) dp_j + (\partial q_i / \partial m) dm \tag{30}$$

$$i = 1, 2, ..., n.$$

Dividing both sides of the equation by q_i and replacing the derivatives by elasticities yields the demand system

$$dq_i / q_i = \Sigma_j e_{ij}(dp_j / p_j) + \delta_i(dm/m) \tag{31}$$

$$i = 1, 2, ..., n$$

where $e_{ij} = (\partial q_i / \partial p_j)(p_j / q_i)$ is the demand elasticity of the ith commodity with respect to a price change of the jth commodity, and $\delta_i = (\partial q_i / \partial m) (m/q_i)$ is the income (expenditure) elasticity of ith commodity.

Given a demand structure consisting of n commodities, a complete ordinary demand system can be defined as a set of linear equations with $n(n+1)$ demand parameters:

$$q_1' = e_{11} p_1' + e_{12} p_2' + ... + e_{1n} p_n' + \delta_1 m'$$

$$\vdots \qquad\qquad \vdots \tag{32}$$

$$q_n' = e_{n1} p_1' + e_{n2} p_2' + ... + e_{nn} p_n' + \delta_n m'$$

where variables q_i', p_i', and m' are respectively the relative changes in quantity, price, and per capita income. These variables can be defined by using the time series data which are usually expressed in index numbers.

To estimate this demand system, the following linear parametric constraints obtained from the classical demand theory are incorporated:

$$\textit{Homogeneity:} \quad \Sigma_j e_{ij} = -\delta_i \qquad i = 1, 2, ..., n \tag{33}$$

$$\textit{Symmetry:} \quad (e_{ji}/w_i) + \delta_j = (e_{ij}/w_j) + \delta_i \tag{34}$$

$$i, j = 1, 2, ..., n$$

$$\textit{Engel aggregation:} \quad \Sigma_i w_i \delta_i = 1 \tag{35}$$

where $w_i = p_i q_i / m$ is a prior fixed value for the expenditure weight of the ith commodity.

An Appraisal of Demand Models

Thus far some representative ordinary demand systems, which are derived either from a utility function or from a direct approximation of conceptual demand model, have been presented. Some of these demand systems may have sound theoretical properties but are difficult to apply and vice versa. The choice of a demand system largely depends on availability of data and on the purpose and priority issue faced by a researcher.

In general, the demand systems generated by the utility function approach satisfy the condition of integrability, a desired property to ensure that a demand system is theoretically consistent. They are, however, not without drawbacks. Conceptually, an infinite variety of functional forms of utility function can be used to generate a demand system. Only a few functional forms discussed here are considered realistic and manageable in applied demand analysis. Thus an application of a particular utility function may lose sight of some potential alternative or more general specification. In particular, the linear expenditure system is rather restrictive in the sense that both inferior goods and complementarity in cross price response are not permitted in the system because of additive utility function.

Most demand systems generated by the utility function approach, except for the simplified version of AIDS system, are nonlinear in parameters. Although some computer software packages for estimating nonlinear regressions are available, the estimation of these demand systems require a heavy workload in computing when large numbers of commodities are included in a demand system. Besides, all of these demand systems require time series data on expenditure shares, which in many cases are not available for food demand studies.

On the other hand, the Rotterdam and the elasticity form demand systems are regarded as an approximation to a conceptual demand model. Although satisfactory approximation to a conceptual demand model may be a problem, some efforts are made in these models to bridge the gap between theory and application by incorporating constraints based on theory. The imposition of fixed demand parameters in these models may be a controversial assumption because some strong restrictions are placed upon the implied utility structure. The assumption is nevertheless a useful approach on empirical grounds; the demand models thus obtained are easily implemented because of their linearity in demand parameters.

Finally, applied demand analysts tend to use elasticity measures to express consumer responses to price and income changes because of easy interpretation and avoiding confusion generated by different "units of measurement" across commodities. Most of these selected demand systems, except for the elasticity form model, should generate elasticities as a function of estimated parameters and endogenous variables such as expenditure shares. These generated elasticities, however, could be unstable estimates because of the stochastic nature of endogenous variables as well as the potential errors of estimated parameters. In the case of the Rotterdam model, it still faces the problem of using expenditure shares as variables. This problem is avoided in the elasticity form model.

Review of Empirical Food Demand Models

This section presents a review of the past studies of food demand and consumption in the United States. Many studies related to food demand (aggregate, food at home, food away from home, or by subcategories) are available in the literature. These studies can be roughly classified into four groups on the basis of methodology. They are (1) using a single equation approach for selected food items, (2) estimating Engel relationships, (3) constructing a food demand elasticity matrix, and (4) using a complete system approach for a food group. The first two categories of study usually attempt to estimate demand parameters for individual commodities. In contrast, the main objective of the last two categories is to estimate a complete set of demand parameters including own-price, cross-price, and income elasticities. We first review the studies based on single equation and Engel relationships, next those constructing food demand elasticities matrices, and then we summarize the studies employing complete demand systems.

Single Equation Food Demand Models

In the 1950s and 1960s, considerable work was published on the demand for particular food products (Buse). The objectives of the widely used single equation approach to model food demand was usually to obtain consumer demand parameters for the food commodities (or groups) of interest, or to search for appropriate explanatory variables to interpret different food consumption patterns, or to evaluate the performance of alternative functional forms and various statistical methods for estimating demand parameters. The most popular functional forms used in these food demand studies were linear, semi-logarithmic, double-logarithmic, and Box-Cox general form. The explanatory variables were usually own price, the prices of selected other foods, and disposable income.

In addition, socioeconomic and demographic variables were sometimes incorporated into a demand function and justified as proxy variables for taste factors. Based on the alternative specifications of error structure, three methods were often used to estimate the demand parameters: (a) ordinary least squares or generalized least squares, (b) limited dependent variable estimation method such as the Tobit model, and (c) maximum likelihood estimation. Table 14.1 presents a survey of recent studies of food demand in the U.S. using a single equation approach.

Table 14.1. Survey of Food Demand Studies in the U.S. Using Single Equation Method.

Study	Data	Commodity	Functional Forms	Estimation Method
Chang (1977)	1935-74 (excl. 1942-47)	Meat	Box-Cox	NMLE[a]
Blaylock & Smallwood (1983)	1960 I-1979 IV Quarterly	Beef	Box-Cox	NMLE
Wohlgenant (1985)	1947-83 (annual)	Beef, pork, poultry, & fish	Fourier	OLS
Raunikar & Huang (1986)	1977-78 Nationwide Food Consumption Survey	Shell eggs	Linear	Tobit
Brown & Lee (1986)	1978 I-1984 III (39 bimonthly data)	6 citrus juices	Double-Log	OLS Mixed Estimation
Lee, Brown, & Schwartz (1986)	1981-82 Panel data	Orange juice (2 brands)	Switching Regression	Two-Stage Heckman Estimation

[a]NMLE refers to Nonlinear Maximum Likelihood Estimation.

Studies of Engel Relationships

Demand analyses using cross-sectional data or other data without price variation information usually focus on Engel relationships or the impacts of income and other socioeconomic and demographic factors on food consumption. This is because cross-sectional data, such as that obtained from a household food consumption survey, has abundant information about household characteristics and socioeconomic and demographic variables but no information to estimate price impacts. Much of the incentive for doing this kind of study came from policymakers with responsibilities for formulating and establishing welfare programs and from food marketing administrators responsible for identifying the target market and developing marketing strategy more efficiently. For instance, the estimation of the equivalent scales for welfare analysis has received much attention over the years.

As pointed out earlier, the proportion of income spent on food away from home has increased dramatically. This trend is partly attributed to demographic changes such as composition and size of the household, women labor force participation, age structure of the population, and life styles. Therefore, many economists working in this area have attempted to analyze expenditures on food away from home. More detailed information on this category of previous studies is summarized in Table 14.2.

Table 14.2. Survey of Studies on Food Consumption in the U.S. Using Engel Relationship, Socioeconomic and Demographic Factors.

Study	Data	Commodity	Functional Forms	Estimation Method
Salathe & Buse (1979)	1955 & 1965 HFCS[a]	Total food & 5 food categories	Linear	Nonlinear Least Squares
Chavas (1979)	1972-73 CEDS (BLS)[b]	17 food categories	Linear	OLS
Redman (1980)	1972-73 & 1973-74 CEDS (BLS)	FAFH[c]	Linear	OLS
Blaylock & Green (1980)	1965 HFCS	Beef, pork, poultry, fish, & eggs	Box-Cox	Nonlinear Maximum Likelihood
Price, Price, & West (1980)	1972-73 Washington State	65 types of fruits & vegetables	Linear	OLS
Huang & Rauniker (1981)	Griffin Consumer Panel	Fresh beef, ground beef, beef roast, & steak	Spline Function	OLS
Smallwood & Blaylock (1981)	1977-78 NFCS (USDA)[d]	FAFH	Linear	OLS
Tyrell & Mount (1982)	1972-73 CEIS (BLS)[e]	8 aggregate commodities including food at home and FAFH	Linear Logit	OLS
Kinsey (1983)	1978 Panel Study of Income Dynamic	FAFH	Linear	Tobit
Haines (1983)	1977-78 NFCS (USDA)	FAFH	Linear	Tobit
Nyankori (1986)	1980 CEIS (BLS)	Total food & 14 selected food categories	Linear Spline	OLS
Capps & Pearson (1986)	1977-78 NFCS (USDA)	8 food categories	Linear	Tobit
Lee & Brown (1986)	1977-78 NFCS (USDA)	FAFH	Linear	Switching Regression

Table 14.2 cont.

Study	Data	Commodity	Functional Forms	Estimation Method
Price (1986)	1977-78 NFCS (USDA)	Total food & 28 food categories	Double-Log	Tobit
Chern & Ferrer (1987)	1980-81 CEIS (BLS)	8 aggregate commodities including food at home & FAFH	Box-Cox	Maximum Likelihood
McCracken & Brandt (1987)	1977-78 NFCS (USDA)	FAFH	Linear	Tobit
Kolodinsky (1987)	1980 CEIS (BLS)	FAFH	Linear	Tobit
Yang (1988)	1985-86 CSFII[f]	FAFH	Linear	Tobit OLS
Basiotis & Young (1989)	1985-86 CSFII	FAFH	Linear	Heckman Two-Step

[a]HFCS = Household Food Consumption Survey.
[b]CEDS = Consumer Expenditure Diary Survey.
[c]FAFH = Food Away From Home.
[d]NFCS = Nationwide Food Consumption Survey.
[e]CEIS = Consumer Expenditure Interview Survey.
[f]CSFII = Continuing Survey of Food Intakes by Individuals.

Elasticity Form Food Demand Systems

Three noteworthy works on constructing a complete disaggregate food demand matrix in the literature are due to Brandow, George and King, and Huang (1985). Brandow employed a synthetic approach to construct a complete structure of demand relationships for 24 foods and one nonfood commodity. The estimated parameters of a demand matrix were constrained to be consistent with the utility maximization. In order to obtain a consistent demand matrix, Brandow adopted the assumption of want-independence (Frisch, 1959) and the previously estimated coefficient of money flexibility of -0.86 and used the direct-price elasticities, income elasticities, and expenditure share from a number of prior studies to derive the parameters of his food demand matrix.

George and King used a similar approach to construct a demand matrix for 49 food commodities and one nonfood commodity. However, the main improvement in their study over Brandow's is that the demand coefficients of commodities were obtained by means of using an uniform estimation procedure on the same sample observations rather than from other prior studies based on different data sources, various time periods, and alternative estimation methods. The data used by George and King covered only the postwar period which had relatively stable consumption patterns.

The major limitations of both studies using a synthetic approach to construct a food demand matrix are related to the estimation procedure, derivation of cross-price elasticities, the problem of statistical reliability, and want-independent assumption. Recently, Huang employed an elasticity form demand system to construct a disaggregate food demand matrix. His model includes 40 food items and 1 nonfood item, and was estimated by a constrained maximum likelihood method using annual observations for 1953-1983.

In addition, two more studies in this category appeared in the literature. One was conducted by Price and Mittelhammer. They used prior information and annual observations for 1949-1973 and then applied a mixed estimation technique to derive a demand matrix at the farm level for 14 fresh fruits. Another study, by Huang and Haidacher, used a constrained maximum likelihood method and parametric restrictions to derive a complete demand matrix for a composite food demand system covering 12 food categories and one nonfood category using annual data for 1950-1981. These five studies using a complete demand matrix approach are summarized in Table 14.3.

Food Demand Systems Derived from Utility Functions

The last category of food demand studies used complete demand systems derived from utility functions. Table 14.4 presents a survey of recent food

Table 14.3. Survey of Studies Using a Food Demand Matrix in the United States.

Study	Data	Commodity	Method
Brandow (1961)	1923-58 annual data	24 food categories & 1 nonfood	Synthetic approach
George & King (1971)	1955 (6060 households), 1965 (15101 households) food consumption survey, & 1946-68	49 food categories & 1 nonfood	Synthetic approach
Price & Mittelhammer (1979)	1949-73 annual data	14 fresh fruits	Mixed Two-Stage Least Squares
Huang & Haidacher (1983)	1950-81 annual data	12 composite food groups & 1 nonfood	Constrained Maximum Likelihood
Huang (1985)	1953-83 annual data	40 food items & 1 nonfood	Constrained Maximum Likelihood

demand studies using a complete system approach. Important findings from this review of previous models can be summarized as follows:

(a)   The linear expenditure system, linear approximate almost ideal demand system, and translog demand system are the three models most often used to estimate food demand;

(b)   The data used in these studies come mainly from annual time series, consumer expenditure survey, or nationwide food consumption survey;

(c)   Food at home, food away from home, and meats are three main categories analyzed in the literature due to their relative importance in food expenditures;

(d)   Estimation methods employed are either maximum likelihood estimation or the iterative seemingly unrelated nonlinear regression method. Both estimation methods have been shown to yield identical results under certain conditions; and

(e)   Except those using the additive utility function, the previous studies analyzed usually employed a small system of less than five commodities or groups of commodities, apparently due to the complexity of computation.

In addition, several studies incorporated habit and demographic factors into the model specification. For instance, Manser and Menkhaus *et al.* used an extended translog function with habit formation to study meat consumption. Eales and Unnevehr and Moschini and Meilke adopted the first-difference LA/AIDS form to capture the dynamic effects on meat demand. Capps and Havlicek employed the translating techniques to include household size and the degree of urbanization in their S_1-Branch system. Kokoski, and Chern and Lee also used the translating method to incorporate family size into their quadratic expenditure system (QES) to analyze the effects of demographic factors on consumption.

A Survey of Estimated Food Demand Elasticities

Table 14.5 provides an extensive, but not exhaustive, survey of previous estimates of food demand elasticities. The estimated elasticities are fairly different among these studies. For instance, the estimated own-price elasticities for beef vary widely. Estimated expenditure elasticities for beef vary from a high value of 1.74 (Menkhaus *et al.*) to a low of 0.34 (Eales and Unnevehr).

Similar variations can be found among the other food commodities shown in Table 14.5. In addition, the level of aggregation for commodity definition and number of commodities included in the system are arbitrary and varied

Table 14.4. Survey of Studies on Food Demand in U.S. Using Complete Demand Systems.

Study	Data	Commodity	Model	Estimation Method
Manser (1976)	1948-72 annual data	Meats, fruits & vegetables, cereal & bakery, & miscellaneous	Translog (TL)	ITSUR
Christenson & Manser (1977)	1947-71 annual data	Fish, beef, poultry, & seafood	Translog	ITSUR
Blackorby, Boyce, & Russell (1978)	1946-68 annual data	Meats (4 types), vegetables (6 types), & fruits (6 types)	Generalized S-branch	FILM
Eastwood & Craven (1981)	1955 - 1978 annual data	Food at home, away from home, & 10 other categories	Extended LES	MLE
Heien (1982)	1947-79 annual data	14 food categories, service, & nondurable goods	Almost Complete Model	NTSLS[a]
Lamm (1982)	1960 I-1980 III quarterly data	Food at home, away from home, & other nondurable goods	Translog	ITSUR
Blanciforti & Green (1983)	1948-78 annual data	11 aggregated commodities including food	AIDS, LES	FILM
Heien (1983)	1967 I-1979 III quarterly data	14 aggregate commodities including 5 food items	Almost Complete Model	NTSLS
Wohlgenant (1984)	1946-68 annual data	Food & nonfood	Fourier TL, GL	Nonlinear Least Squares
Capps & Havlicek (1984)	1972-74 CEDS (BLS)	Ground beef, roasts, poultry, pork, variety meats, & seafood	S_1-Branch	FILM

Table 14.4 cont.

Study	Data	Commodity	Model	Estimation Method
Menkhaus, Clair, & Hallingbye (1985)	1965-81 annual data	Beef, pork, & chicken	Translog	ITSUR
Blanciforti, Green, & King (1986)	1948-78 annual data	Meats, fruits & vegetables, cereal & bakery, & miscellaneous	AIDS, LES	FILM
Kokoski (1986)	1972-73 & 1980-81 CEDS (BLS)	Cereals, meats, dairy, fruits & vegetables, & others	QES	FILM
Huang & Raunikar (1987)	1977-78 NFCS (USDA)	8 food categories	LES	ML
Craven & Haidacher (1987)	1955-78 annual data including food at home & food away from home	11 aggregate commodities	LES-Leser LES-Powell LES-Stone	Leser Power FMLE
Dahlgran (1988)	1950-85 annual data food & nonfood	Beef, pork, chicken, & other	Rotterdam	Stepwise ML
Eales & Unnevehr (1988)	1965-85 annual data food & nonfood	Chicken, beef, pork, & non-meat	LA/AIDS	ITSUR
Heien & Pompelli (1988)	1977 Household Consumption Survey	Steak, roast, & ground beef	AIDS	ITSUR
Chern & Lee (1989)	1980-86 CEIS (BLS) (mean expenditure data)	8 aggregate commodities including food at home & food away from home	QES, LES	ITSUR
Moschini & Meilke (1989)	1967 I-1987 IV quarterly data	Beef, pork, chicken, & fish	LA/AIDS	ITSUR

Table 14.4 cont.

Study	Data	Commodity	Model	Estimation Method
Lee (1990)	1980-86 CEDS (BLS)	18 food categories plus food away from home	Lewbel Full System, LA/ AIDS	ITSUR

[a]NTSLS refers to nonlinear three-stage least squares.

among studies. They were usually dependent on researchers' interests and on data availability.

Demand Models for Forecasting

Despite the previous extensive efforts in estimating food demand systems as reviewed in the preceding section, we found that very few studies dealt with forecasting food demand. Almost all empirical models were evaluated on the basis of theoretical properties (adding-up, homogeneity, and symmetry) and the reasonableness of estimated demand elasticities. Very few of the food demand systems were either evaluated or used for the purpose of forecasting. Nevertheless, several studies conducted careful evaluation of the model's predictive power for within-sample periods. For example, Huang validated his estimated food demand system (41 groups) by means of simulation over the sample period (1953-1983). The forecasting performance based on root-mean-square error and turning points indicates a close relation between actual and simulated values. He suggested that his model can be used as a short-run forecasting device for food consumption, given prices and expenditures. Lee also compared alternative specifications of his LA/AIDS model by computing the index of average information inaccuracy, root-mean-square (RMS) error, RMS-% error (RMSPE), prediction of turning points, and the Merton market timing test. He concluded that one dynamic version performed the best for within-sample forecasts of expenditures of 19 food categories. These validation results, however, provide no basis for selecting one best model for forecasting.

A recent study by Chambers represents one of the few attempts to compare various demand models on the basis of post-sample forecasting. He estimated a linear expenditure system (LES), linear expenditure system with a habit formation (LESH), LA/AIDS, the error component model (ECM), vector autoregression (VAR), and random walk (RW) models, using quarterly data (1956:1 to 1982:4) for the U.K. Post-sample forecasting was conducted for the period of 1983:1 to 1986:2. Based on average information inaccuracies, RMS, RMSPE, and mean absolute prediction error (MPE), he found a simple habit formation model (LESH) to be superior. Based on these comparisons, he concluded that no system of consumer demand equations is going to be

Table 14.5. Survey of Estimated Price and Expenditure Elasticities of Food Demand in U.S.

Study	Commodity	Base Period or Basis for Computation	Elasticities Own-price	Elasticities Expenditure
Manser (1976)	Meats	1959	-0.53[a]	1.11
	Fruit & vegetables		-0.35	0.29
	Cereal & bakery		-0.65	0.18
	Others		-0.94	1.65
Christensen & Manser (1977)	Fish	1971	-0.17[b]	0.37
	Beef		-1.09	1.45
	Poultry		-0.71	0.93
	Seafood		-0.38	0.40
Blackorby, Boyce, & Russell (1978)	Fish	1968	-0.64[c]	0.87
	Beef		-0.27	1.04
	Poultry		-0.63	1.01
	Pork		-0.69	1.13
Eastwood & Craven (1981)	Food at home	1978	-0.23[d]	0.36
	Food away from home		-0.42	0.63
Lamm (1982)	Food at home	1980	-0.16	0.11
	Food away from home		-0.11	0.12
Heien (1982)	Beef	Constant	-0.96	1.27
	Pork		-0.51	0.33
	Chicken		-0.80	0.33
	Eggs		-0.26	-0.39
	Fresh fruit		-3.02	1.99
	Fresh vegetables		-0.35	0.26
Blanciforti & Green (1983)	Meats	Sample mean (1948-78)	-0.57[e]	0.78
	Fruits & vegetables		-0.60	0.67
	Cereal & bakery		-0.55	0.36
	Others		-1.01	1.62
Heien (1983)	Beef	Constant	-0.95	0.94
	Pork		-0.95	0.32
	Broilers		-0.47	0.65
	Milk		-0.33	0.24
	Eggs		-0.15	0.52

Table 14.5 cont.

Study	Commodity	Base Period or Basis for Computation	Own-price	Expenditure
			Elasticities	
Huang &	Meat	Constant	-0.53	0.36
Haidacher	Poultry		-0.68	0.14
(1983)	Fish		0.06	-0.06
	Eggs		-0.14	-0.07
	Dairy		-0.30	0.18
	Fat		-0.15	0.57
	Fruit		-0.37	0.63
	Vegetables		-0.21	0.21
	Processed fru. & veg.		-0.39	0.43
	Cereal		-0.35	-0.29
	Sugar		-0.11	0.44
	Nonalc. beverages		-0.33	0.14
Wohlgenant (1984)	Food	Sample mean (1946-68)	-0.36	0.46
Capps &	Ground beef	Sample mean	-1.58	1.38
Havlicek	Roasts	(1972-74)	-1.83	1.66
(1984)	Steaks		-1.69	1.51
	Other		-1.30	1.11
	Poultry		-1.46	1.28
	Seafood		-1.25	1.10
			-2.24	1.96
Menkhaus,	Beef	1980	-1.39	1.74
Clair, &	Pork		-0.69	0.23
Hallingbye	Chicken		-0.68	-0.69
(1985)				
Huang	Beef	Constant	-0.62	0.45
(1985)	Pork		-0.73	0.44
	Other meats		-1.37	0.06
	Chicken		-0.53	0.36
	Turkey		-0.68	0.32
	Fresh & frz. fish		0.01	0.12
	Canned & cured fish		0.04	0.00
	Eggs		-0.15	-0.03
	Cheese		-0.33	0.59
	Fluid milk		-0.26	-0.22
	Evaporated & dry milk		-0.83	-0.27
	Other fats & oil		-0.22	0.37

Table 14.5 cont.

Study	Commodity	Base Period or Basis for Computation	Elasticities	
			Own-price	Expenditure
Huang (cont.)	Sugar Other 27 food categories (not reported here)	Constant	-0.05	-0.18
Kokoski (1986)	Cereal Meats Dairy Fruits & vegetables Others	Log mean (1972-73 & 1980-81)	-0.77 -0.79 -0.77 -0.72 -0.77	0.88 1.23 0.75 1.08 0.96
Huang & Raunikar (1987)	Cereal & bakery Dairy Red meats Poultry Fish & shellfish Eggs Fruits & vegetables Others	Sample mean (1977-78)	-0.71 -0.81 -0.95 -0.83 -0.68 -0.69 -0.87 -0.92	0.85 0.93 1.21 0.85 0.85 0.80 1.00 1.01
Craven & Haidacher (1987)	Food at home Food away from home	Sample mean (1955-78)	-0.46[c] -0.49	0.31 0.73
Dahlgran (1987)	Beef Pork Chicken	1985	-0.66 -0.58 -0.60	0.44 -0.05 0.20
Chern & Lee (1989)	Food at home Food away from home	Sample mean (1980-86)	-0.98[c] -1.43	0.67 1.51
Eales & Unnevehr (1988)	Chicken Beef Pork Non-meat food	Sample mean (1965-85)	-0.28[c] -0.57 -0.76 -0.64	0.53 0.34 0.28 0.48
Heien & Pompelli (1988)	Steak Roast Ground beef	Sample mean (1977)	-0.73 -1.11 -0.85	1.14 1.37 0.69

Table 14.5 cont.

Study	Commodity	Base Period or Basis for Computation	Elasticities Own-price	Expenditure
Moschini &	Beef	Sample mean	-1.05[g]	1.39
Meike	Pork	(1967 I -	-0.84	0.85
(1989)	Chicken	1987 IV)	-0.10	0.21
	Fish		-0.43	0.31

[a]Indirect translog with habit.
[b]Indirect translog with explicit additivity.
[c]Compensated price elasticity.
[d]Extended linear expenditure system with habit formation.
[e]AIDS with autocorrelation model.
[f]Quadratic expenditure system.
[g]For period after structure change.

completely satisfactory when considering theoretical specification, ease of estimation, and forecasting potential. However, the results from Chambers and Lee suggest that a dynamic model is likely to be better than a static model for forecasting food demand.

A useful forecasting model for food demand should be able to reflect and capture emerging changes in demographic variables and preference structure caused by concerns about health and nutrition. As reviewed earlier, many existing demand models have incorporated demographic variables. Time-series models, which are more suitable for forecasting than cross-sectional models, can accomplish this objective only in a limited fashion because most of the demographic variables, except household age and size, cannot easily be averaged to create consistent time-series data.

Research on incorporating the impacts of health and nutritional concerns in food demand systems remains in the stage of infancy. Two problems are apparent: One is deriving reliable coefficients of demand response to health concerns from historic data; the second is projecting health variables into the future. Recently, Brown and Schrader developed a cholesterol information index and incorporated this variable in their study of the demand for eggs. This index was recently applied by Capps and Schmitz in estimating the demand for meats and fish. Chern *et al.* also used this index in their study of the impacts of health risk belief on the demand for fats and oil. So far, the successes in dealing with issues related to health concerns were limited to the models for a very small subset of food commodities such as fats and oils. These available empirical results show encouraging potential for addressing these important issues in models for forecasting food demand in the future.

Conclusions

This chapter attempts to survey the state-of-the-art in consumer demand modeling. The specifications of the popularly used demand systems are presented and appraised. We also survey and review the existing literature on food demand studies in the United States. This survey shows that many empirical studies are available in the literature. Few models, however, have been used for forecasting. Based on a few studies validating various models for within-sample and beyond-sample predictions, we can only conclude that a dynamic model is likely to be superior to a static one for forecasting. There exists no clear cut evidence on a particular choice of functional form for forecasting purposes.

With respect to the joint research project, our needs for forecasting lie in (1) quantitative and qualitative assessments of the impacts of demographic variables and health concerns on food demand in the medium term (next 10-15 years) and (2) linkage to supply forecasts for the purpose of evaluating surpluses (or shortages) of selected key commodities such as beef, soybeans, corn, and wheat in both the United States and Japan. We need to pay special attention to selection of appropriate food categories in demand modeling so that demand and supply forecasts can be reconciled. In this regard, we need to first identify the set of important agricultural commodities for the joint project and then decide which food groups to include in the demand system. Obviously, we cannot apply the same level of disaggregation for all food groups. In fact, we may have to work with subsets of food items, based on the nonparametric tests or separability assumptions.

To some extent, the choice of a forecasting model depends upon the data base selected for the comparative analyses of food demand in the two countries. The assessment of various data bases for food demand analysis is be provided in the chapter by Buse *et al.* in this book.

References

Barten, A.P.   1966.   Theorie en empirie van een volledig stelsel van vraegvergelijkingen.   Doctoral dissertation.   Rotterdam: University of Rotterdam.

Basiotis, P.P. and H.W. Yang. 1989. Expenditures on food away from home by all-income and low-income households: Analysis using USDA's 1985 and 1986 Continuing Survey of Food Intake by Individuals data. Paper presented at *1989 Annual Meeting of the American Agricultural Economics Association*, Baton Rouge, LA, July 28-August 2.

Blackorby, C., Boyce, R., and Russell, R.R. 1978. Estimation of demand systems generated by the Gorman polar form: A generalization of the S-branch utility tree. *Econometrica* 46:345-64.

Blanciforti, L.A. and R. Green. 1983. An almost ideal demand system incorporating habits: An analysis of expenditures on food and aggregate commodity groups. *Review of Economic and Statistics* 65:513-15.

Blanciforti, L.A., R.D. Green and G.A. King. 1986. U.S. consumer behavior over the postwar period: An Almost Ideal Demand System analysis. Giannini Foundation Monograph No. 40. Berkeley: University of California.

Blaylock, J. and D. Smallwood. 1983. Box-Cox transformation and error term specification in demand models. *Western Journal of Agricultural Economics* 8:68-75.

Brandow, G.E. 1961. Interrelations among demand for farm products and implications for control of market supply. Pennsylvania Agricultural Experimental Station Bulletin No. 680. University Park: Pennsylvania State University.

Brown, D.J. and L. Schrader. 1990. Information on cholesterol and falling shell egg consumption. *American Journal of Agricultural Economics* 72:548-555.

Brown, M.G. and J.Y. Lee. 1986. Orange and grapefruit juice demand forecasts. Pp. 215-232 in O. Capps and B. Senauer, eds., *Food Demand Analysis*.

Buse, R.C. 1986. Is the structure of demand for food changing?: Implications for projections. Pp. 105-129 in O. Capps and B. Senauer, eds., *Food Demand Analysis*.

Capps, Oral Jr. and Joseph Havlicek, Jr. 1984. National and regional household demand for meat, poultry, and seafood: A complete systems approach. *Canadian Journal of Agricultural Economics* 65:98-108.

Capps, Oral Jr. and J.M. Pearson. 1986. Analysis of convenience and nonconvenience food expenditures by U.S. households with projections to the year 2000. Pp. 233-250 in O. Capps and B. Senauer, eds., *Food Demand Analysis*.

Capps, O. and J.D. Schmitz. 1991. A recognition of health and nutrition factors in food demand analysis. *Western Journal of Agricultural Economics* 16:21-35.

Capps, O. and B. Senauer, eds. 1986. *Food Demand Analysis*. Blacksburg, VA: Virginia Polytechnic Institute and State University.

Chambers, M.J. 1990. Forecasting with demand systems, a comparative study. *Journal of Econometrics* 44:363-376.

Chang, H.S. 1977. Functional forms and the demand for meat in the United States. *The Review of Economics and Statistics* 59:355-359.

Chavas, Jean-Paul. 1979. Consumer unit scales and food consumption. Working paper. College Station: Department of Agricultural Economics, Texas A&M University.

Chern, W.S. and Horacio Soberon-Ferrer. 1987. Engel curve estimation for a complete demand system of aggregate expenditure components. In

Proceedings of the 33rd Conference of American Council on Consumer Interests, Denver, CO.

Chern, W.S. and Hwang-Jaw Lee. 1989a. Complete demand systems of nondurable goods and services. In *Proceedings of the 35th Conference of American Council on Consumer Interests*, Baltimore, MD.

Chern, W.S. and Hwang-Jaw Lee. 1989b. Nonparametric and parametric analyses of demand for food at home and away from home. Paper presented at the *1989 Annual Meeting of the American Agricultural Economics Association*, Baton Rouge, LA, July 28-August 2.

Chern, W.S., E.T. Loehman, S.T. Yen, and D.J. Brown. 1991. Information, health beliefs, and the demand for fats and oils. Working paper. Columbus: Department of Agricultural Economics and Rural Sociology, The Ohio State University.

Christensen, L.R. and M.E. Manser. 1977. Estimating U.S. consumer preferences for meat with a flexible utility function. *Journal of Econometrics* 5:37-54.

Christensen, L.R., D.W. Jorgenson, and L.J. Lau. 1975. Transcendental logarithmic utility functions. *American Economic Review* 65:367-383.

Craven, J.A. and R.C. Haidacher. 1987. Comparison of estimates from three linear expenditure system. Pp. 91-113 in R. Raunikar and C.L. Huang, eds., *Food Demand Analysis*. Ames: Iowa University Press.

Dahlgran, R.A. 1988. Changing meat demand structure in the United States: Evidence from a price flexibility analysis. *North Central Journal of Agricultural Economics* 10:165-176.

Deaton, A. and J. Muellbauer. 1980. An almost ideal demand system. *American Economic Review* 70:312-326.

Eastwood, D.B. and J.A. Craven. 1981. Food demand and savings in a complete, extended, linear expenditure system. *American Journal of Agricultural Economics* 63:544-549.

Eales, J.S. and L.J. Unnevehr. 1988. Demand for beef and chicken products: Separability and structure change. *American Journal of Agricultural Economics* 70:521-532.

George, P.S. and G.A. King. 1971. Consumer demand for food commodities in the U.S. with projections for 1980. Giannini Foundation Monograph No. 26. Berkeley: University of California.

Heien, Dale. 1982. The structure of food demand: Interrelatedness and duality. *American Journal of Agricultural Economics* 14:213-221.

Heien, Dale. 1983. Seasonality in U.S. consumer demand. *Journal of Business and Economic Statistics* 1:280-284.

Heien, D. and G. Pompelli. 1988. The demand for beef products: Cross-section estimation of demographic and economic effects. *Western Journal of Agricultural Economics* 13:37-44.

Hicks, J.R. 1956. *A Revision of Demand Theory*. Oxford: Oxford University Press.

Hotelling, H. 1935. Demand functions with limited budgets. *Econometrica* 3:66-78.

Huang, C.L. and R. Raunikar. 1981. Spline functions: An alternative to estimating income-expenditure relationships for beef. *Southern Journal of Agricultural Economics* 13:105-110.

Huang, C.L. and R. Raunikar. 1986. Food expenditure patterns: Evidence from U.S. household data. Pp. 49-65 in O. Capps and B. Senauer, eds., *Food Demand Analysis*.

Huang, K.S. 1983. The family of inverse demand systems. *European Economic Review* 23:329-337.

Huang, K.S. 1985. U.S. demand for food: A complete system of price and income effects. Technical Bulletin No. 1714. Washington, DC: Economic Research Service, U.S. Department of Agriculture.

Huang, K.S. 1988. An inverse demand system for U.S. composite foods. *American Journal of Agricultural Economics* 70:902-909.

Huang, K.S. 1989. A forecasting model for food and other expenditures. *Applied Economics* 21:1235-1246.

Huang, K.S. 1990. An inverse demand system for U.S. composite foods: Reply. *American Journal of Agricultural Economics* 72:239.

Huang, K.S. 1991. U.S. demand for food: A complete system of quantity effects on prices. Technical Bulletin No. 1795. Washington, DC: Economic Research Service, U.S. Department of Agriculture.

Huang, K.S. and R.C. Haidacher. 1983. Estimation of a composite food demand system for the United States. *Journal of Business & Economic Statistics* 1:285-291.

Kinsey, J. 1983. Working wives and the marginal propensity to consume food away from home. *American Journal of Agricultural Economics* 65:10-19.

Klein, L.R. and H. Rubin. 1947-48. A constant utility index of the cost of living. *The Review of Economic Studies* 15:84-87.

Kokoski, M.F. 1986. An empirical analysis of intertemporal and demographic variations in consumer preferences. *American Journal of Agricultural Economics* 68:894-907.

Kolodinsky, Jane. 1987. Female labor force participation and expenditures on food away from home. *Proceedings of the 33rd Conference of American Council on Consumer Interests*, Denver, CO.

Lamm, R.M. Jr. 1982. The demand for food consumed at home and away from home. *Agricultural Economics Research* 34:15-20.

Lee, H.J. 1990. Nonparametric and parametric analyses of food demand in the United States. Ph.D. dissertation. Columbus: The Ohio State University.

Lee, J.Y., M.G. Brown, and B. Schwartz. 1986. The demand for national brand and private label frozen concentrated orange juice: A switching regression analysis. *Western Journal of Agricultural Economics* 11:1-7.

Lewbel, A.   1989.   Nesting the AIDS and translog demand systems. *International Economic Review* 30:349-356.

Manchester, A. January 1991. U.S. food spending and income. Agricultural Information Bulletin No. 618. Washington, DC: Economic Research Service, U.S. Department of Agriculture.

Manser, M.E. 1976. Elasticities of demand for food: An analysis using non-additive utility functions allowing for habit formation. *Southern Economics Journal* 43:879-891.

McCracken, V.A. and J.A. Brandt. 1987. Household consumption of food away from home: Total expenditure and by type of food facility. *American Journal of Agricultural Economics* 69:274-284.

Menkhaus, D.J., J.S. Clair, and S. Hallingbye. 1985. A reexamination of consumer buying behavior for beef, pork, and chicken. *Western Journal of Agricultural Economics* 10:116-125.

Moschini, G. and K.D. Meilke. 1989. Modeling the pattern of structural change in U.S. meat demand. *American Journal of Agricultural Economics* 71:253-261.

Price, D.W. and Mittelhammer. 1979. A matrix of demand elasticities for fresh fruit. *Western Journal of Agricultural Economics* 4:69-86.

Price, D.W., D.Z. Price, and D.A. West. 1980. Traditional and nontraditional determinants of household expenditures on selected fruits and vegetables. *Western Journal of Agricultural Economics* 5:21-35.

Raunikar, R. and C.L. Huang. 1986. Implications of factors affecting food consumption. Pp. 91-103 in O. Capps and B. Senauer, eds., *Food Demand Analysis*.

Redman, B.J. 1980. The impact of women's time allocation on expenditure for meals away from home and prepared foods. *American Journal of Agricultural Economics* 62:234-237.

Roy, R. 1942. *De l'utilite'*. Paris: Hermann.

Salathe, L.E. and R.C. Buse. 1979. Household food consumption patterns in the U.S. Technical Bulletin No. 1587. Washington, DC: Economic Research Service, U.S. Department of Agriculture.

Shephard, R.   1953.   *Cost and Production Functions*.   Princeton, NJ: Princeton University Press.

Smallwood, D. and J. Blaylock. 1981. Impact of household size and income on food spending patterns. Technical Bulletin No. 1650. Washington, DC: Economic Research Service, U.S. Department of Agriculture.

Stone, R. 1954. Linear expenditure systems and demand analysis: An application to the pattern of British demand. *Economic Journal* 64:511-527.

Theil, H. 1965. The information approach to demand analysis. *Econometrica* 30:67-87.

Tweeten, Luther. 1967. The demand for U.S. farm output. *Food Research Institute Studies* 7(3):343-369.

Tyrell, T. and T. Mount. 1982. A nonlinear expenditure system using a linear logit specification. *American Journal of Agricultural Economics* 64:539-546.

Wohlgenant, M.K. 1989. Demand for farm output. *American Journal of Agricultural Economics* 71:241-252.

Wohlgenant, M.K. 1984. Conceptual and functional form issues in estimating demand elasticities for food. *American Journal of Agricultural Economics* 66:211-215.

Wohlgenant, M.K. 1985. Estimating cross elasticities of demand for beef. *Western Journal of Agricultural Economics* 10:322-329

Wold, H. 1944. A synthesis of pure demand analysis, III. *Skandinavisk Aktuarietidskrift* 27:60-120.

Yang, H.W. 1988. Expenditures on food away from home by U.S. low-income households--1985/86. Unpublished Master's thesis. College Park: The University of Maryland.

15

Japanese Agricultural Supply:
Determinants of Workforce in Agriculture and
a Note on Commodity Supply Response
Yuko Arayama

Introduction

After 1975, Japan's net national product (at factor cost) created in agriculture, forestry, and fisheries ceased to increase. As a result, the share of net national product created in agriculture declined to 2.4 percent in 1989 from 8.4 percent in 1965 (Table 15.1). This reduction originated from several channels including a decrease in the number of farm households, decrease of household members per household, and increase of farm household members engaged in off-farm work.

Table 15.1. Net National Product at Factor Cost by Economic Activity (Billion Yen).

	1965	1975	1985	1989
Net national product	26,117	120,362	251,234	286,519
Agriculture, forestry, and fisheries	2,197	7,012	7,496	7,029

Source: Statistical Yearbook of the Ministry of Agriculture, Forestry, and Fisheries.

The number of farm households declined from 5,565,000 in 1965 to 4,194,000 in 1989 (see Chapter 4). The number of farm households whose area of cultivated land is between 0.5 and 2.0 ha decreased the most. On the other hand, the number of farm households with more than 2.5 ha increased, but the absolute number of these farm households is rather small (see Chapter 4). Farm household population followed the same trends as the number of farm households, falling from 30,083,000 in 1965 to 18,975,000 in 1989 (Table 15.2).

Table 15.3 summarizes the number of farm household members classified by annual farm working days and by age. Household members engaged in own farming less than 60 days predominate in Japan. The number of household members engaged in own farming more than 60 days per year has been declining. Household members engaged in own farming display rising average age. In 25 years, the number of household members younger than 29 years old dropped from 1,522,000 to 625,000 in 1989. In addition, the area of cultivated land and aggregated planted area also decreased (Table 15.4).

Table 15.2. Farm Household Population (1,000).

	1965	1975	1985	1989
Total	30,083	23,195	19,839	18,975
Male	14,612	11,241	9,662	9,213
Female	15,472	11,954	10,177	9,762

Source: Statistical Yearbook of the Ministry of Agriculture, Forestry, and Fisheries.

Table 15.3. Number of Household Members Engaged in Own Farming (1,000).

	1965	1975	1984	1989
Working Days				
29 or less		2,218	2,195	2,178
30 to 59		1,337	1,399	1,244
60 to 99		1,290[1]	682	629
100 to 149		---	557	427
150 or more		2,725	1,606	1,304
	1965	**1970**	**1984**	**1989**
Age (Years)				
16 to 29	1,522	1,415	859	625
30 to 39	4,451[1]	1,054	2,249[3]	2,017[3]
40 to 49	---	1,626	---	---
50 to 59	---	1,242	1,542	1,296
60 to 64	1,517[2]	530	543	710
65 or older	---	1,008	1,017	1,134

[1]Including "40 to 59."
[2]Including "65 or Older."
[3]Including "40 to 49."

Table 15.4. Area of Cultivated Land (1,000 Hectares).

	1965	1970	1979	1988
Total cultivated	6,004	5,796	5,474	5,317
Paddy fields cultivated	3,392	3,441	3,081	2,889
Upland fields cultivated	2,650	2,411	2,393	2,428
Total planted area of crops	---	7,619	5,662	5,440

These observations show that the number of workers engaged in agriculture has been declining, and the number of workers in manufacturing and service industries has been increasing as the Japanese economy has experienced economic growth. Thus, the employment structure of developed countries generally has been following Petty-Clark's Law. However, a closer look at the shift of employment structure reveals that the share of employees in each industry and the time pattern of employment differ among prefectures.

This chapter utilizes these prefectural variations to investigate the determinants of employment structure. Employment in manufacturing and service industries was found to be determined by factors within these industries, and employment in agriculture was determined primarily by the degree of economic development. This situation is highly consistent with expected time allocation within farm households, where off-farm work hours are determined first and farm work hours second (Arayama, 1986).

The share of workers engaged in manufacturing is assumed to be exogenous to this model. This assumption does not hold precisely in reality. The difference between the share of workers engaged in service and that in manufacturing turned out to depend on two types of income transfers between prefectures (by government and by private industry) and a demographic factor (the ratio of non-working population to total population).

Employment Structure

Transitional Pattern of Employment Structure

The transitional pattern of employment structure in Japan can be classified into six categories as is shown in Figures 15.1 and 15.2. These two categories are divided into two groups: A category prefectures (Figure 15.1) experiencing an increase in the number of workers over time, and B category prefectures (Figure 15.2) experiencing no increase. The A-1 category is the most common pattern from the viewpoint of economic development. In prefectures such as Tokyo, Osaka, Aichi, and Hyogo, the population has increased rapidly, and the manufacturing and service industries have grown until 1970. After

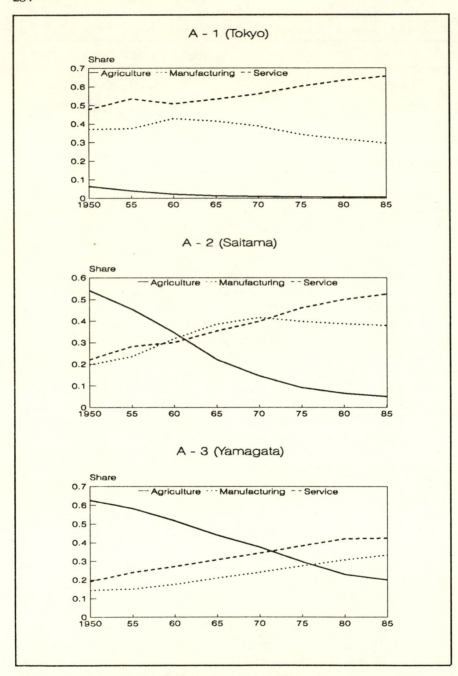

Figure 15.1. Transitional Patterns of Employment Structure.
Source: Population Census of Japan.

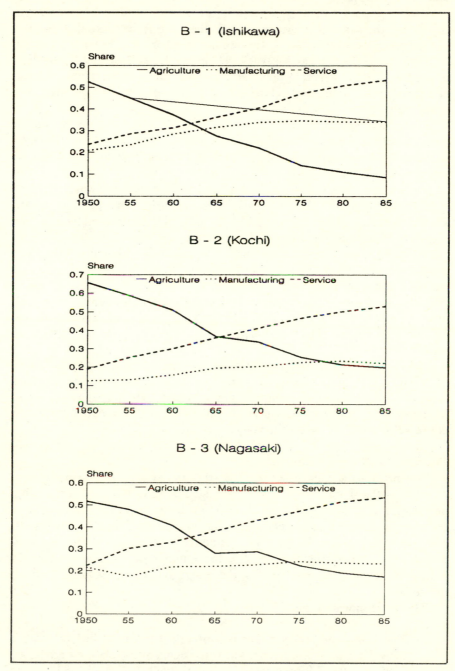

Figure 15.2. Transitional Pattern of Employment Structure.
Source: Population Census of Japan.

this period the share of service workers in the labor force continued to grow, but the share of manufacturing workers in the labor force became constant.

Prefectures classified as A-2, such as Saitama, Kanagawa, and Kyoto show a similar pattern of employment as A-1, but the transition was delayed compared with prefectures classified as A-1. In A-2 prefectures, the manufacturing industry continues to grow.

Prefectures classified as B-1, such as Ishikawa, also followed an ordinal pattern, but the timing showed further delay. The share of workers engaged in manufacturing increased rapidly, reached its peak in 1970, and remained constant thereafter.

Prefectures classified as A-3, B-2, and B-3 show somewhat different transitional patterns. The shares of manufacturing and of services are increasing in A-3. Prefectures classified as B-2 and B-3 increased their service share but their manufacturing share increased very little.

Figure 15.3, summarizing the transitional pattern of each industry for those prefectures, provided three interesting observations. First, the share of workers engaged in service converged to 50 percent, except in some prefectures. Second, the share of manufacturing seemed to have a maximum level, around 40 percent. The maximum level of manufacturing is much lower in some prefectures. Third, the share of agriculture declined steadily for all prefectures.

Another observation is apparent when Figure 15.4 is sorted by the share of workers in manufacturing. In earlier years such as 1950, the share of service was high where the share of manufacturing was high. However, in later years this tendency disappeared, and the share of services tended to converge to about 50 percent for most prefectures.

Population and Employment Structure

The previous section described the transitional aspects of employment structure -- the share of total workers engaged in agriculture, manufacturing, and service in each prefecture. This section will analyze the relation between the number of workers engaged in each industry, the total number of workers, and population. Table 15.5 contains simple correlation coefficients between population, total number of workers, the number of workers engaged in manufacturing, and the number of workers engaged in services for 1960, 1970, and 1980.

This table indicates the following:

1. Population and total number of workers (population in labor force) show the highest correlation. The coefficients of correlation were 0.993, 0.996, and 0.997 for the respective years 1960, 1970, and 1980.
2. Population and the number of workers engaged in services show the second highest correlation. The coefficients of correlation were 0.973, 0.991, and 0.996.

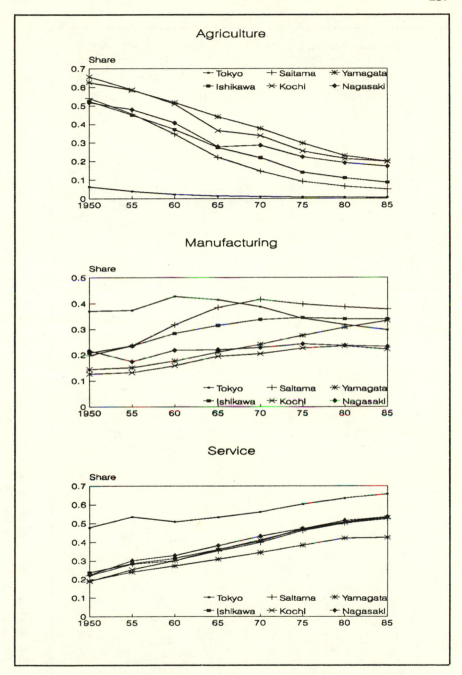

Figure 15.3. Transitional Employment Structure Pattern by Industry.
Source: Population Census of Japan.

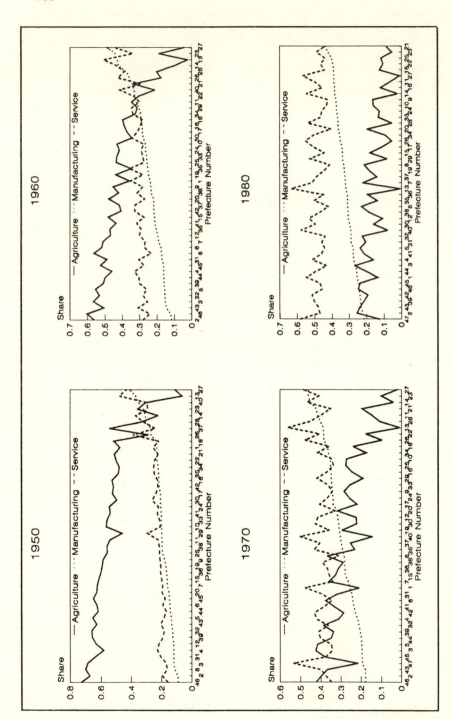

Figure 15.4. Regional Structure of Employment.
Source: Population Census of Japan.

Table 15.5. Correlation Coefficients Between Population, Number of Workers, Number of Workers Engaged in Agriculture, Number of Workers Engaged in Manufacturing, and Number of Workers in Service.

	POP	TOT	AGR	MAN	SER
1960					
POP	1.000	0.993	0.642	0.894	0.973
TOT		1.000	0.671	0.899	0.962
AGR			1.000	0.274	0.461
MAN				1.000	0.953
SER					1.000
1970					
POP	1.000	0.996	0.471	0.941	0.991
TOT		1.000	0.498	0.947	0.985
AGR			1.000	0.250	0.406
MAN				1.000	0.930
SER					1.000
1980					
POP	1.000	0.997	0.421	0.962	0.996
TOT		1.000	0.450	0.968	0.992
AGR			1.000	0.290	0.392
MAN				1.000	0.948
SER					1.000

Source: Population Census of Japan.
NOTE: POP is population, TOT is population in labor force, AGR is workers engaged in agriculture, MAN is workers engaged in manufacturing, and SER is workers engaged in services. Okinawa and Tokyo are excluded from the calculation.

3. Total number of workers and the number of workers engaged in manufacturing shows the third highest correlation. The coefficients of correlation are 0.899, 0.947, and 0.968. This correlation exceeds the correlation between population and the number of workers engaged in manufacturing by about 0.005 in each year.
4. These three sets of coefficients of correlation listed above increased over time.
5. The correlation between population and the number of workers engaged in agriculture and that between the total number of workers and workers engaged in agriculture are lower than 0.5. Furthermore, these correlations have been decreasing over time.

Cause and effect relations among population, the number of workers, the number of workers engaged in manufacturing, and the number of workers engaged in services were implied but by no means proved through these first four facts. The higher correlation between population and service compared with that between population and manufacturing could suggest that the main determinant of the size of the service industry is population (i.e. demand), and that the main determinant for the total number of workers could be the size of manufacturing (i.e. demand for labor). Furthermore, increasing coefficients over time could suggest adjustment in distribution of population, and the redistribution of workers among prefectures towards equilibrium. On the contrary, the number of workers engaged in agriculture has no strong relation with population or with the total number of workers in each prefecture. This weak reaction of agriculture to this changing situation could imply that the number of workers engaged in agriculture could be determined by forces outside of agriculture.

Interregional Variation

This section summarizes the coefficients of variation of four categories of variables that play key roles in understanding the existing interregional variation.[1] Table 15.6 reports the coefficients of variation for the share in the work force of workers engaged in agriculture, manufacturing, and services, respectively. Three observations are apparent. First, the share of workers engaged in services shows the smallest variation among prefectures. This observation corresponds to the convergence of the share of services to 50 percent shown in Figure 15.2. Second, the coefficient of variation for the share of workers engaged in manufacturing has declined over time. Those two facts could indicate that the share of workers engaged in services has been fairly stable, regardless of the level of industrialization, and that the interregional difference in the share of workers engaged in manufacturing has decreased. Third, interregional variation of the share of workers engaged in agriculture has gotten larger over time.

Table 15.7 shows the coefficients of variation for productivity measures. Productivity (PROD-ALL) is Net Prefectural Product divided by the number of workers. PROD-MAN and PROD-SER are labor productivity for manufacturing and services, respectively. According to this table, the variation in productivity for manufacturing is about 0.2 and roughly double that for

---

[1] Okinawa is excluded from calculation due to the data unavailability in earlier years. Tokyo is also excluded because it is considered as outlier in many aspects.

Table 15.6. Coefficient of Variation for Workers Engaged in Agriculture, Manufacturing, and Services among Prefectures.

Year	Share - AGR	Share - MAN	Share - SER
1960	0.26	0.31	0.15
1965	0.31	0.28	0.12
1970	0.34	0.25	0.11
1975	0.39	0.20	0.10
1980	0.39	0.17	0.09
1985	0.43	0.18	0.10

Source: Population Census of Japan.
NOTE: Share - AGR is the share of workers engaged in agriculture and so on. Okinawa and Tokyo are excluded from the calculation.

Table 15.7. Coefficient of Variation for Productivity of Labor.

Year	PROD-ALL	PROD-AGR	PROD-MAN	PROD-SER
1960	0.22	0.18	0.26	0.11
1965	0.18	0.19	0.22	0.09
1970	0.21	0.21	0.24	0.11
1975	0.14	0.17	0.21	0.08
1980	0.15	0.20	0.19	0.08
1985	0.13	0.24	0.21	0.07

Source: Annual Report on Prefectural Accounts.
NOTE: PROD-ALL is Net Prefectural Product / number of workers, PROD-AGR is productivity per worker for agriculture, PROD-MAN is productivity per worker for manufacturing, and PROD-SER is productivity per worker for services. Okinawa and Tokyo are excluded from the calculation.

services. The coefficients of variation have been declining over time except in agriculture.

Table 15.8 reports the coefficients of variation for monthly earnings. Earnings include monthly contractual earnings and one-twelfth of annual special earnings (or "bonuses"). The coefficient of variation of average earnings for all industry and all sizes of enterprise is about 0.1. It is interesting to discover that the interregional variation in the service industry is smaller than in manufacturing.

By comparing Tables 15.7 and 15.8 it is apparent that interregional variation in productivity is larger than in monthly earnings. This difference in interregional variations could have resulted from a situation where workers

Table 15.8. Coefficient of Variation for Earnings (Salary).

Year	SAL-ALL	SAL-MAN	SAL-SER
1970	---	0.12	0.06
1975	0.09	0.10	0.06
1980	0.09	0.10	0.09
1985	0.10	0.10	0.08

Source: Annual Report on Prefectural Accounts.
NOTE: Earnings includes monthly contractual earnings and annual special earnings. SAL-ALL indicates average earnings for all industries and all sizes of enterprise. SAL-MAN is for manufacturing and SAL-SER is for services. Okinawa and Tokyo are excluded from the calculation.

tend to be paid equally regardless of interregional differences in labor productivity. The small interregional variation in monthly earning could be attributed to labor mobility. Somewhat larger interregional variation in productivity compared with that of monthly earning could be attributed to the possible location of each manufacturing site. Less interregional variation for monthly earnings than for labor productivity could affect the employment structure through "income transfer".

Table 15.9 reports the coefficient of variation among prefectures for the ratio of population in the labor force to total population (EPRATIO) and for the ratio of the number of workers engaged in services to total population (EPRAIOS). According to this table, EPRATIO has minimal interregional variation. The difference among prefectures in the ratio of people who are not in the labor force may not affect the employment and sales structure since people consume goods and services regardless of their working status.

Table 15.9. Coefficient of Variation for Labor Force Participation Rate.

Year	EPRATIO	EPRATIOS
1960	0.06	0.13
1965	0.06	0.11
1970	0.06	0.09
1975	0.06	0.07
1980	0.06	0.06
1985	0.05	0.07

Source: Population Census of Japan.
NOTE: EPRATIO is population in labor force / population and EPRATIOS is number of workers engaged in service / population. Okinawa and Tokyo are excluded from the calculation.

Interregional variation in per capita prefectural income has been small and decreased from 1960 to 1975 as is shown Table 15.10.

Fiscal Transfer

All of the prefectures cannot alone raise tax revenue to meet their fiscal demand. The reason for this is twofold. First, local governments cannot take all the tax revenue since a part of the tax belongs to the national tax. Second, the degree of development for secondary or tertiary industry varies prefecture by prefecture. To allow local governments to meet fiscal demand, the central government gives a fiscal transfer under the labels Local Allocation Tax, Local Transfer Tax, and national government disbursements for specific purposes.

The most popular measure of fiscal dependence is the Fiscal Capacity Index (FCI). The Fiscal Capacity Index is defined as basic financial revenue divided by basic financial needs. Table 15.11 reports correlation coefficients between FCI and labor productivity.

FCI and labor productivity show high correlation due to the following reasons: Prefectures where manufacturing has developed can expect higher tax revenue, which results in a higher FCI. It is also true that prefectures with the most developed manufacturing have higher labor productivity. These relations could explain high correlation between FCI and labor productivity.

High correlation between FCI and labor productivity can be also interpreted as a measure of the amount of transfer received by each prefecture. Basic fiscal needs can exceed basic fiscal revenue since there is fiscal transfer from the central government to local governments.

Determination of Employment Structure

As noted earlier, employment structure changes generally follow Petty-Clark's Law characterized by a falling share of agriculture in the economy. However, the transitional pattern of employment structure of each prefecture

Table 15.10. Coefficient of Variation for Per Capita Prefectural Income.

Year	RINCPC
1960	0.23
1965	0.19
1970	0.20
1975	0.13
1980	0.14
1985	0.15

Source: Annual Report on Prefectural Accounts.
NOTE: RINCPC is Net Prefectural Income/population. Okinawa and Tokyo are excluded from the calculation.

Table 15.11. Correlation Coefficients Between the Fiscal Capacity Index (FCI) and Labor Productivity.

FCI	PROD-ALL	PROD-AGR	PROD-MAN	PROD-SER
1960	0.880	0.260	0.779	0.411
1970	0.909	0.052	0.793	0.765
1980	0.825	-0.136	0.694	0.608

Source: Annual Report on Prefectural Accounts.
NOTE: PROD-ALL is Net Prefectural Product / number of workers, PROD-AGR is productivity per worker for agriculture, PROD-MAN is productivity per worker for manufacturing, PROD-SER is productivity per worker for services, and FCI is Fiscal Capacity Index. Okinawa and Tokyo are excluded from the calculation.

is not necessarily consistent with this Law. Matsugi (1987) showed some prefectures were following the developed prefectures with some time lag.

The transitional pattern of employment structure of many prefectures in western Japan, such as Kochi and Nagasaki, is somewhat different from the typical pattern. The share of workers engaged in services has grown without an increase in the share of workers engaged in manufacturing. This transitional pattern of employment structure is contradicting the ordinary interpretation of the process of economic development.

If the service industry is "income initiating" or basic like manufacturing, the reason why the service industry follows the pattern of manufacturing can be explained.[2] For example, some portion of the service sector in Tokyo is "income initiating". Therefore, the share of workers engaged in services in Tokyo has increased regardless of the share of workers engaged in manufacturing. But the service industry in Kochi and Nagasaki is considered as mostly "non-income initiating" or non-basic industry and is a multiple of basic industry.

The share of all workers engaged in service has converged to 40 percent due to a relatively small interregional difference in per capita prefectural income, as shown in Table 15.8. In other words, some portion of income, which does not vary interregionally, tends to be spent on services.

---

[2] Service industry is largely considered as "non-income initiating" or non-basic industry because the demand for service is largely created by income earned through "income initiating" or basic industry such as manufacturing and agriculture.

Furthermore, service is normally locally produced and consumed. Therefore, the share of workers engaged in service has been equalized interregionally. It is also true that the share of workers engaged in service has been increasing since the income elasticity for service demand is high.

Is manufacturing income initiating (basic industry) and services not? Services may not be "income initiating," but the industry is "income generating" without a doubt. Therefore, it is very hard to confirm that the service industry is "non-income initiating." If services are non-basic industry, how can we explain the small interregional variation of per capita prefectural income regardless of the difference in the employment structure?

I will develop here a model which hopefully will make clear two things: (1) that services are not essentially "income initiating", and (2) the determinants for interregional difference in the employment structure.

Manufacturing is assumed to be basic industry, and the size of manufacturing for each prefecture is assumed to be determined exogenously. Because location is determined to a considerable extent by costs not controllable by the local area, this assumption can be justified to some extent. The size of manufacturing determines the number of workers engaged in it. Income is generated through manufacturing. In addition, agriculture is generating income through its operation. On the other hand, service is not non-basic industry because demand for service is derived from the operation of manufacturing. This basic industry demand creates the supply of services, and the service industry generates income while supplying services.

Labor is mobile interregionally. Therefore, earnings will be equalized fairly well among prefectures at each point of time. However, the difference in productivity for manufacturing will remain to some extent due to unique characteristics of each location.

Under these assumptions, it is conceivable that workers in prefectures where labor productivity is lower receive a transfer from other prefectures where labor productivity is high. Workers on the national level could not benefit from this kind of transfer channeled by private companies, but workers in low productivity prefectures are benefitted through this transfer. This transfer is called "private-sector transfer" in this paper. On the other hand, prefectures where basic fiscal needs exceed basic fiscal revenue receive transfer from the central government under the name of the Local Allocation Tax and so on. These "fiscal transfers" become a component of disposable income to residents of each prefecture.

Another factor could increase the total value of expenditure compared with the prefectural income level: People who are not in the labor force, mainly retired workers, spend money. Some people use their saving or pension payments. The share of workers engaged in service industry could increase as the share of people increase who are not in labor force. Furthermore, higher per capita income could increase expenditures on services because the income elasticity of demand for services is relatively high.

Based on the assumptions developed above, the following hypothesis is derived: The extent to which the share of workers engaged in services exceeds that in manufacturing depends on "private-sector transfer", "fiscal transfer", and the share (ratio) of non-working population in the total population.

The hypothesis will be tested by estimating the following equation:

(1) · $\text{SHASM} = b_0 + b_1\text{ALPHA} + b_2\text{P-TRANS} + b_3\text{NEPRATIO} + b_4\text{RINCP} + b5\text{YEAR} + u$

(2) $\text{SHASM} = c_0 + c_1\text{BETA} + c_2\text{P-TRANS} + c_3\text{NEPRATIO} + c_4\text{RINCP} + c5\text{YEAR} + v$

SHASM is defined as the difference between the share of workers engaged in services and that in manufacturing. ALPHA and BETA measure the degree of "fiscal transfer." ALPHA is defined as the difference between basic financial needs and basic financial revenue divided by basic financial needs, and BETA is the difference between basic financial needs and basic financial revenue divided by basic financial revenue. P-TRANS stands for the "private transfer." NEPRATIO is the ratio of non-working population to the total population. RINCP is the net prefectural income per capita. YEAR is trend. u and v are random terms.

Results of Estimation

Three groups of coefficient estimates are reported in Table 15.12. Equations (1) to (5) include time trend (YEAR) and only one other explanatory variable which stands for the hypothesis; equations (6) and (7) include explanatory variables other than RINCP; equations (8) and (9) include all explanatory variables.

Three observations are noted from equations (1) to (5). First, all estimates possess expected signs except RINCP in equation (5) in the first group of equation.[3] Second, equation (4) has the highest coefficient of determination and NEPRATIO also shows the highest t-ratio. Third, equation (3) indicates that the effect of "private-sector transfer" is positive and significant, but P-TRANS is the weakest among all explanatory variables.

Equations (6) and (7) include all explanatory variables other than RINCP, whose coefficient was negative in the first group equation (5). In (6) and (7)

---

[3] This negativity in RINCP can be attributed to a strong correlation between net prefectural income per worker (RINCP) and the share of manufacturing, i.e., RINCP is high in industrialized prefectures.

Table 15.12. Estimates of Coefficient for Difference Between Share of Service and Share of Manufacturing, SHASM the Dependent Variable.[a]

	(1)	(2)	(3)	(4)	(5)	(6)	(7)	(8)	(9)
ALPHA[b]	0.049 (5.149)	—	—	—	—	0.046 (5.353)	—	0.060 (6.425)	—
BETA[c]	—	0.176 (4.242)	—	—	—	—	0.158 (4.335)	—	0.193 (4.932)
P-TRANS[d]	—	—	0.011 (2.317)	—	—	0.011 (2.645)	0.015 (3.336)	0.0001 (3.948)	0.0002 (4.056)
NEPRATIO[e]	—	—	—	1.693 (7.770)	—	2.052 (11.295)	2.106 (11.247)	2.420 (11.600)	2.376 (10.782)
RINCP[f]	—	—	—	—	-34.89 (-4.88)	—	—	24.887 (3.242)	17.536 (2.237)
YEAR	0.006 (3.945)	0.006 (3.590)	0.006 (3.549)	0.006 (4.059)	0.013 (5.71)	0.008 (7.048)	0.008 (6.76)	0.004 (2.354)	0.005 (2.927)
R-Square	0.226	0.180	0.101	0.366	0.212	0.620	0.594	0.650	0.610

Source: Population Census of Japan and Annual Report on Prefectural Accounts.
[a]SHASM = SHAS - SHAM, t-ratio is in parentheses. Okinawa and Tokyo are excluded from the calculation.
[b]ALPHA = (basic financial needs - basic financial revenue) / basic financial needs.
[c]BETA = (basic financial needs - basic financial revenue) / basic financial revenue.
[d]P-TRANS = SAL-ALL - PROD-ALL.
[e]NEPRATIO = (POP - TOT) / POP.
[f]RINCP = Net Prefectural Income / POP.

all the explanatory variable coefficients possess expected signs, and their significance exceeds the 1 percent probability level.

Equations (8) and (9) include all explanatory variables. Coefficients of all variables including RINCP are positive and significant. The sign of RINCP became positive, as appropriate, after controlling effects of other variables on SHASM.

These results support the hypothesis that transfers do play an important role in determining the relative size of the service industry compared with the size of manufacturing. Above all, the transfers given by the central government to local governments help to determine the size of the service industry relative to manufacturing. The ratio of non-working population to total population and income also determine the employment structure.

Conclusion

This study has made the following three points. First, two types of transitional patterns in employment structure characterize Japanese prefectures. Prefectures where manufacturing has developed followed the pattern of the so called Petty-Clark's Law; however, quite a few prefectures in west Japan experienced an increase in the share of workers in service without an increase in the share of workers engaged in manufacturing.

Second, the major determinants for the discrepancy between the share of workers engaged in service and the share in manufacturing have proved to be two kinds of interregional transfers. The first transfer is "fiscal transfer" which is given by the central government to local governments under the name of Local Allocation Tax, and related transfers. The second type of transfer is received by workers in prefectures where labor productivity is relatively low compared with prefectures where the manufacturing sector is well developed. Since interregional variation in earning is smaller than that of labor productivity, workers in prefectures with low labor productivity receive a transfer of income. This kind of transfer is called "private-sector transfer" in this paper. Furthermore, the ratio of non-working population to total population and income level are also found to be crucial determinants of employment structure.

Finally, service and manufacturing industries are different in their nature. Manufacturing is basic "income initiating" industry; service is essentially not so. Major components of output produced in the service industry are classified as "personal" services, serving basic industries such as agriculture and manufacturing. Hence the service industry is small in prefectures with little basic industry.

What implications can be derived from these facts and findings? First, the share of the work force in agriculture is determined mainly by the number of workers in other industries. In other words, factors which have nothing directly to do with agriculture are actually determining the share of the work force in agriculture. Thus policies which promote agricultural production cannot prevent urbanization, but policies which promote industrialization can urbanize the area. The second implication is modeling advice. It has become common to use a multi-sector model to analyze the process of economic development. Such models need to include regional variables to reflect the determination of the employment structures during the process of economic development.

References

Arayama, Yuko. 1986. Time allocation of Japanese farm households. Ph.D Dissertation. Chicago, IL: The University of Chicago.

Kosai, Yasushi. 1990. Yosofuson, sotokubunpu to gijutsuiten. *Higashiajia no Hatten Model: Keizai to Shakai*, pp. 41-58.

Madison, Angus. 1989. *The World Economy in the 20th Century.* OECD Development Center.

Matsugi, Takashi. 1986. *Chiikikeizairon: Chihojidai no Kanosei.* Jikkyo Shuppann.

Matsugi, Takashi. March 1987. Toshi to Sangyo. *Toshimondai Kenkyu* 78:3-18.

Matsugi, T., T. Makido, and N. Okuno. 1990. *Kokusaika to Chiikikeizai: Korekarano Tokaikeizai.* Nagoya University Press.

Minami, Ryoshin. 1981. *Nihon no Keizaihatten.* Toyokeizaishinposha.

Statistics Bureau, Prime Minister's Office. 1983. Jinko no shugyojotai to sangyokosei. *1980 Population Census of Japan* (Monograph Series).

Yamazawa, Ippei. 1986. *Kokusaikeizaigaku.* Toyokeizaishinposha.

Data Sources

Economic Research Institute, Economic Planning Agency, Japan. *Annual Report on Prefectural Accounts.*

Statistics and Information Department, Minister's Secretariat, Ministry of Labor, Japan. *Yearbook of Labor Statistics.*

Statistics and Information Department, Ministry of Labor, Japan. *A Monthly Labor Survey.*

Statistics Bureau, Prime Minister's Office. *Population Census of Japan.*

APPENDIX A

Survey of Japanese Agricultural Supply:
Brief Notes on Elasticity
Yuko Arayama

Very few empirical studies on supply elasticities of agricultural commodities have been found in Japan. Furthermore, existing studies are relatively old and outdated.

According to Akino, the supply of agricultural commodities have been viewed to be inelastic because supply barely responded to a huge decline of price during the Great Depression in the Showa Era. Agricultural supply also did not show significant response to higher prices during the economic boom after World War I. Additionally, the marketing system of commodities reduced the necessity for elasticity studies in Japan. First, Japanese markets for many agricultural commodities are thin except that for rice. That obscures the role of price in markets. Second, agricultural cooperatives have been taking initiatives to determine kind and quantities of commodities their regional members can produce. Each cooperative does not rely on the price mechanism to determine total acreage for planting. Rather, they influence acreage for planting by suggesting the desired acreage to achieve the highest profit. Of course, that makes area in crops a function of profit which is a function of price.

Akino estimated an elasticity of aggregate farm output, and denied the inelasticity of farm output with respect to prices. He attributed the rapid increase in agricultural production after World War II to higher prices in agricultural commodities. Kuroda and Yotopoulos and Kuroda estimated an elasticity of supply for aggregate farm output through a profit function approach. They concluded that: (1) The estimates of profit and factor demand functions are stable and give no evidence of structural transformation during the mid-1960s, (2) the farm firm is rational in following the marginal principles of economics, (3) increasing returns to scale exist in agricultural production, and (4) the farm firm has responded rather elastically to changes in the price of the output. They denied "rigidity of farm output supply" at the microeconomic level.

Nghiep said "Although the striking development of agriculture in Japan has attracted attention of the world and here, and there are relatively abundant data relevant, very few of such studies can be found in Japan." He used the Nerlovian model for the estimation of rice supply. His conclusions were: (1) positive responses of farm producers to price movement, (2) substantially higher price elasticity in the long-run than in the short-run, and (3) rather lower elasticity of supply during the period 1883 to 1919. Nishimura compared the output response to a production costs per hectare with that to output price. He found that production responded to economic returns to production (sales per hectare).

Tsuchiya estimated the elasticities of supply for wheat, rye, and barley. While the elasticity of supply for barley was found rather low even in the long-run, wheat and rye elastically responded to their prices in the long run. Many estimations of supply elasticity were performed by Yuize.

Appendix A Table 15.1 is a brief summary of existing empirical studies on agricultural supply.

Appendix A Table 15.1. Japanese Agricultural Supply Elasticity Estimates.

Crop	Period	Author(s)	Method [a]	Short-Run Elasticity	Long-Run Elasticity
Aggregate	1881-1919	M. Akino	SE	0.0930	---
Farm	1920-1939	M. Akino	SE	0.0704	---
Output	1951-1963	M. Akino	SE	0.3652	---
	1952-1962	Y. Yuize	SN	0.4202	0.5524
	1965	Y. Kuroda &	PF	0.9825	---[b]
	1966	Yotopoulos	PF	0.8950	---[b]
	1967	Y. Kuroda	PF	0.8530	---[b]
	Postwar	Y. Kuroda M. Akino	CD	0.1490	0.4130
Rice & Cereals	1952-1962	Y. Yuize	SN	0.5299	0.7760
Rice	1883-1919	Nghiep	SN	0.0157	0.0492
			LN	0.0500	0.1700
	1918-1928	Nghiep	SN	0.0062	0.0117
			LN	0.1000	0.1800
	1928-1939	Nghiep	SN	0.0506	0.0506
			LN	0.9700	0.9700
	1952-1962	Y. Yuize	SN	0.0962	0.1906[c]
				0.0489	0.0850[d]
				0.8391	1.7512[e]
Wheat & Barley	1952-1962	Y. Yuize	SN	0.0520	---
Wheat	1901-1939, 1955-1960[f]	K. Tsuchiya	SN	0.1900	1.4972[g]
Barley	1901-1939, 1957-1960[f]	K. Tshuchiya	SN	0.0210	0.1171[g]
	1952-1962	Y. Yuize	SN	0.3405	---
Oats	1952-1962	Y. Yuize	SN	0.2750	---
Rye	1901-1939, 1955-1960[f]	K. Tshuchiya	SN	0.1751	1.0491[g]
	1952-1962	Y. Yuize	SN	1.3251	---

302

Appendix A Table 15.1 cont.

Crop	Period	Author(s)	Method [a]	Short-Run Elasticity	Long-Run Elasticity
Beans, Corn, etc.	1952-1962	Y. Yuize	SN	0.1866	---
Red Bean	1952-1962	Y. Yuize	SN	0.0980	0.1683
Broad Bean	1952-1962	Y. Yuize	SN	0.4556	---
Kidney Bean	1952-1962	Y. Yuize	SN	0.0986	0.9670
Soybean	1952-1962	Y. Yuize	SN	0.1283	---
Potatoes	1952-1962	Y. Yuize	SN	0.0919	0.2128
Potato	1952-1962	Y. Yuize	SN	0.0857 0.2006	0.1611[h] 0.3184[i]
Sweet Potatoes	1952-1962	Y. Yuize	SN	0.2580	0.4199
Taro	1952-1962	Y. Yuize	SN	0.1729	0.6793
Vegetables	1952-1962	Y. Yuize	SN	0.2870	---
Cabbage	1952-1962	Y. Yuize	SN	0.1013	0.1198
Carrot	1952-1962	Y. Yuize	SN	0.0989	---
Chinese Cabbage	1952-1962	Y. Yuize	SN	0.0249	---
Cucumber	1952-1962	Y. Yuize	SN	0.0985	---
Eggplant	1952-1962	Y. Yuize	SN	0.1291	---
Onion	1952-1962	Y. Yuize	SN	0.2122	0.3012
Radish	1952-1962	Y. Yuize	SN	0.0299	0.0559
Tomato	1952-1962	Y. Yuize	SN	0.1222	---
Welsh Onion	1952-1962	Y. Yuize	SN	0.0412	---
Fruits	1952-1962	Y. Yuize	SN	0.0350	0.0397
Grapes	1952-1962	Y. Yuize	SN	0.0724	---

Appendix A Table 15.1 cont.

Crop	Period	Author(s)	Method [a]	Short-Run Elasticity	Long-Run Elasticity
Tangerine	1917-1940	H. Nishimura	SN	0.0885	0.1724[j]
	1918-1932	H. Nishimura	SN	0.2984	0.3815[k]
	1933-1941	H. Nishimura	SN	0.5704	0.3270[k]
	1951-1963	H. Nishimura	SN	0.0510	0.2130[k]
				0.0554	0.6204[j]
	1952-1962	Y. Yuize	SN	1.2711	---
Cash Crops					
	1952-1962	Y. Yuize	SN	1.2727	1.6419
Livestock	1952-1962	Y. Yuize	SN	0.4761	0.7889
Beef	1952-1962	Y. Yuize	SN	-0.0251	-0.0598
Eggs	1952-1962	Y. Yuize	SN	0.5893	---
Milk	1952-1962	Y. Yuize	SN	0.1400	---

[a]The methods of estimation are as follows: SE = single-equation estimation, SN = single-equation estimation of a Nerlovian model, PF = system estimation of equations implicitly including first-order conditions by the profit function approach, CD = calculated through the derived demand theory, LN = computed from standardized regression coefficients of the linear function.
[b]Excluding Hokkaido.
[c]Elasticities for all kinds of rice.
[d]Elasticities for paddy rice.
[e]Elasticities for upland rice.
[f]Elasticities are not estimated for before and after World War II. And for 1955/57-1960, the trend of 1901-1939 is applied.
[g]Excluding Okinawa.
[h]Elasticities for all potatoes.
[i]Elasticities for potatoes which are planted in the spring.
[j]The explanatory variable is sales per hectare.
[k]The explanatory variable is output price.

References

Akino, M. 1971. Factor demands and supply elasticities for aggregate agricultural products. *Quarterly Journal of Agricultural Economics* 25-2:217-230.

Kuroda, Y. 1979. A study of the farm firm's production behavior in the mid-1960s in Japan -- A profit function approach. *Economics Studies Quarterly* 30-2:107-122.

Kuroda, Y. and Pan A. Yotopoulos. 1979. A microeconomic analysis of production behavior of the farm households in Japan -- A profit function approach. *The Economic Review* 29-2:116-129.

Le Thanh Nghiep. 1973. Farmer's price response: A study on acreage determination of rice in Japan, 1883-1969. *Review of Agricultural Economics* 29:196-211.

Nishimura, H. 1966. Mikan seisan ni okeru noka no kyokyu hanno. *Journal of Rural Problems* 2-1:7-17.

Tsuchiya, K. 1962. Nogyo keizai no keiryo bunseki. Chapter 7 in *Farmers' Long-Term Response to Prices of Wheat and Barley*. Keiso-Shobo.

Yuize, Y. 1965. On the price responses in agricultural production. *Quarterly Journal of Agricultural Economics* 19-1:107-142.

APPENDIX B

Agricultural Data Available in Japan
Yuko Arayama

The following is a summary list of data sources. The list mainly depends on information included in the *Statistical Yearbook of Ministry of Agriculture, Forestry, and Fisheries*. The ˙ indicates that detailed information is included in the component sources.

A. General

Statistics and Information Department, MAFF˙
   Statistical Yearbook of Ministry of Agriculture, Forestry, and Fisheries
   Statistical Pocket Book of Agriculture, Forestry, and Fisheries

Minister's Secretariat, MAFF
   Economic Relation Tables on Agriculture and Food Industries

Food Agency, MAFF
   Annual Statistics of Food Administration

B. Factors of Production

Costs of Production
Statistics and Information Department, MAFF
   Production Costs of Rice, Wheat, and Barley
   Production Costs of Vegetables
   Production Costs of Fruits and Nuts
   Production Costs of Industrial Crops and Others

Production Costs of Cocoon
Production Costs of Livestock Products

Land
Statistics and Information Department, MAFF*
Statistics of Cultivated Land and Planted Area
Agricultural Structure Improvement Bureau, MAFF
Transfer and Change of Agricultural Land

Labor
Statistics and Information Department, MAFF*
Report of Employment on Farm Household Members
Report of Annual Sample Survey of Agriculture
Report of Farm Household Economy Survey
Statistics of Prices and Wages in Rural Areas
Census of Agriculture

Statistics Bureau, Management and Coordination Agency*
Population Census of Japan

Statistics Bureau, Prime Minister's Office Japan*
Employment Status Survey

Statistics and Information Department, Ministry of Labor, Japan*
Year Book of Labor Statistics
Outdoor Employees' Wage Survey by Occupation

Other Inputs
Statistics and Information Department, MAFF
Statistical Report of Vegetable Seeds Production

Agricultural Production Bureau, MAFF
Handbook of Agricultural Chemicals

Livestock Industry Bureau, MAFF
Monthly Feed Statistics

C. Others

Crop Statistics
Statistics and Information Department, MAFF*
Crop Statistics
Statistics of Agricultural Income Produced
Rice Production by Municipalities

Industrial Crops Statistics
Flower Plants Statistics
Sericulture Statistics
Livestock Statistics
Milk and Milk Products Statistics

Food and Marketing Bureau, MAFF
Oils and Fats Situation in Japan

Crop Insurance
Economic Affairs Bureau, MAFF
Statistical Tables of Agricultural Crops Mutual Relief
Statistical Tables of Field Crops Mutual Relief
Statistical Tables of Horticulture Facilities Mutual Relief
Statistical Tables of Fruits and Fruit Trees Mutual Relief
Statistical Tables of Livestock Mutual Relief

Marketing
Statistics and Information Department, MAFF
Statistics of Production and Shipment of Vegetables
Statistics of Production and Shipment of Fruits and Nuts
Report of Survey on Vegetables and Fruits Wholesale Market
Monthly Statistics of Vegetables and Fruits Marketing
Report of Survey on Marketing Cost of Vegetables and Fruits
Report on Vegetables and Fruits Processing Factory
Report of Follow-up Survey on Prices by Marketing Stages of Vegetables and Fruits
Statistics on Hen Eggs and Poultry Marketing and Statistics on Number of Chicks Hatched
Monthly Statistics on Hen Eggs and Broiler Marketing
Report on Beef Cattle Marketing Structure
Monthly Statistics of Meat Marketing

Agricultural Finance
Statistics and Information Department, MAFF
Statistics on Monetary Flow in Farm Households

The following list includes detailed information for some of the publications. The information includes (1) the name of the publication, (2) the first year of publication, (3) the interval of publication, and (4) the main contents of the publication.

(1)   *Statistical Yearbook of Ministry of Agriculture, Forestry, and Fisheries*
(2)   1886

(3)   **Annual**
(4)   **Farm household**
       Agricultural land
       Materials for agricultural land
       Crops
       Sericulture and raw silk production
       Livestock and poultry
       Production costs of agricultural products
       Prices and wages in rural areas
       Farm Household economy
       Forestry
       Index number of agricultural and forestry production
       Income of agriculture and forestry
       Marketing of agricultural and forestry products

(1)   *Statistical Pocket Book of Agricultural, Forestry, and Fisheries*
(2)   **1952**
(3)   **Annual**
(4)   ******

(1)   *Statistics of Cultivated Land and Planted Area*
(2)   **1966**
(3)   **Annual**
(4)   **Area of cultivated land**
       Area of cultivated land expanded or ruined
       Aggregate of planted area of crops and utilization rate of cultivated land

(1)   *Report of Employment on Farm Household Members*
(2)   **1958**
(3)   **Annual**
(4)   **Increase and decrease of farm household members**
       Newly employed to other industries by type of employment and separated employees from other industries by type of separated
       Newly employed and separated employees by industries
       Temporary workers away from home
       Employment status of new graduates in farm households
       Present occupation of separated employees from regular work
       Past occupation of newly employed in regular work

(1)   *Report of Annual Sample Survey of Agriculture*
(2)   **1961**
(3)   **Annual**
(4)   **Number of farm households and farm household population**

Number of farm households by size of cultivated land
Number of farm households and area of rented cultivated land from others
Number of farm households by full-time and part-time status
Number of part-time farm households by kind of side job
Number of farm households by type of farming
Number of farm households by agriculture labor force, owned
Number of farm households and area by size of paddy field rice planted area
Farm household population
Number of farm household members by working status
Number of household members engaged in own farming
Population mainly engaged in own farming
Core persons mainly engaged in own farming
Number of persons engaged in farming by kind of side job
Number of major agricultural implements on farms

(1)   *Report of Farm Household Economy Survey*
(2)   1951
(3)   Annual
(4)   Summary of farm household economy
Agricultural gross income
Agricultural and non-agricultural expenditures
Non-agricultural gross income
Living expenditures
Working members, working hours, and area under management
Agricultural fixed capital value and property of farm households
Deposits and debts
Index numbers of consumption level in rural areas
Index numbers of consumer prices in rural areas

(1)   *Statistics of Prices and Wages in Rural Areas*
(2)   1946
(3)   Annual
(4)   Index numbers of agricultural products
Index numbers of materials for agricultural production
Index numbers of price by commodity
Index numbers of material prices for living necessities
Index numbers of wages in rural areas

(1)   *Census of Agriculture*
(2)   1950
(3)   Every 5 years
(4)   Number of farm households

Farm household population
Employment status
Land
Crops
Livestock and sericulture
Agricultural implements
Forestry

(1)   *Population Census of Japan*
(2)   1920
(3)   Every 5 years
(4)   Population and area
Sex and age
Marital status
Nationality
Education
Labor force status
Employment status
Industry
Occupation
Socio-economic group
Time of last move and place of previous residence
Place of work or schooling
Type of household
Family type of household
Economic type
Source of household income
Specific household
Housing
Major metropolitan area and range of distance

(1)   *Employment Status Survey*
(2)   1956
(3)   Every 3 years
(4)   Basic tables
Annual working days and weekly working hours
Income
Secondary job
Desire for work of working persons
Desire for work of persons not working
Change of type of activity and change of place of residence
Work history
Household
Family structure and children

(1)   *Year Book of Labor Statistics*
(2)   1952
(3)   Annual
(4)   Labor force survey
Survey on employment trends
Employment security statistics
Survey on employment management
Survey on employment conditions of the aged
Labor productivity statistical survey
Basic survey of wage structure
Outdoor employees' wage survey by occupation
Occupational wage survey of forestry employees
General survey on wages and working hours system

(1)   *Crop Statistics*
(2)   1959
(3)   Annual
(4)   Area of cultivated land
Area of cultivated land expanded or ruined
Planted area of rice, wheat and barley, and potatoes and sweet potatoes
Production of rice, wheat and barley, and potatoes and sweet potatoes
Total planted area of crops
Utilization rate of cultivated land
Crop damages

(1)   *Statistics of Agricultural Income Produced*
(2)   1961
(3)   Annual
(4)   Gross agricultural output and agricultural income produced

16

American Agricultural Supply
Richard E. Just

Introduction

Understanding agricultural supply is crucial for analyzing basic economic and policy issues of agriculture. Agricultural price analysis, knowing how agricultural markets function, investigation of the effects of alternative environmental policies, and evaluation of the impacts of new technology all depend fundamentally on understanding agricultural supply. Nevertheless, estimates of agricultural supply elasticities in the literature are diverse and conflicting (Henneberry and Tweeten). The unexplained variation in agricultural supply equations is large and greater than for demand equations. This relatively poor quality of information on supply can be attributed to several important problems: (1) errors in representing price expectations; (2) the role of natural and biological phenomena associated with weather, insects, and disease; (3) strong and changing effects of government programs; and (4) strong and irregular effects of asset adjustment and new technology (Tomek and Robinson).

This paper critically reviews the methodology and depth of understanding of agricultural supply in the United States. Many of these comments apply to agricultural supply in other countries as well. Practices used to measure agricultural supply are critically evaluated. Then some suggestions are offered on research strategies for coping with the important problems surrounding agricultural supply measurement. Seemingly, the effort to measure agricultural supply has waned as diverse approaches have produced varying and conflicting estimates and as traditional approaches have come to be viewed as mundane. Consequently, the stock of knowledge about agricultural supply has been depreciating. On the other hand, needed innovative efforts and approaches for dealing with the basic underlying problems have not been forthcoming.

Traditional Approaches

Traditional agricultural supply analysis has been reviewed at length elsewhere (Askari and Cummings, 1976, 1977; Coleman; Henneberry and Tweeten). Some duplication of these efforts is necessary here to present a complete picture of agricultural supply analysis in the United States and to provide an adequate backdrop for the critical discussion of this paper. However, much of the discussion here is a methodological critique geared toward suggestions for future improvements in agricultural supply analysis.

The Nerlovian Model

Undoubtedly, the most common approach to agricultural supply analysis has been estimation of supply equations using the Nerlovian model (see Table 16.1 for a representative, though not exhaustive, set of supply studies). The overwhelming popularity of the Nerlovian model stems from convenience. As it is usually applied, the Nerlovian model involves a simple linear regression of the quantity supplied, Q_t, on price, P_t, and the lagged dependent variable, i.e.,

$$Q_t = \alpha_0 + \alpha_1 P_t + \alpha_2 Q_{t-1}. \tag{1}$$

Estimation of this model produces both a short-run elasticity of supply, $\alpha_1 P_t / Q_t$, and a long-run elasticity of supply, $[\alpha_1/(1-\alpha_2)] P_t / Q_t$. The limited response can be attributed to either a tendency of price expectations, P_t^e, to respond in a limited way to current price,

$$P_t^e - P_{t-1}^e = \delta(P_{t-1} - P_{t-1}^e), \tag{2}$$

with supply,

$$Q_t = \beta_0 + \beta_1 P_t^e, \tag{3}$$

following the Nerlovian adaptive expectations model, or a tendency to adjust output slowly due to habit persistence, costs of adjustment, or technological/institutional rigidities following the Nerlovian partial adjustment model, i.e.,

$$Q_t - Q_{t-1} = \delta(Q_t^* - Q_{t-1}), \tag{4}$$

Table 16.1. American Agricultural Supply Elasticity Estimates.

Crop	Region	Period	Author	Method[a]	Short-Run Elasticity	Long-Run Elasticity
Wheat	U.S.	1909-32	Nerlove	SN	.47 - .93	--
		1948-74	Morzuch et al.	SS	.46 - .52	--
		1969-77	Chambers & Just	SS	.50	--
		1976	Rojko et al.	SM	.20[b]	2.55[c]
		1960-80	Liu & Roningen	SE	--	.25[c]
		1960-80	Tyers	SE	.45	.80
	Texas	1957-79	Shumway	PF	.43	--
Corn	U.S.	1909-32	Nerlove	SN	.09 - 1.02	--
		1969-77	Chambers & Just	SS	.55	--
		1960-80	Liu & Roningen	SE	--	.09[c]
	Midwest	1963-74	Whittacker et al.	SS	.22	--
	Iowa	1948-80	Tegene et al.	SN	--	.20
	Kentucky	1960-79	Reed & Riggins	SN	.34 - .56	.93 - 2.07
	Texas	1957-79	Shumway	PF	.07	--
Rice	U.S.	1976	Rojko et al.	SM	--	.90[c]
		1960-80	Liu & Roningen	SE	--	.16[c]
		1960-80	Tyers	SE	.35	.75
		1962-81	Ito et al.	ST	.11	.31
	Texas	1957-79	Shumway	PF	.72	--

314

Table 16.1 cont.

Crop	Region	Period	Author	Method[a]	Short-Run Elasticity	Long-Run Elasticity
Coarse Grains	U.S.	1976	Rojko et al.	SM	--	2.40[c]
		1960-80	Liu & Roningen	SE	--	.09[c]
		1969-80	Tyers	SE	.40	.75
	Various	1946-79	Saez & Shumway	PF	-4.40 - .27	--
	ND & SD	1950-70	Weaver	PF	.64 - .74	--
Oilseeds	U.S.	1976	Rojko et al.	SM	--	3.27[c]
Soybeans	U.S.	1969-77	Chambers & Just	SS	.64	--
		1960-80	Liu & Roningen	SE	--	.10[c]
	Various	1946-66	Houck & Subotnik	SN	.75 - 3.30	--
Other Oilseeds	U.S.	1960-80	Liu & Roningen	SE	--	.25[c]
Cotton	U.S.	1960-80	Liu & Roningen	SE	--	.25[c]
	Various	1905-32	Brennan	SN	.31 - .37	--
		1946-79	Saez & Shumway	PF	-.19 - 1.50	--
	Southwest	1909-32	Nerlove	SN	.20 - .67	--
	Texas	1957-79	Shumway	PF	.25	--
Livestock	U.S.	1911-58	Griliches (1960)	SN	.20 - .30	.70
		1921-66	Tweeten & Quance	ST	.38	2.90
	ND & SD	1950-70	Weaver	PF	.56 - 1.01	--
	Various	1946-79	Saez & Shumway	PF	-.96 - .43	--

Commodity	Region	Years	Source			
Beef	U.S.	1976	Rojko et al.	SM	--	.30
		1976	Liu & Roningen	SE	--	.01[c]
		1960-80	Tyers[d]	SE	.13	.50
Pork	U.S.	1924-37	Dean & Heady	SN	.28 - .46	--
		1937-56	Dean & Heady	SN	.30 - .60	--
		1961-72	Meilke et al.	SN	.16	.43
		1961-72	Meilke et al.	SP	.17 - .24	.48
		1976	Rojko et al.	SM	--	.50
		1976	Liu & Roningen	SE	--	.05[c]
		1960-80	Tyers[d]	SE	.33	.81
Milk	U.S.	1978	Rojko et al.	SM	--	.40
	Various	1931-54	Halvorson (1955)	SS	.03 - .22	--
	West	1927-57	Halvorson (1958)	SN	.13 - .17	.40 - .44
		1941-57	Halvorson (1958)	SN	.18 - .31	.15 - .89
		1958-68	Prato	ST	0	--
	CA	1953-68	Chen et al.	SN	.38	2.54
		1953-68	Chen et al.	SP	.16	2.52
Potatoes	U.S.	1930-58	Zusman	SS	.07 - .16	.06 - .46
	Various	1955-55	Estes et al.	SN	.13 - 2.05	.35 - 2.05
	CA	1929-53	Mundlak et al.	SS	.10 - .38	--
		1950-73	Shumway & Chang	PG	2.23	4.00
Tomatoes	U.S.	1954-77	Hammig	SN	.05	.20
		1919-55	Nerlove & Addison	SN	.16	.90
	CA	1967-75	Chern & Just	SN	.49 - 1.13	--

Table 16.1 cont.

Crop	Region	Period	Author	Method[a]	Short-Run Elasticity	Long-Run Elasticity
Lettuce	U.S.	1954-77	Hammig	SN	.02	.34
		1954-77	Hammig et al.	SN	.42	---
		1919-55	Nerlove & Addison	SN	.03	.16
	CA	1950-73	Shumway & Chang	PG	.23	1.70
Cabbage	U.S.	1954-77	Hammig	SN	.05	.11
		1919-55	Nerlove & Addison	SN	.36	1.20
Cantaloupe	U.S.	1919-55	Nerlove & Addison	SN	.02	.04
	CA	1950-73	Shumway & Chang	PG	.57 - .58	11.0 - 12.3
Carrots	U.S.	1954-77	Hammig	SN	.03	.23
		1934-55	Nerlove & Addison	SN	.14	1.00
Celery	U.S.	1954-77	Hammig	SN	.06	.32
		1919-55	Nerlove & Addison	SN	.14	.95

		Study	Period	Method		
Aggregate Farm Output	U.S.	Griliches (1959)	1911-57	WA	.28 - .30	1.20 - 1.32
		Griliches (1960)	1920-57	SS	.10	.15
		Tweeten & Quance	1921-66	ST	.16	.19
		Tweeten & Quance	1921-41	ST	.08	.31
		Tweeten & Quance	1948-66	ST	.16	.31
		Tweeten & Quance	1921-66	ST	.25	1.79
		Tweeten & Quance	1921-66	WA	.26	1.52
		Antle	1910-46	PF	1.35	---
		Antle	1947-78	PF	.43	---

Source: For original sources, see Henneberry and Tweeten.

[a] The methods of estimation are as follows: PF - system estimation of equations implicitly including first-order conditions by the profit function approach, PG - estimation by fitting the results of a programming model, SE - system estimation of equilibrium equations, SM - elasticities used in a simulation model based on many other published studies, SN - single-equation estimation of a Nerlovian model, SP - single-equation estimation with a polynomial lag structure, SS - simple single-equation estimation with naive expectations, ST - computed from elasticities estimated for separate structural components, WA - weighted average of estimated input demand elasticities.

[b] Derived by Sarris and Freebairn from Rojko *et al.*

[c] Elasticity with respect to world price.

[d] Tyers estimated elasticities for ruminant and non-ruminant meats rather than for beef and pork.

where Q_t^* is the equilibrium output associated with the current price,

$$Q_t^* = \beta_0 + \beta_1 P_t. \tag{5}$$

In either case, equations (2) and (3) or (4) and (5) can be solved to find that the estimated coefficients in equation (1) are $\alpha_0 = \delta\beta_0$, $\alpha_1 = \delta\beta_1$, and $\alpha_2 = 1 - \delta$.

In various applications, the supply variable is quantity (weight or volume) produced or marketed while in others it is production units (acreage planted, acreage harvested, or head of livestock). In some applications, the price variable is paralleled by a yield variable and in some the price variable is replaced by returns per production unit, e.g., price times yield. In some cases, the price variable is deflated by a consumer price index, an index of input prices, or an index of prices of other crops. In some cases, additional terms are added in equations (3) or (5) and thus in equation (1) to represent the effects of other variables such as government program controls, weather, and risk.

Because of this great simplicity of representing a variety of intuitive phenomena, a large majority of agricultural supply studies use this approach. In fact, Askari and Cummings' extensive 1976 survey of econometric evidence on agricultural supply response focuses exclusively on Nerlovian models because of their predominance in the literature. However, applications of Nerlovian models have many problems relating to model estimation and specification.

Stochastic Specification and Estimation Problems

The problems of estimation stem from the correlation of stochastic disturbances in equation (1) that arise from basic stochastic disturbances in equation (3). A simple white noise disturbance in (3) causes both serial correlation and correlation of the disturbance with the lagged dependent variable in (1). As a result, ordinary regression estimates are biased and inconsistent. Alternatively, if the Nerlovian model represents strictly a partial adjustment phenomena, then these problems do not apply. That is, a simple white noise disturbance in equation (5) preserves the desirable properties of ordinary regression for estimating equation (1).

These problems, methods to discern the presence of problems, and methods to correct problems are discussed at length by Dhrymes. Unfortunately, many of the studies using the Nerlovian model in the literature neither use estimation methods to correct for these problems nor test for their presence. Dhrymes finds that the best approach is to include the complete structural expectation representation in the estimating equation so any lagged quantity represents a partial adjustment. Thus, the estimating equation becomes (3) rather than (1) or, combining both the adaptive expectations and the partial adjustment models, P_t in (5) is replaced by P_t^e obtaining

$$Q_t = \alpha_0 + \alpha_1 P_t^e + \alpha_2 Q_{t-1} \tag{6}$$

where P_t^e in either is replaced by the difference equation solution of (2),

$$P_t^e = \sum_{k=0}^{\infty} \delta(1-\delta)^k P_{t-k-1}.$$

This approach easily adapts to consideration of other forms of expectation mechanisms and testing the applicability of alternative expectation mechanisms. Nevertheless, few studies use this approach because a nonlinear estimation method is required.

Specification of Price

Some of the problems of specification are discussed at length by Askari and Cummings (1976, 1977). They attribute many of these problems to the necessity of using time series data over an extended period of time for estimation. One difficulty is that the appropriate measure of price may be changing over time. For example, if price is deflated by a consumer price index to represent what is of value to the farmer, the appropriate basket of goods of importance to the farmer may be changing over time. If the price is deflated by an index of prices of inputs, technology may be changing over time so that the appropriate weights of input prices should be changing. If the price is deflated by an index of prices of competing crops, the set of competing crops may be changing over time. In the latter two cases, the weights determine the relative cross elasticities of supply with respect to input and other output prices and, unfortunately, these weights are often established by means that do not relate directly to suppliers, e.g., through a general index series, if they are included at all.

Specification of Expectations

Another difficulty is that the appropriate representation of expected prices may be changing over time. Errors in measurement of price expectations are important because they translate into errors in estimated supply elasticities. One problem with the Nerlovian model is that observed price changes may not always suggest a change in price expectations for the following production period. For example, an unusually high price can occur either with a one-time crop failure or a permanent increase in demand. The assumption in equation (2), however, is that price expectations change by a constant proportion, β, of the error of expectations regardless of the source of the price change. In reality, the proportion by which price expectations change will likely differ depending on whether the farmer perceives price changes to be permanent or transitory.   For this reason, some have suggested that the adjustment parameter, β, should depend on factors such as output (Fisher, Chapter II). This suggestion, however, has rarely been implemented.

Distributed Lag Analysis

Some have suggested that price changes must persist for several periods before they are translated into changes in expectations. This has led to the use of lag distributions other than the geometric lag distribution associated with equations (2) and (3). Some of these methods include frequency domain regression and Box-Jenkins analysis.   The problems with these kinds of generalizations are threefold. First, they introduce additional parameters that may be difficult to identify with limited data. Second, the form of the lag distribution that fits best tends to depend heavily on the time period used for estimation.   Third, no clear framework explains the form of these distributions; thus, use of the estimates outside of the sample period is likely to be inappropriate.

In fact, any lag distribution that remains constant over time is generally inconsistent with the motivating explanations that weights on price changes depend on their perceived permanence or that price changes must persist for several years before they are incorporated into expectations.   These explanations imply that if a price change does not persist then it is disregarded. In any conventional distributed lag model, the lag weights are constant so the effect is simply to delay the price impact -- not alter the effect according to consistency or perceived permanence. This problem can only be taken into account if the lag weights depend on consistency of prices from period to period or some factors that explain perceived permanence.

The difficulty here is that most of the formal literature on price expectations in the tradition of Muth generates price expectations schemes whereby the importance of observations diminishes with time lags.   This occurs whenever a stable stochastic process underlies changes in the structure of the economy (Just, 1977). In reality, changes may occur erratically from time to time but the magnitude or permanence of effects is initially unclear. If this problem is important, then expectations mechanisms need to be refined to consider uncertainty with respect to structural change by implicitly including tests for consistency over time with lag weights determined accordingly. This approach, however, would lead to a more tightly structured model of the role of past prices whereas the literature has tended to the opposite approach of free-form estimation.

Rational Expectations

Alternatively, applications in the literature have turned to representation of expectations by rational mechanisms. These mechanisms suppose that the decision maker has a complete understanding of the market economy generating prices and can thus calculate a "reduced-form" price expectation based on the exogenous variables of a model representing that economy. The difficulties here are as follows. First, even the best available econometric techniques are often inadequate for determining with much confidence how a market economy generates prices. Second, even if the operation of the market economy is understood, one still has the problem of forecasting the exogenous variables. Third, the way rational expectations are usually generated, they offer little improvement over the more ad hoc Nerlovian or free-form approaches.

One way of generating a rational expectations mechanism is to solve a theoretical market model for a rational expectation equation which then specifies the expectation in terms of other parameters estimated in the market system. The problem here is that if the model has a continuous and stable stochastic structure with additional random forces affecting the market and its evolution each period, then the rational expectation is represented by a simple function of the lagged price assuming current stochastic forces are unknown at the time of decision making (Turnovsky). Another common way of generating rational expectations for purposes of estimating a supply equation similar to equations (3) or (6) is to regress observed prices on all exogenous variables available. While this method is theoretically defensible with abundant data in a stable environment, it is subject to identification problems because of the multiplicity of exogenous variables that are potentially important and because spurious correlations in unstructured reduced form specifications tend to make the results heavily dependent on the sample period. In the small sample case, these "expectations" can fit prices too closely and thus cause the elasticity of supply to be underestimated.

Finally, as either of these approaches are traditionally applied, no mechanism is included to allow different effects depending on whether recent phenomena are considered temporary or permanent. Ideally, this should be determined within the rational model but in practice this can only be done with the exogenous variable forecasts used by such decision makers. The 1973 Soviet grain deal, however, suggests the difficulty of sufficiently generalizing expectation models and gives an example of the kind of information that is needed to improve agricultural supply models. In 1973 following this deal, many farmers perceived that the U.S. Secretary of Agriculture encouraged farmers to plant "fence row to fence row," indicating that a new era of U.S. agricultural demand had arrived. Undoubtedly, the response to the large price increase of 1973 for wheat and feed grains was then much larger than if farmers had been better informed or uninformed by the Secretary. Thus, without tempering the role of the 1973 price increases, conventional techniques would overestimate supply elasticity as a result of this problem. This problem suggests price expectation mechanisms must include a wide range of information that makes identification difficult. Alternatively, survey data on price expectations is needed from farmers to improve agricultural supply estimation.

Future Expectations

One approach that has found some use in the literature is to represent price expectations by futures market prices (e.g., Morzuch *et al.*; Weaver). This approach is justified under certain assumptions by theoretical results that have demonstrated a separation of production and futures market trading decisions (e.g., Feder *et al.*). However, not all crops have futures markets and farmers using futures markets suffer from basis risk and transactions costs. Thus, direct applicability has been subject to debate. Nevertheless, futures prices generally do a better job of incorporating information available at the time of planting decisions than other types of expectations based on annual data where prices are more closely associated with harvest time. Also, because of the way other expectation mechanisms are applied in practice, futures expectations are more effective in current practice for dealing with the wide range of information that can affect price expectations. Unfortunately, empirical studies to date have been unable to discern clearly which expectation mechanism or combination of them applies.

Specification of the Process of Adjustment

Another major problem of specification in the Nerlovian model and its successors is the partial adjustment mechanism. The mechanism in equation (4) is justified variously by technological and institutional rigidities, costs of adjustment, habit formation, and risk. The model assumes that only a fixed proportion of the desired adjustment may be accomplished regardless of how great the desired adjustment. This assumption is clearly absurd. The adjustment process can be improved if the specific phenomena affecting speed of adjustment are represented. This problem is important because errors in specification of the adjustment mechanism translate directly into errors of estimation of long-run supply elasticities.

Limited Adjustment and Costs of Adjustment

One of the primary causes of slowness to adjust is the cost of adjustment. Buying new implements or adapting machinery to new crops is costly. Learning costs may also slow adjustments. Factors that affect these costs affect the rate of adjustment. Also, the ability to adjust may depend on institutional factors such as government acreage limitations that can be better modelled explicitly. Alternatively, slowness to adjust may depend on technological and biological factors such as the ability to expand a livestock herd or bring a grove or vineyard to bearing age. Some have attempted to determine the lags in responses to price changes for these reasons with data-based, free-form distributed lag analysis (e.g., Dean and Heady; Chen *et al.*).

Again, however, one should bear in mind that economic conditions may affect the speed of adjustment even with biological processes because of the possibility of using additional inputs or altering production practices. Generally, it is advantageous to represent the adjustment phenomena by separate equations explaining investment, maturity, and culling or removal rather than lumping all of this into a flexible lag distribution. The reasons are threefold. First, the reasons for lags and, thus, changes in them can be represented in the model, thereby leading to better specification. Second, when data are available for the relevant variables, more econometric efficiency is possible by breaking the responses into separately estimated components. Third, knowledge about the underlying biological or technological phenomena can be brought to bear on correct assessment of the parameters in a structural model of the various processes underlying adjustment. For example, a detailed structural specification allows one to impose plausibility with respect to the aging process and age required for maturity.

Asset Fixity

Asset fixity has been a topic of great debate in agriculture. One of the problems is the inconsistency in the way asset fixity is usually modelled and the way it really works. The common concept is that the more fixed an asset, the longer it takes to change it once a decision is made to do so. In reality, however, most asset levels can be changed substantially within a year although a large change may be more costly. Land is traditionally viewed a highly fixed factor but yet marginal lands can be broken up, resodded, or moved in and out of production within a year. A more useful concept of fixity is based on length of service. A highly fixed asset remains productive over a long period of time so that ordinarily it must be used over a long period of time to be economical. This implies that adjustment of more fixed assets will tend to occur when price changes are expected to last longer. Indeed, with the 1973 Soviet grain deal, many farmers adjusted long-term assets substantially expecting long-term high prices which then left them poorly situated for the later financial crisis.

These considerations suggest that better estimates of supply depend on developing better estimates of the perceived permanency of price changes. Because the term of expectations applicable to factors of different fixity vary, econometric identification and efficiency suggest that multiple equations are needed. Otherwise, short-run and long-run expectations will tend to be collinear and the role of fixed assets versus variable assets will be difficult to discern.

These considerations also raise the possibility of different responses to price increases as opposed to price decreases. Tweeten and Quance examined this proposition some time ago and concluded that some differences exist. However, with the instability of internationalization that occurred during the 1970s and 1980s, a careful analysis with a better representation of asset fixity is needed. At the aggregate level, breeding herds can be liquidated through slaughter but may take time through the normal biological process to replace. The commodity boom of the 1970s may also have caused a tendency to overproduce given sunk costs -- after false permanent expectations induced heavy investment in machinery. These hypotheses can only be properly investigated in a complete model of asset fixity that differentiates the role of short- and long-term expectations. This seems to be a much more plausible approach to estimation of long-run supply elasticity to the extent that available data can identify the role of longer-term price expectations. To the extent that identification of expectations is not possible, the Nerlovian framework may be leading to false confidence in an over-simplified model.

Habit Formation and Risk Aversion

Similar comments about structural modeling apply to habits and preferences although the knowledge base of the profession is more lacking. For example, the work of Just, Zilberman, Hochman, and Bar-Shira suggests that farmers tend to follow accepted practices but modify practices in response to the profit motive. In other words, habits persist when they are not very costly but they are modified when much better opportunities arise. Other studies have used cost-of-learning models to explain the process of adoption of new technology. These considerations again suggest absurdity of the partial adjustment model whereby the same proportion of change is made regardless of how much is needed. Explicit models of the role of risk applied in supply response analysis have shown that a structural representation of risk response as opposed to estimation of an ad hoc Nerlovian partial adjustment model can lead to a quite different interpretation of the data (Just, 1976).

Government Programs

Changing government programs present one of the most difficult problems for agricultural supply assessment in the United States. Not only are policy instruments varied frequently but the set of active policy instruments has been changed often for the major commodities. The major policy instruments that have been used at various times over the past 40 years include target and support prices; base acreages, acreage set asides, diversion programs, acreage reduction programs, acreage retirement programs, and allotments; the farmer owned reserve program with its support, release, and call prices; crop insurance; disaster assistance; and subsidized interest rates among others. All of these instruments affect behavior and cropping patterns on the farm and thus factor directly into agricultural supply. (In addition, current supply depends on public decisions to sell government stocks into commercial markets.) For the most part, participation has been voluntary, which further complicates modeling. Some studies have attempted to take into account how these policy variables can be represented systematically in traditional agricultural supply models (Just, 1973; Houck and Ryan). For the most part, however, government programs have been represented by adding a simple government program variable such as acreage diversion, allotment, or a price support as a regressor in the standard supply model in equations (1) or (6).

As argued later in this paper, far more sophisticated approaches are possible and useful.

Econometric Model Structure and Estimation Efficiency

One of the broad lessons learned from agricultural supply and agricultural policy models generally is that more structured models that break measurements into observable components give more accurate, efficient, and plausible estimation (Just, 1990; Rausser and Just). These empirical findings parallel theoretical findings in econometric theory whereby structural systems of equations are generally more efficient than reduced form or single equation estimators. For example, essentially all of the general econometric models of the agricultural economy carrying through to the commercial econometric vendors evaluated by Just and Rausser estimate agricultural supply by components consisting of separate equations for yield, acreage, inventory adjustment, and herd size. Other studies such as Rojko *et al.* and Liu and Roningen have applied this methodology but imposed certain coefficients and relationships judgmentally, which has led some to call them simulation models. Similar techniques are applied on a more limited scale to assess agricultural supply, for example, by Ito *et al.*, using acreage/yield components and by Tweeten and Quance using production/inventory components and animal-units/yield-per-animal components. Developing better structural representations based on practical understanding has helped greatly to improve supply assessment and holds considerable promise for further refinement.

Accounting for Weather, Insects, and Disease

The principles are particularly pertinent to estimation of the effects of weather, insects, and disease. Various efforts have been made to include indexes of rainfall, humidity, frost, etc. (e.g., Love). However, because these factors are essentially unpredictable, measurement of their effects does not markedly improve supply measurement except insofar as it helps to identify other factors affecting supply. More importantly, structured models that include equations reflecting how farmers' translate their price expectations into action are needed. Structured models separate the economic decisions from the major random vulnerabilities of agricultural yields. As Askari and Cummings argue, planted acreage rather than harvested acreage or production generally gives better measurement of how farmers actually translate their expectations into action. Yield responses to prices are also desirable to measure but generally less precise results are possible.

Structured Models Based on Economic Theory

While the above discussion argues for structuring supply models econometrically (separating estimated equations) to the extent that data allows, further structure can also be imposed on the basis of economic theory to aid in model identification. For example, economic theory suggests that certain relationships must hold among elasticities. Imposition of these relationships can bring additional data to bear on estimation of supply and/or reduce the number of parameters that need to be estimated thus improving identification of others. The earliest of these models springs from the work of Griliches (1959) and was later applied by Tweeten and Quance. Griliches noted that the aggregate supply elasticity is the weighted average of all demand elasticities of inputs with respect to the price of output with weights based on the elasticity of output with respect to input quantity. He thus estimated aggregate supply elasticity from aggregate demand estimates. Tweeten and Quance compared the results of three methods for estimation of aggregate supply elasticity: direct estimation, a structural estimator consisting of crop and livestock components for production units and yields, and the input demand elasticity approach of Griliches. The structural and input demand elasticity approaches yielded similar results but the direct approach yielded a short-run elasticity 60 percent less and a long-run elasticity over 90 percent less (see Table 16.1). A further possibility would be to combine the system of demand equations used to estimate the input demand elasticities with a direct output supply equation and the Griliches elasticity identity to form a full information system for estimating aggregate supply elasticity. Or the output supply equation in this system could be replaced by its component parts. Such an approach has not been used but would be useful to resolve inconsistencies among methodologies.

The input demand elasticity approach has rarely been used for assessing agricultural supply mainly because input data by commodity are not readily available. For example, public aggregate data sources include input prices but no information on quantities of inputs by commodity. As a result, this methodology has been useful essentially only for estimating aggregate supply where input quantities by crop are not needed.

The Programming Approach

The programming approach has been used to assess agricultural supply by creating a programming model that describes behavior by a region or representative farms subject to prices and resource availability. By solving the model with various prices, supply relationships can be traced (Hazell and Norton). Some have further resorted to econometric estimation of the resulting relationships which obtains continuous approximations from which elasticities can be calculated rather than step functions (Shumway and Chang). One of the great strengths of the programming approach is that cross effects of input prices and other output prices are inherent in the model and can be easily derived. Programming models also do not require long time series of data as do econometric approaches. However, coefficients in the model are often estimated on the basis of only one or a few data points. Statistical precision of supply results is difficult to evaluate. Thus, the precision of results may be poor with little warning to the researcher. Also, programming models are typically calibrated by "playing" with the constraints. Quance and Tweeten (1971) found that, unless results are arbitrarily restrained, programming models provide absurdly high estimates of input demand and product supply elasticities. On the other hand, too much "playing" can cause underestimation of supply elasticities. Depending on how they are applied, programming models can also suffer from a restrictive representation of technology, short-run versus long-run adjustment, price expectations, aggregation problems, and/or representative farms. It suffices to say that while programming models have proven useful in specialized planning exercises, they have not been widely used for supply estimation.

Duality

Duality is one of the few methods of assessing agricultural supply that has gained increasing interest over the past twenty years. Following the earlier work by Shephard, McFadden recognized econometric simplifications made possible by a duality between production and profit functions. The appeal of the dual approach is that one can easily derive all of the firm's input demands and output supplies in a consistent way from one specification of the profit function. This facilitates imposition of theoretical consistency among all of the estimated supplies and demands and implicitly includes the first-order conditions associated with the firm's behavioral criteria. Furthermore, because the derivation of supply and demand specifications from the profit function involves simple differentiation, much more complex forms can be used. With the primal approach by comparison, derivation of consistent supply and demand specifications involves solution of a complex nonlinear set of first order conditions based on a production function specification. Previously, the level of complexity for these purposes was limited to very simple production function forms such as a Cobb-Douglas (Marshak and Andrews). Another advantage of the dual approach is that it requires data on prices of inputs which are generally observable in aggregate public form rather than quantities of inputs which often are not available.

The dual approach, however, has not been without problems. First, applications (e.g., Weaver; Shumway; Antle) have not yielded both short- and long-run elasticities. In its conventional form, the profit function approach considers all factors variable and, thus, long-run response is obtained in the short run (e.g., Weaver). The methodology has been generalized to consider restricted profit functions where some inputs are held fixed. This approach can be applied to obtain short-run elasticities (e.g., Shumway) but then a longer-term approach needs to be used to determine fixed factor adjustment to obtain longer-term elasticities.

Another problem of duality is that it assumes profit maximization. Profit maximization is the most popular behavioral assumption in economics. But risk aversion has been verified empirically in agricultural supply (Just, 1974; Pope and Just) and this invalidates the profit function approach (Pope).

Aggregation is also a problem that can invalidate the relationships imposed by duality. The dual framework applies to a single, profit-maximizing firm but the technology, land quality, prices, and, thus, the set of active crops and livestock can differ among firms. Aggregation over the associated corner solutions can cause the systematic relationships imposed across estimated supplies and demands to fail. Another problem of the dual approach pointed out by Shumway, Pope, and Nash is that some of the most important inputs in agriculture such as land are fixed inputs but easily allocable across production activities. A means of dealing with this problem in the dual approach has been developed only recently by Chambers and Just (1989) and is quite cumbersome. Finally, the dual approach faces all of the same problems representing price expectations as do other approaches.

Ad Hoc Modeling, Alternative Methodologies, and Variability of Estimates

In summary, traditional measurement of supply has been characterized mainly by direct econometric estimation of ad hoc supply equations for quantity or acreage. These equations have tended to follow the Nerlovian approach or some modification whereby price expectations are represented by a fixed lag distribution and/or slowness to adjust is represented by lagged dependent variables. Improvements have been attempted by considering rational expectations mechanisms and more econometrically structured representation of adjustment mechanisms (particularly for perennials and livestock). For the most part, however, traditional supply studies do not explicitly generate cross elasticities of supply and do not take account of relationships that exist among inputs and outputs. If prices of other outputs are included, typically only one or two important competitors are considered or an index of competing crop prices is included so that the relative cross elasticities are determined by weights in the index. While duality holds new promise for generating theoretically defensible elasticities and cross elasticities, the studies thus far need refinement and generalization particularly with regard to the role of fixed inputs and input allocations.

Table 16.1 gives some representative results of American agricultural supply studies to date. In one sense, these results appear quite uniform in that almost all short-run elasticities are between zero and 1 (in fact, most are between zero and .5) suggesting that agricultural supply is inelastic in the short-run. However, the results are considerably more variable in the long run, ranging from zero to over 12 in one case. Even for the short-run, however, the estimated elasticities differ by orders of magnitude.

Some of these differences can be attributed to the importance of the crop, its substitutes, the share of the suitable acreage it occupies, and the associated potential for adjustment. For example, a specialty crop such as cantaloupe may plausibly have a high supply elasticity for this reason. A dominating crop such as wheat or corn would have less elasticity. A broad commodity group like coarse grains or aggregate output should have even lower elasticity.

Because of the inability to produce new animals without a normal growing cycle, short-run livestock supply elasticity is also likely to be small. While these relationships tend to hold in Table 16.1, many contrary relationships are evident, e.g., the small elasticities estimated by Hammig for specialty crops.

Even for the short-run, however, the estimated elasticities vary by more than an order of magnitude for the same commodity in about half of the cases (corn, coarse grains, cotton, livestock, milk, potatoes, tomatoes, lettuce, cantaloupe, and aggregate farm output). Where do these differences come from? Some differences can be attributed to differences in estimation method (e.g., lettuce, cantaloupe, and aggregate output). Some can be attributed to the time period of estimation (e.g., milk, tomatoes). But for several commodities (corn, coarse grains, cotton, livestock, and potatoes), estimates varying by more than an order of magnitude are obtained by the same author(s) using the same methodology on the same set of data. This is not surprising to many practitioners but is likely quite disturbing to businessmen and public decision makers who need to rely on these estimates. Anyone who has attempted estimation of ad hoc supply equations knows that a small change in specification such as adding a competing crop price or a government program variable sometimes can drastically change the results.

New Directions for Improved Supply Assessment

With this wide variation in results, the challenge is to find new avenues for improving estimates of agricultural supply. Some promising directions are suggested by the improvements that have been made previously. These include imposing additional plausible structure that reduces the burden on econometric identification; imposing more consistency in the application of techniques and interpretation of data; improving the knowledge base and modeling of firm level decisions to change production activities; developing better global functional representations; specific consideration of the process of technology development that comes into play in long-run supply response; as well as the suggestions above for representing more carefully the underlying processes of behavior, expectations formation, and asset adjustment.

These suggestions involve drawing together more sources of information to gain better understanding by consistent, conceptually plausible, and simultaneous interpretation of available data. One exercise that Askari and Cummings' used to make sense out of the wide variation in estimated supply elasticities was to regress them on factors that potentially explain the variation. They found significant explainable variation of supply elasticities across crops due to crop area, irrigation (fixed investment), price risk, yield risks, income level, and literacy. If common behavioral criteria motivate a given group of farmers to grow several different crops as these results suggest, then the behavioral criteria embodied in one supply equation should apply to another supply equation associated with the same decision maker(s). This relationship can be exploited to improve estimates of supply.

Complete Models of Firm Decision Problems

One possible source of additional structure and improved estimation of supply that is only beginning to be exploited is economic theory. Estimation of agricultural demand has considered theoretical consistency of relationships among markets for some time (e.g., Brandow; George and King; Huang). These efforts have provided the most useful and reliable estimates of cross elasticities of demand available. One argument that has been used against imposing theoretical structure is that it forces the researcher to make an assumption about the behavioral criteria and technology underlying supply. Preferably, data should determine supply without imposing behavioral and technological assumptions. However, limited data availability, a rapidly changing economic environment, and the persistent problem of econometric identification in traditional supply studies have proven that purely data-based supply estimation has not been successful. Data availability and econometric techniques are simply not sufficient to determine functional form and coefficients of all potentially important variables or, in other words, to discern among all possible behavioral and technological possibilities. For example, Askari and Cummings (1977) in their critique of traditional approaches to supply estimation note that the correct specification depends on what motivates the farmer to change output. That is, even in traditional ad hoc supply specifications these types of assumptions are imposed implicitly. If behavioral and technological assumptions must be imposed implicitly in any case, then why not impose them in a systematic way that allows more efficient estimation? This approach also holds potential for estimating more plausible functional forms. For example, the system approach in demand has shown that all demands cannot be linear in prices and income as were estimated historically. For supply, even for a single-output profit-maximizing firm, a supply equation linear in output price as in the case of the Nerlovian model implies a very peculiar linear average cost curve.

Programming models were the first widely used approach to agricultural supply analysis imposing consistent behavioral criteria and technological relationships among alternative supplies and demands. Their success, however, was limited for other reasons. Duality approaches have greatly enhanced this potential although other refinements are needed in application. Both represent complete models of firm decision making and implicitly include representations of technology and behavioral criteria with the associated first-order conditions. This section is largely a discussion of potential for enhancing and integrating these approaches to agricultural supply estimation.

According to economic theory, the structure of supply is tied to the structure of production functions, cost functions, and profit functions. Theoretically, supply is based on firm theory and aggregation over firms. Yet estimation of corresponding concepts from firm theory has become far more sophisticated than standard direct estimation of supply. Production, cost, and profit function estimation has been found far more efficient when complete models of the firm are considered. Econometric theory implies that all observable, nonredundant equations should be jointly estimated to gain efficiency (Just, Zilberman, and Hochman). For a simple single-output problem, the production function approach under profit maximization can be characterized by the production function and first-order conditions for each input (Marshak and Andrews) which taken together are sufficient to determine supply. This compares to the similar input elasticity approach of Griliches discussed above but is more efficient because it considers the complete system as if Griliches had also estimated supply simultaneously with demands imposing parameter restrictions among supply and demands as dictated by theory. In this way, the complete modeling approach to firm supply decisions integrates some of the traditional approaches to attain consistency of relationships and thus efficiency of estimation.

More generally, the complete modeling of the firm supply decision can be attained for a fully joint multi-output technology by estimating all of the supplies and demands associated with the profit function which implicitly include the first-order conditions as well as the production technology under the behavioral assumption of profit maximization. For many agricultural applications, however, a more realistic representation of farm-level decision making is obtained by considering nonjointness of some inputs and allocatable fixity of others (Just, Zilberman, and Hochman). For example, where land, water, tractor hours, and fertilizer are allocated among land parcels with separate production functions applying to each land parcel and some factors such as land held fixed at the farm level, further structural relationships can be imposed in either the primal (production function) or dual (profit function) approaches. This then integrates many of the conceptually plausible aspects of traditional programming models. The important point in all of these cases, however, is that many of the estimable relationships have parameters in common so that joint estimation permits more efficiency for each individual parameter than if only the supply function is estimated. The problem in each application then becomes determining the appropriate scope of estimation given data availability.

To consider these possibilities in more detail, suppose agricultural production problems are characterized by (a) production relationships which describe the outputs as functions of the input allocations,

$$q_i = f_i(X_{1i}, ..., X_{ni}), \qquad (7)$$

(b) the behavioral criterion described by its associated conditions, e.g., the first order conditions for profit maximization,

$$p_i \partial f_i / \partial X_{ji} = w_j,\tag{8}$$

(c) accounting relationships that tie total input use (purchases), x_j, to the allocations, e.g.,

$$x_j = X_{j1} + \dots + X_{jm},\tag{9}$$

and (d) a determination of which of the allocatable inputs are fixed in total over the relevant time horizon as opposed to freely available at market prices.

For example, the problem of profit maximization in the context of relationships such as equations (7) and (9) can be represented as

$$max\ p'q - w'x$$
$$s.t.\quad q = f(X)\tag{10}$$
$$Xe = x$$

where p is an m by 1 vector of output prices, q is an m by 1 vector of output quantities, w is an n_v by 1 vector of variable input prices, x_v is an n_v by 1 vector of total variable input quantities, X is an m by n matrix of variable input allocations, $e = [1 \dots 1]'$, x is an n by 1 vector of total input quantities, $x' = [x_f'\ x_v']$, and x_f is an n_f by 1 vector of fixed allocatable input quantities. By developing a Lagrangian and deriving first order conditions, one finds that the solution to this problem is characterized by conditions

$$p = \lambda;\quad \phi_v = w;$$
$$\lambda_i \partial f_i / \partial X_{ji} = \phi_j,\ j=1,\dots,n,\ i=1,\dots,m;\tag{11}$$
$$q = f(X);\quad Xe = x$$

where λ is an m by 1 vector of shadow prices associated with the production function constraints and $\phi = [\phi_f'\ \phi_v'] = [\phi_1 \dots \phi_n]$ is a vector of shadow prices associated with the accounting relationships. This gives $2m+n+n_v+mn$ nonredundant equations in $3m+2n+n_v+mn-1$ variables (see Just, Zilberman, and Hochman).

The number of observable equations in (11) depends on how many variables are observed. The maximum number of nonredundant equations that can be expressed solely in terms of observable data under quite general conditions is the number of observable variables less the number of exogenous variables. The number of exogenous variables is $m+n-1$ which includes the $m+n_v-1$ prices in p and w (considering one price as the numeraire under homogeneity) and the n_f quantities of fixed inputs in x_f. Several likely cases with associated maximum numbers of nonredundant equations are as follows. For observed data (q, p, x, w, X), i.e., where all data other than shadow prices are observed, one can solve λ and ϕ out of (11) obtaining

$$p_i \partial f_i / \partial X_{ji} = w_j, j = n_f + 1, ..., n, i = 1, ..., m;$$

$$q = f(X); \quad Xe = x; \tag{12}$$

$$p_i \partial f_i / \partial X_{ji} = p_1 \partial f_1 / \partial X_{j1}, j = 1, ..., n_j, i = 2, ... m,$$

which has $nm + m + n_v$ nonredundant observable equations for estimation.

Next, let the input allocation matrix be partitioned as $X = (X_f' \, X_v')'$ where the first n_f rows (in X_f) represent the fixed input allocations and the last n_v rows (in X_v) represent the variable input allocations. Then where the variable input allocations are not recorded and observed data are (q, p, x, w, X_f), one can solve the system in (12) for $X_v = X_v(p, w, x_f)$ and aggregate obtaining $x_v = X_v e = x_v(p, w, x_f)$ to replace the first $n_v m$ equations. Then X_v can be replaced accordingly in the last $n_f(m-1)$ relationships, obtaining the system

$$x_v = x_v(p, w, x_f); \quad q = f(X); \tag{13}$$

$$X_f e = x_f; \quad p_i \partial f_i^* / \partial X_{ji} = p_1 \partial f_1^* / \partial X_{j1}, j = 1, ..., n_f, i = 2, ..., m,$$

where f_i^* denotes evaluation of the derivatives at $X_v = X_v(p, w, x_f)$ which has $n_f m + m + n_v$ nonredundant equations for estimation.

If no input allocations are recorded and observed data consist of (q, p, x, w), one can further solve X_f out of (13) obtaining

$$p = p(q, x), \quad w = w(q, x), \quad h(q, x) = 0, \tag{14}$$

which has $m + n_v$ nonredundant equations. This is simply a system of inverse supplies and demands plus a single equation input-output relationship. Note, however, that the input-output relationship is not simply a technological relationship. Rather, it is a reduced form equation summarizing the interaction of behavioral and technical information in the larger underlying but unobservable system. Alternatively, equation (14) can be represented equivalently as

$$q = q(p, w, x_f), \quad x_v = x_v(p, w, x_f), \tag{15}$$

which also provides $m + n_v$ nonredundant equations corresponding to the standard application of duality with the profit function approach (e.g., Weaver; Shumway; Antle).

A Synthesis of Methodologies for Supply Analysis

A comparison of the systems in equations (12)-(15) demonstrates how information is often thrown away in supply estimation and efficiency is thus lost. If the systems in equation (14) or (15) are estimated when data are available to estimate equation (13), or if (13) is estimated when data are available to estimate (12), then efficiency is lost and the estimates tend to be more erratic. Nevertheless, a closer fit is likely obtained when only a part of the system is estimated. This likely gives the researcher a false sense of precision and can explain poor performance of supply models outside of the sample period. This problem is somewhat akin to the problem of pretest estimation bias in econometrics. If a researcher chooses to fit only a partial representation of the supply problem and chooses to report estimates for the part where the best fit is obtained, then the significance statistics are not appropriate.

The most common situation of data availability in the United States is probably closest to (13). Available data include output prices and most variable input prices (used by the dual profit function approach), most variable input quantities aggregated across crops (used implicitly in the input demand approach by Griliches, 1959), output quantities (used individually in various supply studies), and land allocations among crops (used in acreage response studies of supply). Nevertheless, the most common approach has been to estimate a single supply equation corresponding to one of the equations in (14) solved for quantity-dependent form, i.e., quantity regressed on a price and an acreage variable representative of asset fixity. The Griliches approach of using input elasticities basically corresponds to using only the n_v input demand equations in (14). In this context, the dual approach of equation (15) is clearly a major advance in consistent interpretation of data and efficient estimation of supply. However, it still falls far short of the potential of equation (13) because an additional $n_f m$ estimable relationships are ignored. As Chambers and Just (1989) have shown, these considerations can be incorporated into a dual approach corresponding to (13) by providing more structure for the problem. That is, by defining individual profit functions for each production activity, $\pi_i = \pi_i(p_i, w, X_{fi})$ where X_{fi} is the *i*th column of X_f, (13) can be written equivalently as

$$q = q(p,w,x_f); \quad \pi_i = \pi_i(p_i,w,x_f), \; i = 1,...,m; \; X_f e = x_f;$$

$$\partial \pi_i(p_i,w,X_{fi})/\partial X_{ji} = \partial \pi_1(p_i,w,X_{f1})/\partial X_{j1},$$

$$j = 1,...,n_f, \; i = 2,...,m. \tag{16}$$

This system has the typical advantage of duality allowing more functional flexibility than is tractable with the primal approach in (13). However, with a multiplicity of profit functions that all have flexible form, this approach can result in very large numbers of parameters even for modest problems (see the application by Chambers and Just, 1989). In addition, other considerations as discussed below are important.

To complete this methodological synthesis of traditional supply analyses, note that the programming approach corresponds to the basic problem in equation (10) which is, in fact, a nonlinear programming problem. If the production technology follows fixed proportions for individual outputs, i.e., $q_i = f_i(X_{1i}, \dots, X_{ni}) = \min_j (X_{ji}/a_{ji})$, then the problem in (10) becomes a linear programming problem as has typically been used in agricultural programming models where the technology matrix is $A = \{a_{ij}\}$. This characterizes programming models of supply as the opposite extreme from single-equation supply models that disregard available data. Programming models alternatively demand more data than are available at the aggregate level. These needs are filled by making simplistic technology assumptions and gathering scant observations on representative farms for needed coefficients.

By comparison, the approach in equations (13) or (16) represents a blending of the traditional methodologies of direct supply estimation and programming models tailored to the data available for supply estimation. The modern applications of duality also represent a blending of these approaches but the methodology is not tailored to exploit available data.

Firm Level Decisions to Change Production Activities and Implications for Modeling Changes in Elasticities

Frequently, estimates of elasticities vary considerably with respect to the time period of estimation. For example, Antle's aggregate supply elasticity drops from 1.35 to .43 between adjacent time periods (Table 16.1). Rosine and Helmberger present an interesting application of the Marshak-Andrews methodology to estimate how elasticities in equations (7) and (8) -- which implicitly determine supply -- change annually over time for U.S. agriculture. The results demonstrate a continual annual change with a significant long-term trend explained by the technology coefficients identified through first-order conditions. These kinds of refinements are needed to generate models that explain changes in supply elasticities in order to gain usefulness of models beyond the sample period.

In addition, historical agricultural supply analysis has resulted in very poor estimation of cross supply elasticities. In fact, for the most part, they are not estimated. One reason is that microeconomic models of acreage allocation are poor. Programming models can produce drastic changes in acreage with small changes in prices but farmers are not so ready to abandon traditional activities as programming models sometimes suggest. On the other hand, econometric models are generally very poor in explaining differences in cropping patterns among farms. When the models of the profession perform poorly in reflecting individual farm behavior, questions arise about whether these structures are sufficiently applicable for aggregate supply estimation.

Generally, micro level econometric studies of production and supply have been extremely limited in the United States. Few truly micro level data sets have been developed and those in government hands have restricted use because of confidentiality considerations. A new generation of models and research is needed at the micro level and can help to improve the quality of supply models. As noted earlier, some recent research has shown that farmers may stay with accepted practices when the deviation from profit maximization is not great but that major changes tend to cause profit maximizing adjustments (Just, Zilberman, Hochman, and Bar-Shira). Models with costs of learning and adjustment also offer possibilities for better understanding the allocation of farm resources among alternative production activities.

As a result of the poor state of positive modeling of farm-level decision making, the profession has not produced good positive models of intercrop acreage response. Econometric models of acreage allocation tend not to reflect the phenomena whereby two crops may be highly competitive and thus have large direct and cross price elasticities of supply when the relative profitabilities of the two are similar, but may not be competitive with only a ten or twenty percent change in one of the prices. Thus, a relatively plausible price change can greatly alter the elasticities. Programming models, on the other hand, can have abrupt changes between zero and infinite elasticities with small changes in prices. When these problems are troublesome, programmers tend to add "calibration" or "habit" constraints so the sensitivities of the results suit the intuition of the researcher. Both of these approaches ignore the real underlying relationships and leave the profession with poor models of how elasticities and cross elasticities change in response to changing prices and other conditions.

Other factors that affect changes in supply elasticities include expectations of permanence of current conditions, changes in cropping toward or away from perennials, changes in technology, and changes in government programs and policy instruments. When a larger part of acreage is tied up in 30-year tree crops, supply response for other crops is likely to be much smaller. Important innovations have been made to improve the structural representation of planting, removal, and bearing acreage for perennials (French and Matthews) but the implications for cross effects on other crops have not been developed. Similarly, if technologies with expensive and specialized machinery like the mechanical tomato harvester are adopted, then supply response will likely decrease (Chern and Just) and this will likely cause cross elasticities to decrease for the whole set of competing crops.

Efforts to estimate agricultural supply elasticities must also recognize the dependence of own price elasticities on the extent to which cross elasticities are included. If an own elasticity is estimated without conditioning on prices of other outputs, then the resulting estimate tends to be an equilibrium estimate that measures quantity response taking into account equilibrium adjustments in other markets. Similarly, if an own elasticity is estimated without conditioning on the prices of inputs, then the resulting estimate is an equilibrium elasticity that tends to take account of equilibrium adjustment in input markets in response to changes in output price (Just, Hueth, and Schmitz). These considerations tend to be overlooked in practice but can have important implications for how the elasticities should be used. For example, suppose input prices tend to get bid up over a sustained period of high prices but not for a short-lived price increase. Then a supply elasticity estimated without conditioning on input prices over a period of stable or long-term price changes may be inapplicable for a period of short-term price volatility.

To some extent, using complete models of firm decision making can help to improve the focus on needed estimation of cross elasticities. However, unless the models are further developed to account for the issues that affect functional structure, the forthcoming estimates of cross elasticities are likely to be misleading. Another difficulty that will be encountered in efforts to carry complete models of firm decision making to the market level of application is aggregation. When different firms are involved in different sets of production activities, the associated corner solutions may make some properties applicable at the firm level inapplicable at the aggregate level. Similar problems are encountered in using individual consumer models at the aggregate level. These problems call for more work on aggregation of specifications which may lead to better consideration of distributional issues in aggregate specifications and/or development and use of more disaggregated data.

Flexible Functional Forms Versus Global Functional Structure

One of the great attractions of the dual approach is that more flexible functional forms are tractable than with the primal approach. Most applications can claim a second order approximation of the true profit or cost function (although imposition of theoretical constraints on parametric relationships reduces the flexibility somewhat from a true second order approximation). These properties have made researchers more comfortable with the choice of functional forms compared to the traditional approach of ad hoc econometric specification. In another sense, however, these properties may be providing a false sense of security. The problem is that smooth functions with continuous first and second order derivatives may not apply. This is particularly true given characteristics of government programs in agriculture where many policy instruments are imposed as one-sided limits (e.g., price supports and acreage limitations). Also, while one approximation may apply with one set of data or in one time period, a different approximation may apply for another. Thus, applicability outside of the sample period may be limited. Finally, while one may start with a second-order approximation of the profit function, the associated supply curve will only be a first-order approximation because it is a derivative. Understanding the changes in supply elasticities that occur over time may depend more heavily on achieving a globally reasonable functional structure rather than a close approximation to any particular point on the supply curve. In this context, the second-order flexible functional forms of the dual approach might be only a little less ad hoc than the traditional approach. Given that frequent changes in government programs have been one of the primary causes of poor information on supply, it seems that a better avenue to understanding of supply elasticity and how it changes is to refine our representation of the global role of government program instruments rather than finding an nth order local approximation. This is particularly true where many farms are involved in voluntary government programs with frequent shifts in and out of participation.

In supply analyses that account for the voluntary nature of government programs, a typical approach to modeling acreage response has been to specify a linear acreage equation

$$A = A(\pi_c, \pi_n, \pi_a, A_{-1}, G_v) \tag{17}$$

where π_c is anticipated short-run profit per acre under (voluntary) compliance with government programs, π_n is anticipated short-run profit per acre under noncompliance, π_a is anticipated short-run profit per acre from production of alternative crop(s), A_{-1} is lagged acreage representing production fixities as in the Nerlovian case, and G_v is the government payment per acre for voluntary diversion beyond the minimum (see, e.g., Rausser; Love). In this formulation, the levels of profit under compliance and noncompliance are assumed to pick up the change in voluntary compliance. (Dual approaches have not yet been applied in a way that meaningfully captures the compliance-noncompliance relationship.)

An approach that imposes more globally-relevant structure on the data is as follows. Suppose first that free market acreage follows $A = A_f(\pi_n, \pi_a, A_{-1})$. Then when government programs are voluntary, the nonparticipating component of acreage would follow this free market equation on the nonparticipating proportion of farms so nonparticipating acreage is

$$A_n = (1 - \phi) A_f(\pi_n, \pi_a, A_{-1}) \tag{18}$$

where ϕ is the rate of participation in the diversion program. For participating acreage, theory suggests that participation in a voluntary program and access to its price subsidies would tend not to be attractive unless the acreage limitations were effective. Thus, participating acreage is largely determined by program limitations with perhaps some minor modifications associated with departures from this general rule, e.g.,

$$A_p = B\phi(1 - \theta) - D(G_v) \tag{19}$$

where B is the program base acreage, θ is the minimum proportion of base acreage required to be diverted for participation, and D describes additional voluntary acreage diversion beyond the minimum as a function of the payment per acre for additional diversion. The estimating equation for total acreage given the participation level is obtained by combining equations (18) and (19),

$$A_t = B\phi(1 - \theta) - D(G_v) + (1 - \phi) A_f(\pi_n, \pi_a, A_{-1}). \qquad (20)$$

To determine the level of participation in this framework, each farmer i is assumed to participate if anticipated profit per acre (given diversion requirement and payment considerations) is greater under compliance than under noncompliance $(\pi_c^i > \pi_n^i)$. Assuming that individual perceived profits differ by an amount characterized by some stochastic distribution across farmers, the participation rate at the aggregate level can be represented by a profit relationship, e.g., in the logistic case

$$ln \frac{\phi}{1 - \phi} = \phi^*(\pi_n, \pi_c). \qquad (21)$$

To consider further structure, suppose that short-run profit per unit of land under noncompliance follows $\pi_n = P_m Y_a - C$ where P_m is the anticipated market price, Y_a is the anticipated actual yield, and C is the short-run production cost per unit of land. Then given the structure of major government programs for, say, wheat and corn, short-run profit per unit of land (producing plus diverted) on complying farms follows

$$\pi_c = (1 - \theta - \mu)\pi_p + \theta G_m + \mu \, max(G_v, \pi_p) \qquad (22)$$

where μ is the maximum proportion of base acreage that can be diverted in addition to minimum diversion, G_m is the payment per unit of land for minimum diversion, G_v is the payment per unit of land for voluntary diversion beyond the minimum, and π_p is the short-run profit per unit of producing land under compliance,

$$\pi_p = [max(P_t, P_m) \, Y_p + max(P_s, P_m) \, max(Y_a - Y_p, 0)$$
$$+ \, max(r_m - r_g, 0) \, P_s \, Y_a - C] \qquad (23)$$

where P_t is the government target price, Y_p is the program yield, P_s is the price support, r_m is the market rate of interest, and r_g is the government subsidized rate of interest on commodity loans under the program.

The latter term in equation (22) suggests no voluntary additional diversion if $G_v < \pi_p$ and voluntary additional diversion to the maximum is $G_v < \pi_p$. Equation (23) reflects the complicated relationship through which a participating farmer is entitled to at least the target price on his program yield, at least the (lower) support price on all of his production, and gains an additional interest subsidy on a loan against his stored crop (at harvest time) evaluated at the support price. These benefits must be balanced against the opportunity loss of having to divert some land from production reflected by (22).

The relationships in equations (22) and (23) do not necessarily apply exactly. For example, an uncertain anticipated market price may be discounted by a farmer compared to a target or support price which is known with certainty at the time of acreage decisions. Also, not all farmers place their crop under federal loan to take advantage of the interest subsidy. Nevertheless, (22) and (23) apply as reasonable global approximations. By comparison, the large number of highly correlated variables with numerous qualitative relationships suggests significant problems with purely data-based econometric identification and makes the possibility of obtaining even plausible signs remote with estimation of ad hoc or flexible forms. If further refinements to improve the approximation are desired, introducing them into a structure consistent with operation of the major government programs holds more promise of producing understanding of how supply elasticities vary with major shifts outside of sample data used for estimation.

To illustrate the difference in performance of the approach in equation (17) compared to that in equations (20) and (21), both were used to estimate acreage response of wheat and of feed grains in the U.S. over the period 1962 to 1982 and then to forecast acreage in the 1983-1986 period. (See Just, 1990, for a detailed specification of the models and data used for the analysis.) The results are given in Table 16.2. The results for equation (20) take the participation rate as exogenous whereas the results where the model is specified as equations (20) and (21) include forecasting errors for the participation rate as well.

In the case of feed grains, the ad hoc formulation in equation (17) leads to a much smaller standard error in the sample period than the structural form in equation (20) even though the structural form performs better than the ad hoc form in ex ante forecasting of the post-sample period. The model combining equations (20) and (21) obtains an even lower standard error. In the case of wheat, the structural form fits the sample data better than the ad hoc form and performs substantially better in ex ante simulation.

This superior performance of the structural model carries through when errors in forecasting the participation rate are also considered. The reason the structural form can outperform the ad hoc model even in the sample period is that nonlinearities and kinks in response over a wide range of policy parameters put a premium on global properties of the function. The participation rate over the sample period ranges from zero (a kink point) to nearly 90 percent. As a result, the effects of profits with and without compliance cannot be well represented by a smooth approximating function following (17).

Table 16.2. The Performance of Structural Versus Ad Hoc Models: The Case of U.S. Wheat and Feed Grain Acreage.

Crop Error	Model Definition[a]	Estimation Period	Forecast Period	Standard Error Within Sample	Standard Post-Sample
	(Equation)			(Mil. Acres)	(Mil. Acres)
Wheat	(17)	1962-82	1983-86	4.41	14.90
Wheat	(20)	1962-82	1983-86	3.32	6.21
Wheat	(20), (21)	1962-82	1983-86	b	9.07
Feed Grains	(17)	1962-82	1983-87	1.73	6.40
Feed Grains	(20)	1962-82	1983-87	6.26	6.38
Feed Grains	(20), (21)	1962-82	1983-87	b	5.50

[a]See the text for equations which define the various models.
[b]No within sample error is computed since the model is derived by combining the estimated equations corresponding to (6) and (7).

By comparison with this structured approach, a flexible function approach is likely to be inadequate on two grounds. First, mathematically a flexible form with continuous first and second derivatives cannot approximate well all of the kinks that can occur in equations (22) and (23). Second, the flexible approach demands too much data. The models in equations (17) or (18) through (26) have 10 variables which with a second-order flexible function would require over 100 parameters for a single crop. Time series data on annual crops are simply not available in that abundance. These arguments should not be taken to say that duality cannot be used but that some structure more consistent with government program operation needs to be imposed. Typically the only qualitative term in (23) that has fit easily into dual approaches is $max(P_t, P_m)$ which is conveniently used in place of the standard product price.

Technological Change and Induced Innovation

Finally, consider the role of technological change in agricultural supply. As mentioned in the introduction, strong and irregular effects of new technology have been major impediments to agricultural supply analysis. In traditional models of agricultural supply, technology change in most commonly represented by a simple time trend (Askari and Cummings, 1977). Although widely used, a time trend can hardly represent irregular waves of new technology affecting a particular crop such as was the case with hybrid corn and it has no possibility of reflecting the induced technology development that occurs in response to long-term price changes. Again, the traditional methodology tends to approximate a given period of time in a way that will likely not hold outside of the sample period. Alternatively, all of the effects of asset fixity, and habit formation as well as long-term technological change are summarized in the Nerlovian partial adjustment mechanism. This ties the rate of technology development, a process that is not in farmers' hands, to the rate at which farmers are willing to adjust assets or habits in response to prices.

The phenomena that govern technology development are very different than those that govern switching among crops or production activities on a farm. The lags on returns to research are different. The source of funds to finance research is different. The regulatory environment and institutions are different. Technology development is likely the major source of long-term supply response. It makes little sense to estimate its role on the basis of a partial adjustment coefficient that measures the extent to which a farmer will change from one year to the next. This implies that the Nerlovian partial adjustment framework may well give a poor assessment of long-term supply elasticity.

A classical view might be that agricultural supply should be conditioned on available technology rather than include the effects of price induced adjustments in technology. To follow this approach, however, estimated supply relationships must first be adequately conditioned on available technology. If they are not adequately conditioned as many estimated equations in the literature are not, then the resulting estimates will necessarily include the effects of technology development implicitly. On the other hand, if properly conditioned, then the extensive work on technology development in the literature can be employed to improve assessments of long-term technology development. When used in conjunction with a properly conditioned agricultural supply relationship, these elements explaining technological development will give a useful assessment of long-term supply response. This is another way in which additional structure can be imposed to improve supply assessment.

Perhaps a useful approach to capture the structure of long-term supply response would be to use a restricted profit function approach where each set of fixed factors is determined using a term of price expectations associated with the period of time over which the fixed factors would be in service. That is, the dual approach applied to a longer time horizon with longer-term price expectations could be used to represent how fixed factors are changed at the outset of that time period. Then if the profit function in each case depends on some exogenous representation of the level of technology development, a complete structure of long-term response would be obtained once a model of technology development was incorporated. As it has been applied in the past, however, the dual approach has been inadequate for these purposes. The issue of price expectations has been addressed poorly. The term of price expectations has not been tied to the applicable time period of the corresponding input decision. This will require greater consideration in the designation of fixed versus variable inputs and in the applicable time horizons than has been the case previously. It will also raise issues of tractability in trying to specify a consistent representation of the decision problem across time periods except for simple self-dual forms.

Conclusions

Estimates of American agricultural supply have varied considerably over time, crops, and methodologies. These variations need to be understood to facilitate use of supply estimates beyond the sample period. These problems can be addressed by developing a more complete representation of the underlying farmer decision problems tailored to data availability, estimating it efficiently by imposing cross-equation relationships in full-information techniques, developing better global structural representation of the functional forms, developing better representation of expectations formation and the applicability of longer-term expectations, developing a more structured representation of asset adjustment and technology development, and renewing efforts to study and represent micro level farm behavior positively.

A serious problem facing the agricultural economics profession and the users of their analyses is that efforts to measure agricultural supply elasticities have seemingly diminished since interest in their estimation peaked in the 1950s, 1960s, and 1970s. As a result, the stock of knowledge regarding agricultural supply is aging. One reason is that the traditional techniques of supply estimation are regarded as mundane and unworthy of publication in refereed journals. The profession and users of their results badly need updated estimates for many agricultural commodities. Many new directions are possible for improving the methodology of agricultural supply estimation. Pursuing these directions has the potential for once again generating interest, creativity, and publishability and thus revitalizing agricultural supply analysis.

References

Antle, J. 1984. The structure of U.S. agricultural technology. *American Journal of Agricultlural Economics* 66:414-421.

Askari, H. and J.T. Cummings. 1976. *Agricultural Supply Response: A Survey of the Econometric Evidence.* New York: Praeger Publishers.

Askari, H. and J.T. Cummings. 1977. Estimating agricultural supply response with the Nerlove Model: A survey. *International Economic Review* 18:257-292.

Brandow, G.E. August 1961. *Interrelations Among Demands for Farm Products and Implications for Control of Market Supply.* Pennsylvania Agricultural Experiment Station Bulletin 680.

Brennan, M.J. 1958. Changes in cotton acreage in the Southeast: Implications for supply functions. *Journal of Farm Economics* 40:835-844.

Chambers, R.G. and R.E. Just. 1981. Effects of exchange rate changes on U.S. agriculture: A dynamic analysis. *American Journal of Agricultural Economics* 63:32-45.

Chambers, R.G. and R.E. Just. 1989. Estimating multioutput technologies. *American Journal of Agricultural Economics* 71:980-995.

Chen, D., R. Courtney, and A. Schmitz. 1972. A polynomial lag formulation of milk production response. *American Journal of Agricultural Economics* 44:77-83.

Chern, W.S. and R.E. Just. September 1978. *Econometric Analysis of Supply Response and Demand for Processing Tomatoes in California*. University of California, Giannini Foundation Monograph No. 37. Berkeley, CA.

Dean, G.W. and E.O. Heady. 1958. Changes in supply response and elasticity for hogs. *Journal of Farm Economics* 40:845-860.

Dhrymes, P.J. 1971. *Distributed Lags: Problems of Estimation and Formulation*. San Francisco: Holden-Day.

Estes, E., L. Blakeslee, and R.C. Mittelhammer. 1982. Regional and national impacts of expanded Pacific Northwest potato production. *Western Journal of Agricultural Economics* 7:239-252.

Feder, G., R.E. Just, and A. Schmitz. 1980. Futures markets and the theory of the firm under price uncertainty. *Quarterly Journal of Economics* 94:317-328.

Fisher, F. 1962. *Apriori Information and Time Series Analysis*. Amsterdam: North-Holland Publishing Co.

French, B.C. and J.L Matthews. 1971. A supply response model for perennial crops. *American Journal of Agricultural Economics* 53:478-490.

George, P.S. and G.A. King. March 1971. *Consumer Demand for Food Commodities in the United States with Projections for 1980*. Giannini Foundation Monograph No. 26. Berkeley: University of California.

Griliches, Z. 1959. The demand for inputs in agriculture and a derived supply function. *Journal of Farm Economics* 41:309-322.

Griliches, Z. 1960. Estimates of the aggregate U.S. farm supply function. *Journal of Farm Economics* 42:282-293.

Halvorson, H.W. 1955. The supply elasticity of milk in the short-run. *Journal of Farm Economics* 37:1186-1196.

Halvorson, H.W. 1958. The response of milk production to price. *Journal of Farm Economics* 40:1101-1112.

Hammig, M.D. 1978. Supply response and simulation of supply and demand for the U.S. fresh vegetable industry. Unpublished Ph.D. dissertation, Washington State University.

Hammig, M.D. and R.C. Mittelhammer. 1980. An imperfectly competitive market model of the U.S. lettuce industry. *Western Journal of Agricultural Economics* 5:1-12.

Hazell, P.B.R. and R.D. Norton. 1986. *Mathematical Programming for Economic Analysis in Agriculture*. New York: MacMillan Publishing Company.

Henneberry, S.R. and L.G. Tweeten. 1991. A review of international agricultural supply response. *Journal of International Food & Agribusiness Marketing* 2:49-95.

Houck, J.P. and M.E. Ryan. 1972. Supply analysis for corn in the United States: Impact of changing government programs. *American Journal of Agricultural Economics* 54:184-191.

Houck, J.P. and A. Subotnik. 1969. The U.S. supply of soybeans: Regional acreage functions. *Agricultural Economics Research* 21:99-108.

Huang, K.S. December 1985. *U.S. Demand for Food: A Complete System of Price and Income Effects*. ERS Technical Bulletin No. 1714. Washington, DC: U.S. Department of Agriculture.

Just, R.E. 1977. The existence of stable distributed lags. *Econometrica* 45:1467-1480.

Just, R.E. 1973. An investigation of the importance of government programs in farmers' decisions. *American Journal of Agricultural Economics* 55:441-452.

Just, R.E. 1974. An investigation of the importance of risk in farmers' decisions. *American Journal of Agricultural Economics* 56:14-25.

Just, R.E. 1976. Spectral analysis of stochastic properties in regression: An application in supply response identification. *American Journal of Agricultural Economics* 58:712-720.

Just, R.E. 1990. Modelling the interactive effect of alternative sets of policies on agricultural prices. In L.A. Winters and D. Sapsford, eds., *Primary Commodity Prices: Economic Models and Policy*. Cambridge, England: Cambridge University Press.

Just, R.E., D.L. Hueth, and A. Schmitz. 1982. *Applied Welfare Economics and Public Policy*. New York: Prentice-Hall, Inc.

Just, R.E. and G.C. Rausser. 1981. Commodity price forecasting with large-scale econometric models and the futures market. *American Journal of Agricultural Economics* 63:197-208.

Just, R.E., D. Zilberman, and E. Hochman. 1983. Estimation of multicrop production functions. *American Journal of Agricultural Economics* 65:770-780.

Just, R.E., D. Zilberman, E. Hochman, and Z. Bar-Shira. 1990. Input allocation in multicrop systems. *American Journal of Agricultural Economics* 72:200-209.

Ito, S., E.J. Wailes, and W.R. Grant. 1985. Asian rice elasticities. Pp. 20-25 in RE-45, *Rice Outlook and Situation Report*. Washington, DC: ERS, U.S. Department of Agriculture.

Liu, K. and V. Roningen. 1985. *The World Grain-Oilseeds-Livestock (GOL) Model: A Simplified Version*. International Economics Division ERS Staff Report No. AGES850128. Washington, DC: U.S. Department of Agriculture.

Love, H.A. 1987. Flexible public policy: The case of the United States wheat sector. Unpublished Ph.D. dissertation, University of California, Berkeley.

Marshak, J. and W.H. Andrews. 1944. Random simultaneous equations and the theory of production. *Econometrica* 12:143-206.

McFadden, D. 1978. Cost, revenue, and profit functions. In M. Fuss and D. McFadden, eds., *Production Economics: A Dual Approach to Theory and Applications*. New York: North-Holland.

Meilke, K.D., A.C. Zwart, and L.J. Martin. 1974. North American hog supply: A comparison of geometric and polynomial distributed lag models. *Canadian Journal of Agricultural Economics* 22:15-30.

Morzuch, B.J., R.D. Weaver, and P.G. Helmberger. 1980. Wheat acreage supply response under changing farm programs. *American Journal of Agricultural Economics* 62:29-37.

Mundlak, Y. and C.O. McCorkle, Jr. 1956. Statistical analysis of supply response in late spring potatoes in California. *Journal of Farm Economics* 38:553-569.

Nerlove, M. 1956. Estimates of the elasticities of supply of selected agricultural commodities. *Journal of Farm Economics* 38:496-508.

Nerlove, M. and W. Addison. 1958. Statistical estimation of long-run elasticities of supply and demand. *Journal of Farm Economics* 40:861-880.

Pope, R.D. 1982. To dual or not to dual? *Western Journal of Agricultural Economics* 7:337-351.

Pope, R.D. and R.E. Just. 1991. On testing the structure of risk preferences in agricultural supply analysis. *American Journal of Agricultural Economics* 73:743-748.

Prato, A. 1973. Milk demand, supply, and price relationships, 1950-1968. *American Journal of Agricultural Economics* 55:217-222.

Quance, Leroy and Luther Tweeten. 1971. Comparability of positivistic and normative supply elasticities for agricultural commodities. Pp. 451-459 in *Policies, Planning, and Management for Agricultural Development*. (Papers and Reports, 14th International Conference of Agricultural Economists, Byelorussian State University, Minsk, USSR, August 23-September 2, 1970.) Oxford: Institute of Agrarian Affairs.

Rausser, G.C. 1985. *Macroeconomics of U.S. Agricultural Policy*. Studies in Economic Policy. Washington, DC: American Enterprise Institute for Public Policy.

Rausser, G.C. and R.E. Just. 1981. Using models in policy formation. In *Modeling Agriculture for Policy Analysis in the 1980s*. Kansas City, MO: The Federal Reserve Bank of Kansas City.

Reed, M.R. and S. Riggins. 1981. A disaggregated analysis of corn acreage response in Kentucky. *American Journal of Agricultural Economics* 63:709-711.

Rojko, A., D. Regier, P. O'Brien, A. Coffing, and L. Bailey. 1978. *Alternative Futures for World Food in 1985*. Foreign Agriculture Report No. 146. Washington, DC: U.S. Department of Agriculture.

Saez, R.R. and C.R. Shumway. 1985. *Multiproduct Agricultural Supply Response and Input Demand Estimation in the United States: A Regional Profit Function Approach*. Technical Report No. 85-3. College Station: Texas Agricultural Experiment Station, Texas A&M University.

Sarris, A.H. and J. Freebairn. 1983. Endogenous price policies and international wheat prices. *American Journal of Agricultural Economics* 65:214-224.

Shephard, R.W. 1953. *Cost and Production Functions*. Princeton, NJ: Princeton University Press.

Shumway, C.R. 1983. Supply, demand, and technology in a multi-product industry: Texas field crops. *American Journal of Agricultural Economics* 65:748-760.

Shumway, R.C. and A.A. Chang. 1977. Linear programming versus positively estimated supply functions: An empirical and methodological critique. *American Journal of Agricultural Economics* 59:344-357.

Shumway, C.R., R.D. Pope, and E.K. Nash. 1984. Allocatable fixed inputs and jointness in agricultural production: Implications for economic modeling. *American Journal of Agricultural Economics* 66:72-78.

Tegene, A., W.E. Huffman, and J.A. Miranowski. 1988. Dynamic corn supply functions: A model with explicit optimization. *American Journal of Agricultural Economics* 70:103-110.

Tomek, W.G. and K.L. Robinson. 1977. Agricultural price analysis and outlook. In Lee R. Martin, ed., *A Survey of Agricultural Economics Literature: Volume 1*. St. Paul: University of Minnesota Press.

Turnovsky, S.J. 1979. Futures markets, private storage, and price stabilization. *Journal of Public Economics* 12:301-327.

Tweeten, L.G. and L. Quance. 1969. Positivistic measures of aggregate supply elasticities: Some new approaches. *American Journal of Agricultural Economics* 51:342-352.

Tyers, R. 1984. *Agricultural Protection and Market Insulation: Analysis of International Impacts by Stochastic Simulation*. Research Paper No. 111. Development Studies Center and Australia-Japan Research Center. Canberra: Australian National University.

Weaver, R. 1983. Multiple input, multiple output production choices and technology in the U.S. wheat region. *American Journal of Agricultural Economics* 65:45-56.

Whittaker, J.K. and R.L. Bancroft. 1979. Corn acreage response-function estimation with pooled time-series and cross-sectional data. *American Journal of Agricultural Economics* 61:551-553.

Zusman, P. 1962. Econometric analysis of the market for California early potatoes. *Hilgardia* 33:539-668.

17

The Political Economy of Rice in Japan
Susumu Yamaji and Shoichi Ito

Introduction

Rice is the major crop and staple food in Japan. Despite the decline in the share of rice in general agricultural production and food consumption, rice is still the most important food for the Japanese people. The country has approximately 3.5 million rice producers and each Japanese consumes on average about 70 kilograms of rice annually.

The hot recent issue has been whether Japan should open up its rice market to foreign rice. This issue first was spurred in 1986 when the American Rice Millers Association filed, before the U.S. Trade Representative, a complaint against Japan over its closed rice market. The high domestic rice price relative to the world price has been widely criticized. On the other hand, in Japan there is strong support for maintaining domestic supply essential to Japanese food security.

Historical Perspective

Rice has remained an important cultural component in Japan. Rural Japanese society is heavily influenced by institutions that developed out of the need for cooperative action to control irrigation and to ensure community security for rice production. Modern urban corporate society still pays homage to the rice culture in year-end ceremonies similar to traditional rituals seeking divine protection for the rice harvest (USDA). The deep roots of government involvement in the rice sector have become strongly woven into the political fabric, reflected currently in the ruling Liberal Democratic Party (LDP) which has relied upon the rice producer cooperatives for its important rural power base (Okimoto).

Following the Rice Riots of 1918 and 1920, which were caused by major rice shortages in the cities due to the increased rice demand associated with

World War I, the Rice Law of 1921 was established and subsequently replaced by the Rice Control Law in 1933 (Hayami). These laws allowed the government to indirectly intervene in the rice market by establishing a means of purchasing, selling, storing, and restricting imports so that market prices would be maintained between floor and ceiling prices. However, these measures were insufficient to stabilize production, consumption, and prices. As Japan became involved with World War II, the Rice Distribution Control Act was enacted in 1939 to allow the government to directly influence rice supply and distribution.

The law was replaced by the Food Control Act of 1942, which made direct government intervention permanent. This act included nearly all other food commodities in addition to rice (Hayami; MAFF, Policy Division). Producers were expected to deliver all rice production to the government under the new law even if government prices were lower than market prices. During the recovery from World War II, the Food Emergency Measure Act was promulgated in 1946 as a more forceful law authorizing the government to expropriate undelivered rice (Hayami).

As the economy recovered, the compulsory delivery system was changed to a voluntary delivery system in 1955, under which each producer agreed to deliver a specific amount of rice. As economic growth continued and consumer prices increased in the 1960s, rice consumption began to decline while production increased due to high government producer purchase prices. Consequently, rice surpluses became a serious problem for the government.

The Food Control Act, enacted during the food shortage period, was not compatible with an abundant food period. Year 1969 was a milestone for Japanese rice policies because the government introduced the rice diversion program. The voluntary delivery system, which had been in effect since 1955, was replaced by a quantity allotment system in 1971 (MAFF, Policy Division). Under this system, the government does not necessarily purchase more than the limit or quota assigned to individual producers.

Beginning in 1969, rice was classified into two categories, direct-government-controlled rice and indirect-government-controlled rice. Direct-government-controlled rice is distributed through government channels as before. The indirect-government-controlled rice does not go through government purchase operations, but the government still controls production and monitors prices. The indirect-government-controlled rice was established due to the pressure of an enormous government budget deficit created by large rice purchases. To avoid having all rice purchased by the government, the indirect rice category was designed to introduce a free market channel for the rice sector, particularly for high quality rice. A scheme to allow different qualities of rice was implemented in 1972. These changes were formally legalized in 1981 and facilitated a flexible and more market-oriented rice production and distribution system. The proportion of indirect-government-controlled rice has increased over time. By 1989, it accounted for nearly 60 percent of the total direct and indirect-government-controlled rice in Japan.

In 1990, a free market was finally introduced for a limited amount of rice. Auctions were held once in Tokyo and Osaka in 1990, but they were scheduled to be held more often in 1991. Despite some regulations for submission of rice and changes in prices offered by tenders, this system is another milestone towards a free market system for rice in Japan.

Overall Plan

The Minister of the Ministry of Agriculture, Forestry, and Fisheries (MAFF) designs an overall plan for supply, distribution, and consumption of rice. This plan, established and announced every year, is the basis for controlling production and marketing of rice in Japan. The Minister consults with the governors of the states (or ken in Japanese) to develop a distribution plan detailing when and what quality of rice is to be produced and distributed to the individual states during the rice marketing year.

The Minister of MAFF allocates the national rice production goal to the individual states. The governor in each state then reallocates to the individual counties (or shi, cho, or son in Japanese). The mayor in each county reallocates to each community. The community actually finalizes the allocation process to individual producers. Once a limit for each producer is determined, the producer signs for delivery of rice only up to the allocated amount of rice. The total amount of rice allocated to each producer is divided into two categories, direct-government-controlled rice and indirect-government-controlled rice (Figure 17.1).

Actual delivery of rice to the government is controlled step by step. At harvest, rice is dried, hulled, and packed into 60 kilogram paper sacks by the producers. The packed brown rice is then delivered to the first handlers by the individual producers. If there is a discrepancy between estimated and harvested amounts, adjustments between surplus and deficit are made by the individuals or regions. Inspection and grading of each rice pack takes place at the time of delivery to the first handlers. Each pack shows the producer's name, grade, variety, and whether it is direct- or indirect-government-controlled rice.

Handlers at all levels must be licensed by MAFF. Agricultural cooperatives of the Nokyo system generally are the dominant first handlers at the local level. The number of Nokyo acting as first handlers was 3,656 in 1988 (MAFF Food Agency). Another certified organization for handling rice is known as the National Staple Food Handlers' Cooperative, or Zenshuren in Japanese. There were 1,520 Zenshuren first handlers in 1988. However, more than 95 percent of the 3.2 million rice producing/marketing households ship their rice through Nokyo (Zenchu). Since June 1988, the first handlers have been allowed to collect rice from any area in their respective state without being restricted to their local area. In order to encourage new

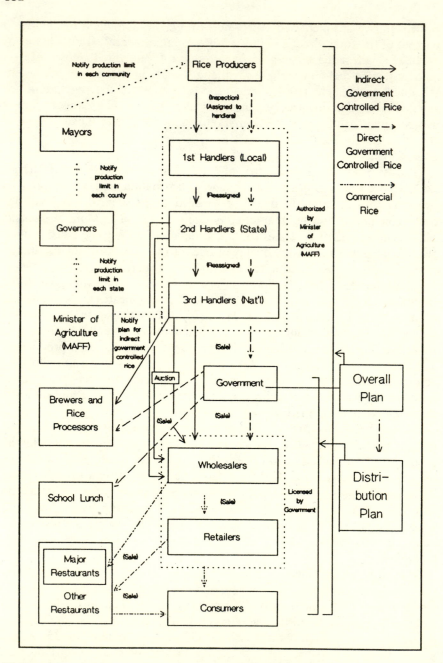

Figure 17.1. Structure of Government Control Over Production and Marketing.
Source: MAFF, *Shokuryo Kanri no Genjo*, December 1990.

handlers, in 1988 the government relaxed the requirements for first handlers in terms of size of institution, length of experience, and volume to be handled.

After the first handlers, the rice then goes to the second handlers, typically state-level federations of the individual first handlers. In 1988, there were 47 Nokyo-related second handlers, one in each state, while the number of Zenshuren-related second handlers was only 42.

Rice is transferred to the third handlers who are the national federations of the two systems. The Nokyo-related third handler is called Zen-noh (National Federation of Agricultural Cooperatives Association for Supply and Marketing) and the other is Zenshuren. Both direct- and indirect-government-controlled rice is transferred to the third handlers. The title of ownership of rice, however, is not transferred from the individual producer until the third handler finally sells the rice. The direct-government-controlled rice is sold only to the government at the government floor prices, while indirect-government-controlled rice is sold to wholesalers, usually at negotiated prices, which are usually much higher than government prices due to the higher quality of the rice. The second route, which became available in 1988, is for the second handlers to sell the indirect-government-controlled rice directly to the wholesalers in the same state. This new channel was designed to encourage faster distribution of high-quality rice based on market-oriented demand.

More recently, a third route has been created for indirect-government-controlled rice. This is an auction in which tenders are invited to bid. This is conducted by the Price Determining Organization for Indirect-Government-Controlled Rice (PDO) which was organized in August 1990 and is currently funded entirely by MAFF. According to the operating rules of the PDO, the amount of rice auctioned at this market should not be less than 20 percent of the total indirect-government-controlled rice annually. Further, fluctuation of prices for each brand of rice has to be within 10 percent of its previously established base price. Auctions are supposed to be held once a month in both Tokyo and Osaka, although they were held only a few times in 1990/91 due to the recent introduction of the route.

Current Concern for Self-Sufficiency

Total agricultural imports to Japan have been increasing in both volume and value since the 1960s. Japan has become the largest agricultural importer in the world, importing $8 billion from the U.S. alone in 1986. The self-sufficiency rate of food, in terms of calorie intake, declined from 73 percent in 1965 to 49 percent in 1988. Thus, domestic political concern for maintaining self-sufficiency in rice has increased, while the high level of protection has become a point of contention in trade liberalization discussions. However, public opinion in Japan on opening the rice market is changing. According to opinion polls taken in May 1990, 60-65 percent of the Japanese people expressed support for opening the rice market completely or in part (*The Daily Yomiuri*; *Asahi Shimbun*).

More recently, some powerful politicians in the LDP (the ruling party) have hinted at opening up the market under a quota system (*Nihon Keizai Shimbun*). Such an opinion from the LDP may reflect their desire to successfully conclude the Uruguay Round multilateral trade negotiations.

The Position of the Japanese Government
Toward GATT Negotiations

The Japanese Diet has affirmed the policy of self-sufficient rice production three times during the last 11 years. The first time was in April 1980 when U.S. President Jimmy Carter ordered an embargo against the Soviet Union to protest the Soviet Union's invasion of Afghanistan. The Japanese felt that the U.S. betrayed them by using food as a weapon. The Japanese were greatly disappointed to learn that the U.S. still considered the food embargo a political strategy. The resolution to raise the self-sufficiency rate in all the important food markets including rice was unanimously voted for in the Lower House.

The second resolution was brought up in the midst of the nation's emergency rice imports from South Korea in July 1984. Due to bad weather in Japan, domestic rice production was insufficient to meet demand. Japanese rice growers became furious with the government because this happened while a mandatory rice diversion program was in place to avoid an oversupply. The producers insisted that the imports were necessitated by governmental mismanagement in estimating demand and supply of rice.

The latest resolution was in September 1988. The background which gave rise to this resolution was quite different from the last two cases. This time, the Rice Millers Association (RMA) in the U.S. filed a second petition against the closed Japanese rice market. In Japan, the action of the RMA was taken seriously and this raised an unprecedented issue over the closed market and high prices of rice. Despite such a hot issue, however, both the Upper and Lower Houses unanimously voted for a policy to provide all rice domestically. The unanimous votes of the entire Diet have been the backbone of the Japanese governmental policy at the GATT negotiations (*Nihon Nogyo Shimbun*). This strongly indicates that not only the rice growers but also consumers support the closed rice market.

Some top ranking representatives from the LDP and Koumeito, the third largest party in the Japanese Diet, hinted at allowing minimum access by foreign grown rice. However, rice growers and some consumer groups have taken a strong position against such a move. In July 1991, the Agricultural Cooperative organization held the largest conference and demonstration ever, bringing 50,000 rice growers and supporters from all over the country to

Tokyo to protest any motions to allow rice imports. This was to show their strong opposition to opening the rice market under any circumstances.

The Japanese GATT negotiators mirror the position of the government and the politically strong opinions in their home country. Accordingly, Japan would not alter its position of a closed rice market unless other countries take drastic measures. An example is for the U.S. to give up protection of some of its markets from imports.

Rice Growers: A Political Base

The number of Japanese rice-producing households has been steadily decreasing over the last quarter century as explained in earlier chapters. This has mirrored the decline in total farm households. However, the 3 million plus rice-producing households still account for the majority of farmers and account for three-quarters of total farm households in Japan (Table 17.1). Rice-producing-marketing households are defined as rice-producing households that market more than 60 kilograms of brown rice during the rice market year (November-October). They number 2.4 million and account for more than half of farm households.

Table 17.1. Total Farm Households, Rice-Producing Households, and Rice-Producing-And-Marketing Households in Japan, 1960-1988 (1,000 Households).

Year	Total Farm Households	Rice-Producing Households	Rice-Producing-And-Marketing Households
1961	5,906	5,275	3,348
1962	5,829	5,220	3,363
1963	5,750	5,158	3,343
1964	5,667	5,087	3,339
1965	5,665	5,036	3,317
1966	5,498	4,978	3,422
1967	5,419	4,922	3,518
1968	5,351	4,864	3,500
1969	---	4,792	3,468
1970	5,402	4,569	3,205
1971	5,261	4,361	3,045
1972	5,170	4,183	2,937
1973	5,157	4,073	2,893
1974	5,081	4,063	2,935
1975	4,953	4,039	2,974

Table 17.1 cont.

Year	Total Farm Households	Rice-Producing Households	Rice-Producing-And-Marketing Households
1976	4,891	3,997	2,955
1977	4,835	3,947	2,947
1978	4,788	3,870	2,880
1979	4,742	3,802	2,826
1980	4,661	3,721	2,603
1981	4,614	3,645	2,636
1982	4,567	3,592	2,592
1983	4,522	3,532	2,560
1984	4,473	3,475	2,605
1985	4,376	3,437	2,591
1986	4,331	3,368	2,546
1987	4,284	3,297	2,470
1988	4,240	3,214	2,385

Source: MAFF Food Agency, 1987 and 1990.

Table 17.2 shows that the average rice farm in Japan is very small. More than half of the total rice area in Japan was on rice farms smaller than 1.0 hectares (2.5 acres) in 1988. Farms larger than 5 hectares accounted for only 5.1 percent of rice area. Even in terms of rice-producing-marketing households, the number of farms smaller than 1 hectare accounted for nearly 80 percent of the total. The small size of rice farms mirrors the small scale of Japanese farms in general. All farms in Japan in 1989 averaged only 1.27 hectares per farm.

Table 17.2. Total Areas Planted and Number of Rice Farmers by Size of Hectares to Rice per Farm, Japan, 1988 (Percent).

	Hectares						
	< 0.5	0.5-1.0	1.0-1.5	1.5-2.0	2.0-3.0	3.0-5.0	> 5.0
Area planted	24.3	26.4	16.1	10.0	10.5	7.4	5.1
Farmers[a]	47.3	30.8	11.1	4.9	3.7	1.7	0.6

Source: MAFF Food Agency, 1990.
[a]Farmers in this table are rice-producing-and-marketing households.

Two factors, small farm size and the high degree of mechanization relative to other crops, have contributed to the fact that rice in Japan is produced predominantly by part-time farmers. In 1989, rice area planted by full-time farmers accounted for only 261,000 hectares (13 percent of total), while part-time farmers and part-time farmers who hold other jobs accounted for 577,000 hectares (29 percent) and 1.16 million hectares (58 percent), respectively (Table 17.3). In comparison with figures for 1986, the trend is towards more part-time production.

More than half of the Japanese area planted to rice in 1986 and 1989 was farmed by producers whose agricultural income were less than half of their total household income. This comparison, over a relatively short time period, suggests a substantial change over a longer time period. Small size farms are usually inefficient. One of the major reasons for their uneconomical production is that operators have a strong feeling that they would be shamed and lose face if they left their farms barren. In other words, it is a tradition of shame culture that makes them grow rice despite an economic loss.

Costs of Production

Table 17.4 shows production costs by farm size in 1988. Total costs per hectare and per 60 kilograms of brown rice decrease by 39 percent as size increases from less than 0.3 hectares to more than 5 hectares. Labor costs per hectare decrease from U.S. $5,608 for farms less than 0.3 hectares to U.S. $2,518 for farms greater then 5 hectares, a 55 percent decrease. Direct labor hours per hectare of rice production range from a high of 663 hours for farms smaller then 0.3 hectare to a low of 298 hours for farms larger than 5

Table 17.3. Rice Area Planted by Producer Type, Japan, 1986 and 1989.[a]

	1986		1989	
	1,000 Hectares	**% of Total**	**1,000 Hectares**	**% of Total**
Full-time	340	15	261	13
Part-time	682	31	577	29
Part-time but hold other jobs	1,209	54	1,161	58
Total	2,231	100	1,999	100

Source: MAFF Food Agency, 1987 and 1990.
[a]Definition of full-time, part-time, and part-time-but-hold-other-jobs producers are those whose farm incomes account for more than 90 percent, 50-90 percent, and less than 50 percent, respectively, of their total household incomes.

Table 17.4. Costs of Rice Production by Farm Size, Japan, 1988 (US$ per Hectare).[a]

		Farm Size (Hectares)				
	Average	< 0.3	0.5-1.0	1.5-2.0	3.0-5.0	> 5.0
Fertilizers	728	787	761	664	687	612
Chemicals	587	706	613	585	528	431
Fees/borrowing	706	1,584	884	494	386	234
Equipment	3,486	4,305	3,951	3,159	2,586	2,371
Labor	3,983	5,608	6,656	3,401	2,786	2,518
By-products	-342	-537	-382	-306	-239	-274
Interest	656	847	738	580	489	472
Rent	2,432	2,130	2,134	2,655	3,049	2,649
Total	13,700	17,298	14,749	12,559	11,603	10,492
Yield (kg. brown)	5,170	5,230	5,060	5,280	5,430	5,190
Cost/60 Kg. brown[b]	159	198	175	143	128	121
Cost/cwt., rough	95	119	105	86	77	73
Gross income	12,126	12,257	11,947	12,696	12,771	11,039
Net income[c]	5,083	2,883	4,169	6,413	7,175	5,831
Labor (Hrs./Ha.)	481	663	541	418	354	298

Source: Wailes, Ito, and Cramer.
[a]Numbers are rounded.
[b]Costs per 1 cwt. rough rice = costs per 60 kilograms brown rice * 0.8/60 kilograms * 45 kilograms (100 lbs.).
[c]Net income = gross income - total costs (excluding interest, rent, own labor, and by-products).

hectares. In addition to labor, more efficient utilization of equipment and lower average expenditures for fees and borrowing contribute to size economies.

Large-scale farms may be able to cut costs substantially. A farm in Shiga Prefecture grew rice on 9.66 hectares, mostly rented land, and sold 53.4 tons of brown rice. The total production cost per 60 kilograms of brown rice was 10,094 Yen, about half of the average production cost in 1988 over all farms (Okamura). These data suggest that farm size/structure is a major constraint to lowering the national average cost of rice production and that substantial cost reductions could be achieved in Japan by enlargement of farms. However, even on relatively large Japanese farms, rice production is costly relative to the world rice price. Current average rice production costs in Japan are several times higher than those in major rice exporting countries such as Thailand and the U.S.

Diversion Programs

The rice area planted and production in Japan steadily increased until 1967 due to governmental incentives to producers. As rice consumption leveled off in the early 1960s and then began to decrease, the build-up of rice stocks began to put pressure on the government budget. In 1969, a rice diversion program was introduced for the first time in Japanese history. Government stocks, which were as low as 0.52 MMT of brown rice in 1965, reached a level of 7.2 MMT in 1970. This volume exceeded 70 percent of the 1970 production.

Diversion programs have been implemented continuously since then. The details of the programs are well documented by Wailes, Ito, and Cramer. Rice diversion programs have been practically mandatory for all rice producers although there are many kinds of government subsidies. Under the current diversion program, the Rice Farming Establishment Program announced in 1987, MAFF set a target level of government stocks at 1.5 MMT. The rice diversion target was increased from 600,000 hectares (the equivalent of 2.9 MMT of brown rice) in 1986 to 770,000 hectares (3.65 MMT) for the 1987-89 period due to decreased consumption. The diversion target during the 1990-92 period has been further increased to 830,000 hectares (4.05 MMT).

Farmer compliance with the diversion programs has been high and in many years has exceeded the target. The strict adherence is not based as much upon the economic incentives of the diversion subsidies as it is upon the obedience of producers to government requirements which are reinforced by community and peer pressure. Producers and communities who fail to reduce rice area and marketed volume to their allocated level are required by the government to add an area equivalent to the area of overproduction to the next year's regular diversion allocation. Further, if the rice area reduction is not achieved satisfactorily in a certain region, the government may withhold other kinds of subsidies from the region. Due to these strict controls under the series of rice diversion programs, the rice area planted decreased by 35 percent from 3.17 million hectares to 2.08 million hectares from 1969 to 1989.

The diversion programs have been costly to the government, however. Expenditures were large from the outset with 184 billion Yen spent in 1971 when the government aggressively implemented the rice diversion program after the two initial trial years. After rising to 380 billion Yen in 1980, expenditures decreased over time but they were still as high as 163 billion Yen (U.S. $1.07 billion) in 1989 (Table 17.5).

Table 17.5. Japanese Government Expenditures on the Rice Market, 1986-90 (Million U.S. Dollars).[a]

Year	Net Cost of Procure- ment	Indirect Rice Control	Processor and Feed	Market Manage- ment	Diversion Program	Total Subsidies
1986	459	615	111	1,107	1,480	3,770
1987	588	668	116	1,107	1,487	3,966
1988	-58	732	160	1,076	1,706	3,616
1989	-80	845	195	1,166	1,646	3,772
1990[b]	-129	820	186	1,110	1,074	3,060

Source: Wailes, Ito, and Cramer.
[a]Excludes indirect subsidies, such as those for land and irrigation improvements.
[b]Preliminary.

Determination of Government Procurement and Selling Prices

The Food Control Act of 1942 specifies that government procurement prices must be set at a level that covers the cost of production and provides financial security for producers. The specific method of determining the government procurement price has been modified from time to time.

The Rice Price Advisory Committee was created in 1949. This committee is responsible for evaluating the government procurement price as proposed by the MAFF. The committee is comprised of 25 members appointed by the MAFF Minister and representing producers, consumers, and other groups. Each year, a government procurement price, calculated by MAFF, is proposed by the Minister to the Committee. The Rice Price Advisory Committee then provides its evaluation and response to the government. The Prime Minister, the Ministers of Finance and MAFF, and others in the Executive Cabinet make the final decision on the rice procurement price, taking into account the response from the Rice Price Advisory Committee. Usually this process is completed in July of each year.

The process leading to the actual price determination is very complicated and highly political (Figure 17.2). Even though the Ministry has used the same method for calculating the government procurement price since 1960, estimates by different interest groups using the same method vary widely, reflecting their own biases. MAFF tends to calculate conservatively so that the government expenditures will be as small as possible. On the other hand, the producer groups such as the agricultural cooperatives (called "Nokyo" for short) and the LDP, representing the interests of producers, estimate higher prices than typically proposed by MAFF to the Rice Price Advisory Committee.

Nokyo has a major role in marketing rice. The fees for handling and storage are important income sources for the Nokyo cooperative organization.

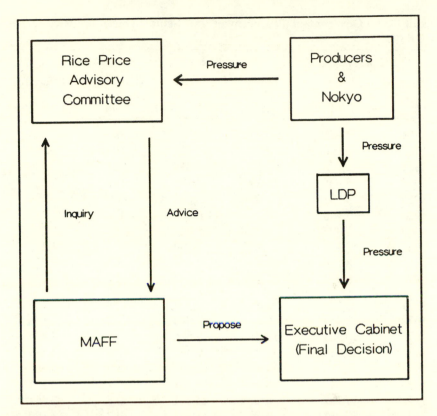

Figure 17.2. The Process of Determining Government Rice Procurement Price.

Accordingly, Nokyo exercises strong political pressure to increase the rice procurement price each year, often summoning several thousand members from across the nation to conduct lobbying and demonstrations in Tokyo. In addition, the LDP places pressure on the government in support of Nokyo. Due to opposing positions by its members, the Rice Price Advisory Committee often faces difficulties in developing a consensus decision for MAFF.

Government procurement prices tend to reflect these pressures. It is often said that the government rice procurement price is a "political price." It is also observed that determination of the rice procurement price is apt to favor producers during a year when the general election is held. Nevertheless, the procurement price is primarily tied to the costs of production (Table 17.6).

Determination of the rice selling price is also specified in the Food Control Act. The government selling price must take into account household expenditures, the consumer price index, and other economic conditions in order to stabilize family expenses (Yamada). The process for determining the

Table 17.6. Government Procurement and Selling Prices for Rice, Japan, 1961-1991.

Year	Procurement Price (Yen/Ton)	Change[a] (%)	Selling Price (Yen/Ton)	Change[b] (%)	Difference[c] (Yen/Ton)
1961	4,421	6.2	4,326	-0.6	-95
1962	4,866	10.1	4,314	-0.3	-552
1963	5,268	8.3	4,819	11.7	-449
1964	5,985	13.6	4,783	-0.7	-1,202
1965	4,538	9.2	5,632	17.8	-906
1966	7,140	9.2	6,107	8.4	-1,033
1967	7,797	9.2	6,009	-1.6	-1,788
1968	8,256	5.9	6,939	15.5	-1,317
1969	8,256	0.0	7,497	8.0	-759
1970	8,272	0.2	7,442	-0.7	-830
1971	8,522	3.0	7,377	-0.9	-1,145
1972	8,954	5.1	7,846	7.2	-1,108
1973	10,301	15.0	7,806	-0.1	-2,495
1974	13,615	32.2	10,256	32.0	-3,359
1975	15,570	14.4	12,205	19.0	-3,365
1976	16,572	6.4	13,451	10.2	-3,121
1977	17,232	4.0	14,771	9.8	-2,461
1978	17,251	0.1	15,391	4.2	-1,860
1979	17,279	0.2	15,891	3.2	-1,388
1980	17,674	2.3	15,891	0.0	-1,783
1981	17,756	0.5	16,391	3.15	-4,365
1982	17,951	1.1	17,033	3.9	-918
1983	18,266	1.8	17,673	3.8	-593
1984	18,668	2.2	18,327	3.7	-341
1985	18,668	0.0	18,598	1.5	-70
1986	18,668	0.0	18,598	0.0	-70
1987	17,557	-6.0	18,130	-2.5	573
1988	16,743	-4.6	18,130	-1.5	1,114
1989	16,743	0.0	18,396	1.5	1,653
1990	16,500	-1.5	18,396	0.0	1,896
1991	16,392	-0.65	18,203	-1.0	1,811

Source: MAFF Food Agency, various issues; Nihon Nogyo Shimbun.
[a]Change in procurement prices relative to previous year.
[b]Change in selling prices relative to previous year.
[c]Difference is defined as selling price minus procurement price.

selling price of rice is basically the same as that for the procurement price. MAFF tentatively determines the selling price and requests the advice of the Rice Price Advisory Committee (see Figure 17.2). A major difference between the determination process for the procurement price and that for the selling price is that consumer lobbying activities seeking lower selling prices are substantially less intense than are activities by producers seeking higher procurement prices.

Rice Consumption

Household food consumption accounts for approximately 90 percent of total rice consumption in Japan. Per capita annual household consumption decreased sharply from 118.3 kilograms of milled rice in 1962 to 71.0 kilograms in 1988 -- a 49 percent decline. Ito *et al.* studied the relationship between rice consumption and income levels in Asian countries. They found that in Asian countries, where per capita annual rice consumption historically has been above 100 kilograms per capita, rice consumption decreases, after first reaching a peak, as income rises. With greater income per capita, Asians substitute more desired foods for rice. Japanese consumers have followed this pattern. As the Japanese economy has grown especially during the last three decades, diets have diversified to include larger shares of dairy products, meats, wheat products, and other foods.

The government and the Nokyo organizations have financially supported a variety of programs to encourage rice consumption. However, they have not been able to reverse the decreasing trend. Per capita rice consumption is likely to continue to decrease in the future unless substantial changes occur in the demand structure and policies.

Conclusion

Whether Japan should open its rice markets or not depends not only on economic factors but also on cultural, emotional, and environmental factors. The rice issue in Japan is highly political. Even consumer organizations often support the closed rice market in fear that an open rice market would lead to an insecure supply of foreign food products and to domestic agricultural depression.

Regarding the current GATT negotiations, there is a gap between new continent countries and old continents (including Asia). For rice in particular, South Korea, Taiwan, China, and Japan share the same idea that free trade in food may diminish food security. While most Asian countries already depend heavily on imported food, they feel that their own staple food, rice, should be fully supplied domestically. The Declaration of Geneva by the World Council of Churches, an international group of people who are concerned with food security and environmental protection in developed and developing countries and chaired by Sicco L. Mansholt, reads "Every nation must retain the right: (a) to achieve the level of self-sufficiency of food and food quality they deem appropriate, and (b) to protect economic and social sustainability of their rural societies." This criticizes the current atmosphere of the GATT. It is argued that contemporary GATT agreements, established almost a half century ago, may not be compatible with the situation today and that the agreements should be relaxed and adjusted to the situation in each country.

Because rice producers have such strong political power, together with support from consumer groups, it is quite difficult for Japan to open its markets. The LDP lost its continuous majority of seats at the national election of the Upper House in 1988. It is well understood that the loss was in part due to low support from the agricultural sector for the LDP, reflecting the government decision to remove the quota system for beef and citrus.

The Koumeito, the third largest political party after the LDP and the Socialist Party, is the only party which formally agreed to partially open the Japanese rice market. A major industrial organization, the Japan Federation of Economic Organizations (Keidanren) has also insisted on opening the market during the last few years. However, the political power against opening the market is much stronger at this moment.

References

Asahi Shimbun. June 4, 1990. 65 percent approves liberalization of rice imports.

The Daily Yomiuri. June 6, 1990. Poll: 60 percent favor opening nation's rice market.

Hayami, Yujiro. 1972. Rice policy in Japan's economic development. *American Journal of Agricultural Economics* 54:19-31.

Ito, Shoichi, E. Wesley F. Peterson, and Warren R. Grant. 1989. Rice in Asia: Is it becoming an inferior good? *American Journal of Agricultural Economics* 71:32-42.

Ministry of Agriculture, Forestry, and Fisheries (MAFF), Food Agency. Various issues. *Beika ni Kansuru Shiryo (Data Related to Rice Prices).* Tokyo, Japan.

Ministry of Agriculture, Forestry, and Fisheries (MAFF), Food Agency, Policy Division. Various issues. *Shokuryo Kanri no Genjo (Food Control Situation).* Tokyo, Japan.

Ministry of Agriculture, Forestry, and Fisheries (MAFF), Statistics and Information Department. 1990. *65th Statistical Yearbook of the Ministry of Agriculture, Forestry, and Fisheries, Japan 1988-89.* Tokyo: Nourin Toukei Kyoukai Publishing Company.

Nihon Keizai Shimbun (Japan Economic Journal). May 20, 1991. Partially open the market -- Kanemaru approves liberalization of rice market under condition of compensating producers.

Nihon Nogyo Shimbun (Japan Agricultural Press). February 22, 1991 through March 5, 1991 series. Rice and the Diet's resolutions.

Nihon Nogyo Shimbun (Japan Agricultural Press). July 5, 1991. 0.65 percent reduction on 1991 government procurement price.

Okamaura, H. 1989. Daikibo Inasaku Nouka no Keiei Bunseki (A Management Analysis on Large Scale Rice Farm). Unpublished thesis. Shiga, Japan: Faculty of Agriculture, Shiga Prefecture Junior College, Kusatsu.

Okimoto, Daniel I. 1988. Political inclusivity: The domestic structure of trade. In Takashi Inoguchi and Daniel I. Okimoto, eds., *The Political Economy of Japan*, Vol. 2. Stanford, CA: Stanford University Press.

United States Department of Agriculture. 1990. Japan's food security: Reality and illusion. *Agricultural Outlook*. AO-164. Washington, DC: USDA.

Wailes, Eric J., Shoichi Ito, and Gail L. Cramer. February 1991. *Japan's Rice Market: Policies and Prospects for Trade Liberalization*. Report Series 319. Fayetteville: Arkansas Agricultural Experiment Station, University of Arkansas.

Yamada, Hiroshi. 1984. Economics of Food Control Act and Nokyo. Chapter 4 in Hiroshi Yamada and Takuji Sakurai, eds., *Kome no Keizaigaku (Rice Economics)*. Tokyo: Fumin-Kyokai Publishing Company.

Zenchu (Central Union of Agricultural Cooperative). 1989. *Kome no Subete: Seisan kara Shouhi made (Everything about Rice: From Production to Consumption)*. Tokyo: Ieno-Hikari Kyokai Publishing Company.

18

A New Phase for Rice in Japan: Production, Marketing, and Policy Issues
Kenji Ozawa

Introduction

The Japanese people face a time of difficult decisions in choosing a rice policy for the country. Rice policy is one of the most controversial policy issues in Japan. Rice policy has been strictly regulated through the rice marketing system (Shokkan Seido) based on the Food Control Act. It seems that all policy matters relating to rice, from production to distribution, are under strict government control. However, the function of Shokkan Seido has recently changed, especially in the rice marketing system.

This chapter examines recent changes in the rice marketing system and the function of Shokkan Seido. Recent changes in the producing regions due to the changes in the rice marketing system are briefly discussed. In discussing what kind of rice policy Japan should pursue, it is necessary to understand what changes are taking place in the rice marketing system, the function of "Shokkan Seido," and emerging trends in rice production. After examining these points, policy alternatives for Japan are proposed based on viewpoints important for future rice policy.

The Function of Food Control Systems

Direct government intervention of rice based on the Food Control Act of 1942 includes three major areas: pricing, distribution channels, and trade. For example, rice distribution is under strict government control through specification of the distribution channels. Handlers at all levels, from the farmgate to the retail level, must be licensed by MAFF or the local government.

However, the Food Control Act has been amended to adapt to the changes in the political and economic environment such as economic development, the demand-supply situation of rice, government budgets, and the weakening political power of farmers. These amendments have restructured the rice marketing system. Changes can be divided into four time periods.

First, semi-controlled or voluntary rice (Jishu Ryūtuumai) was introduced in 1969. Before that, all marketed rice (legally admitted) was government rice (Seifu Mai). In the case of government rice, the Food Agency is responsible for collecting and purchasing the rice from the farmers through specified first handlers (mostly local farmers' cooperatives) and then the rice is sold to licensed wholesalers. The rice price is strictly regulated from the farmgate to the retail level. However, in case of semi-controlled rice, cooperatives sell directly to wholesalers at a price negotiated between representatives of the cooperatives and the wholesalers. In addition, semi-controlled rice is a higher quality rice that commands a higher price than government-purchased rice and its price fluctuates reflecting demand-supply conditions (Figure 18.1). But, semi-controlled rice is not free market rice because the government gives farmers subsidies to promote its marketing and the distribution channels are the same as in the case of government rice.

Second, the negative margin of government rice disappeared in the mid-1980s. The producers' rice price was higher than the consumers' price and this price difference continued to be large until the mid-1970s. This negative margin was based on the overall protection policy of both producers and consumers. However, as the budget deficit problem became more and

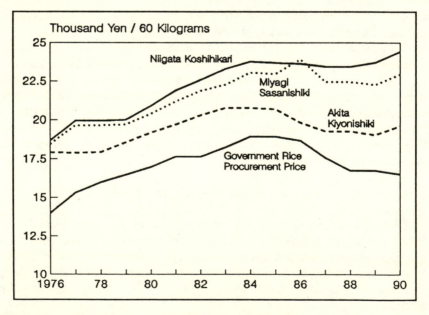

Figure 18.1. Market Price of Semi-Controlled Rice.
Source: MAFF.

more serious, the negative margin began to decrease and in 1986 the consumers' price has been higher than the producers' price. Since then, the gap between the consumers' price and the producers' price has widened and in 1990 the consumers' price was higher than the producers' price by about 10 percent. This disappearance of the negative margin and the increase in the consumers' price has promoted free-market rice. Instead of participating in the government's acreage reduction program, some farmers prefer to sell their rice to illegal handlers. If this behavior of rice producers prevails, it is inevitable that Shokkan Seido will collapse.

Third, production of semi-controlled rice has increased greatly since 1985 under MAFF promotion of production and marketing. The background of this MAFF measure is that the demand for rice has shifted to higher grades and the surplus problem of government rice has become serious. Also, the strict intervention of the government has become criticized as "out of date" by the Advisory Committee of Administrative Reform (Rinchō). Therefore, measures by MAFF have been taken to introduce more market orientation and encourage competition in rice marketing between each farmers' cooperatives for semi-controlled rice.

Fourth, the Rice Trade Board (Kakaku-Keisei Kikou) was established in 1990 to make markets function better in semi-controlled rice. Twenty percent of semi-controlled rice is transacted through the Rice Trade Board. In the case of such transactions, secondary handlers (most of them are farmers' cooperatives of each prefecture) and wholesalers gather and bid on the rice at an auction. The rice price reached through the auction becomes the standard price for the transaction of the remaining 80 percent of the semi-controlled rice. Thus, introduction of market elements has brought a more effective rice transaction price with the establishment of the Rice Trade Board.

During the four periods described above, government control of rice marketing has diminished and the amount of government-rice has declined. Now, three kinds of rice, namely, government rice, semi-controlled rice, and free market rice are marketed. Among them, the largest portion is semi-controlled rice which makes up 70 percent of the legally marketed rice. It is difficult to specify the exact amount of free market rice because it is illegal, but its marketing quantities are estimated to be between 1 and 2 million tons. Therefore, some researchers say that the Japanese rice marketing system is a mixed system of free competition and government control. Now, government control is confined to implementing the acreage reduction program based on overall demand-supply prospects, deciding the floor rice price, stabilizing the fluctuations of rice price through management of inventory, specifying the distribution channels, and, finally, prohibiting rice imports.

Most points of debate concerning a rice policy for the future center on to what degree at what market levels and for what purposes should government intervention be maintained. Another very important and controversial issue is whether Japan should allow minimum access of foreign rice. Before addressing other issues, we must first address the purpose of government control in the domestic rice market.

A New Phase of Rice Production

In 1990, Japan had about 2.85 million hectares of paddy fields. Some 30 percent of them, about .85 million hectares, was set aside through the government's acreage diversion program. Some 3.2 million farm households (75 percent of all farm households) were engaged in rice production in 1988. Some 25 percent of them produce rice only for home consumption and, therefore, don't sell any rice. Most rice producers in Japan are very small-scale, part-time farmers who derive most of their income from off-farm sources. Most rice producers are elderly. Only a few large-scale, full-time farmers depend totally on rice for their income.

Rice production in Japan has decreased gradually with changes in food consumption patterns (Figure 18.2) and with the recent changes in the rice marketing system. Keen competition in rice marketing between second handlers, that is, farmers' cooperatives of each prefecture, has led to competition of rice production between major rice producing regions. One result of this keen competition has been rapid changes in rice varieties produced. Although Sananishiki and Koshihikari have been the two main

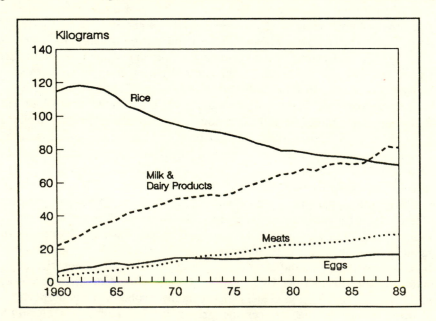

Figure 18.2. Long-Term Food Consumption Trends.
Source: MAFF.

varieties of semi-controlled rice for many years, the share of Sananishiki has declined recently. In contrast, Akitakomachi, Kirara has become popular.

With this increased competition, regional differentiation between dominant producing areas and areas of declining production is taking place. Major producing regions of high quality rice are the Hokuriku and Tōhoku regions. Within the Hokuriku region, Niigata is the most advanced area in producing the superior rice variety Koshihikari. Other prefectures in the Hokuriku region are Toyama, Fukui, and Ishikawa. The Koshihikari rice produced in these three prefectures also commands a higher price in the market, although not as high as that produced in the Niigata area.

Next to the Hokuriku region which produces Koshihikari varieties of semi-controlled rice, the Sansanishiki and Akitakomachi varieties produced in the Tōhoku region, including the Miyagi, Yamagata, and Akita prefectures, are ranked as the second highest grade in the market. But recently, consumers' demand preference has shifted from Sansanishiki to Koshihikari and with this, the price difference between them has widened. Although Tōhoku is the largest rice producing region, accounting for 27 percent of the total rice production in Japan, it's position as the main rice producing region has declined. To recover its position, the Tōhoku region and each prefecture in this region are very eager to develop excellent new varieties to compete with Koshihikari (Figure 18.3).

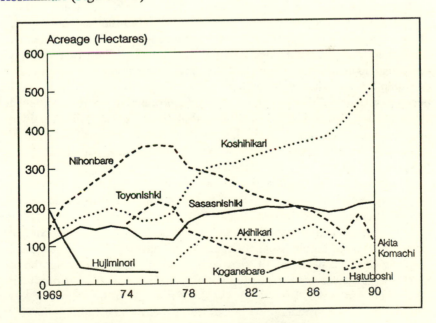

Figure 18.3. Planted Acreage of Main Rice Varieties.
Source: Food Agency.

Besides these two regions, some parts of Kanto, Kyushu, and Hokkaido are suitable for rice production and there is some potential for these regions to remain rice producing areas. Among them, some prefectures of Kanto, for example Ibaragi and Tochigi, produce rather high quality semi-controlled rice and, because these prefectures are adjacent to a metropolitan area, they can take advantage of favorable market access.

In contrast, Kyushu and Hokkaido are far from a metropolitan area. Their lack of market access is compensated by low-cost and relatively abundant agricultural resources such as farmland and labor. The average farm size is much larger in Hokkaido than in any of the other regions. Taking advantage of scale economies, rice producers in Hokkaido can produce rice at a relatively lower cost. For example, production cost per 60 kilograms of rice is 11,509 Yen for farms with more than 3 hectares, compared to 21,125 Yen for those with less than 3 hectares. Another point is that farmers in Hokkaido can't produce high quality rice because of its less favorable weather. So, rice produced in Hokkaido has been classified into the lowest grade of government rice. However, since introduction of semi-controlled rice, Hokkaido has made an effort to overcome its weak market position. It has recently developed excellent new varieties such as Yukihikari and Kirara. These varieties are now marketed as semi-controlled rice and they command a higher price in the market.

Because of its larger scale and recent efforts, Hokkaido will be able to survive as a rice producing region. Rice production in the remaining regions of Tosan, Kinki, Shikoku, and Chugoku is more vulnerable to setbacks from changes in markets, technology, and policies. Most of the rice produced in these regions is of inferior quality and is mainly for home consumption. As consumption has shifted to higher quality rice, the surplus problem has become serious in these regions and rice production there has declined substantially. There is little possibility that these regions will remain rice producing areas especially in the less favorable rural areas such as the hilly and remote countryside far away from a metropolitan area. Abandoned paddy fields in these areas have increased remarkably.

These less favorable areas have few off-farm employment opportunities and young people leave the rural areas to find employment opportunities elsewhere. Rice production activities tend to be shouldered by the elderly; after their retirement abandoned paddy fields will be left uncultivated. In short, rice production in Tosan, Kinki, Shikoku, and Chugoku will not be sustainable.

Thus, the recent trend of rice consumption and changes in the rice marketing structure have promoted the regional division of rice production. As a result, Hokuriku, Tōhoku, Hokkaido, Kyushu, and some parts of Kanto will remain as rice production regions. But, we must bear in mind that there is little room for expanding rice production even in these regions. For example, in Hokuriku, although most rice producers are part-time farmers who continue to produce rice as a side-business, their rice production will not pay them enough and farm work is too wearisome for younger people. On the other hand, it's very difficult for full-time rice farmers to enhance their productivity by expanding their scale of operation. The difficulties of expanding rice production and increasing its productivity are problems of profitability and land accumulation.

Some Japanese neoclassical economists insist that by abolishing government regulations on rice production and bringing down the rice price, the land rental and sales market will be activated and larger-scale farms will be created. Their argument is based on the assumption that if the rice price is lowered significantly, part-time farmers will give up rice production and their paddy fields will be transferred to the larger-scale operators. In fact, bringing down the rice price substantially may discourage larger-scale operators and decrease their numbers. This problem is closely related to the profitability of rice production by scale of operation. Too little is known of the influence of rice price on promoting larger-scale operators.

Second, neoclassicists underestimate the complexities of the Japanese land problem. In Japan, the price of farmland, except that located in less favorable areas, is not decided through a land rate of return, that is, its price is much higher than the level derived from current land returns in farming. Even if small-scale part-time farmers give up rice production, they may cling tenaciously to their paddy fields and may not be willing to sell or rent them. To them, disposing of farmland inherited from ancestors is dishonorable and renting off a small parcel of fields is too much trouble. Instead of renting, they will continue to hold on, waiting until their farmland can be sold for non-agricultural purposes such as road construction or housing development. They have plenty of opportunity for windfall gains. To activate the land rental market, municipalities, farmers' organizations, and farmers themselves must cooperate to devise measures which will persuade landowners to rent their idled farmland.

In Japan, the high economic growth rate has adverse effects both on agriculture and the market for farmland. Market factors, by themselves, don't provide economic incentives to move agricultural resources to more efficient larger-scale farms. On the contrary, market factors may reduce the profitability of larger-scale operators.

Conclusions

An appropriate rice policy must take account of the social, political, and economic factors. In Japan, a great many people are concerned about the rice problem. The main reason is because rice is a traditional food and a crop in which Japan is self-sufficient. Many Japanese are concerned that they will face severe food shortages if rice production disappears and events beyond their control interrupt continuous import of foods. In addition, rice reflects Japanese agricultural interests in general, so it tends to be considered the final stronghold of Japanese agriculture. From these concerns arises the key concept of food security.

Japan's self-sufficiency rate in grain currently is as low as 30 percent and, therefore, Japan must depend on food imports. If a worldwide poor harvest or a catastrophe such as a big war occurred, a great many Japanese would not be provided with a minimum amount of indispensable food. (And no one can assume that such a situation will never occur.) At that time, Japan's food security would be seriously threatened. Also, if Japan's self-sufficiency rate continues to decline, its position in diplomatic negotiation of agricultural issues will become vulnerable. Of course, we should think of food security from a wider point of view and place a higher value on international cooperation. However, Japan has good reason to be concerned about food security because of its low self-sufficiency rate for food. For the sake of food security, we must maintain the productive capacity of agriculture.

Besides food security, the many other policy issues concerning rice include economic as well as social and environmental aspects. From the economic aspect, rice generates much income for rural economies. Revenues from rice comprise about 30 percent of all farm revenues and rice is still the largest source of farm income. In addition, rice affects the rural economy through intra-industry relationships. If rice production continues to decline, economic conditions of the main rice producing regions such as Hokuriku and Tōhoku will deteriorate further. Within the social aspects, rice production provides employment opportunities for people in the rural areas, especially the elderly. Securing such opportunities for these people will become more and more important with emerging urban social problems. In Japan, high economic growth has promoted drastic concentration of population in metropolitan areas. This concentration has caused serious housing and other social problems in the cities. In a sense, rice production has played an important role in the social welfare in the rural areas by restraining movement to cities.

In terms of environmental aspects, we must remember an important fact: Paddy fields play the role of giant dams. They hold reserve water and prevent flooding disasters caused by heavy rainfall.

We may say that the high economic growth rate of Japan has promoted the rapid decline of rice production, because terms of trade and profitability of rice have become unfavorable as economic growth has occurred. There-fore, if left alone, rice production will continue to decrease in Japan. Faced with this situation, we have to examine what policy option is feasible or desirable.

The most important and controversial policy matters concerning rice production are price and land problems. Which level of rice price is most appropriate to nurture large-scale operators and to enhance productivity without disrupting the employment opportunities for aged people. Which land policy is feasible to activate a land rental system and concentrate farmland among the more efficient farmers?

Maybe the most feasible rice policy is a market-oriented policy supplemented by various policies taking into consideration the various public interests. Rice policy in Japan will be closely related to which direction the rest of Japanese society and the economy proceed.

References

Food Agricultural Policy Research. 1991. America no kome, Nihan no kome (Americans rice and Japanese rice).

Hayami, Yujiro. 1988. *Japanese Agriculture Under Siege*. New York, NY: Macmillan Press.

Mochida, Keizoou. 1991. *Nihon no Kome (Japanese Rice)*. Chikuma Press.

Saheki, Naomi. 1986. *Kome Ryūtuu Sisutemu (System of Rice Marketing)*. Tokyo: Tokyo University Press.

Saheki, Naomi. 1987. *Shokkan Seido (Food Control System)*. Tokyo: Tokyo University Press.

Wailes, E.J. *et al*. 1991. Japan's rice market. Fayetteville: Arkansas Agricultural Experiment Station.

19

Rice and Food Security in Japan: An American Perspective

Eric J. Wailes, Kenneth B. Young, and Gail L. Cramer

Introduction

The Japanese government spends the equivalent of billions of dollars on its rice program annually and bans rice imports to achieve self-sufficiency as a means of ensuring food security. As Japan has moved into an increasingly dominant role in the world economy, international pressures combined with changes in opinions by the Japanese public have brought a reexamination of the value of this costly program. The status of rice in Japan and the issue of food security from an American perspective are addressed in this chapter.

Status of Rice in Japan

It is difficult for most Americans to understand the special status still accorded the rice industry in Japan, the most economically advanced country in Asia. Rice has remained deeply ingrained in the culture of Japan as the historical source of livelihood and wealth. Thus, the Japanese have strongly resisted any reduction in rice production capacity of their nation and increasing dependence on rice imports. The desire for food security also stems from the memory of the famine that followed World War II. The present ruling Liberal Democratic Party has traditionally relied upon the rice producer cooperatives for its important rural power base (Okimoto; Fujitani). This linkage explains the current inertia against reform of rice policy and the strong political interest in continued protection of the Japanese rice industry. This political linkage is strengthened by the commitment and control of substantial resources, including both budget and employees, by the Food Agency of the Ministry of Agriculture, Forestry, and Fisheries.

Japan has maintained self-sufficiency in rice production by means of an extremely high producer price support program with protection from imports and use of government payments to control the domestic supply on the market. The current producer rice price in Japan is approximately 7 to 10 times the average world market price. Domestic supply is controlled by a combination of government procurement and storage operations and paid land diversion. Total annual direct costs of the government's rice program averaged about $3 billion during the 1980s, including $1.67 billion as of 1989 for land diversion (Wailes, Ito, and Cramer).

The program supports many small farmers. More than half of the 2.38 million rice marketing households in Japan are part-time farmers with less than one hectare of rice. Rice production in Japan has benefitted from labor-saving technology and mechanization which along with significantly higher returns to labor in the non-agricultural sector has allowed many rice land-owners to seek nonfarm employment while also producing a rice crop (Nakayasu). Thus, the size structure of rice farming in Japan, unlike livestock and horticultural crops, has remained relatively static (MAFF), despite the existence of substantial size economies (Inamoto). Rigidities in land transfers have thus emerged as a significant source of disequilibrium and inefficiency in Japan's rice economy, as noted by Hayami and Kawagoe.

Rice production area has declined from 3.17 million hectares in 1969 to 2.08 million in 1989. The area diverted to control rice supply was 0.77 million hectares in 1989. As a result of land diversion, total production was reduced from a record level of 14.5 million tons (brown) in 1967 to 10.6 million in 1989. Diverted land is allocated to various other crops including wheat, soybeans, sugarbeets, buckwheat, perennial crops, vegetables, and tobacco. Average rice yield per hectare has continued to increase over time (Figure 19.1). This has been primarily due to varietal improvements and chemical imports but also to the diversion programs as less productive land is generally used for alternative crops. Severe reductions in yield occurred in 1964-65, 1971, 1976, and 1980-83 because of adverse weather conditions. To replace stocks, 150 thousand tons of rice had to be imported from South Korea in 1984. However, average rice yield increased by more than 25 percent from 3,900 kilograms (Kg) per hectare (Ha) (brown) in 1965 to a peak level of 5,170 kilograms in 1984 (Figure 19.1).

Increased rice yield and a reduction in rice consumption since the 1960s resulted in excessive stocks by 1970. Per capita rice consumption declined from 118.3 kilograms (milled) in 1962 to only 71.0 kilograms in 1988 as a result of changes in diet (Figure 19.2). The government was forced to initiate the acreage diversion program in 1969 to avoid further surpluses. Current diversion payments per hectare range from $876 for vegetables and tobacco crops to $2,920 for alternative grain crops (Wailes, Ito, and Cramer). This compares with an estimated rice production cost per hectare of $13,700 in 1988 including $2,432 for land rent. Average production cost per ton of rice (brown) in Japan was $2,650 in 1988. (For the sake of comparison, average

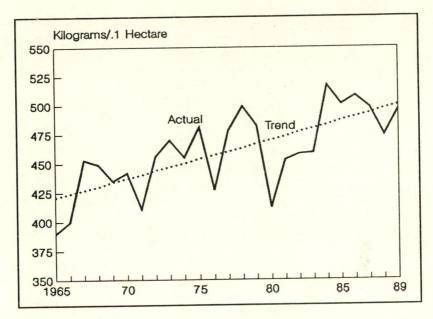

Figure 19.1. Actual and Trend Japanese Rice (Brown) Yields.

estimated costs in California in 1988 were $1,710 per hectare and $270 per ton (Salassi *et al.*).)

The market distribution system is controlled by the government through production targets, licensing of marketing agents, and price controls. A major change in this structure has been the growth in the semi-controlled market channel under which exchange of rice is negotiated more freely in regard to market supply and demand for a particular rice variety and quality. In 1991, further liberalization was pursued through the development of monthly rice auctions in Tokyo and Osaka.

Comparison of Japanese and U.S. Rice Programs

There are some basic similarities in the operation of Japanese and U.S. rice programs. Both are intended to protect the income of rice farmers, maintain a national base acreage in rice production, and, at the same time, implement supply control to confront the problem of excess supply capacity. Similar features include a government price guarantee involving a procurement price in Japan versus a target price in the U.S. A mandatory acreage diversion program is implemented through direct payments to producers in Japan. In the U.S., adherence to acreage reduction targets is a requirement for voluntary loan and income support program participation. Both countries have subsidized government storage programs. Both have subsidized schemes to stimulate sales or consumption through school lunch programs and other surplus disposal methods. And in both countries, the

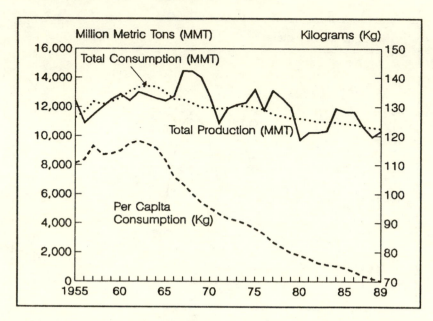

Figure 19.2. Japanese Rice Production, Total Consumption, and Per Capita Consumption.

guaranteed producer prices, whether procurement prices or target prices, are generally set above the average market level and various government subsidies are used to help maintain viability in the rice industry.

A fundamental difference between the two programs is that the U.S. program allows the market price of rice to fluctuate relatively free of intervention as imports are subject to only a minor duty whereas the market price in Japan is directly controlled by the government and is extremely high compared to international prices. This necessitates a virtual ban on imports. The approximate average difference in the U.S. between the internal market price and the guaranteed target price was about 31 percent over the period 1981-88 for Arkansas, the major rice production state (USDA). The average 5-month domestic market price for 1981-88 in Arkansas for which government program payments are calculated was $8.49 per hundredweight and the government target price was $11.15 per hundredweight; thus the estimated average deficiency payment was $2.66 per hundredweight. This deficiency payment was paid only for production from the eligible rice base acreage at the established program yield in 1988. Farmers had to idle 25 percent of their rice land in 1988 as unpaid land diversion and the national average program yield was 121.5 hundredweight per hectare compared to the harvested yield of 137.8 hundredweight per hectare. Producers did not receive any return on this idled cropland to comply with requirements of the program. The unpaid land diversion system is used in the U.S. to control national rice production to avoid buildup of surpluses. The percentage diverted varies from year to year.

The U.S. method of supporting farm income from the government budget may not be a feasible alternative in Japan. Japan has relied more directly on the implicit consumer tax to pay for the producer price and income support. The current support price is 6 to 8 times what the free market price would be if imports were not banned (Cramer *et al.*). The government's budget exposure would make it difficult for Japan to maintain self-sufficiency in rice production if imports were not restricted.

Issue of Food Security

Japan has pursued the concept of food security as a justification for limiting trade liberalization in the current GATT negotiations. The country contends that trade restrictions, as necessary, should be permitted in order to remain self-sufficient in rice production. Although most Japanese probably think that they have food security by maintaining self-sufficiency in rice production, this is, as noted by Hayami, largely an illusion.

It is argued that Japan's rice policy is not consistent with the concept of food security and further that the policy results in self-sufficiency in only a narrow sense. In order to discuss this issue the concept of food security requires definition. Williams and Grant reviewed numerous definitions and offered their composite which we will adopt for the purpose of discussion in this chapter.

> Food security for a given country is access by the population of the country, and particularly by low-income consumers, to an ample, timely, reliable, stable supply of nutritionally adequate food at a reasonable cost on a long-term basis (p.2).

As argued by Williams and Grant, policies that enhance food security for a country include those that: (1) improve availability, reliability, and stability and/or (2) make food more accessible at a reasonable cost.

Does Japan's rice policy fit either of these two policy categories? In general, Japan's rice policy does not make more rice available, in fact it reduces availability through diversion of acreage and a ban on foreign supplies. Japan's supply of rice has not been necessarily any more reliable nor stable than foreign supplies. As noted below, the variability in stocks-to-utilization has been much higher for Japan than for the rest of the world's rice market. It is worthy to note that as recently as 1984 Japan had to rely upon South Korea to meet its rice needs. The rice policy has not improved accessibility to rice due to production control as well as the high implicit consumer tax which reduces the overall purchasing power of the Japanese consumer. Finally, depending upon quality equivalence, Japan's consumer price is 4 to 6 times higher than the delivered price of rice from export suppliers. This magnitude of difference is perceived by the U.S. as unreasonable. Industrial users of rice in Japan have claimed the cost to be unreasonable and Japanese public opinion has shifted in favor of opening the market to conceivably benefit from lower prices.

It may be further argued that Japan's rice policy is not even self-sufficient in a broad sense. Japan's modern rice production system is in fact very dependent on imported inputs, in particular, crude oil through its refined products such as fertilizers, chemicals, and fuels used heavily in the Japanese rice production system. The traditional farming system included only hand labor, some buffalo draft, use of natural fertilizer, and almost no chemicals or motor power. The modern system is very capital intensive, and requires high use of imported oil, mechanized transplanting, weeding, harvesting, and artificial drying. Imports are also necessary to supply ingredients for chemical fertilizers and for plant protection.

An estimated budget for modern rice production in Japan with comparisons to Thailand and the U.S. is shown in Table 19.1. The major

Table 19.1. Comparative Rice Production Budgets for Japan, Thailand, and the United States, 1984 (Yen per Metric Ton).

Cost Item	Japan	Thailand	United States[a]
Seeds/seedlings	5,629	928	1,830
Fertilizers	22,149	997	3,201
Agricultural chemicals	14,496	148	1,758
Fuel	8,370	67	5,535
Other raw materials	4,654	NA	NA
Water	11,442	428	1,559
Feeds and custom charge	17,826	1,424	7,601
Capital improvements	8,701	NA	NA
Agricultural machinery	84,750	493	5,016
Cattle/draft power	NA	3,688	NA
Labor	110,191	10,723	2,393
Subtotal	288,208	18,896	28,893
Interest	15,379	3,281	1,523
Land rent	63,135	4,846	9,115
Economic cost	366,722	27,023	39,531
Milled yield (MT/Ha)	4.92	1.18	5.50

Source: Adapted from Tsujii, Table 1.1.
[a]California.

foreign exchange components in production are embodied in fertilizers, agricultural chemicals, fuel, and machinery. Without imports, necessary for these critical inputs, the estimated rice yield would be reduced substantially. Thus, it is evident that Japan would not likely sustain self-sufficiency in rice production without an assured supply of crude oil and other imported inputs.

The limited and temperate climatic rice production area in Japan is also vulnerable to adverse weather conditions and risks of disease that affect stability of production as illustrated in Figures 19.1 and 19.2. Although rice is still the traditional staple food in Japan, per capita consumption of milled rice has decreased over the period 1960-1988 from 114.9 kilograms per year to 71.0 kilograms per year and has been projected by MAFF to fall to 55 kilograms by the year 2000. At the same time meat consumption in kg. per capita increased from 5.2 to 28.2, fish products consumption increased from 27.8 to 37.0, egg consumption increased from 6.3 to 16.4, milk and dairy product consumption increased from 22.9 to 80.9, and wheat consumption increased from 25.8 to 31.5 (MAFF). Consequently, rice has lost it's significance as a food staple and is less important for food security than formerly. The decline in rice consumption is also continuing in spite of high government expenditures to promote rice consumption ($170 million in 1990). It is clear that the net effect of government policies has been to discourage rice consumption through high prices. It is conceivable that the government would be much more successful in promoting rice consumption by moving to lower retail prices with the importation of lower priced rice. It is clear that even if Japan self-supplies 100 percent of its rice consumption, total food calorie self-sufficiency will continue to decline, as rice becomes less significant in the Japanese diet.

Provision for at least some rice imports would enhance food security in Japan compared with relying exclusively on domestic production. While there are many countries that export rice, there are far fewer that export the high quality japonica rice demanded by the Japanese consumer. Trade relations would probably have to be developed well in advance to assure a stable supply of the type and high quality demanded by Japanese consumers. Increased food security can also be achieved with various supplemental policy measures, such as food stockpiling, direct foreign investment, bilateral food supply contracts, and research and development (see Table 19.2).

Japanese consumers currently have a strong preference for high quality japonica rice as produced in their own local temperate climate. However, this type of rice is by no means unique to Japan and is currently exported by Australia and California, with the potential for exportable production in other countries (Table 19.3). While the current varieties of japonica rice grown in these countries may differ from Japanese rice varieties, these differences can be adjusted to accommodate the Japanese market. California, for example, produced high quality Japanese varieties on over 10 percent of its rice acreage

Table 19.2. Alternative National and International Measures to Achieve Food Security.

	National	International
Stock measures	Central Government stocks	Coordinated national stocks Regional stocks Emergency stocks
Production measures	Input subsidies Water management Research and development Disease control Price policies	Fertilizer supply scheme Research centers Production assistance
Consumption measures	Consumer subsidies Improved distribution State distribution Price policy Waste reduction	Food entitlement Targeted consumption schemes
Trade measures	Bilateral contracts Futures markets Trade policy Collective buying Foreign exchange reserves	Trade liberalization Food aid Commodity agreements Special borrowing facilities
Other	Market information and analysis Export earning stability	Information schemes Monetary facilities Nonfood trade measures

Source: McCalla and Josling. Reprinted by permission of McGraw-Hill.

in 1990. Japonica rice of suitable quality can potentially be grown in other countries or areas with additional variety testing and economic incentive. It is recognized that Japanese consumers are highly sensitive to quality and will pay substantial premiums for high quality rice (Wailes *et al.*).

Total current annual consumption of brown rice is about 10.6 million metric tons (MMT) in Japan including 1.5 million metric tons used for industrial processing. Except for certain products such as pilaf and those requiring glutinous rice or flour, the quality requirement for processing demand in Japan is much less stringent than for direct consumption. About half of processed rice is used for sake. This demand could be satisfied by almost any type of rice. It is interesting to note that while Japan prohibits imports of uncooked rice, restrictions on imports of semi-processed or finished products are comparatively small. There are no quotas, and tariff rates range

Table 19.3. Japonica Rice Trade Volume, 1986-87.

Country/Region	Quantity
	(1,000 MT)
Importers	
Canada	41
Eastern Europe	340
EC-10	108
Japan	19
Madagascar	0
Oceania	90
Other Africa	81
Other Asia	222
Other N.C. America	454
South Korea	0
Syria	26
Taiwan	0
USSR	161
Total Quantity	1,542
Exporters	
Australia	142
China	0
Italy	617
North Korea	346
Spain	108
U.S.-California	329
Total Quantity	1,542

Source: Cramer *et al.*

from 6 to 35 percent, depending upon the ingredients other than rice (Parker). The equivalent of over 13,000 metric tons of rice were imported in the form of semi-finished or finished rice products in 1989, primarily from Thailand and the U.S. This is an unusual import policy -- most industrial countries tend to restrict imports of value-added, manufactured goods more so than commodities.

Options for Japanese Rice Policy

Japan has come under increasing international pressure to liberalize trade in rice, particularly in the recent GATT negotiations. However, the simple solutions suggested by some observers fail to reckon with the complexity of rice in Japan. In view of the current public sentiments and special significance accorded rice production in Japan, relinquishing rice self-sufficiency as the primary policy of food security will be difficult (Wailes *et al.*). Our perception of the situation in Japan is that the political will has developed to a point where there are good prospects to proceed with some degree of trade liberalization. However, it will likely be a gradual process and there will undoubtedly need to be at least some continued protection of income for rice farmers. The larger issue is the need for structural reform such that larger size farming units can benefit from size economies and provide a more competitive domestic supply in Japan. Japanese consumers also have to be convinced that they are not being forced to give up any food security and that they will continue to have a dependable rice supply of the type and quality that is produced domestically.

An important unresolved issue is what level of self-sufficiency and preservation of national base acreage should be maintained. Rice production in Japan is not likely to be sustainable at the current level because of the rising international pressures to allow at least some minimum level of rice imports but also because domestic public opinion is becoming less resistant to opening the rice market. Japan is likely to face continued international pressure on the issue of rice trade liberalization because of its export-oriented economy and the growing sensitivity of many countries to bilateral trade deficits with Japan. Therefore, it is probable that Japan will soon initiate some steps to liberalize trade in rice.[1]

A low risk option for Japan to initiate liberalized trade would be to maintain the present national base area for rice by continuing income protection for rice farmers and allow restricted rice imports. There would no longer be 100 percent self-sufficiency in rice but the national production capacity could be preserved. The internal market price of rice in Japan would be reduced if this option were followed, although not to the world market level. The revenue collected from import tariffs would be used to compensate farmers, e.g., with supplemental deficiency payments to continue income protection. Of course, this option may not be totally satisfactory to the international community because the imports would likely be subject to heavy tariffs. But this might be acceptable as a first step in trade liberalization in contrast to continuing the present complete ban on imports. This initial restricted trade policy would help to reduce international pressure for trade liberalization as some trade would be opened. And consumers could benefit

---

[1] A report in the Yomiuri Shimbun newspaper on May 30, 1991 indicated that Prime Minister Toshiki Kaifu had decided to allow rice imports with a maximum limit of 5 to 10 percent of domestic use. A formal announcement and details of the decision have not been made, however.

from a reduced price. A major part of Japanese production would be left intact, thus helping to preserve stability.

This initial restricted trade option could be relaxed in the future with increased liberalization of trade, reduced tariffs, and perhaps reduced rice production in Japan over time as importation of rice becomes a more accepted practice and Japan becomes more confident of the ability of the world rice market to provide dependable supplies. However, it seems important from the standpoint of Japanese domestic politics and public approval to initiate the opening of the rice market on a time schedule under the control of the Japanese people -- so they do not feel they are being forced to give up their rice industry. Otherwise, it would appear to be very difficult to get the approval of farmers and other political interests to initiate any trade liberalization. The gradual process of trade liberalization also seems appropriate to allow time for the Japanese to establish market connections for acquiring the qualities of rice they desire. For example, they may have to provide technical assistance to prospective exporters on the use of preferred rice varieties and milling practices to accommodate specific Japanese tastes in rice. A gradual process will also provide time for Japanese agriculture to restructure itself to produce rice at lower costs and improve varieties such that a much higher proportion than currently produced is of the highest, most demanded varieties.

The option of gradual trade liberalization discussed above is not a recommended policy for Japan to follow but only our perspective of how trade liberalization could most easily be initiated in view of the public concern on this issue. Most analysts from rice exporting countries have not addressed this problem in Japan and may not agree with our notion that rice trade liberalization in Japan is likely to be more successful if it is gradually implemented. We understand that rice trade liberalization remains a very sensitive public issue in Japan. Accordingly, it seems preferable to pursue a rational, low risk, and politically acceptable solution to Japan opening rice trade rather than causing ill will in Japan by pressuring the country into possibly regrettable decisions.

Long-Term Outlook for Security of Rice Imports

The fundamental problem of protectionist measures as currently used in Japan is that they prohibit voluntary transactions that would otherwise take place among domestic producers/consumers and foreign producers/consumers. Free trade commitments should not be considered as concessions that governments make to each other but the distribution of rights among governments and their citizens. They provide assurances to citizens that they can engage in economic transactions with foreigners free from politically imposed obstacles (Vanberg).

From a policy perspective, the international pressure on Japan with regard to its reluctance to submit to trade liberalization for rice is based on the fact that Japan's export sales of manufactured products are especially concentrated in grain-producing countries. Therefore, the case of rice market protection in Japan is not a matter of a preferred trade isolation policy but rather is a more complex domestic social and political problem involving vested interests in the current rice industry and general public fear of giving up the illusion of self-sufficiency in a traditional staple food.

As far as general food security is concerned, there seems to be no cause for alarm that the world's population and demand for food will outstrip our capacity to produce. Unlike many developing countries for which foreign exchange constraints creates an over-riding logic for a self-sufficiency oriented food security policy, Japan is foreign exchange rich. Furthermore, the cereal requirement for Japan is small compared to total world production (Table 19.4). Data covering the period from 1960 to 1990 on the stocks-to-utilization ratio for world grain (rice, wheat, and coarse grains) reveal a coefficient of variation of 0.15, while it was 0.27 for rice alone. However, for Japan which attaches much importance to food security, the coefficient of variation of rice stocks-to-utilization was 1.0 for the period 1960-1988. While rice stock levels in Japan have been influenced by other factors, the large variation in rice stocks-to-use in Japan relative to the rest of the world suggests that food security through stable domestic stocks has been of little importance in Japan.

Of course the international market for rice is much thinner than for cereals such as wheat, and particularly so for high-quality japonica rice. The thin market has translated into more volatile prices, due mainly to the isolation of the three major high-quality japonica consuming nations -- South Korea, Taiwan, and Japan. It must be noted however that despite the price volatility in the world rice price, even its highest peaks have reached only a level of less than half the domestic Japanese rice price. The import ban on high quality japonica rice in Japan, South Korea, and Taiwan has contributed directly to world price instability given the lack of an equilibrating adjustment through consumption and/or stocks. However, there is substantial capacity to expand production of this type of rice if demand increased. High quality japonica currently sells at a discount to indica rice in the U.S. because of the more limited demand for japonica rice. Increased domestic consumption in the U.S. has been mainly for indica varieties rather than japonica. Total U.S. rice production is currently about 155 million hundredweight (rough) of which 72 percent is indica and 28 percent is japonica. This proportion could be changed if there was increased export demand for japonica rice. Most other exporters of japonica rice also have excess capacity to produce if their export market expanded. China is currently a sporadic exporter and would probably require technical assistance to improve milling practices to supply a high-quality japonica rice but with trade liberalization would have high potential to supply the market in Japan.

The growth rate of Asian rice yields and total rice production declined in the 1980s (Table 19.5). The growth in demand for rice in Asia is forecast at 2.1-2.6 percent per year in the 1990s (Rosegrant and Pingali). The recent

Table 19.4. World Production, Consumption, and Net Imports of Cereals, 1990 (Million Metric Tons).

Region/Country	Production	Consumption	Net Imports
Developed			
United States	310	220	-80
Canada	58	26	-26
EC-12	170	144	-22
Other Western Europe	19	15	-3
South Africa	9	11	2
Japan	11	38	26
Australia	23	9	-15
Centrally Planned	671	694	33
Eastern Europe	94	99	3
USSR	223	244	26
China	333	329	-4
Developing	486	550	61
Mexico/C. America	25	41	7
Brazil	34	41	6
Argentina	22	10	-10
Other S. America	13	18	5
N. Africa	21	40	20
Other Africa	44	53	7
South Asia	208	210	2
Southeast Asia	86	88	1
East Asia	27	72	44
World Total	1,767	1,739	0

Source: ERS/USDA.

[a]Regional totals include some high-income countries not treated in this table.

decline in growth of Asian rice production is attributed to reduced research expenditures, declining irrigation investment, degradation of irrigation infrastructure, low world rice prices, a declining yield gap (due to a stagnant technological yield frontier), decreased growth and declining efficiency in fertilizer use, and increased losses due to pests.

However, there are good prospects for major breakthroughs in yield potential from changes in plant architecture and the exploitation of hybrid vigor (Rosegrant and Pingali). The estimated increased yield potential is 20-25 percent. New approaches (alien gene transfer, use of novel genes, horizontal resistance, etc.) are also being used to improve yield stability through durable resistance to diseases and insects. Fertilizer efficiency can be

Table 19.5. Annual Growth Rates in Rice Area, Production, and Yield, Asia, 1961-88 (Percent).

Region	1961-72[a]	1972-81	1981-88	1961-88
Asia[a]				
Area	1.00	0.66	0.02	0.59
Production	3.30	3.32	1.52	3.08
Yield	2.28	2.64	1.50	2.47
South Asia[b]				
Area	1.37	1.24	-0.07	0.86
Production	2.00	3.14	1.01	2.21
Yield	0.62	1.88	1.08	1.33
Southeast Asia[c]				
Area	0.68	1.45	0.62	0.86
Production	2.76	3.99	2.24	3.31
Yield	2.07	2.50	1.61	2.42
China[a]				
Area	2.15	-0.66	-0.62	0.29
Production	4.01	2.54	1.81	3.23
Yield	1.83	3.23	2.45	2.93
India				
Area	0.62	0.97	0.05	0.60
Production	1.92	1.03	3.27	2.48
Yield	1.29	2.05	3.21	1.87

Source: For China, State Statistical Bureau, Ministry of Agriculture. For all other countries, FAO data tapes.
[a]For Asia and China, first period trends are for 1964-72. Asia includes South Asia, Southeast Asia, China, and India.
[b]South Asia includes Bangladesh, Nepal, Pakistan, and Sri Lanka, excluding India.
[c]Southeast Asia includes Burma, Indonesia, Kampuchea, Laos, Malaysia, Philippines, Thailand, and Vietnam.

improved with more balanced use of fertilizer and improved timing and placement. Pest control can be improved with greater use of integrated pest management. Other major improvements can be achieved by upgrading extension services and increasing irrigation investment. Increased prices would also induce increased production of rice by expanding input use and shifting land from other crops into rice.

Conclusions

Self-sufficiency in rice production has been achieved in Japan under a policy of food security. This achievement is not only an illusion but has been costly to the Japanese government and consumer, and to rice producers in the rest of the world. That food security is only an illusion is based on the facts: (1) critical rice production inputs must be imported, (2) the role of rice in the Japanese diet has diminished dramatically, (3) Japan's rice stocks-to-utilization have been more unstable than for rice in the world market, and (4) Japan's rice policy does not provide a more available, reliable, and stable supply at a reasonable cost. Counting only the direct expenditures, costs to the government have been above $3 billion per year through the 1980s, while at the same time consumers have paid 4 to 6 times the world price for high quality japonica rice.

The ban on rice imports has imposed significant externalities on the world rice market in the form of more volatile prices and a lower volume and value of trade. This policy has contributed to a significant resource misallocation in Japan and abroad. Rice policy in Japan is a result of the traditional economic, cultural, and political role that rice has played for many centuries. However, it is clear that the post-war land reform brought a significant legacy in the form of rigidities in the land market, preventing needed changes in the size of farming units to achieve size economies. International pressures have now brought about a critical examination of this policy. Japan's increasingly dominant role in the world economy requires that it open its economy to justify continuation of benefits from a world market open to its exports. The complexity and intensity of the rice issue in Japan, however, calls for problems to be solved gradually. Existing excess supply capacity in the rest of the world as well as structural reform within Japan's farm economy can translate into a competitive but dependable source of supply for Japan's consumers. GATT proposals providing for minimum access and a gradual reduction in trade barriers can provide the opportunity for Japan to adjust its rice policy, maintain a system of food security, and alleviate the international pressure for opening its market.

References

Cramer, Gail L., Eric J. Wailes, Stanley S. Phillips, and John M. Goroski. November 1991. The impact of liberalizing trade in the world rice market. Special Report 153. Fayetteville: Agricultural Experiment Station, University of Arkansas.

Fujitani, Chikuji. 1991. Japan's agricultural cooperatives. In Committee for the Japanese Agriculture Session, eds., *Agriculture and Agricultural Policy in Japan*. XXI IAAE Conference, Tokyo. Tokyo: University of Tokyo Press.

Hayami, Yujiro. 1988. *Japanese Agriculture Under Siege*. New York: Macmillan and St. Martin's Press.

Hayami, Yujiro and Toshihiko Kawagoe. 1991. Farm mechanization, scale economies, and structural change. In Hayami and Yamada, eds., *The Agricultural Development of Japan, A Century's Perspective*. Tokyo: University of Tokyo.

Inamoto, Shiro. 1991. Technical progress in agricultural production and its contribution to international competitiveness. In Committee for the Japanese Agriculture Session, eds., *Agriculture and Agricultural Policy in Japan*. XXI IAAE Conference. Tokyo: University of Tokyo Press.

Kamegai, Kiyoshi. March 1990. *An International Comparative Study of Rice Economy and Policy Among the United States, Thailand, and Japan*. A Final Report of an International Scientific Research Program of the Ministry of Education, Science, and Culture, Japan.

McCalla, A.F. and T.E. Josling. 1985. *Agricultural Policies and World Markets*. New York: MacMillan.

Ministry of Agriculture, Forestry, and Fisheries (MAFF). February 1990. Structural changes in Japan's agriculture. *Japan's Agricultural Review*, Vol. 18.

Ministry of Agriculture, Forestry, and Fisheries, Ministries Secretariat, Research Division, Supply, and Demand for Food (Shokuryo Hyo). Tokyo, 1990.

Nakayasu, Sadako. 1991. Japan's agricultural structure: Characteristics and changes. In Committee for the Japanese Agriculture Session, eds., *Agriculture and Agricultural Policy in Japan*. XXI IAAE Conference. Tokyo: University of Tokyo Press.

Okimoto, Daniel I. 1988. Political inclusivity: The domestic structure of trade. In Takashi Inoguchi and Daniel I. Okimoto, eds., *The Political Economy of Japan*, Vol. 2. Stanford, CA: Stanford University Press.

Parker, James. June 1990. U.S. scoring sales in Japan's processed rice product market. *AgExporter*. Washington, DC: Foreign Agricultural Service, United States Department of Agriculture.

Salassi, Michael, Mary Ahearn, Mir Ali, and Robert Dismukes. March 1990. *Effects of Government Programs on Rice Production Costs and Returns, 1988*. Agriculture Information Bulletin No. 597. Washington, DC: Economic Research Service, United States Department of Agriculture.

Tsujii, Hiroshi. March 1990. International comparison of rice policies and the world rice trade conflicts. P. 18 in Kiyoshi Kamegai, ed., *An International Comparative Study of Rice Economy and Policy Among the United States, Thailand, and Japan*. Japan: Kyoto University.

United States Department of Agriculture. July 1989. *Rice Situation and Outlook Yearbook*. RS-55. Washington, DC: Economic Research Service, USDA.

Wailes, Eric J., Shoichi Ito, and Gail L. Cramer. February 1991. *Japan's Rice Market: Policies and Prospects for Trade Liberalization*. Report Series 319. Fayetteville: Arkansas Agricultural Experiment Station.

Williams, Gary W., and Warren R. Grant. 1990. Food security and the multilateral trade negotiations: The case of Japanese Rice. (Mimeo.) College Station: Texas A & M University.

Vanberg, Victor. December 1990. *A Constitutional Political Economy Perspective on International Trade*. Annual Meeting of International Agricultural Trade Research Consortium held in San Diego, CA.

20

Impacts of Trade Arrangements on Farm Structure and Food Demand: A Japanese Perspective
Keiji Oga

Introduction

The Japanese economy owes much of its growth to international trade arrangements set forth in the General Agreement on Tariffs and Trade (GATT) principles. Japanese trade policy formulated in the early 1960s featured gradual reductions in import quotas. The Basic Guide of Trade and Foreign Exchange Liberalization Programs of 1960 set the trade policy guidelines for Japan including for agricultural products. This trade policy was one of the fundamental precedents of the Agricultural Basic Law enacted in 1961 although it did not explicitly prescribe agricultural trade policy (Henmi).

Japanese agricultural border protection has relied mainly on import quotas which are unacceptable, in principle, under the GATT rules. Following its basic trade policy, the Japanese government relaxed import quotas in recent years. As a result, Japanese dependency on imported food increased from 25 percent in 1965 to 51 percent in 1988 in energy terms. Dependency on imported grain rose from 38 percent to 70 percent in the same period (MAFF). Barriers remain, but Japan has done more than other developed countries in recent years to open its agricultural market to the world.

This paper first presents an overview of the Japanese import situation for agricultural products. Second, it discusses the impacts of beef import liberalization on demand and trade. Third, it reviews some projected effects of rice import liberalization. And finally, I comment on the impacts of agricultural trade liberalization on farm structure.

Japanese Import of Agricultural Products

Japanese imports of agricultural products reached $26.5 billion in 1989, about 30 times the value in 1960. Japan is the world's largest net importer of agricultural products. The United States is the single biggest supplier of the imported food with a market share of about 40 percent. Japan is the largest importer of feed grains and soybeans in the world (ERS/USDA). Japan is the third largest importer of wheat after the former Soviet Union and China. The United States has been the largest supplier of soybeans but its market share has been declining and it is being replaced in part by South American countries. Japan ranks second to the U.S. in beef import volume, but is the largest beef importer in terms of value. The main suppliers of Japanese beef imports are Australia and the U.S.

In 1989, Japan replaced the U.S. as the world's largest pork importer (excluding intra-EC trade). Major suppliers are Denmark (39 percent), Taiwan (32 percent), U.S. (14 percent), and Canada (9 percent). Taiwan was the largest pork supplier to Japan before 1987, but since then it has lost its market share while Denmark and the U.S. have gained.

Japan continues to be the world's largest poultry importer. Poultry imports are mostly chicken. Major suppliers are the U.S. (38 percent), Thailand (33 percent), Brazil (14 percent), and China (10 percent). Although the U.S. has maintained its position as the leading poultry exporter to Japan in terms of volume, its share has been declining while Thailand's share has been increasing. Thailand already is the leading supplier in terms of value. Japan ranks second to the U.S. in cheese imports (excluding intra-EC trade).

In 1988, Japan decided to abolish import quotas on beef, oranges, processed cheese, and other items following the GATT panel conclusion and negotiations with the U.S. and Australia. By the end of 1992, the number of agricultural and fishery products under import quota will fall to 13. Tariffs remain on many products but Japan has opened up much of its agricultural sector to world trade, giving impetus to the ongoing GATT negotiations. Japan is the only developed country which has continuously opened its food market to the world and has increased its dependency on imported food. This is contrary to some views presented in reports such as the ABARE report.

Impacts of Beef Import Liberalization

Following the Japan-U.S. beef and citrus agreement in June 1988, the beef import quota was expanded sharply in the latter half of fiscal 1988. A gradual and transitional import liberalization was implemented at this time, although formal abolishment of the import quota started in April 1991. The impacts of the expansion of beef imports on the Japanese market give some insights into future meat trade (Mori and Gorman).

In the transitional period, the retail price of high-end domestic beef has been steady, while imported beef price has dropped sharply due to increased import volume (Figure 20.1). This trend also can be observed at the wholesale level after 1985 with a sharp expansion of beef imports (Figure 20.2). Product differentiation based on quality differences is the major factor in the widening price gap. In general, Japanese consumers prefer marbled and tender beef to imported lean beef (ABARE). Domestic beef is chilled fresh while most imported grain-fed beef is frozen. Imported grass-fed beef is hard and lean. Because of these quality differences, the consumers of domestic beef and imported beef are quite different (Table 20.1). Generally speaking, domestic beef is consumed at home and in high-class restaurants (Namiki). Imported grain-fed beef is consumed at popular family restaurants and somewhat at home. Imported grass-fed beef is used for processing for ground beef and hamburger mixed with other foodstuffs.

Similar product differentiation can be observed for pork and chicken consumption. Domestic fresh meats are consumed mainly at home while imported meats are consumed at family restaurants or at fast-food shops. Thus imported meat demand grows fast while domestic meat demand is maintained although it shows signs of stagnating.

Table 20.2 shows projections of Japanese meat consumption, production, and imports from 1995 to 2000. Beef projections were made by adjusting

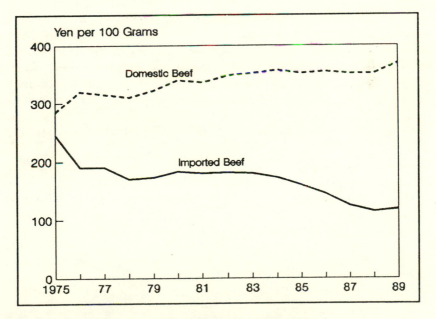

Figure 20.1. Retail Price of Beef in Tokyo, 1975-1989.
Source: General Affairs Agency, Japan.
Note: Shoulder, 2nd grade and imported beef is frozen.

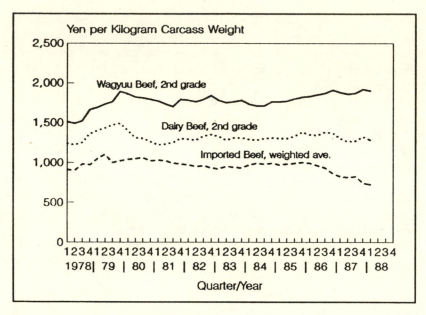

Figure 20.2. Wholesale Prices of Domestic Beef and Imported Beef, Tokyo.
Source: MAFF.

domestic production to 1990 estimates, based on simulation results of the
Japanese beef model (Oga). Pork and poultry consumption figures are based
on MAFF projections. Production estimates of pork and chicken are calculated using elasticity of production with respect to consumption in 1980 and 1988
because simple projections tend to underestimate demand and over-estimate
production -- perhaps reflecting analysts' hopes of maintaining

Table 20.1. Distribution of Domestic Beef and Imported Beef in Japan, 1986.

	Domestic	Imported	Total
Quantity (1,000 Tons)			
Home Consumption	261	46	307
Processing	8	69	77
Restaurant, etc.	109	70	179
Total	378	185	563
Market Share (%)			
Home Consumption	69	25	55
Processing	2	37	14
Restaurant, etc.	29	38	32
Total	100	100	100

Source: Livestock Bureau, MAFF.

Table 20.2. Japanese Meat Demand and Supply Projections to Year 2000 (Slaughtered Weight, 1,000 Tons).

		Actual		Estimate	Projection	
Commodity	Item	1980	FY 1988	1990	1995	2000
Beef[a]	Production	431	556	547	616	694
and	Consumption	597	774	1,103	1,469	1,863
Veal	Net Imports[b]	172	225	563	853	1,169
Pork	Production	1,430	1,559	1,537	1,568	1,600
	Consumption	1,646	1,813	2,086	2,223	2,370
	Net Imports[b]	207	272	499	655	770
Poultry	Production	1,120	1,325	1,429	1,562	1,707
	Consumption	1,194	1,466	1,744	2,003	2,300
	Net Imports[b]	80	115	302	441	593
Other	Production	4	6	7	8	9
Meat	Consumption	258	230	187	142	121
	Net Imports[b]	254	223	170	150	130

[a]Beef projections: Adjusted following 1990 estimates based on "Impact of Beef Import Liberalization;" poultry and pork projections: Consumption based on MAFF projections to year 2000, production calculated using elasticity of production to consumption in 1980-1990, and net imports calculated by consumption minus production.
[b]Actual and estimates of net imports in 1980, 1988, and 1990 are not equal to the balance of consumption and production because of stock change.

self-sufficiency ratios.   Net imports are calculated as balances between consumption and production.

Projected results show that beef imports could double from 563,000 tons (in carcass weight basis) in 1990 to 1,169,000 tons in 2000. Japan could be the world's largest importer by year 2000, not only in terms of value but also in terms of volume, even if U.S. beef imports maintain about the same volume in the future. Pork imports could be 1.5 times as large as the 1990 level, keeping Japan the world's largest pork importer. Poultry imports are projected to double from 302,000 tons in 1990 to 593,000 tons in 2000. Thus, Japan would continue to be the world's largest importer of poultry meat.

As a result of the stagnant production of meat, consumption of feed grains which are almost entirely imported have stagnated since the late 1980s. The meat projections shown above imply the stagnation or even decline of feed grain and soybean imports in 1990s after accounting for the possible moderate increase in feed efficiency. Dyck came to the same conclusion, reflecting the impact of beef import liberalization on feed grain consumption in Japan. Expansion of feed grain imports accompany the expansion of domestic livestock production.

Impacts of Rice Import Liberalization

One of the focus points of agricultural trade negotiations underway in the Uruguay Round of GATT is whether or not Japan will open its rice market to the world. The importance of rice in Japanese agriculture is well known and documented by Wailes and others. Rice in Japan may be comparable to the importance of the livestock sector to western countries. Rice accounts for about one-third of the gross value of agricultural production, and one-third of Japanese per capita calorie intake comes from rice.

The Japanese Government has intervened heavily in rice production, distribution, and trade. Producer subsidy equivalents (PSEs), calculated by OECD (Table 20.3), show that rice accounts for about 60 percent of the total PSE value. We should not talk about Japanese agricultural protection in general but should make clear distinction between the highly protected rice market and other fairly open markets.

As import quotas of beef and processed cheese have been abolished and tariffs are being reduced, rice remains the only major agricultural product which is protected significantly by the current Japanese trade regime. When we think of the impacts of future trade policy reform, rice import liberalization is the most important issue. The Rice Policy Research Group chaired by Morishima has made comprehensive studies on impacts of Japanese rice import liberalization (Morishima *et al.*). This paper focuses on a few of the economic impacts on price, production, and imports.

Most of the past studies on the economic impacts of agricultural import liberalization naively assumed product homogeneity (Tyers and Anderson,

Table 20.3. Producer Subsidy Equivalents for Japan.

	1980 (Bil. Yen)	1980 (%)	1985 (Bil. Yen)	1985 (%)	1986 (Bil. Yen)	1986 (%)	1987 (Bil. Yen)	1987 (%)	1988 (Bil. Yen)	1988 (%)	1989 (Bil. Yen)	1989 (%)
Gross Total PSE												
Wheat	123	3.0	169	3.2	181	3.1	170	3.3	180	3.8	158	3.4
Coarse Grains	72	1.8	70	1.3	69	1.2	67	1.3	69	1.5	61	1.3
Barley	72	1.8	70	1.3	69	1.2	67	1.3	69	1.5	61	1.3
Rice	2,252	55.1	3,343	63.1	3,586	62.4	3,129	61.3	2,695	56.7	2,707	58.2
Soybeans	44	1.1	50	0.9	52	0.9	52	1.0	43	0.9	42	0.9
Sugar	57	1.4	107	2.0	100	1.7	95	1.9	86	1.8	78	1.7
Sugar Beet	30	0.7	60	1.1	59	1.0	53	1.0	47	1.0	40	0.9
Net Unit PSE												
Milk	566	13.8	667	12.6	728	12.7	647	12.7	639	13.5	630	13.6
Beef	395	9.7	471	8.9	574	10.0	507	9.9	526	11.1	477	10.3
Pork	394	9.6	238	4.5	291	5.1	312	6.1	390	8.2	369	7.9
Poultry	77	1.9	77	1.5	60	1.0	54	1.1	50	1.1	49	1.1
Eggs	110	2.7	103	1.9	109	1.9	74	1.4	73	1.5	77	1.7
Net Total PSE	4,089	100.0	5,294	100.0	5,749	100.0	5,107	100.0	4,750	100.0	4,649	100.0

Source: Tables of CSE and PSE 1979-1989, OECD, Paris, 1990.

Roningen and Dixit, Oga).   But the experience of Japanese beef import liberalization has highlighted the critical importance of product differentiation.

Japonica rice is different from indica rice.   Rice produced in Japan is exclusively japonica rice, except for some which is produced for processed food or liquor use.   However, indica rice is dominant and japonica rice almost negligible in the world rice market.   A study on the impacts of Japanese rice liberalization taking this product differentiation into account was presented in 1988 in an annex paper to the Petition of the Rice Council for Market Development and the Rice Millers' Association pursuant to Section 301 of the U.S. Trade Act (Bateman).   With an open Japanese rice market, Bateman calculated that the Japanese rice price would decline 59 percent, the world japonica price would rise 233 percent, the world indica price would rise 82 percent, Japanese production would decline 2.85 million tons, and U.S. rice exports would increase by 1.80 million tons in the short run.   His calculations are moderate compared to the study results which assumed a homogeneous rice market.

A group of researchers at the University of Arkansas incorporated rice product differentiation in their spatial equilibria model of world rice (Cramer *et al.*).   They separated rice trade into high-quality indica, low-quality indica, and japonica varieties.   The results of worldwide free trade shows that Japan's rice imports increase from nearly zero to 8.2 million metric tons.   The U.S. export price of japonica rice increases from $229 per metric ton (MT) to $566 per MT and U.S. export volume increases from 343,000 tons to 710,000 tons.

Recently Dixit and Roningen presented SWOPSIM simulation results showing that recognition of product differentiation in the rice market could alter the economic implications of Japanese policy reform.   According to their calculations, Japanese rice imports would be 3.1 million MT in the case of no substitution possibilities between japonica rice and indica rice compared to 5.1 million MT in the case of full substitution.   Japanese rice producer price falls by 56 percent in the case of imperfect substitution compared to the 77 percent in the case of perfect substitution.   Japanese rice production decreases by 20 percent assuming differentiated rice while production declines 41 percent when rice is treated as a homogeneous product.

Kusakari studied further the impact of rice trade liberalization in relation to quality differentiated demand of Japonica rice.   Even though direct food consumption of rice in Japan has been gradually declining, high quality rice consumption has been increasing while medium and the standard quality rice consumption has been declining.   Based on the estimation of own- and cross-demand elasticities for quality differentiated rice, he showed that the decline of producer rice would be 30 to 37 percent when the imported rice is assumed to be the same quality as the standard quality rice in Japan -- depending on supply elasticity (-0.5 and -1.2).   These figures are much less than the 67 and 72 percent declines calculated by Peason and Oga, respectively.   As a result, rice production would fall 35 and 37 percent compared to 33 and 73 percent in the case of perfect substitution.

He also calculated the effects assuming that the imported japonica rice in the same quality as the medium rice in Japan. In this case, the decline of producer price would range from 55 to 47 percent and the decline of production would range form 55 to 59 percent.

Kusakari's calculations are based on the small country assumption that Japanese rice trade does not influence world prices. Japan is no small country in the rice trade market. We need a world model incorporated the product differentiation not only between indica and japonica rice but also quality differentiation within japonica rice. japonica rice exporters are the United States and Australia in the current rice trade situation, but we have to take into account that potential production and exports of Japonica rice from other countries in the long run.

The impacts of Japanese rice trade policy reform on food demand would be focused around the extent of substitution of imported rice for domestic rice, but the impacts on other food demands have to be studied further.

Impacts of Agricultural Trade Liberalization on Farm Structure

The Japanese agricultural market has been opened for most sectors except rice, a part of dairy products, and other minor items. High tariffs remain on some imports, however.

Opinions about the effects of agricultural trade liberalization on farm structure are divergent. On the one hand, Agricultural Cooperatives have the view that agricultural trade liberalization will ruin Japanese agriculture and sharply reduce cultivated land for crops. On the other hand, some writers such as Kano believe that removal of agricultural protection will give greater opportunity to large farmers to better utilize their farm size and efficiency, perhaps making Japan's rice sector an exporting industry. The performance of Japanese agriculture in the past 30 years of gradual trade liberalization and the recent study cited in the previous section rejects both of these extreme positions.

Farms with at least one full time male dominate production in most sectors expect rice as shown Table 20.4. The impacts of agricultural liberalization on these sectors would be mostly indirect and much smaller than the impacts on the rice sector.

As for the rice sector, no quantitative simulation results show that rice production expands in either volume or value with trade liberalization. Even the most optimistic combination of 30 percent decline of price and 35 percent decline of production in Kusakari's estimates implies a 50 percent decline of gross rice production value.

Under such expectation very few farmers would expect to expand their rice operation. Surviving rice growers would be mostly part time farmers who would not care much about profitability. Part time farming already dominates and is extending as we saw from Table 20.4. Trade liberalization would accelerate this trend. Most young farmers are engaging in sectors other than rice; rice production is supported by older farmers who still have significant influence in rural areas.

This paper does not discuss comprehensive impacts of agricultural trade liberalization, but I will make a few comments on non-economic effects. We can view food security as a kind of public accident insurance. The cost for food security is like insurance dues which depend on accident possibilities and our willingness to bear the certain annual costs of risk premiums or to bear the high cost but low probability of food shortfall. We cannot avoid studying the food security problem in relation to the possibilities of war -- even if Japan is not directly involved in the war. Many Japanese people think the food security problem must be viewed in the context of the food shortage during and after the World War II (Kada). Studying food security in the broad perspective of military security policy involves issues of food security that are emotional and intangible and hence cannot be resolved on a scientific basis.

Another non-economic concern is the water and land conservation role of paddy field cultivation. This side effects should be calculated in relation to the cost or payment to farmers for alternative measures such as forestation or keeping paddy fields as preservatory ponds.

In a similar vein, impacts on regional economies should be studied in relation to the effects and cost of alternative or compensatory measures to develop rural economies. Another issue is the value of land for farm production versus urban development.

Table 20.4. The Production Share of Core Farmers.

	1979	1989
Agriculture	59	57
Rice	33	28
Vegetable in Facility	91	76
Vegetable in Field	69	56
Fruit	66	59
Serviculture	48	68
Broiler and Egg	67	79
Pork	78	78
Dairy	92	90

Source: MAFF.

Concluding Remarks

Critics of protectionist Japanese agricultural trade policy need to recognize that Japan has already opened up most of its market to the world. The residual trade barriers -- having significant importance to trade, production, and consumption -- are import quotas on rice and to a lesser extent butter and non-fat milk.

Policy reform of the Japanese rice trade would have enormous effects not only on economic but also political, social, and cultural life in Japan. Compared to a radical reform, a gradual reform would ease burdens. Continued study of various dimensions of the impacts of agricultural trade liberalization can provide a sounder basis for policy decisions.

References

ABARE. 1990. *Effects of Liberalization of North Asia Beef Import Policies*.

ABARE. 1988. *Japanese Agricultural Policies: Time of Change*.

Bateman, M.J. 1988. Economic effects of Japan's rice policy on the U.S. and world rice economies. Annex paper to the *Petition of the Rice Council for Market Development and the Rice Miller's Association, pursuant to Section 301 of Trade Act of 1974*.

Cramer, G.L., E.J. Wailes, S.S. Phillips, and J.M. Garoski. 1990. The impact of liberalizing trade on the world rice market. Paper presented at *1990 Annual Meeting of American Agricultural Economics Association*.

Dixit, P.M. and V.O. Roningen. 1991. Reforming Japanese rice policies: Importance of product differentiation. Paper presented at *1991 Annual Meeting of American Agricultural Economics Association*.

Dyck, J.H. 1991. Pacific trade in feedstuffs. Paper presented at *1991 Annual Meeting of American Agricultural Economics Association*.

ERS/USDA. 1990. *Pacific Rim*.

Hemmi, K. 1987. Agricultural reform efforts in Japan. Pp. 24-26 in D.G. Johnson, ed., *Agricultural Reform Efforts in the United States and Japan*.

Kada, R. 1989. Issues of food security and agricultural trade liberalization: A Japanese perspective. In *Agricultural Policies of Japan*. Food and Agriculture Policy Research Center.

Kano, Y. 1987. Toward an independent and healthy agricultural industry. *Journal of Japanese Trade and Industry*.

Kusakari, H. 1991. Quality differential demand and import liberalization of rice. Pp. 146-174 in M. Morishima *et al.*, *Projected Impact of Rice Import Liberalization*.

MAFF. 1991. *White Paper on Agriculture*. Japan.

MAFF. 1990. *Long-Term Prospects of Agricultural Products to 2000*. Japan.

Mori, H. and W.D. Gorman. 1988. Quantitative considerations in the Japanese beef market. *Keizaironshu*, Senshu University.

Morishima, K. *et al.* 1991. *Projected Impacts of Rice Import Liberalization.*

Namiki, M. 1989. Beef liberalization and retail/wholesale prices. In Food and Agricultural Policy Research Center, ed., *New Developments in Beef Liberalization.*

OECD. 1990. *Tables of Producer Subsidy Equivalents and Consumer Subsidy Equivalents 1979-1989.*

Oga, K. 1989. Impacts of beef liberalization on production, consumption, and price. *Quarterly Report of National Research Institute of Agricultural Economics.*

Oga, K.. 1988. *International Rice Market and Japanese Rice Import Liberalization Problem.*

Roningen, V.O. and P.M. Dixit. 1991. Reforming agricultural policies: The case of Japan. *Journal of Asian Economics.*

Tyers, R. and K. Anderson. 1986. Distance in world food markets. Background paper for the World Bank. *World Development Report.*

Wailes, E.J., S. Ito, and G.L. Cramer. 1991. Japan's rice market. Fayetteville: University of Arkansas.

21

The Impact of Trade Arrangements on Farm Exports: A U.S. Perspective
Dermot J. Hayes

Introduction

The United States is the world leader in exporting raw agricultural commodities such as wheat and corn, yet its share of the more value-added commodities such as meat and meat products is small. This chapter examines why the United States can dominate world commodity markets but export few products made from these commodities. The chapter focuses on the trade-offs between feed-grain exports and meat exports; however, much of what is presented could just as easily apply to cotton and textiles, wheat and flour, or lumber and furniture. The meat/feed-grain example was chosen because farmers produce both meat and feed grains and therefore are more interested in lost export opportunities for livestock products than for flour or furniture.

This chapter begins with an overview of U.S. trade patterns and the U.S. share of the world market for the important temperate agricultural commodities. The chapter then discusses three possible reasons for the dominance of the United States as an exporter of raw commodities and its lack of success in exporting processed agricultural commodities such as meat. Finally, with an eye toward the future, the chapter discusses how Pacific Rim trade patterns will change once the bias against value-added exports is removed.

Trade Shares

Figures 21.1 through 21.6 present world wheat, coarse grain, soybean, soybean meal, beef, and pork market shares held by major exporting countries. It is clear from these figures that the United States holds large shares of world raw commodity markets but is only a minor player in world meat markets. U.S. producers and policymakers are often surprised to discover that 80 percent of world trade is in high-value agricultural products. To many U.S. producers, agricultural exports mean wheat, corn, and soybeans, but the United States holds large shares of these markets in part because the rest of the world is busy turning commodities into processed products *before* exporting them. The United States exports 3 percent of its processed food production, whereas the average for members of the Organization for Economic Cooperation and Development (which includes the United States) is 21 percent.

Hogs can be viewed as opportunities for repackaging corn as meat, yet the United States is a net importer of hogs and a major exporter of corn. There are at least three possible explanations for this phenomenon. First, it may be more economical for food-importing countries to meet marginal livestock product demand by importing feedstuffs with which to breed and fatten animals domestically. Second, transportation technology may limit meat exports because of the perishable nature of these products. And finally, there may be political reasons for food-importing countries to ensure that additional meat needs are met from producing animals domestically with imported feedstuffs. Another political element is heavy subsidies to high-value exports by the European Community, driving out competing exporters. The following sections examine each potential reason.

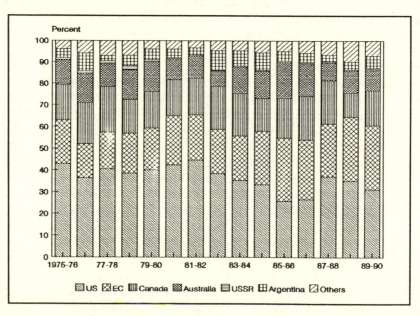

Figure 21.1. Shares of World Wheat Exports by Major Exporters, July-June 1975-76 to 1989-90. (1982-83 to 1989-90, EC is EC-12.)
Source: PS & D View '91.

Economics

If only economic issues were important, we could model the food import decision as if it were being made by a profit-maximizing firm. We could solve a linear programming problem that would have as variables the relative costs and productivity of labor, feed, and capital and the relative costs of transporting meat and feed grains. Now I will examine how the relative costs of labor and feed differ among countries in the region and how the cost of transporting meat compares with the cost of transporting feed grains.

Labor costs in many Pacific Rim countries are low but increasing rapidly. In Japan, however, labor costs have already exceeded those in the United States, so it is worthwhile to pay particular attention to this case. Presumably other countries in the region will eventually follow Japan's lead and increase their wage rates relative to those in the United States.

The Japanese poultry sector is very efficient, whereas pork and beef producers tend to run smaller, less efficient operations than do their counterparts in the United States. This situation is evidenced by the 50 percent and 70 percent tariffs (as measured by the difference between world and internal Japanese prices) currently protecting these industries.

Table 21.1 shows the relative efficiencies of the Japanese and South Korean livestock industries. These numbers reflect actual feed-grain use

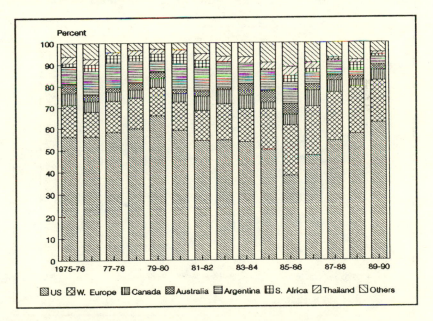

Figure 21.2. Shares of World Coarse Grain Exports by Major Exporters, July-June 1975-76 to 1989-90.
Source: PS & D View '91.

Table 21.1. Pounds of Feed Grains Required to Produce One Pound of Liveweight, by Country.

	Cattle	Hogs	Poultry
United States	7.00	4.00	1.70
South Korea	8.00	6.80	5.00
Japan	7.58	4.80	3.20

Sources: Japan and South Korea: Harris *et al.*, 1990; United States: Discussion with Iowa State University Cooperative Extension Service Staff, August 1991.

per unit of liveweight produced, differ markedly from the theoretical limits used by scientists, and may not be fully comparable across countries. Nevertheless, neither Japan nor South Korea has any advantage over the United States in producing meats with feed grains.

Transporting one pound of boneless chilled boxed meat from the Midwest to Japan costs approximately ten times more than transporting one pound of feed grains (Midwest Agribusiness Trade Research and Information Center 1990). To compare relative transportation costs, we must determine how

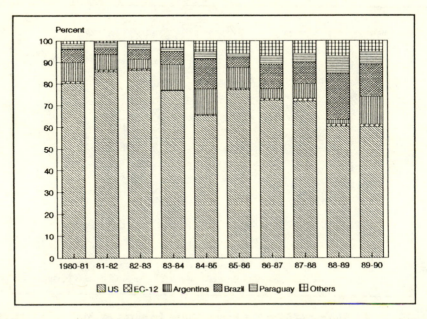

Figure 21.3. Shares of World Soybean Exports by Major Exporters, October-September 1980-81 to 1989-90.
Source: PS & D View '91.

many pounds of corn it takes to produce one pound of boxed beef, pork, and poultry, respectively.

To compute these costs, assume that the food-importing country has utilized almost all domestic sources of roughage and feed and that it must import the feed-grain requirements of the breeding stock and the meat animals. Also, for purposes of direct comparison, assume that feed-conversion efficiencies (FCEs) and production methods are comparable to those achieved in the United States. Production of a beef calf requires feeding approximately 1.1 cows for a full year. Some of the cow feed may be used for additional milk production or to feed the calf. Also, some of the feed will need to come from roughage -- either imported or domestically produced. Allocating five pounds of imported feed per day for the calf results in 365 days x 1.1 x 5 pounds = 2,007 pounds of corn. Assuming seven pounds of grain per pound of liveweight gain requires an additional 7,700 pounds of corn to produce a 1,100-pound steer yielding approximately 55 percent, or 605 pounds of beef. Therefore, to produce 605 pounds of beef requires 9,707 pounds of imported corn -- a 16 to 1 ratio.

We have ignored two important factors in these calculations. First, not all of the 605 pounds will be sold internationally. A more accurate figure would be 400 pounds (after the larger bones, offals, excess fat, and less valuable

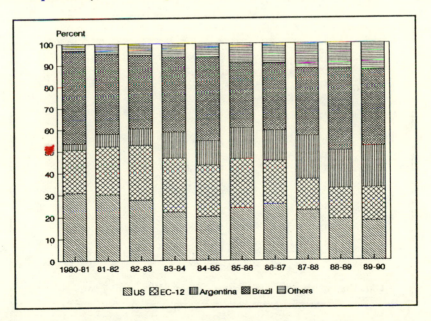

Figure 21.4. Shares of World Soybean Meal Exports by Major Exporters, October-September 1980-81 to 1989-90.
Source: PS & D View '91.

cuts have been removed). Second, and more importantly, we have ignored the ability of meat importers to select only those cuts that are most in demand in the domestic market. Japan, for example, imports predominantly middle cuts of beef, pork loins, and chicken legs. Any consideration of these factors would serve to increase the corn import-to-meat ratio beyond 16 to 1. The transportation logistics clearly favor beef imports in this example.

Pork production requires approximately 182 pounds of corn to feed one sow to produce one piglet with a lifetime FCE of 4. An additional 960 pounds of grain are required to produce a 240-pound hog, which in turn will produce approximately 168 pounds of pork. The final ratio is approximately 7 to 1. The ratio for poultry meat production would be between 3 to 1 and 4 to 1. One can therefore conclude that the transportation logistics favor importing grain to produce poultry and that they are neutral regarding pork imports. Despite liberal import policies for both feed grains and poultry, Japan has imported most of its additional poultry needs, indicating that the ratios just presented are conservative.

Technology

Historically it has been necessary to transport feed grains, live animals, or frozen meat because fresh (chilled) meat is highly perishable. Frozen meat

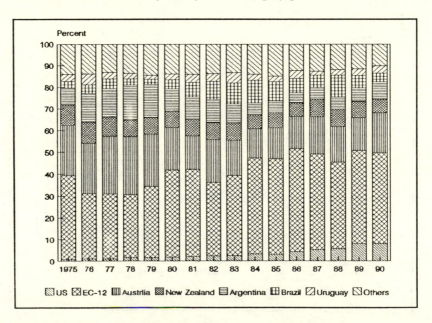

Figure 21.5. Shares of World Beef and Veal Exports by Major Exporters, Calendar Years 1975-90. (Includes Intra-EC Trade; From 1983 to 1990 EC is EC-12.)
Source: PS & D View '91.

loses value, particularly in Japan, where it is discounted by 30 percent. When considered as a transportation cost, this 30 percent discount could help explain the low U.S. share in world meat markets. Because the United States is surrounded by two oceans, U.S. exports are diminished by quality deterioration induced by long periods of surface transportation.

Recent developments have removed this deterioration allowing Midwestern meat exporters to send chilled (not frozen) meat to Asia by using surface transportation. Three technologies are responsible for these changes: (1) slaughterhouses have reduced microbial contamination by washing carcasses with dilute acids (vinegar) and by reducing surface contact in boning halls, (2) vacuum packing of meat primals has decreased aerobic activity on the meat, and (3) transportation companies have provided refrigerated containers that can be loaded in the Midwest and shipped via truck to trains that carry the containers to a ship. In Japan, this transportation process is reversed. These intermodal containers avoid the need for risky transportation and reduce damage caused by mishandling. The transportation cost ratio quoted earlier is based on this intermodal technology.

These three new technologies are still in their infancy and not widely used. One might hypothesize that, as demand for these technologies grows, their costs will fall; however, this process is not likely to occur for grain

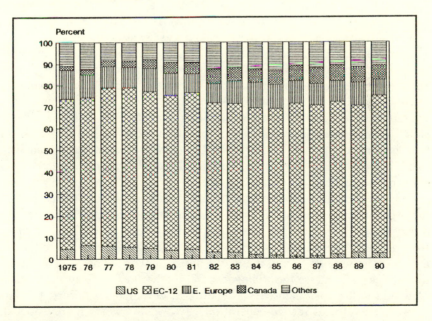

Figure 21.6. Shares of World Pork Exports by Major Exporters, Calendar Years 1975-90. (Includes Intra-EC Trade.)
Source: PS & D View '91.

transportation technologies. Other features that will contribute to continued reductions in the meat/feed-grain transportation ratio are the expansion of double-decker freight trains and international acceptance of boxed beef in Asian markets.

One may therefore conclude that, although transportation barriers may have existed in the past, technological developments in the way meat is processed and transported have begun to remove these barriers.

Politics

The U.S. Department of Agriculture has estimated that the income multiplier for primary commodities is 1.86, whereas for high-value agricultural products it is 2.88. Each dollar of bulk grain export sales generates $1.86 of national income whereas each dollar of livestock exports generates $2.88 of national income. This means that, if the United States began exporting feed grains in the form of meat, employment would increase by approximately 50 percent if employment multipliers are the same as income multipliers. The same argument can and has been made to justify the protection of domestic livestock industries by food-importing countries.

Taken as a whole, Asia has only 0.14 acres of arable land per person. Farm sizes throughout much of Asia, including Japan and South Korea, average 3 acres or less. As Asian countries enter the development phase, it is important that their agricultural sectors do well. A prosperous agricultural sector provides a tax base to help finance industrial development. Also, a prosperous agricultural sector helps to reduce the trauma of an inevitable decrease in the proportion of the population working in agriculture. Farmers with small acreage allotments can remain viable so long as they expand into livestock production. Intensive poultry, hog, beef, and dairy production operations do not require much land so long as a plentiful commercial market supply of feed grains is available. It is therefore not surprising that almost all food-importing countries in the Pacific Rim (with the exception of Hong Kong and Singapore) use barriers to restrict livestock product imports while allowing feedstuffs to enter freely.

Farmers and their urban offsprings make up a significant political force in these countries, and consumers feel more secure when livestock is produced domestically -- even with imported foodstuffs -- than when it is purchased from abroad. There are, however, political forces that may eliminate this bias against meat imports. First, the world has recently become a safer place to live, which may reduce the willingness of city dwellers to finance protection of domestic livestock industries. Second, as development occurs, the farm lobby loses votes as second-generation city dwellers worry more about the price of food than about the welfare of asset-rich farmers. Third, these countries often look to the United States as an export market, which enhances the political power of groups exporting to the United States and, in turn, the clout of U.S. trade negotiators. It is perhaps not coincidental, therefore, that first Japan and then South Korea have begun to remove barriers against meat imports. Taiwan also has begun to restrict the growth of its hog industry in an effort to control pollution. Japan, the most advanced country in the region, now imports significant quantities of beef, pork, and poultry. South Korea imported approximately one-half of its beef needs in 1990 but is still self-sufficient in pork and poultry.

Future U.S.-Asian Trade Patterns

Because personal incomes are increasing markedly in Asia, a region comprising 58 percent of the world's population, demand for livestock products -- domestic or imported -- will increase. Many Asian countries are unwilling to import meats from countries contaminated with the virus responsible for foot-and-mouth disease, so additional imports of beef or pork will come from North America, Scandinavia, or the Antipodes. In addition, the United States currently dominates world broiler and feed-grain markets.

U.S. producers have a particular interest in the composition of expanding Asian imports. If imports consist primarily of feed grains, then any increase in U.S. agricultural exports will be comprised of corn and soybeans. If, however, the additional imports consist of meats, U.S. producers will need to expand both grain and livestock production.

The United States will also need to evaluate its competitive situation because it might lose markets to grass-fed beef produced on land that cannot produce feed grains. The U.S. government and commodity markets also have an interest in the composition of this trade. Current government promotional and data collection efforts are primarily targeted toward raw commodities, and futures traders of livestock products have historically ignored international developments.

Earlier in this chapter, I identified three possible reasons for the relative inability of U.S. agriculture to capture world meat markets. These restrictions have recently begun to disappear. On the economics side, for example, relative wage rates in the United States have fallen. Technical barriers to chilled meat exports have been removed, and the cost of transporting meat is decreasing relative to the cost of transporting feed grains. Political justification continues for prohibiting meat imports, but Japan and South Korea have begun to remove these asymmetric barriers. I hypothesize that, as the rest of the countries in the Pacific Rim reach a phase in development at which urban interests outweigh rural interests, barriers against meat imports will be removed.

Table 21.2 shows how U.S. agricultural exports have trended from 1982 to 1990. Two features are worth mentioning. First, the nominal value of meat and meat products has increased by 260 percent and for poultry by 180 percent, whereas the nominal values of grains, feeds, oilseeds, and oilseed products have been flat or falling. Second, the 1989/90 value of animal and

Table 21.2. Value of U.S. Agricultural Exports (Million U.S. Dollars).

	Fiscal Year							
	1982/83	1983/84	1984/85	1985/86	1986/87	1987/88	1988/89	1989/90
Total	34,769	38,027	31,201	26,309	27,876	35,316	39,637	40,182
Animals and animal products	3,748	4,218	4,075	4,353	5,014	6,057	6,538	6,553
Meats and meat products	926	929	906	1,102	1,300	1,797	2,355	2,457
Beef and veal	405	447	478	539	734	1,009	1,421	1,495
Pork	150	138	73	81	105	228	305	341
Variety meats	267	273	294	326	355	411	423	369
Other	104	72	61	66	106	149	207	251
Poultry and poultry products	451	413	393	455	594	647	724	854
Poultry meats	281	280	257	282	406	424	510	631
Chicken (fresh or frozen)	224	218	210	240	361	366	442	518
Other	57	62	47	43	45	59	68	113
Dairy products	349	393	414	431	491	536	475	348
Nonfat dry milk	148	187	184	221	221	229	145	20
Butter	59	76	66	40	18	11	32	98
Cheese	34	36	27	26	32	46	29	36
Other dairy	108	95	136	144	220	250	268	194
Fats, oils, and greases	593	703	608	477	417	545	531	459
Hides and skins	997	1,318	1,325	1,440	1,666	1,837	1,713	1,796
Other animals and animal products	432	462	431	538	547	696	740	641
Grains and feeds	15,050	17,304	13,285	9,472	9,059	12,573	16,821	15,694
Wheat (unmilled and flour)	6,166	6,731	4,428	3,463	3,084	4,640	6,258	4,412
Unmilled	5,910	6,497	4,264	3,260	2,877	4,469	6,004	4,209
Flour	256	234	164	203	207	170	255	203
Rice (paddy milled)	874	897	677	648	551	734	955	829

Table 21.2 continued.

			Fiscal Year					
	1982/83	1983/84	1984/85	1985/86	1986/87	1987/88	1988/89	1989/90
Grains and feeds cont.								
Feed grains and products	6,582	8,217	6,884	3,817	3,752	5,193	7,374	8,093
Barley	114	274	146	63	242	226	211	220
Corn	5,717	7,023	5,788	3,291	3,048	4,324	6,109	6,929
Grain sorghum	661	829	856	386	391	564	910	811
Oats	1	2	1	3	2	1	1	2
Other feed grains	89	89	93	75	69	78	141	132
Feeds and fodders (e.g., oilcake)	1,193	1,216	1,004	1,286	1,455	1,721	1,849	1,826
Corn byproducts	630	666	531	729	783	846	787	778
Other	563	550	473	557	672	875	1,062	1,048
Other grains and feeds	235	243	293	258	217	285	384	533
Oilseeds and products	8,721	8,602	6,195	6,271	6,308	7,692	6,629	6,098
Soybean meal	1,449	1,181	833	1,113	1,325	1,469	1,332	994
Soybeans	5,866	5,734	3,876	4,174	4,205	5,000	4,085	3,939
Soybean oil	462	633	558	292	223	437	404	339
Other oilseeds and products	944	1,054	927	693	555	786	807	827
Other products								
Fruits and preparations (e.g., juices)	1,152	1,047	1,001	1,089	1,281	1,462	1,536	1,860
Fruit juice	222	223	200	148	185	252	264	328
Nuts and preparations	508	548	686	677	769	906	858	929
Vegetables and preparations	990	999	946	997	1,176	1,280	1,542	2,079
Tobacco	1,487	1,433	1,588	1,318	1,203	1,297	1,274	1,373
Cotton (e.g., linter)	1,683	2,395	1,945	678	1,419	2,136	2,040	2,704
Sugar and related products	108	142	137	144	199	205	282	388

Source: U.S. Department of Agriculture.

animal product exports is greater than the value of wheat and oilseed exports and approximately equal to that of corn exports. This increase in animal product exports has caught many by surprise. I hypothesize that this trend will continue well into the next century as U.S. meat exports replace U.S. feed-grain exports.

Conclusions

U.S. agricultural export patterns, in contrast to those of the rest of the world, are predominantly commodity-oriented. This pattern can be explained by economic, technological, and political barriers. These barriers to meat trade recently have diminished, which explains the relative increase in meat exports. This trend is expected to continue until the United States displays an agricultural export trade pattern of value-added products similar to that of other developed countries.

References

Harris, David, Andrew Dickson, Greg Corra, and Walter Gerardi. 1990. *Effects of the Liberalization of North Asian Beef Import Policies*. Canberra, Australia: Australian Bureau of Agricultural and Resource Economics.
Midwest Agribusiness Trade Research and Information Center (MATRIC). 1990. *Meat Marketing in Japan*, edited by Dermot J. Hayes. Ames, IA: MATRIC, Iowa State University.
PS&D View '91. November 1991. Users manual and database. Washington, DC: U.S. Department of Agriculture.
U.S. Department of Agriculture. Various issues. *Foreign Agricultural Trade of the United States (FATUS)*. Washington, DC: U.S. Department of Agriculture, Economic Research Service.

22

Regional Research: Possibilities for the Organization and Management of International Cooperative Research

*Roland R. Robinson, John A. Naegele,
and Paul L. Farris[1]*

Introduction

The first state agricultural experiment stations in the United States were established over 100 years ago. The concept of public support of agricultural research in the United States was adapted from early publicly supported research ventures in Great Britain and Germany. Between 1875 and 1888 fifteen state agricultural experiment stations were established without federal aid (True, pp. 82-106). The Hatch Act was passed in 1887 and federal funding began in 1888. The state agricultural experiment stations now form a nation-wide system with one station in each state with California, Connecticut, and Georgia each having two.

The stations have made enormous contributions to the agricultural industry, to the fundamental understanding of biological and economic systems, and to the welfare of the nation's citizens. The experiment station system has survived and progressed over a long period of time because it has made the necessary adjustments and modifications as new conditions and problems have emerged.

A historical review of the system, however, reveals a substantial "lag" between the perception of needed changes by station administrators and scientists and the public action needed to bring about the support to initiate these changes. Examples include latent support for economic research in the

---

[1] The views expressed do not necessarily represent nor reflect the policies of the Cooperative State Research Service, U.S. Department of Agriculture.

1920s and marketing research in 1946. The lag was also evident in the long period between the expressed need for cooperative research and the formalization and federal funding of what is now the regional research program. Currently, there is growing awareness of the need for international cooperative research.

With globalization of world markets, United States agriculture now faces serious new problems and challenges. Scientists in other countries are becoming more actively involved, along with U.S. researchers, in analyzing problems that cut across national boundaries. It is an appropriate time for the station system to extend its horizons and enlarge the support and capacity of its research programs in providing the new knowledge and technology needed by United States industry to maintain and expand its position in the competitive environment of the new global economy. Many current international problems and opportunities did not exist and, therefore, were not considered in drafting most of the federal legislation that now provides federal funding of station research.

The focus of this paper is on new challenges for the regional research program, a major innovation in the way research is organized, administered, and conducted. It is our belief that the regional research concept and its administrative structure and processes offer an excellent mechanism for the organization and conduct of international cooperative research. In our judgment, international cooperative research, building on the U.S. regional research model, is the best approach to organize and conduct the research that will provide the comprehensive knowledge base and technology for United States agriculture to maintain its leadership role in the future world economy. Our concept of international cooperative research is simply a team, or organized committee, of researchers made up of participants from all countries who share a common problem and have described their approach to solving the problem with a commonly affirmed set of objectives.

This chapter includes a brief historical overview of the origins and development of the State Agricultural Experiment Station (SAES) system; the emergence of the need for cooperative regional and national agricultural research; the origin, development, and administration of the regional research program; and trends in funding for the program and implications for future support. Finally, the paper addresses the emerging need for international cooperative research and strategies for moving the regional research program into the international arena -- what we consider to be its next stage of evolutionary development.

Evolution of Cooperative Agricultural Research

Several events prior to World War II contributed significantly to the emergence of cooperative agricultural research by the State Agricultural Experiment Stations and the establishment of the regional research program

(Knoblaugh, pp. 191-194). Research workers at the experiment stations and USDA research agencies organized regional conferences for the purpose of promoting the more effective use of resources and the exchange of information. Based in large measure on these conferences, the USDA began to enter into agreements with certain stations to conduct cooperative work. These were formal arrangements and the agreements specified the leaders of the projects, the objectives to be completed, procedures to be used, the cooperative system or division of efforts and responsibilities, physical location, and plans for publication. These cooperative contracts were confined to the USDA and a specific station and did not involve a collection of stations. The USDA funded the contracted work and reimbursed the stations for the travel costs of collaborators.

The Purnell Act

Economic stress in agriculture and the enormous problems of the industry and rural areas after World War I increased awareness of the need for economic research to deal with problems that cut across state boundaries. At both the state and national levels pressures were intensified for additional federal support for station research programs and for cooperative research activity. More regional conferences were conducted and experiment station directors approved travel for station scientists to attend. The Purnell Act, passed in 1925, increased support for station research and specifically noted greater emphasis on economic and sociological investigations. However, no provision was made in the Act for the support of cooperative research.

Station and federal administrators continued their efforts to expand cooperative research. Plans were formulated to promote and develop Federal-State cooperation under six national projects. Special subject-matter committees were established, each with an advisory administrator, to formulate plans for cooperative projects. A committee of directors was formed to clear each set of plans. This represented the first time an attempt was made to organize and conduct cooperative regional research on a formal basis. Although these planning exercises did result in more cooperative research between the stations and the USDA, they did not result in more cooperative research among the stations. In fact, in 1931, a Joint Committee on Projects and Correlations of Research recommended that the special projects committees, established in 1925, be discontinued. Although these efforts were disappointing in terms of formalizing and conducting regional research, the experience helped to form the knowledge base necessary for putting in place the regional research program in subsequent years when federal funding became available.

The Bankhead-Jones Act

The Bankhead-Jones Act passed in 1935 provided additional federal funds for station research programs. It also provided the impetus for increased cooperative research. The Act provided for the establishment of regional laboratories with federal funds available for the travel of collaborators. This dispersion of federal research facilities and personnel in the various states increased contact between the USDA and station researchers and expanded opportunities for cooperative work. Again, the support was for cooperative work between the USDA and the stations and not among the stations.

The Research and Marketing Act of 1946: Federal Legislation to Promote the Foundation and Support of Cooperative Research

The regional research provision of the Research and Marketing Act of 1946 resulted from the convergence of three major forces. First was the growth of the agricultural industry that expanded the geographical scope of industry problems. Agricultural leaders, concerned about the possibility of commodity surpluses and declining farm prices after World War II, turned to marketing to help deal with prospective problems. Answers could not be found by concentrating resources on isolated and limited state components of those problems. Markets were far removed from areas of production. The efficient marketing and distribution of commodities had to be studied in the context of regional and national marketing and distribution systems. It was logical that provisions for both regional and national marketing research be incorporated in the same Act.

The second major force was the concern of Congress about duplication of research efforts. The regional research mechanism appeared to be an excellent way to achieve coordination of research between the USDA and the stations and among the stations.

Finally, the directors and USDA administrators had historically stressed the need for the cooperative approach to broaden the scope of research and more efficiently use research resources (Knoblaugh, p. 195). So what had earlier appeared to be futile efforts to organize and conduct regional research by the stations became, in reality, a valuable knowledge and experience base to facilitate the organization and development of regional research programs when federal funding became available. In fact, an entire regional research program, including the administrative structure and 52 regional projects, was put in place by the time funding became available.

Funding of Regional Research, 1946-89

In addition to establishing the framework for regional research, the Research and Marketing Act of 1946 provided for ongoing federal support. No more than 25 percent of Hatch funds was to be used on approved regional projects. In 1950, expenditures of designated federal regional research funds (RRF) were $1,161,628 according to the Regional Research Office, CSRS. By

1970, CRIS data showed RRF expenditures were over $11 million and in 1989 were more than $35 million.

Relative Changes in Support for Regional Research

Figure 22.1 provides a perspective on relative shares of support for the regional research program for the 1970-74 period compared to the 1985-89 period. In the 1970-74 period, 32.4 percent of support for regional research came from RRF, 15.5 percent from other Hatch, 5.3 percent from other federal (primarily USDA), and 46.8 percent from nonfederal (primarily state) sources. By the 1985-89 period, the relative shares had shifted significantly. The nonfederal share increased to 66.6 percent and the relative support from RRF had declined to 17.7 percent. The relative support from other Hatch had declined while the relative support from other federal sources had increased.

Change in Relative Importance of Regional Research in SAES Programs

Figure 22.2 highlights the fact that regional research during the past two decades has been growing relative to total station research programs. Of total state experiment station expenditures for all purposes, spending on regional research projects rose from 11.2 percent in 1970-74 to 14.9 percent in 1985-

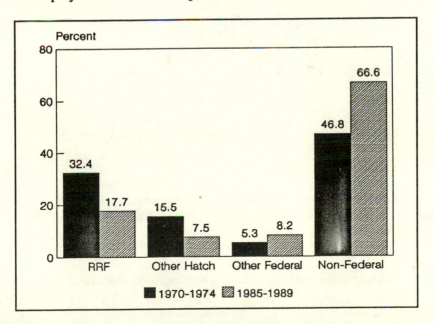

Figure 22.1. Percent of Total Regional Research Funds from Indicated Federal and Non-Federal Sources, SAES, 1970-1974 and 1985-1989.
Source: CRIS data provided by John Myers, CSRS.

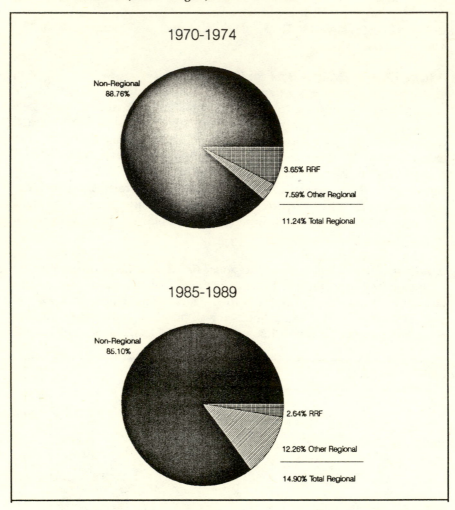

Figure 22.2. Percent of Total SAES Funds Allocated to Regional and Non-Regional Research and Share Accounted for by RRF Funds, 1970-1974 and 1985-1989.
Source: CRIS data provided by John Myers, CSRS.

89, even though the RRF contribution declined relatively from 3.65 percent of the SAES total in 1970-74 to 2.64 percent in 1985-89.   Over time the regional research program received more and more support from nonfederal funds, primarily state appropriations.   It is becoming essentially a station program. These trends in the support for regional research have been gradual and consistent between the two time periods and are expected to continue in the future.   The federal regional research framework and program, even though federal support is declining relatively, continues to be a valued program as demonstrated by growing station support.

Growth in Real Dollars and in Average Support per Project

Table 22.1 shows that total spending on regional research, in nominal dollars, rose from $4.36 million in 1950 to over $221 million in 1991. The increase in deflated dollars was also substantial. But the RRF amount in nominal dollars leveled off in the 1980s and declined in real terms.

Active regional research projects numbered 70 in 1950 and 191 in 1991. Numbers totalling around 200 in the mid-1960s were above that level in the 1980s (Table 22.2). Total spending per project from all funding sources rose from $62.3 thousand in 1950 to over $1 million in 1991. RRF expenditures per project rose from $16.6 thousand in 1950 to $194.7 thousand in 1991. When adjusted for inflation, federal regional research funds (RRF) per project trended downward after the mid-1970s, although total SAES expenditures per regional project have continued to increase in real terms. State support largely made up the difference.

The increase in support per regional project reflects both the increasing costs of doing research and more participants per project. For example, participation in several agricultural economics regional projects grew

Table 22.1. Regional Research Expenditures in Nominal and Deflated Dollars, Total and Designated Federal Regional Research (RRF) Funds, Selected years 1950-91 (Million Dollars).

| | Expenditures on Regional Research | | | |
| | Total (All Sources)[1] | | RRF Funds | |
Year	Nominal	Deflated[2]	Nominal	Deflated[2]
1950	4.36	18.12	1.16	4.83
1955	9.03	33.74	2.82	10.53
1960	17.15	57.94	5.88	19.85
1965	21.16	67.07	9.38	29.74
1970	34.79	89.62	11.17	28.78
1975	68.53	127.36	16.41	30.49
1980	118.76	144.13	26.64	32.33
1985	183.45	170.49	35.62	33.10
1991	221.66	162.75	37.20	27.31

Source: Regional Research Office, CSRS, prior to 1970, CRIS data provided by John Myers, CSRS, afterward.
[1]Includes RRF, Other Hatch, Other Federal and Non-Federal Funds.
[2]Deflated by the Consumer Price Index (1982-84 = 100).

substantially as problem coverage moved from regional to national and international in scope.

Economics expenditures under regional projects accounted for 13.2 percent of total SAES spending on regional research in 1991, according to CRIS data. This proportion was larger than the 6.6 percent share of economics research in total SAES spending for all purposes in that year. Marketing economics spending on regional projects in 1991 made up 6.9 percent of the regional total. For total SAES expenditures, marketing economics accounted for 2.7 percent in 1991.

Changes in CSRS Administered Programs

Figure 22.3 shows that, in 1970, about 93 percent of the federal funds administered by CSRS were used to support Hatch (73.3 percent) and regional research (19.3 percent) programs. Very small percentages of CSRS administered funds were then used for special grants and other programs. The competitive grant program in CSRS did not exist. By 1991, the share of CSRS administered funds allocated to Hatch and regional research programs had declined to about 65.2 percent (49.6 percent to Hatch and 15.6 percent

Table 22.2. Average Expenditures Per Active Regional Research Project, Total and RRF Funds, Selected Years, 1950-91 (Thousand Dollars).

| | | Expenditures per Active Project | | | |
| | | Total (All Sources)[1] | | RRF Funds | |
Year	Number of Active Projects	Nominal	Deflated[2]	Nominal	Deflated[2]
1950	70	62.3	258.8	16.6	68.9
1955	120	75.3	281.2	23.5	87.8
1960	198	86.6	292.6	29.7	100.3
1965	202	104.6	331.7	46.4	147.2
1970	183	190.1	489.7	61.1	157.3
1975	186	368.5	684.7	88.2	164.0
1980	219	542.3	658.1	121.6	147.6
1985	244	751.8	698.7	146.0	135.7
1991	191	1160.5	852.1	194.7	143.0

Source: Regional Research Office, CSRS, prior to 1970. CRIS data provided by John Myers, CSRS, afterward.
[1]Includes RRF, Other Hatch, Other Federal and Non-Federal Funds.
[2]Deflated by Consumer Price Index (1982-84 = 100).

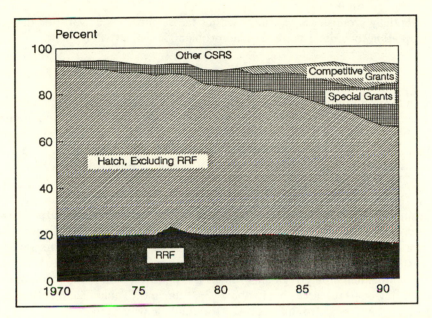

Figure 22.3. Percent of CSRS Funds Allocated to Major Programs, 1970-1991.
Source: CSRS data provided by John Myers, CSRS.

to regional research). While total dollars allocated to Hatch and RRF increased until the mid-1980s, the proportional support for Hatch and regional research declined significantly. Impressive gains were made in the support for special grants, which received 18.7 percent of CSRS administered funds, competitive grants 8.3 percent, and other programs 7.9 percent in 1991.

Summary Observations

Regional research has remained a vital part of SAES research for nearly half a century. The regional framework offers institutional flexibility and adaptability to undertake research projects in which collaboration among researchers from various institutions can be complementary and productive. Regional projects have in the past varied widely in terms of numbers of participants, agencies involved, budgets, purposes, and organizational configurations. Benefits apparently were recognized, as regional research grew in relative importance in the state agricultural experiment stations and accounted for approximately 15 percent of total SAES programs in the late 1980s. Although federal RRF support as a proportion of total SAES activities has been relatively small, and was down to 2.2 percent in 1991, the influence of the total regional research program has spread far beyond the direct products of the research, with further potential in the future. There is a potentially promising opportunity within the regional framework for further adaptation to address newly defined problems.

Potential for Globalization of Regional Research

One of the first significant developments in regional research under the Research and Marketing Act of 1946 was the shift from regional to national projects, particularly in agricultural economics. This was in response to nationwide economic problems. But some problems in other areas were also national in character. Currently, very few regional projects have participants only from within a particular region.

National or interregional research projects, whose scope went beyond regional administrative boundaries, began in 1950 with IR-1. The purpose was to coordinate a national effort to collect, evaluate, preserve, and distribute a superior potato germ plasm (Kerr, p. 100). In 1955, IR-2 was formed to provide virus-free ornamental tree stock (Kerr, p. 100). However, the current level of funding of interregional projects is a relatively small proportion of the total regional research fund, about 3.4 percent (Table 22.3). Because interregional projects require off-the-top funding, which means that all states contribute, not all directors are equally supportive. Costs and benefits vary among states. Some individual station directors see little, if any, benefit from off-the-top funding for some projects.

As a consequence, the regional project framework, rather than interregional, is being used to deal with broad problems, some international in scope. Four regional projects are currently under way dealing with international trade. Projects in the Southern and North Central regions are active while two in the Western region are planning and coordination type projects. However, participation in those projects includes primarily U.S. researchers.

The next logical development in the regional research program is to move toward international cooperative research (ICR). The movement toward free trade with Canada and Mexico are examples where pressures will emerge for international collaboration. International projects will not only investigate problems of international dimensions but, more importantly, will allow participation by multiple countries that have common concerns and problems. The benefits of the research promise to be just as great as the benefits from the cooperative regional and national research conducted domestically. The regional research program with nearly half a century of demonstrated effectiveness, both in terms of administration and research performance, in our judgment is the appropriate mechanism to manage this emerging development.

Some Emerging Examples of Multi-Country Participation

A brief survey of the regional research files in CSRS reveals that international research involving participants from other countries is already

Table 22.3. Summary of Allotments of the Regional Research Fund, Hatch Act, as Amended August 11, 1955, to Cooperative Regional Projects of the State Agricultural Experiment Stations, Fiscal Year 1990, Ending September 30, 1990.

NORTH CENTRAL REGION	$10,371,780
NORTHEASTERN REGION	6,694,272
SOUTHERN REGION	9,355,199
WESTERN REGION	7,784,667
Subtotal	$34,405,918
IR-1, Potato Introduction	$114,990
IR-2, Virus-Free Tree Fruit Clones	209,244
IR-4, Clearances of Chemicals and Biologies	347,424
for Minor or Special Uses	204,400
IR-5, Current Research Information System	197,400
IR-6, National and Regional Analysis, Evaluation, Planning, and Financing of Agricultural Research	90,555
IR-7, Chemistry and Atmospheric Deposition	
Subtotal	$1,194,013
Grand Total	**$35,599,931**

Source: Regional Research Office, CSRS.

beginning to edge into the regional research program. For example, representatives from four Canadian research institutions are formal and active participants with substantial resource commitments in the NE-103 project, Post Harvest Physiology of Fruits. The representatives are from the Horticulture Department, University of Guelph; the Horticulture Research Institute, Vineland, Ontario; and the Agriculture Canada Stations at Kentville, Novia Scotia and Summerland, British Columbia. The regional project lists 20 participating project leaders, eleven from states in the U.S., five from the USDA, and four from Canada. The project outline for W-164, Post Harvest Technology and Quarantine Treatments for Insect Control in Horticulture Crops, lists informal participation of representatives from institutions in Australia, Canada, and New Zealand. This participation is classified as informal because the participants have no contributing work built into the project outline nor commitments of resources. A representative from Japan participates on an informal basis in W-177, Domestic and International Strategies for U.S. Beef, and a U.S.-Canadian team cooperates in WRCC-70, Economic Impacts of the U.S.-Canadian Trade Agreement. A few other regional projects have some international involvement and further participation is developing.

Personnel from the Department of Agricultural Economics and Rural Sociology, The Ohio State University are working with Japanese scholars in developing a joint U.S.-Japan research proposal dealing with comparative analyses of food consumption patterns and agricultural structure in the two countries. A proposal to formalize the arrangement was presented to the Committee of Nine (C/9) at their January 1991 meeting. It was rejected, not because of lack of merit of the proposal, but, because it had not been routed first through a regional association of directors for recommendation before being forwarded to C/9. Also, it apparently did not have a sponsor to be considered as an international project with off-the-top funding from the regional research fund. S-216, Food Consumptions Patterns and Consumer Behavior, is developing plans for including an international component in a new regional project. Given the precedence of international participation in regional projects, S-216 has an excellent possibility for productive research involving foreign collaborators.

The Ohio State University is also providing leadership in organizing an international project proposal involving U.S. and Western European researchers. The international team proposes to examine the impacts of EC-92 on food industries. This is being done under the Core Group of NC-194, The Organization and Performance of World Food Systems: Implications for U.S. Policy.

Proposed Strategies for Organizing and Conducting ICR

The precedent for conducting international cooperative research in the regional research program has been established. However, in these projects, the cooperators are mostly Canadian with two distinct advantages. They are nearby neighbors and they speak English which reduces travel costs and removes communication barriers. With the precedence established, using regional research funds and the administrative structure are feasible options to organize and conduct international cooperative projects with Canada and Mexico. These types of proposals, however, must originate in one of the four administrative regions, be approved by a regional research committee of the regional association of directors, be endorsed by the association, and be forwarded to the C/9 and CSRS for approval (Figure 22.4). Because travel costs are relatively low, the holding of technical committee meetings in Mexico and Canada have a good chance of being approved. The organization of the planning-type technical committee can be approved at the regional level.

However, the major barrier to ICR, involving the U.S. and more distant countries, such as those in Western European or the Pacific Rim, is transportation costs of U.S. participants. While the CSRS has no constraints on the use of federal or regional research funds for overseas meetings, the decision to use these funds to support the travel of individual station researchers rests with their respective station directors. In the projects mentioned above involving Japanese, Australian, and New Zealand

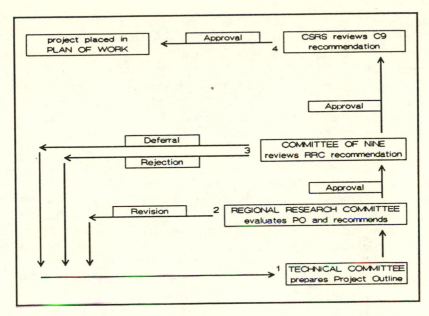

Figure 22.4. Regional Research Project Flow: Origin to Approval.
Source: Regional Research Office, CSRS.

cooperators, technical committee meetings have been held in the U.S. and the travel costs are therefore borne by the foreign participants. In the longer run, adequately organizing, supporting, and conducting ICR on a larger global scale within the context of the existing regional research program would probably require substantial changes in regional research procedures, funding mechanisms, and even philosophy of the program.

As regional research has evolved over the years, three major components have emerged that form the foundation of any cooperative research project. These are the technical committee, the regional project outline, and the administrative advisor (and attendant structures and processes). The project outline is an essential document not only for organizing the work of the technical committee but also for facilitating communication between the technical committee that requires resources to conduct the research and the administrative components that authorize the expenditures of funds. The latter would include the Regional Research Committees of the Regional Associations of Directors, the Committee of Nine (C/9), and the CSRS.

The emergence of formalized ICR will certainly require a modification of existing regional research administrative arrangements and processes and perhaps a new operations manual covering the administration, planning, coordination, conduct, and accountability for ICR projects. Our efforts focus only on a prototype of an ICR outline (Appendix I). Further we have concentrated on only the basic components of an ICR project outline. In drafting the prototype outline we drew heavily on the CSRS report "Preparation, Evaluation, and Approval of Regional Research Fund Project Outlines." We essentially built international dimensions into selected components of the regional research project outline presented in the document. The outline is a first attempt but it may be useful in preparing a first draft of an ICR project format. In the draft, we are anticipating ICR with international participation on a par with U.S. participation. In fact, U.S. participants may be in the minority, in which cases the major part of the resources may come from non-U.S. sources.

The modification of current regional research administrative structures and processes to accommodate ICR will come at a later date as needs arise. This assumes, of course, an expanded ICR program involving significant levels of new federal funding. As one looks at the progression of developments in cooperative research, the question is not a matter of whether there will be international cooperative research, but when it will happen and how it will be organized and managed. It is our judgment that the organization and management in the context of the U.S. regional research program offers the best available and proven option for the successful launching and management of an ICR program. Of course, this is premised on the vision and leadership of both the researchers and administrators involved in the regional research program.

Strategies for the Funding of ICR

The suggestions made in this section are based on historical precedence. An early competitive grants program administered by the CSRS (at the time, the State Experiment Station Division or SESD) was the 204(b) program of the Research and Marketing Act of 1946. A special appropriation established under this section of the Act was used to support marketing research projects on a competitive basis to be conducted by the stations. The funds could be used to support other cooperative marketing activities conducted by agencies of state governments. The program was funded at the $500,000 level but appropriations were discontinued in 1964. As a separate line item in the budget, 204(b) funding did not compete with Hatch marketing or regional research program funding. The evaluation and selection of marketing research proposals were carried out by SESD in cooperation with the Experiment Station Marketing Research Advisory Committee (ESMRAC). The funding of proposals was through cooperative agreements between the stations and SESD. The management and funding processes were similar to the ones currently used by the CSRS Cooperative Grants Office.

Our suggestion is that the regional research program (Section 3(c)3 of the Hatch Act) be amended to include an ICR component, separately funded but a part of the regional research program. This amendment would bring back the 204(b) concept but make the program a part of the regional research program. Therefore, while the federal funding of the regional research program would be on the basis of equity principles, the funding of ICR would be on the basis of competitive principles. As a part of the regional research program, ICR would be managed in the traditional partnership basis under the C/9-CSRS administrative structure. We are further suggesting that the ICR program be non-matching, the same as competitive grants, and earmarked for agribusiness research or research that contributes to improving the overall competitive position of U.S. agriculture and agribusiness in global markets.

Meeting Current Realities

The above suggestion is consistent with current realities in the federal support of experiment station research programs. One is the decline in federal support for the regional research program which has been offset by increasing support from state sources. Therefore, the program is increasingly becoming a station-driven program in terms of support and leadership. For example, state support for the regional research program increased from 46.7 percent of total funding in the 1970-74 period to 66.6 percent during the 1985-89 period, while RRF support declined from 32.4 percent to 17.7 percent between the two periods. The proposed program would increase the federal support of the regional research program, bringing it more in balance with state support, establish an international presence in CSRS which it currently does not have, and enhance the leadership position of the Regional Research Office in regional and international research.

Second, is the inherent conflict in the regional research program between off-the-top funded projects and the support for conventional research projects. Any increase in the proportion of the limited RRF allocated to the former type projects reduces the amount available to support the latter type projects. Since the funding of the proposed ICR program would be additive rather than competitive, it would remove the potential conflict between the support for conventional and ICR projects.

The third reality is the emergence of the global economy and the need and national concern for enhancing and maintaining the competitive position of U.S. agriculture and agribusiness in global markets.

Fourth is the marked change in emphasis recommended in a recent GAO report on USDA programs. The report calls for greater emphasis on strategic international marketing and agribusiness.

The third and fourth realities are, of course, highly related and provide the rationale for the earmarking of ICR funds for international marketing and agribusiness research. This rationale in our judgment is further supported by the following statements from the GAO report:

USDA agencies rarely employ strategic marketing -- a range of practices that identify consumer needs and develop products and delivery systems to satisfy those needs -- to help U.S. agribusiness better compete in both export and domestic markets. Program and policy emphases generally favor the production-oriented philosophy that contributed to agriculture's post-World War productivity boom. While productivity remains important, reliance on production-oriented philosophy means risking the loss of opportunities in food processing and marketing, the fastest-growing aspects of global agribusiness (GAO p. 1).

The report further states:

Such products (value-added) provide greater benefits to the exporting nation because processing adds jobs, economic output, and government revenues (p. 2).

According to the report,

Agribusiness includes all the interrelated private and public policy-making enterprises, from farm supply, farming, and processing, through distribution to the ultimate consumer (p. 1).

The conclusions and recommendations presented in the GAO report are not an isolated incident but are essentially consistent with the findings of several other studies issued over the past 10 years or so.

The fifth reality is the demonstrated capacity of the regional research program to manage and conduct cooperative research effectively with an increasingly broad scale of participation. Having such a program in place would enormously reduce start-up and administrative costs of a new program.

Conclusions

The historical approach employed in this paper shows how experience of the past can provide instructive guidelines in formulating agricultural science policy and funding agricultural research programs. An important example is regional research.

As we have seen, cooperative research has evolved through several stages over a long period of time. Early station research focused on state problems. The first cooperative efforts were between the stations and the various research agencies of the USDA. Although, station and USDA administrators and researchers had the vision and articulated the need for cooperative research on a broader scale, it was a number of years before federal funding became available to establish a formal structure and process for cooperative research.

Two additional stages then occurred in the formal structure of regional research. One was the move toward problems national in scope and participation by scientists from states and agencies outside the regions administering the projects. The next evolutionary phase is now beginning. Increasing numbers of foreign scientists are joining regional projects on a formal and informal basis or making contacts with U.S. scientists involved in regional research projects. The regional research program is again serving as a fitting institutional mechanism and framework to accommodate this new development, just as it was in the movement from regional to national research.

Despite success of the regional research program, the relative support from federal sources over the years has declined while that from state sources has increased. The stations apparently place a higher priority and assign a greater value to cooperative research than does the federal research establishment.

The recommendation proposed in this paper is for an international cooperative research program, supported with federal funds and administered as a component of the existing regional research program. The proposal builds on historical precedence, follows a well established procedure, and meets current and emerging realities. It would increase the relative amount of federal support for cooperative research, give much needed visibility to ICR at the national level, fit in with the shift from equality to competitive principles in the support of federally funded research projects, utilize an existing cost-effective administrative structure, and respond to the growing interest in international research collaboration. The proposal is consistent with the long recognized need for a major shift in program emphasis as articulated by the GAO and several other reports. The recommended program represents an effective approach to generating new knowledge and technology beneficial to all participants and needed by U.S. agriculture to help meet emerging competitive challenges in the global marketplace.

References

Kerr, Norwood Allen. 1987. *The Legacy, A Centennial History of the State Agricultural Experiment Stations, 1887-1987.* Columbia: Missouri Agricultural Experiment Station, University of Missouri-Columbia.

Knoblaugh, H.C., E.M. Law, W. P. Meyer, B.F. Beacher, R.B. Nestler, and B.S. White. May 1962. *State Agricultural Experiment Stations, A History of Research Policy and Procedure.* Miscellaneous Publication No. 904. Washington, DC: United States Department of Agriculture.

True, Alfred Charles. June 1937. *A History of Agricultural Experimentation Research in the United States, Including a History of the United States Department of Agriculture, 1607-1925.* Miscellaneous Publication No. 251. Washington, DC: U.S. Department of Agriculture.

United States General Accounting Office. January 1991. *U.S. Department of Agriculture, Strategic Marketing Needed to Lead Agribusiness in International Trade.* Report to the Secretary of Agriculture. GAO/RCED-91-22.

APPENDIX

Prototype: International Cooperative Research
Project Outline

Title: A brief, clear, specific statement of the nature and international scope of the problem to be investigated.

Justification: An overall assessment of the problem to be investigated in a global, regional, or participating countries context.   Clearly state the importance of the problem to agriculture, rural life, consumers and science in each of the participating countries and the need and advantages of the international approach compared to an individual country approach. What are the expected contributions of the research to alleviating the problem, enhancing the well-being of users and the advancement of science?   More specifically, the following points need to be addressed in the justification statement:

- Importance and scope of problem - What is the importance and scope of the problem in terms of the size of the agricultural industries and the population groups affected in the participating countries. What is the significance of the problem identified relative to national research priorities in the participating countries. Is there a consensus and a formalized research agenda in the participating countries that supports the planned work, and is the proposed research consistent with the priorities on the national agendas?
- Benefits from the International Cooperative Approach - Why cannot this research be conducted just as effectively by one country and what are the special advantages and benefits from the international approach?
- Impacts of Research - What are the likely beneficial impacts of the research results in each of the participating countries? What is the degree of transferability of the new knowledge and technology generated by the committee and its application to problem solutions in the different participating countries? What are the likely beneficial impacts of the research results on industries, population groups, and the advancement of science in each participating country. Are the results mutually beneficial to participating countries or will conflict in national goals result.

Related Current and Previous Work: What is the current status of knowledge on the problem to be investigated-both in published literature and the research underway. U.S. participants will make an assessment of related research underway from CRIS information. Other participants will use existing research information systems in their respective countries to make these surveys and assessments. After a collective assessment of research underway and literature survey of completed work, the status of global knowledge bearing on the problem will be determined. Based on this analysis, the relevance of existing knowledge will be ascertained and the additional knowledge needed to resolve the problem will be determined. This will result in concentrating research resources on the generation of new and relevant knowledge to fill the gaps needed to attack the problem and to avoid the duplication of research efforts in countries involved in the effort. All relevant information sources will be identified and documented.

Objectives: Develop clear and concise statements of researchable objectives and arrange in a logical sequence. The number and scope of objectives stated should be realistic and achievable within the constraints of the resources committed and the project time-frame designated. More specifically, the set of objectives stated should:

- Clearly and concisely define what is to be accomplished in the proposed project.
- Be achievable within the constraints of available resources and time.
- In the statement of objectives (ends to be achieved) exclude all procedural processes (means to achieved ends) such as exchange of information, coordination of research, development of standardized techniques, identification of sources and collection of data, etc.

Procedures: Describe the working plans and methods to be used in accomplishing each stated objective. The division of effort and assignment of responsibilities should be stated in the procedures under each objective. Also, committee and subcommittee structures and their relationship to the objectives and leadership roles and responsibilities should be described. More specifically this section should:

- Describe the time-phased plan of work and the research methods to be used to accomplish each stated objective.
- Describe methods(models/simulations) that are to be uniformly applied in the analysis of data and draw conclusions about problem solutions on a global, regional, and participating country basis.
- Describe standardized questionnaires or survey instruments to be used by all international participants in centralized data collection and collective analyses.

- Describe the division of effort, assignment of responsibilities and expectations of participants and agreed to time frames for accomplishing specific tasks and plans.

Organizational Structure: Describe the organizational structure of the international technical committee, with delineation of specific aspects of organization such as executive committee and its functions, subcommittees and their specific functions, program coordinators/managers, subcommittee leadership, and membership and responsibilities.

23

Discussion Group Summary
Tim Mount

Overview[1]
Leader: Ryohei Kada

Four papers were presented in this opening session. Two described the "Organization, Institutions and Policy" of agriculture, and two papers described "Food Structure and Consumption".

According to Goto and Imamura (Chapter 2), the history of Japanese agricultural policy revolves around the balancing of efficiency and equity. The average farm size is relatively small and not large enough to support a family without additional off-farm income. Furthermore, the distribution of farm sizes has remained relatively stable over time. Rice is the dominant crop, and, recently, over-production has led to government restrictions on production.

In Chapter 5, Tweeten observed that the situation in the U.S. is very different because average size is large and has increased over time. The primary policy objective is to preserve family farms. Because farms have consolidated and grown in size, they are still economically viable. On small farms, off-farm income is required to survive even with existing support programs. Furthermore, environmental problems are often worse on small farms when farming is not the major source of income.

Morishima *et al.* (Chapter 8) observe that caloric consumption in Japan has reached a plateau, but the proportion of calories coming from protein and fat is still increasing, particularly from the latter. Currently, the Japanese diet

---

[1]These subsections refer to discussion group sessions and papers presented at the International Association of Agricultural Economists meeting in Tokyo (see Preface). The chapter numbers refer to the chapters in this book.

is well balanced with roughly a third of calories coming from each of the three major food groups. Some concern exists about the increasing amount of fat in the diet. Demographic factors are important determinants of differences in patterns of food consumption among families, particularly the increase in expenditures on food away from home.

In the U.S., the demand for food is driven by consumer tastes as well as economic factors (Chapter 11). This has resulted, for example, in the substitution of poultry for beef. Increased awareness of health issues has resulted in concern about saturated fat, cholesterol, and sodium consumption. The food industry has responded by producing new products such as low-fat yogurt. Demographic factors are important determinants of demand in the U.S. as in Japan, and the increased number of women in the paid workforce has expanded demand for convenience foods. One interesting contrast is that expenditures on food away from home are substantially higher in the U.S. than in Japan.

Data Bases and Methodology
Leader: Tim Mount

Four papers were presented in the session: two on "Consumer Demand", and two on "Agricultural Supply". Both papers on consumer demand identified the main sources of data on food consumption. Similarities existed in sources on disappearance data, nutritional surveys, and consumer expenditure data. Data on prices and quantities comprising expenditures are available in Japan, but in the U.S., only expenditure data are available. Commercial data are not readily available for research purposes in Japan, according to Buse *et al.* (Chapter 13).

Methods used to estimate models of food demand are similar in the U.S. and Japan. They range form single equation models to complete demand systems. However, these models use somewhat highly aggregated groups of commodities. More work needs to be done to incorporate demographic factors into models, particularly when modeling the demand for disaggregated commodities.

In contrast to the comparison of demand analysis between Japan and the U.S., the approaches to supply are very different in the two countries. In the U.S., methods are closely parallel between demand and supply analysis. Just (Chapter 16) noted limitations of single equation models of supply. A number of desirable improvements in the methods were discussed. A problem is that professional interest in research on supply has diminished in the U.S.

Arayama (Chapter 15) focused on determinants of the supply of labor in agriculture in Japan. Because many commodity prices are administered by government, supply elasticities for crops are of less interest in Japan than in the U.S. The approach to understanding the supply of rice was to predict the supply of labor to non-agricultural activities (manufacturing and services) and to treat agricultural supply as a residual. The overall implication is that one must understand the behavior of non-agricultural sectors to understand agricultural supply.

Demand, Supply, and Structure:
The Special Case of Rice in Japan
Leader: Luther Tweeten

Two papers were presented from a Japanese perspective (Chapters 17 and 18), and one from an American perspective (Chapter 19). The structure of rice markets in Japan is complicated. The rationale for the high support price of rice is "food security", but the true meaning of this term in Japan has important historical components. Because Japan produces only 30 percent of its grain consumption, the support for agriculture is politically acceptable. All but one of the political parties and all local governments are against opening rice markets. Although some organizations support opening rice markets, all consumer organizations are aligned with farmers and are against such a change. These organizations do not necessarily reflect the views of the typical consumer.

The demand for rice by households is for high quality without much regard for price. In contrast, the demand for rice by food processors and restaurants is much more responsive to price. This latter market is growing and is the most likely outlet for American rice. However, if rice production is reduced in marginal production regions, the paddy fields may deteriorate and it would be difficult to renovate them in a genuine food emergency. Furthermore, paddies help prevent flooding. Therefore, preserving rice farms has a positive effect on the environment.

The view of Japanese rice policy in the U.S. is understandably different than it is in Japan. The goal of self sufficiency in rice under current policies is considered to be an illusion because inputs in production must be imported, and the variability of the ratio of stocks to utilization is higher in Japan than in international markets. Restrictions on imports have brought high costs for farm support in Japan and have caused misallocations of resources within Japan and in international markets. New policies can be considered for a gradual liberalization of rice imports.

Trade, Summary, and Future Directions
Leader: Yuko Arayama

Two papers were presented on the "Impact of Trade Arrangements on Farm Structure and Food Demand" from the Japanese perspective (Chapter 20) and the American perspective (Chapter 21). The question posed for the U.S. was why agricultural exports were mainly raw products (grain rather than processed products (meat). The explanations were economic (high costs of transportation), technical (long distances make it impractical to export chilled meat), and political (until recently, Japanese markets have been restricted). However, new technological developments make it possible to export chilled meat from the U.S., making it practical and economic to export more meat.

The view in Japan is that its policies for rice are very different from those for other commodities. Imports of grains, dairy products, and meat have increased substantially in response to trade liberalization, and Japan is the leading importer of these commodities. Remaining quotas are required to maintain a minimum capacity for domestic production. The rationale for protecting rice producers is food security, but the retirement of older farmers will gradually reduce the domestic production of rice.

About the Contributors

Yoshihisa Aita, is head of the Consumption Section of the National Research Institute of Agricultural Economics (NRIAE) at the Ministry of Agriculture, Forestry, and Fisheries (MAFF) in Tokyo, Japan. He received his B.S. and M.S. degrees in agricultural economics from the University of Tokyo in 1976 and 1978, respectively. From 1978 to 1989, he worked at the National Research Institute of Agricultural Economics. He worked as a research coordinator for the Agriculture, Forestry, and Fisheries Research Council Secretariat at MAFF in 1989-90. He was head of the Commodity Section of NRIAE, MAFF in 1990-91 before becoming head of the Consumption Section. His research areas are mainly food consumption and food demand analysis in Japan, comparative studies of food consumption among East Asian countries, and studies of the food industry.

Yuko Arayama, is an associate professor in the Department of Economics at Nagoya University. He received his B.S. in agricultural economics from Kyoto University and his M.A. (1981) and Ph.D. (1986) degrees in economics from the University of Chicago. His research fields are time allocation of households and determination of employment structure.

Elaine Asp, is a food scientist and associate professor in the Department of Food Science and Nutrition at the University of Minnesota. Her research includes projects on cereals and cereal-based food products and on the economic and nutritional effects of special eating plans. Dr. Asp received her Ph.D. in home economics/food science and nutrition from the University of Minnesota. She is a co-author of the recent book, *Food Trends and the Changing Consumer*.

Rueben C. Buse, is a professor in the Department of Agricultural Economics at the University of Wisconsin. He received his B.S. and M.S. degrees from the University of Minnesota and his Ph.D. from Pennsylvania State University. He has devoted his research career to the economics of household behavior and food consumption. Consumer expenditure surveys and data quality issues have also been an important focus of his research. He is the author of an introductory text in agricultural economics, another in econometrics, edited volumes on food demand and data needs, and has also authored many papers and monographs related to household consumption behavior and data problems in research.

Wen S. Chern, is a professor of agricultural economics at The Ohio State University. His current research covers food and nutrition consumption and food demand estimation in Taiwan, Mainland China, Japan, Korea, and the United States, as well as energy demand assessment in LDCs. He is particularly interested in modeling the impacts of health risk concerns on food demand and its application to fats and oils. He earned his B.S. in agricultural economics from National Chung Hsing University in 1964, his M.S. in agricultural economics from the University of Florida in 1969, and his M.S. in statistics and Ph.D. in agricultural economics from the University of California at Berkeley in 1971 and 1975, respectively.

Gail L. Cramer, is L.C. Carter Professor of Agricultural Economics at the University of Arkansas, Fayetteville. His teaching and research interests have centered in grain marketing and policy. Current research includes trade liberalization, grain quality, comparative costs of production studies, marketing rice by-products, and analyzing government rice policies. He received his B.S. degree in agricultural economics from Washington State University in 1963; his M.S. from Michigan State University in 1964; and his Ph.D. in agricultural economics from Oregon State University in 1967. He conducted grain marketing research at Montana State University from 1967 to 1987, Harvard University (1974-75), and Winrock International (1978-80).

Selahattin Dibooglu, is a graduate student in the Economics Department at Iowa State University. He is currently working on his Ph.D. dissertation which involves modelling exchange rates. He received his M.A. degree in economics from Ankara University in 1988. His research interests include time series behavior of exchange rates and applied microeconomics (production efficiency, agricultural policy).

David Eastwood, is a professor in the Department of Agricultural Economics and Rural Sociology at the University of Tennessee. He has a Ph.D. in economics from Tufts University (1972). His interests are in the areas of consumer demand, the economics of information, and food retailing. Dr. Eastwood is the author of *The Economics of Consumer Behavior*, has authored or co-authored numerous articles in scholarly journals and chapters in books, and is a past editor for the *Journal of Consumer Affairs*. He is a co-leader of the Scan Data Project which focuses on the management of supermarket scan data.

Paul L. Farris, is a professor emeritus of the Department of Agricultural Economics at Purdue University. Dr. Farris received his B.S.A. from Purdue University in 1949, his M.S. from the University of Illinois in 1950, and his Ph.D. from Harvard University in 1954. He was a Purdue faculty member from 1952 to 1990 where his duties consisted mainly of research, teaching, and advising graduate students in the areas of agricultural marketing, price analysis, and public policy. He served as Head of the Department of Agricultural Economics at Purdue from 1973 to 1982. Since 1984 he has worked part-time with the Cooperative State Research Service, USDA.

Natsuki Fujita, is an associate professor of agricultural economics at the University of Tokyo, Japan. He devoted his earlier research to agricultural and development economics while working as an economist at the Institute for Developing Economies in Japan in 1974- 85 and as a fellow at the East-West Resource Systems Institute in the U.S. in 1985-86. He earned his B.A. from the University of Tokyo and his M.A. and Ph.D. from the University of Pennsylvania.

Junko Goto, is a Ph.D. candidate in the Urban Planning Program at the University of California, Los Angeles. During 1981-88 she was a research staff member of the Rural Development Planning Commission (noson kaihatsu kikaku iinkai), a juridical foundation located in Tokyo. She was involved with a variety of planning and policy related studies on rural Japan while extending her research to rural development problems in other advanced economies. She earned her B.S. in agro-biology from the University of Tokyo in 1978 and her M.S. in landscape architecture from the University of Wisconsin in 1981. After she began the Ph.D. program at UCLA in 1988, she focused on a historical and comparative study of agricultural and rural development in East Asia. Since 1991, she has been engaged in her dissertation project on the topic of rural revitalization in Japan.

Arne Hallam, is an associate professor of economics at Iowa State University. Dr. Hallam received his Ph.D. from the University of California-Berkeley in 1983. His research is in the areas of production economics, econometrics, and welfare economics. He has worked on a wide variety of national and international problems including work on disease control, pest management, macroeconomic policy, and technology adoption. His recent work has emphasized issues of size and structure in agriculture.

Dermot J. Hayes, is an associate professor of agricultural economics at Iowa State University. He received a Bachelor of Agricultural Science degree from University College in Dublin in 1981 and a Ph.D. from the University of California-Berkeley in 1986. His primary research area is international trade and policy.

Stephen J. Hiemstra, is a professor in the Department of Restaurant, Hotel, Institutional, and Tourism Management at Purdue University where he has been since 1983. He was educated as an agricultural economist at Iowa State University, B.S. and M.S., and at the University of California-Berkeley in the area of food marketing. Prior to coming to Purdue, he worked for the U.S. Department of Agriculture at both the Economic Research Service and the Food and Nutrition Service. At ERS he was head of the Food Consumption Section for several years and edited the *National Food Situation*. At FNS he was chief economist for the agency and in charge of evaluating all of the domestic food assistance programs. At Purdue, he is director of his department's Ph.D. program and focuses his research on the foodservice industry.

Kuo S. Huang, is an agricultural economist with the Economic Research Service, U.S. Department of Agriculture. He received his B.S. and M.S. degrees in agricultural economics from National Taiwan University and his M.A. in statistics and Ph.D. in agricultural economics from the University of California at Berkeley. His major research interests are in the areas of econometrics and consumer demand. He received the ERS Administrator's Excellence Award for his research in developing a model to estimate complete demand systems for food commodities. He also received recognition for his research from the American Agricultural Economics Association and the Southern Agricultural Economics Association.

Naraomi Imamura, has been a professor of agricultural economics in the Department of Agricultural Economics at the University of Tokyo since 1982. He was an associate professor at Shinshu University in 1968-74 and at Tokyo University in 1974-82. He earned his Ph.D. in agricultural economics from Tokyo University in 1963. His current research covers food and land use systems policies in Japan, Mainland China, and other Asian countries. He was president of the Agricultural Economics Society of Japan in 1990-92.

Shoichi Ito, is an associate professor in the Department of Information Science at Tottori University. His research areas include agricultural policy and marketing focusing on international rice markets. He is currently the project leader of a "Study on World Production Potential and Marketing of Japonica Rice" funded by the Ministry of Education, Japan. He is also involved with research for agricultural development of the Mu Us Shamo Desert in Inner Mongolia, China. He earned his B.S. in agricultural economics from Miyazaki University in 1977, his M.S. in agricultural economics from the University of Arkansas, and his Ph.D. in agricultural economics from Texas A&M University. In addition, he was a journalist for a newspaper in Tokyo during 1977-81.

Richard E. Just, is a professor of agricultural and resource economics at the University of Maryland. From 1975 to 1985 he was a professor of agricultural and resource economics at the University of California, Berkeley, where he formerly received his M.A. (1971, statistics) and Ph.D. (1972) degrees. From 1972 to 1975 he was a professor of agricultural economics and statistics at Oklahoma State University where he formerly received his B.S. (1969) degree. He is a fellow of the American Agricultural Economics Association and a former editor of the *American Journal of Agricultural Economics*. His research has ranged widely among fields in agricultural production, trade, policy, development, resource, and environmental issues is widely cited.

Ryohei Kada, is an associate professor in the Department of Agricultural and Forestry Economics at Kyoto University. He received his B.S. and M.S. degrees in agricultural economics from Kyoto University in 1971 and 1973, respectively. He received his M.A. and Ph.D. degrees in agricultural economics from the University of Wisconsin-Madison in 1975 and 1978, respectively. He joined the faculty at Kyoto University in 1977. Dr. Kada has held several research assistant positions over the years at both Kyoto University and the University of Wisconsin-Madison. Dr. Kada was also a visiting professor at the University of Wisconsin-Madison in 1988. His research has been on rural and human resource development, including part-time farming.

Michio Kanai, is Director of the Foreign Agriculture Division, National Research Institute of Agricultural Economics (NRIAE) at the Ministry of Agriculture, Forestry, and Fisheries (MAFF). He received his B.S., M.S., and Ph.D. degrees in agricultural economics from the University of Tokyo in 1964, 1966, and 1985, respectively. He worked in the Planning Division of the NRIAE, MAFF in 1968-73, in the Farm Management and Land Utilization Division, National Institute of Agricultural Sciences, MAFF in 1973-78, and in the Agriculture Division, United Nations Economic and Social Commission for Asia and the Pacific (ESCAP) in 1978-80. He studied at the University of Hawaii, Iowa State University, and the University of Minnesota in 1969-71 and 1973-74 as an East-West Center grantee. His areas of expertise are: (1) individual food consumption, (2) comparing food consumption patterns, (3) the sugar economy, and (4) the development economy of Asia and the Pacific.

Jean Kinsey, is a consumer economist, Professor, and Director of Graduate Studies in the Department of Agricultural and Applied Economics at the University of Minnesota where she teaches "Economics of Food and Consumer Policy" and "Human Capital and Household Economics." Her research interests include consumer credit, food consumption trends, and the effect of food prices on consumer confidence. Dr. Kinsey received her Ph.D.

in agricultural economics from the University of California at Davis. She is a co-author of the recent book, *Food Trends and the Changing Consumer*.

Hwang-Jaw Lee, is an associate professor in the Graduate School of Business Administration at Tunghai University, Taichung, Taiwan. He earned his B.S. in agricultural marketing from National Chung-Hsing University in 1979, his M.B.A. from Tunghai University in 1979, and his Ph.D. in agricultural economics from The Ohio State University in 1990. His teaching and research interests are in the areas of demand and consumption analysis, consumer behavior, and marketing management.   His current research includes estimation of complete food demand systems in Taiwan, functional forms of meat demand systems in Taiwan, aggregation of demand functions, and examination of store attitude and store patronage behavior.

Vicki A. McCracken, is an associate professor of agricultural economics at Washington State University. She received her B.S. in economics and foods and nutrition from Indiana University in 1978, and her M.S. and Ph.D. degrees in agricultural economics from Purdue University in 1981 and 1984, respectively.   Dr. McCracken's teaching interests are in the areas of agricultural price analysis and agricultural statistics and econometrics. Past research efforts include analyzing retailer and consumer behavior in retail food markets and estimating consumer demand for foods consumed away from home. Current research efforts include analyzing domestic consumer nutrient and commodity demand and hedonic price analysis.

Masaru Morishima, is a professor of agricultural economics at the University of Tokyo. He received his B.S. degree in civil engineering from the University of Tokyo in 1957, and his M.S. and Ph.D. degrees in agricultural economics from the University of Tokyo in 1960 and 1963, respectively. He worked in the Farm Management and Land Utilization Division, National Institute of Agricultural Sciences in the Ministry of Agriculture, Forestry, and Fisheries in 1964-75 and was an associate professor of agricultural economics at the University of Hokkaido in 1975-78 and at the University of Tokyo in 1978-84. He served as a vice president of the Japan Agricultural Economics Association in 1988-90.   Recent published work includes "Issues of Modern Beef Economy," "A Perspective on Paddy Farming," and "Estimated Effects of Rice Import Liberalization."

Tim Mount, is Director of the Cornell Institute of Social and Economic Research and a professor of resource economics in the Department of Agricultural Economics at Cornell University. He received his Ph.D. in 1970 from the University of California-Berkeley. His research and teaching interests include econometric modelling and policy analysis relating to the demand for fuels and electricity and to environmental policies. Currently, he is conducting research on the implications for long-run planning of incorporating the costs of environmental damage from emissions.

John A. Naegele, is Hubbard Professor of Biology at the University of New Hampshire. He received both his B.S. and Ph.D. degrees in entomology at Cornell University. After receiving his Ph.D. in 1952, he joined the faculty at Cornell University and served in the Department of Entomology in teaching and research for 11 years. In 1964 he became Head of the Waltham Field Station and Head of the Department of Environmental Sciences at the University of Massachusetts and in 1974 became the Associate Dean of Research of the College of Food and Natural Resources and Associate Director of the Massachusetts Agricultural Experiment Station at the University of Massachusetts. He moved to the USDA in Washington and became Chief of Party of an Agricultural Research Service-sponsored program in Pakistan. In 1979 he returned to Washington to serve as Assistant Administrator of the Agricultural Research Service and then served as International Coordinator for the Science and Education Administration. He joined the Cooperative State Research Service as Principal Scientist and became Deputy Administrator with principle responsibilities in the Regional Research Program. In 1991 he assumed the Hubbard Chair of Biology where he is now involved in the planning and funding of a major biological sciences complex.

Mitsuhiro Nakagawa, is a senior researcher for the Foreign Agriculture Division of the National Research Institute of Agricultural Economics at the Ministry of Agriculture, Forestry, and Fisheries. He received his B.S. degrees in biology and agricultural economics from the University of Tokyo in 1978 and 1980, respectively. His major areas of research include agricultural productivity, agricultural trade issues, and agricultural policy reform.

Tokumi Odagiri, is a senior professor of economics in the Department of Economics at Takasaki City University. His previous appointment was as an assistant professor at the University of Tokyo in 1989-92. He earned his M.A. in agricultural economics from the University of Tokyo in 1984. His current research covers farm structure and rural development in Japan. He is primarily concerned with problems of agriculture in mountainous and less-favored areas in the EC and Japan.

Keiji Oga, is a senior research fellow at the National Research Institute of Agricultural Economics in Tokyo and a visiting research fellow at the International Food Policy Research Institute in Washington, DC (1990-93). He joined the Ministry of Agriculture, Forestry, and Fisheries after graduate from Tokyo University in 1967. He served the Ministry mainly in the policy planning office. He worked for the Foreign Agriculture Service as an econometrician in charge of developing a World Food Model in 1977-80. He moved to the Research Institute in 1983, developed commodity projection models, and analyzed of impacts of beef and rice import liberalization of Japan.   He has developed a multi-commodity, multi-country dynamic projection model called the International Food Policy Simulation Model (IFPSIM) for personal computers.

Kenji Ozawa, is a professor in the Department of Economics at Niigata University.   He was formerly with the Foreign Agriculture Division of the National Research Institute of Agricultural Economics (NRIAE), Ministry of Agriculture, Forestry, and Fisheries (MAFF).   He became a research officer of the NRIAE in 1971 before beginning work in the Foreign Agriculture Division.   He earned his B.S., M.S., and Ph.D. degrees in economics from the University of Tokyo in 1966, 1968, and 1990, respectively.   In addition, he studied at the University of Illinois in 1977.   His areas of expertise are (1) the structure of American agriculture, (2) farm policy in the U.S., (3) agricultural trade issues between Japan and the U.S., and (4) the rice economy in Japan.

David W. Price, is a professor of agricultural economics at Washington State University.   He received his B.S. in dairy science in 1957 from The Pennsylvania State University, his M.S. in agricultural economics from the same university in 1959, and his Ph.D. from Michigan State University in 1965. Dr. Price's research interests have focused on consumption economics with emphasis on age-sex equivalent scales, evaluation of government feeding programs, and hedonic analyses of food products.   He is currently a member of the Steering Panel which directs a research project estimating the effects of past releases of radionuclides from plutonium production operations at Hanford, Washington.

Dorothy Z. Price, is a professor in the Department of Child, Consumer, and Family Studies at Washington State University.   She earned a B.S. in home economics and journalism from the Pennsylvania State University and a Ph.D. in family economics from Michigan State University.   Her research interests have centered on studies of decision making in varied contexts and more recently have concentrated on decision making of consumers both in the U.S. and in other countries, particularly those in the Pacific Rim.   She served as department chair from 1976-1983 and is currently departmental coordinator of graduate programs.

Roland R. Robinson, is principal agricultural economist with the Cooperative State Research Service of the U.S. Department of Agriculture.   Dr. Robinson was trained at George Washington University, where he received his B.S. in biological sciences, and the University of Maryland where he received his M.S. in animal science and Ph.D. in agricultural economics.   He also completed a post-doctoral program in research administration at George Washington

University. He joined the Economic Research Service, USDA in 1960 and the Cooperative State Research Service, USDA in 1961. He provides national leadership in agricultural economics research programs conducted by the Land Grant Universities and State Agricultural Experiment Stations. He currently has major responsibility for the nationwide regional research program in agricultural economics.

Manabu Sawada, is an associate professor in the Department of Agricultural Economics at Obihiro University of Agriculture and Veterinary Medicine, Obihiro, Japan. He received his B.S., M.S., and Ph.D. degrees in agricultural economics from Hokkaido University in 1976, 1978, and 1984, respectively. Dr. Sawada's research areas are mainly food consumption and agricultural policy. His current research includes food demand estimation in Japanese households and applied welfare analysis of the Japanese sugar and starch policy.

Yutaka Sawada, is a professor of economics at Hokusei Gakuen University. In addition, he was a visiting professor in the Department of Agricultural Economics at the University of British Columbia from August 1990 to July 1991. He received his B.S. and M.S. degrees in agricultural economics from Hokkaido University in 1972 and 1974, respectively. His current research interests are changes in meat demand in Japanese households and beef trade liberalization.

Benjamin Senauer, is a consumer economist and Professor in the Department of Agricultural and Applied Economics at the University of Minnesota where he teaches courses in "Applied Microeconomics," "Consumption Economics," and "Food Marketing Economics." His research focuses on consumer food demand and on food economics and policy. Dr. Senauer received his Ph.D. from the Food Research Institute at Sanford University. His is a co-author of the recent book, *Food Trends and the Changing Consumer.*

Bernard F. Stanton, is a professor of agricultural economics at Cornell University. His primary research interests are related to the structure of agriculture and production economics. He teaches courses in food and agricultural policy and research methodology and assists with extension programs in public policy, outlook, and farm management. He received a B.S. in agriculture from Cornell (1949), an M.S. from the University of Minnesota (1950), a Diploma Agricultural Economics from Oxford University (1951), and a Ph.D. from Minnesota (1954). He joined the faculty at Cornell University in 1953. He was chairman of the Department of Agricultural Economics from 1968-76. He is a member of the American Agricultural Economics Association, served on its Executive Board (1974-80), was President (1979-80), and was made a Fellow (1983). He is a member of the International

Association of Agricultural Economists, is President of the Fund for holding its conferences and was Vice President for Program (1988-91).

Nobuhiro Tsuboi, is a chief at the international research section of the National Agriculture Research Center, Ministry of Agriculture, Forestry, and Fisheries in Tsukuba. He graduated from Tokyo Agricultural University in 1966 and earned a Ph.D. in agricultural economics from the University of Tokyo in 1986. He devoted his earlier research to the rural development of Nepal in 1972-76 and rural finance and agricultural cooperative activities in Japan in 1976-90. His current research covers land and water use systems in rural areas, agricultural cooperative activities, and farm management systems in Japan.

Luther Tweeten, is the Anderson Professor of agricultural marketing, policy, and trade in the Department of Agricultural Economics and Rural Sociology at The Ohio State University. He received his B.S. in agricultural education from Iowa State University in 1954, his M.S. in agricultural economics from Oklahoma State University in 1958, and his Ph.D. in economics from Iowa State University in 1962. His research emphasizes public policy for agriculture and regional, national, and international economic development and trade. He has extensive international experience in Europe, Africa, Asia, and South America. Dr. Tweeten served as President of the American Agricultural Economics Association in 1980-81 and was selected a Fellow of the Association in 1983.

Thomas I. Wahl, is an assistant professor of agricultural economics at Washington State University and is associated with the International Marketing Program for Agricultural Commodities and Trade Center (IMPACT). Dr. Wahl received his Ph.D. from Iowa State University in 1989. Areas of interest include international trade and marketing, demand analysis, and policy modeling.

Eric J. Wailes, is a professor of agricultural economics at the University of Arkansas, Fayetteville. His teaching and research interests are in the area of agricultural marketing, trade, and policy. His current research focuses on the analysis of the global rice economy including the effects of grain quality and product differentiation, pricing efficiency, and policy reform. He earned his B.S. in agricultural economics from Cornell University in 1972 and his Ph.D. in agricultural economics from Michigan State University in 1983.

Susumu Yamaji, is a professor in the College of Economics at Tokai University in Kanagawa, Japan. He has studied world food supply and demand, Japan-U.S. agricultural trade issues, Chinese agricultural policies in the 1980s, population growth in developing countries, and the relationship of journalism and agricultural policy. He earned his B.S. at Kyoto Institute of Technology in textile science in 1953. Immediately after his graduation, he became a journalist for the *Nihon Keizai Shimbun (Japan Economic Journal)*. He was an editorial writer during 1969-84. He retired in 1984. After his retirement from the *Journal*, he took his current position as professor. He served as a member of the Rice Price Council and was president of the Japan Agricultural Journalists' Association for eight years.

Kenneth B. Young, is currently a research associate at the University of Arkansas, Fayetteville. He has extensive research and consulting experience in agricultural marketing and development in Asia, Africa, and the Caribbean. He is currently conducting research on the marketing of rice by-products. He earned his B.S. and M.S. degrees in agricultural economics at the University of Manitoba. His Ph.D. in agricultural economics was completed at Montana State University in 1971.